IN VIVO

The Cultural Mediations of Biomedical Science

PHILLIP THURTLE and ROBERT MITCHELL, Series Editors

IN VIVO: THE CULTURAL MEDIATIONS OF BIOMEDICAL SCIENCE
is dedicated to the interdisciplinary study of the medical and life sciences,
with a focus on the scientific and cultural practices used to process data,
model knowledge, and communicate about biomedical science. Through
historical, artistic, media, social, and literary analysis, books in the series
seek to understand and explain the key conceptual issues that animate and
inform biomedical developments.

The Transparent Body: A Cultural Analysis of Medical Imaging
by José Van Dijck

*Generating Bodies and Gendered Selves: The Rhetoric of Reproduction
in Early Modern England*
by Eve Keller

*The Emergence of Genetic Rationality: Space, Time, and Information in American
Biological Science, 1870–1920*
by Phillip Thurtle

Bits of Life: Feminist Studies of Media, Biocultures, and Technoscience
edited by Anneke Smelik and Nina Lykke

Life as Surplus: Biotechnology and Capitalism in the Neoliberal Era
by Melinda Cooper

HIV Interventions: Biomedicine and the Traffic between Information and Flesh
by Marsha Rosengarten

Bioart and the Vitality of Media
by Robert Mitchell

Affect and Artificial Intelligence
by Elizabeth A. Wilson

Darwin's Pharmacy: Sex, Plants, and the Evolution of the Noösphere
by Richard M. Doyle

The Clinic and Elsewhere: Addiction, Adolescents, and the Afterlife of Therapy
by Todd Meyers

The Pulse of Modernism: Physiological Aesthetics in Fin-de-Siècle Europe
by Robert Michael Brain

THE PULSE OF MODERNISM

Physiological Aesthetics in Fin-de-Siècle Europe

ROBERT MICHAEL BRAIN

UNIVERSITY OF WASHINGTON PRESS

Seattle and London

© 2015 by the University of Washington Press
Printed and bound in the United States of America
Composed in Meridien and Univers, typefaces designed by Adrian Frutiger
19 18 17 16 15   5 4 3 2 1

All rights reserved. No part of this publication may be reproduced or
transmitted in any form or by any means, electronic or mechanical, including
photocopy, recording, or any information storage or retrieval system, without
permission in writing from the publisher.

UNIVERSITY OF WASHINGTON PRESS
PO Box 50096, Seattle, WA 98145, USA
www.washington.edu/uwpress

LIBRARY OF CONGRESS CATALOGING-IN-PUBLICATION DATA
Brain, Robert Michael, 1959–
The pulse of modernism : physiological aesthetics in Fin-de-Si?cle Europe /
Robert Michael Brain.
      pages   cm. — (In Vivo)
Includes bibliographical references.
ISBN 978-0-295-99320-1 (hard cover : acid-free paper) —
ISBN 978-0-295-99321-8 (pbk. : acid-free paper)
1. Aesthetics—Physiological aspects. 2. Modernism (Aesthetics)—Europe.
3. Modernism (Literature)—Europe. 4. Modernism (Art)—Europe. I. Title.
BH301.P45B73 2015
111'.85094—dc23

2014040342

The paper used in this publication is acid-free and meets the minimum
requirements of American National Standard for Information Sciences—
Permanence of Paper for Printed Library Materials, ANSI Z39.48–1984.∞

For Parisa

Why is there such a thing as beauty in sound, color, scent, or rhythmical
movement in nature? What causes beauty to emerge? . . . Art is the greatest
stimulant to life: how could one understand it as aimless, as useless, as *l'art
pour l'art?*

Friedrich Nietzsche, *Twilight of the Idols* (1889)

A bit later, some innovators emboldened themselves. They deliberately
broke with conventions, demanding no more than their instinct for rhythm
and the sensitivity of their ear, the cadences and the musical substance of
their verses. Their attempts also depended on the theoretical research found
on the works of phoneticians, and on the recordings of the voice. . . . In
the period between 1880 and 1890, several hardy spirits undertook to
construct a doctrine of art derived from then fashionable theses of psychophysics. The study of sensibility by the methods of physics, research into
the (hypothetical) correspondence of sensations, the energetic analysis of
rhythm, were all enterprises not without effect on painting and poetry.

Paul Valéry, "Existence du symbolism" (1936)

[The work of art bears] a hidden rhythm—still more vital that we perceive
it ourselves—of our soul, similar to those sphygmographic traces that automatically inscribe the pulsations of our blood.

Marcel Proust, "Sur la lecture,"
preface to John Ruskin, *Sésame et les lys* (1906)

Contents

Acknowledgments

MANY YEARS OF WORK AND AN ENORMOUS AMOUNT OF SUPPORT has made this book possible. Early research was carried out with fellowships from the German Academic Exchange Service (DAAD) and the University of Cambridge Renaissance Trust. Much of the subsequent research was carried out during fellowships at the Max Planck Institute for the History of Science in the research groups of Lorraine Daston (1998, 2000, 2010) and Otto Sibum (2003, 2005). Further research was conducted with a Harvard University Tozzer Faculty Research Grant (1999), a University of British Columbia HSS/SSHRC Research Grant, and a visiting professorship at the Department of the History of Science and Ideas at Uppsala University. I am also grateful for the generosity of my faculty colleagues at the University of British Columbia, especially Danny Vickers and Anne Gorsuch, for patience and support in various forms, including permitting me to take time off to complete this project.

Several people provided critical late-stage assistance with the manuscript. My colleagues Alexei Kojevnikov and Neil Safier read chapters and provided crucial advice, as well as practical and moral support. I am deeply indebted to two anonymous referees, one of whom I now know to be John Tresch, for lengthy reports brimming with skill, insight, professionalism, and generosity that helped me improve this book in many ways; to John and the second referee, whoever you are, my enduring gratitude. Special thanks to Audra Wolfe of the Outside Reader for providing timely and indispensable developmental editing expertise. John Pickstone read the completed manuscript and made numerous helpful suggestions. I am also grateful for precise copyediting help from Eric Michael Johnson and, especially, Ken Corbett, who worked beyond the call of duty in the face of critical deadlines. Working with Tim Zimmerman, my editor at the University of Washington Press, has been a pleasure. Many thanks as well to Phillip Thurtle and Robert Mitchell, the In Vivo series editors, for good advice and strong support.

At the University of British Columbia (UBC) I have been blessed with talented and humane colleagues in the Department of History and in the Science, Technology, and Society (STS) Program. Each of my colleagues has helped in different ways, and I thank them all. In the History Department I received especially critical help from Jessica Wang, Alejandra Bronfman, Joy Dixon, Michel Ducharme, Dianne Newell, and Ivan Avakumovic. In the STS Program Alan Richardson, Brandon Konoval, Margaret Schabas, Adam Frank, John Beatty, Judy Segal, Sylvia Berryman, and Keith Benson have been great comrades. Several graduate students, especially Geoff Bil, Kelly Whitmer, Katie Joel, and Jasmina Karabeg, provided help and inspiration of many kinds. Beyond my home departments several more UBC colleagues have provided valuable assistance: Richard Cavell, Nancy Gallini, Tom Kemple, Darrin Lehman, Dom Lopes, and Geoff Winthrop-Young.

At Harvard I also had much help from splendid colleagues, students, and friends. Mario Biagioli, Peter Galison, and Everett Mendelsohn were especially generous with their time and sagesse. Further thanks to Allan Brandt, Anne Harrington, Jimena Canales, Peder Anker, Debbie Coen, Coventry Edwards-Pitt, Adriane Gelpi, Michael Gordin, Edward Jones-Imhotep, David Kaiser, Stephanie Kenen, Eric Kupferberg, Sidney Kwiram, Matt Jones, Ziad Obermeier, Alejandro Kaufmann, Giuliana Bruno, Michelle Murphy, Matt Price, Peter Buck, Steven Shapin, and Susan Lanzoni.

It is a special pleasure to record my appreciation of Simon Schaffer, whose vision and commitment to the history of science and its place within the broader picture of intellectual life has inspired all of my research and teaching. I would also like to extend special thanks to Lorraine Daston for long-standing support and exemplary academic leadership. Much of the material of this book began with my doctoral dissertation written under the supervision of Robert G. Frank Jr., to whom I remain very grateful for many forms of guidance. John Pickstone read the entire manuscript and made many remarks that improved the work and saved me from several errors.

My specific debts to scholars fill the notes of this book, but two scholars deserve special mention for their influence on my work: Henning Schmidgen, whose many studies of the experimental systems of nineteenth-century physiology have transformed my understanding and set an example of outstanding scholarship; and Linda Dalrymple Henderson, for her generosity and trailblazing work on the sciences and arts around 1900.

Over the many years of work that has gone into this book, I have been helped by numerous friends and colleagues: Ken Alder, Daniel Andersson, Mitchell Ash, Jim Bennett, Charlotte Bigg, David Bloor, Christophe Bonneuil, Cornelius Borck, Francesca Bordogna, Fae Brauer, Soraya de Chadarevian, Michael Dettelbach, Dani Eshet, Robert Marc Friedman, Jean-Paul Gaudillière, Peter Geimer, Rémy Guerinel, Michael Hagner, Ernie Hamm, Mark Hansen, Arne Hessenbruch, Myles Jackson, Nick Jardine, Doug Kahn, the late Lily Kay, Evelyn Fox Keller, Mimi Kim, Friedrich Kittler, Julia Kursell, Sophie Lachapelle, Antonia Lant, Barbara Larson, Tim Lenoir, Andreas Mayer, Massimo Mazzotti, Hélène Mialet, Mara Mills, Iwan Morus, Sybille Nikolow, Anca Pauley, Irina Podgorny, Ted Porter, Hans-Jörg Rheinberger, Robert J. Richards, Bart Ryan, Haun Saussy, Armin Schäfer, Wolfgang Schäffner, Richard Schiff, Sam Schweber, Adam Shapiro, Otto Sibum, Skúli Sigurdsson, Richard Staley, Mary Terrall, Joseph Vogl, Keith Wailoo, Andy Warwick, Simon Werrett, Alison Winter, Michael Wintroub, and Norton Wise.

Finally, my enormous gratitude to my parents, Marvin and Dorothy Brain, is tinged with regret that they did not live to see the completion of a project that owes so much to their support and inspiration. Indeed, it was my father's professional interest in the physiology of vision and avocational passion as a painter and student of art history that first implanted in me some of the questions engaged in this book. Ruth Petit and Lola Johnson have given limitless love and support for longer than I can remember. Sohrab Mehrkhodavandi and Doulat Zienabad-Kianian provided tireless love and support while I was completing the manuscript. My daughters, Guita and Roya, came into the world while this book was coming together and have brought joy to every day of my life with their incessantly vibrating protoplasm. My deepest thanks go to my wife, Parisa Mehrkhodavandi, without whom this book would probably never have seen the light of day. I dedicate it to her with profound love and appreciation.

Some material in this book has previously appeared in the following publications: "Genealogy of Zang Tumb Tumb: Experimental Phonetics, Vers Libre, and Modernist Sound Art," Grey Room: Architecture, Art, Media, Politics, no. 43 (2011): 88–117; "How Edvard Munch and August Strindberg Contracted Protoplasmania: Memory, Synesthesia and the Vibratory Organism in Fin-de-Siècle Aesthetics," Interdisciplinary Science Reviews 35, no.

1 (2010): 7–38; "Protoplasmania: Huxley, Haeckel, and the Vibratory Organism in Late Nineteenth-Century Science and Art," in *The Art of Evolution: Darwin, Darwinisms, and Visual Cultures*, edited by Fae Brauer and Barbara Larson (Lebanon, NH: University Presses of New England, 2009), 92–123; "The Pulse of Modernism: Experimental Physiology and Aesthetic Avant-Gardes circa 1900," *Studies in History and Philosophy of Science* 39 (2008): 393–417; "Protoplasmania: Vibratory Organism and 'Man's Glassy Essence' in the Later Nineteenth Century," in *Zeichen der Kraft: Wissensformationen 1800–1900*, edited by Thomas Brandstetter and Christof Windgätter (Berlin: Kadmos Verlag, 2008), 198–227; "Representation on the Line: The Graphic Method and the Instruments of Scientific Modernism," in *From Energy to Information: Representation in Science, Art, and Literature*, edited by Bruce Clark and Linda D. Henderson (Stanford, CA: Stanford University Press, 2002), 155–178; "Standards and Semiotics," in *Inscribing Science*, edited by Timothy Lenoir (Stanford, CA: Stanford University Press, 1998), 249–85; and, with M. Norton Wise, "Muscles and Engines: Indicator Diagrams and Helmholtz's Graphical Methods," in *Universalgenie Helmholtz. Rückblick nach 100 Jahren*, edited by Lorenz Krüger (Berlin: Academie Verlag, 1994), 124–48, reprinted in *The Science Studies Reader*, edited by Mario Biagioli (London: Routledge, 1998), 51–66.

My apologies to anyone I have forgotten, and with great gratitude to all.

Introduction

I N 1877, A REVIEWER FOR THE *LONDON EXAMINER* NOTED AN "INVASION of the region of aesthetics by natural science."[1] Grant Allen's *Physiological Aesthetics* had just appeared, introducing British readers to a burgeoning European science of aesthetics that was carried out under various rubrics. The philosopher William James, who was trained as a painter and physician, avidly followed the nascent field, summing up the climate of opinion by noting that physiologists, while "industriously exploring the functions of the brain," had not yet attended to "the aesthetic sphere of the mind, its longing, its pleasures and pains, and its emotions."[2]

But there was more at stake in these researches than simply the extension of physiology to a new domain of human function. This domain—art—held a hallowed place in the moral imagination of the nineteenth century as the critical refuge of voluntarism, intentionality, and freedom of the will. Science and art had been cast in a two-cultures divide between allegedly creative individualist artists and communal law-bound scientists, famously expressed in Claude Bernard's famous dictum that "art is I, science is we."[3] The invasion of science into aesthetics threatened the system of détente between the two cultures and all the cherished assumptions it upheld.

Painters, poets, and composers encountered physiological aesthetics through various channels, either working directly in physiology laboratories or taking their lessons from critics, aestheticians, and other intermediaries. Beginning in the 1880s artists adopted ideas, instruments, and techniques from experimental physiology to reconfigure the human sensorium and devise new formal languages of art, including notions of rhythm, automatism, abstraction, empathy, and montage, all of which contributed to the making of new fluid, plastic forms of art in painting, poetry, and music. By the eve of the First World War the artists' experiments with physiological aesthetics had brought a dramatic transformation in the very idea of art itself, in the new formal innovations and techniques of abstraction that, coupled with new models of creation and reception of art, of embodied spectatorship, came to be called modernism.

The Pulse of Modernism: Physiological Aesthetics in Fin-de-Siècle Europe charts these developments by zigzagging between nineteenth-century workshops and physiology laboratories, filled with professors and students attaching industrial instruments to the bodies of living organisms, and the lonely studios of painters toiling on their canvases; between lectures intoned by Sanskrit philologists expounding on the phonetics of the ancient Indian Vedas, and the bohemian cabarets where vanguard poets tested the rhythms of new unconventional modes of declaimed speech and versification. This study takes its methods from a rich and growing literature on early modernism that has developed at the intersections of the cultural history of science, studies of literature, art, and the sciences, and the wider discipline of science studies over the past several decades.[4]

AESTHETICS MEETS PHYSIOLOGY

The late nineteenth-century term *physiological aesthetics* might seem lexically jarring, a meeting of two disciplines with utterly different aims and purposes. Yet, the modern notion of aesthetics began, as Terry Eagleton reminds us, as an eighteenth-century "discourse of the body."[5] For early aestheticians like Alexander Baumgarten, aesthetics concerned itself primarily with the sensory infrastructure of the human body, with questions of the nature and essence of art only arising as a secondary concern.[6] The body took on its importance as the site from which values were derived, in clear opposition to the excessive claims of absolute reason; discussions of aesthetic value usually refused to credit answers that did not take into account the muscular structure of the eye or the nervous pathways of joy and disgust.[7] Aesthetics was therefore primarily an enterprise aimed to dissolve rational law into custom and habit and "to identify it with the human subject's own pleasurable well-being, so that to transgress that law would signify a deep self-violation."[8] Depending on circumstances, aesthetic discourse could either ratify the status quo in a common physiology or disrupt the ideology of convention by unleashing a rhythm of rebellion that targeted the common basis of custom, affection, and sympathy. Aesthetics did both in the nineteenth century, as William James noted when he contrasted "the grotesque stuff called Aesthetics in the systems of German philosophers, from Baumgarten and Kant downwards," with approaches to art "from below," namely the physiological and laboratory approaches that examined how line, color, sound, or perception of movement produced a corresponding movement in the beholder's eye muscles, breathing, vascular system, or bodily musculature, stimulating either fellow feeling or revulsion.

Because of its original eighteenth-century emphasis on *soma*, aesthetics was well positioned to ride the wave of the laboratory revolution in experimental physiology in the nineteenth century. Historians of scientific physiology have emphasized the driving role of medicine in the expansion of the nineteenth-century discipline, but aesthetics remained a key concern of leading physiologists, from early laboratory pioneers like Johannes Mueller, Jan Purkyně, and Kaspar Tourtual, to midcentury leaders like Hermann Helmholtz, Ernst Brücke, and Emil Du Bois-Reymond, to later figures like Max Verworn.[9] This meant, as Nick Jardine has splendidly argued, that the emphasis on visual techniques and the modernism of the laboratory space was understood as an "aesthetic accomplishment" by nineteenth-century physiologists.[10] But it also meant that questions of the physiology of artistic perception retained an important place in the work of leading experimental physiologists throughout the discipline's ascent to cultural prominence in the nineteenth century.

In our time, however, experimental physiology has often become an ancillary discipline, making it easy to forget that in its late nineteenth-century heyday it featured the most high-profile, numerous, and highly funded network of laboratories of any scientific discipline, which often provided the model for the disciplinary expansion of physics, chemistry, and other laboratory sciences.[11] The enormous cultural prestige of experimental physiology in the late nineteenth century drew it regularly into the public eye and attracted many talented scientists to the field. As it expanded, experimental physiology widened its compass to a broad range of scientific questions, both fundamental and applied, from investigations into basic functions of life, to a vast array of problems with medical application, and to a large field of applications related to practical problems of industry and agriculture, aesthetics, fine arts, and other cultural questions. It was therefore hardly surprising when physiologists began to weigh in on questions of art in the late 1860s and 1870s.

While some of this work was directed to meliorating lay appreciation of art, physiological aesthetics also aimed to put artistic practice on new, scientifically informed footing. Writing from Berlin in 1879, the American psychologist G. Stanley Hall reported the excitement around the scientific investigation of aesthetics yet wondered whether artists might ever learn from the laboratory.

> Ought artists to credit it as an additional proof of the accuracy of the Greek eye, that if the horizontal lines of the Parthenon slightly incline to the right and left it is to compensate the slight distortion of every horizontal line to the normal eye, or that some attitudes of a galloping horse, instantaneously photographed by a new method, correspond to equine postures found upon Elgin marbles, if at the same time other details, no less observable and perhaps more serviceable, like perpendicular visual directions in the columns of ancient temples, and the second d phase of the horse's spring, etc., are, so far as known, ignored in Greek art? Should German poets listen to Brücke, e.g., when he writes on a revolving drum the mathematical time relations of anapests, spondees, caesuras, accents, verse-forms, borrowed from the classics, logically unusable, or others, hitherto unknown, possible, or shows the natural sub-rhythms of the muscles of the chest, larynx, etc.? Should painters listen to Helmholtz on the laws of saturation, intensity, and contrast of colors, even if he points out errors in the great masters? Should architects trouble themselves about such average impressions respecting proportion as Fechner has collected?[12]

As several of Hall's examples suggest, lessons from the laboratory were material as well as cognitive; or rather, their cognitive content could not be easily separated from the instruments and experimental setups used in the investigations.

These examples illustrate the principal theme of this book: the exchange between physiology and the arts hinged less on textual resources than on the transfer of physiologists' *experimental systems*—the configurations of measuring instruments, material techniques, and living substances that constituted the core scientific work and furnished exemplars of certified knowledge.[13] My central argument is that the exchange between experimental physiology and the avant-garde arts of the late nineteenth century involved transfer of the elements of the experimental systems developed in nineteenth-century physiology laboratories. Scientists, and then artists, drew epistemic and aesthetic possibilities from the experimental systems of physiology, especially the systems using graphical recording methods, remaking the most basic notions of aesthetic materials and creating a powerful new vehicle for materializing questions that could be investigated within the media of the arts. This meant that characteristics of the physiologists' experimental systems became recognizable features of the new arts: early modernism was deeply imprinted with these materialities of the laboratory.

This is one reason why fin-de-siècle physiological and evolutionary aesthetics differ fundamentally from analogous projects in the cognitive neurosciences today that examine questions of art, beauty, and taste. Cognitive neuroscientists would seem to hold a distant mirror to scientific culture circa 1900 when they conduct fMRI studies of the amygdala responding to landscape paintings or portraits, or of the orbitofrontal cortex in the presence of the aroma of freshly baked bread, or of the anterior insula in subjects faced with visceral emotional provocations.[14] Yet, separated by more than a century, the materiality of the experimental systems of 1900 and 2010, respectively, were entirely different: fin-de-siècle physiologists lacked good instrumental access to the brain and so studied such phenomena along peripheral psychophysiological pathways accessible to the methods and instrumental armamentarium of nineteenth-century science. It is true that many of the physiologists who appear in this book would have been unsurprised by recent proposals that artworks function as attentional strategies, or that sensorimotor processes, in the form of action simulations, produce empathic feelings in the observer related to the visible traces of artists' creative gestures, such as brushwork or signs of the movement of the artist's hand.[15] But both the fin-de-siècle physiologists' questions and their answers were formulated in the terms allowed by their experimental systems—rhythm, arrest, duration, ideomotor sympathy, and so on. Similarly, the artists who reformed their craft in light of experimental physiology produced art that reflected both the material and cognitive characteristics of fin-de-siècle laboratory setups.[16] In many instances, early modernist artists extended the questions posed intrinsically by the experimental systems but not easily answered within the constraints of the laboratory: art was a way of exploring or recontextualizing the physiologists' questions and, sometimes, drawing out their implications for society at large. In this sense, my story bears closer resemblances to current work in bioart than to the experimental studies of cognitive neuroscience.[17]

Specialists in science studies will recognize that my account relies heavily on the literature of laboratory studies and the "sociology of translation" of intramural laboratory activities to extramural settings. Bruno Latour's early work is of course fundamental to my thinking about the laboratory as generator of inscriptions that circulate and expand the effects of the laboratory in space and time.[18] Although I have not followed Latourian methods or ideas closely or literally, they nevertheless suffuse this study. Indeed, the whole story could be described as a historical sociology of translation, that is, the formation of mediators—human and nonhuman—into agential networks. More concretely, much of the fascination of the late nineteenth-century physiology laboratory for artists, aestheticians, and philosophers grew from the hybrid ontological status of its scientific objects, suspended between natural facticity and artificial creation. For the artists these objects suggested new modes of existence, new modes of recomposing artworks, bodies, and societies with a new ontology of intensities. Latour's conceptual vocabulary, which is indebted to several key fin-de-siècle thinkers, often illuminates these relations very effectively, even if he denies that they (or anybody else) were ever modern.[19]

POLITICAL AESTHETICS

Or maybe it depends on what one takes modernism to be. In *The Pulse of Modernism* I contend that the early modernist artists who reshaped their craft in the image of experimental physiology found not only resources for formal innovation but also the grammar of a new social and political language. Once the artists' conceptions of aesthetic materials—painted image, spoken (or written) word—had been partially reimagined after the materialities of the laboratory, the artists began to project new possibilities or potentials from the intimately known practices of their crafts. The specific effects of artistic techniques on the beholder's sensorium and visceral and emotional life came fully into focus, and with this understanding art became the focus of a utopian impulse to reinvent civil governance as a mode of engineering the sensory, affective, and pulsatile life of societies.

This impulse was not entirely new, of course. When Friedrich Nietzsche encountered French physiological aesthetics in the late 1880s, he proclaimed France, not Germany, as "the real soil for Wagner." Decades earlier Richard Wagner had, of course, imagined the "art-work of the future" as a kind of technology for remaking social life, including the moral, sensory, and psychological character of viewing and listening publics.[20] Nietzsche immediately grasped that the new physiological studies of art might give many contemporary artists stronger purchase on their Wagnerian ambitions to shape society with their work. "After all, art is nothing but a kind of applied physiology," he concluded.[21]

Although *le wagnérisme* defined the predominant idiom for this utopian idea of art in the 1880s, it had deeper roots in an earlier nineteenth-century Paris that the avant-garde of the early Third Republic were eager to revive. Seeking to overcome the triumph of standardizing capitalism, positivism, and bourgeois mores, many young independent artists of the 1870s and 1880s found their touchstone in the collaborations of scientists and artists in the period spanning the Restoration and July Monarchy (from the defeat of Napoleon to the revolution of 1848). Neo-impressionist painters found their precursors in the collaborations of painter Eugène Delacroix and chemist Michel-Eugène Chevreul, whose scientific theories of color enabled the artist to create dynamic, pulsating surges of chromatic contrasts and irregular forms, in what Michael Marrinan has called an "aesthetics of confrontation."[22] The social unity of scientists and artists corresponded with the André-Marie Ampère's critical notion of "technaesthetics," described by John Tresch as a concept "of art as a series of rational, repeatable procedures aided by technology" and based on "a labor theory of aesthetic effects."[23] Ampère's technaesthetics underwrote a variety of different forms of spectacle in the 1830s—panoramas, phantasmagoria, and not least, the new modes of opera of Giacomo Meyerbeer and Berlioz—that laid the basis for Wagner's notions of the total work of art (*Gesamtkunstwerk*).[24]

Key figures in the 1880s avant-garde frequently invoked the 1830s precedents. Charles Henry, for example, was by turns affectionately nicknamed by his friends, the poets Gustave Kahn and Jules Laforgue, as *le savant*, for his self-fashioning after the mathematician, technologist, and mystic Count Hoëne-Wro ski; *l'artiste,* for his aesthetic theorizing; and *le phalanstère,* for his dreams of rekindling old Saint-Simonian passions for an avant-garde striving toward utopias based on the fusion of science, labor, industry, art, and love.[25] Yet for Henry and his avant-garde comrades the new science of physiological aesthetics provided a powerful resource for aesthetic and social control that neither *technaesthetique* nor *wagnérisme* possessed.

By the early 1890s the larger vision of physiological aesthetics had gained enough traction that voices of dissent, anxiety, and outright opposition began to be heard. Some intellectuals, like the young Paul Valéry, quickly drew the ominous conclusion that if art produced such calculable and predictable effects, it was a source of power in the world as formidable as a charismatic politician or a large technology.[26] Art, Valéry thought, was also amoral and therefore, in the end, cruel, since it wielded its power indiscriminately. Far more influential than the young Valéry, however, was the strident oppositional voice of writer and neurologist Max Nordau, whose *Degeneration* (1892) diagnosed the key menace to fin-de-siècle society in physiological aesthetics and the art inspired by it.[27]

Through Nordau's work the very idea of a "fin-de-siècle" condition became synonymous with physiological aesthetics. Although *Degeneration* was a shrill jeremiad, it struck a chord that continued to resonate as the new art became the dominant model of art across Europe. By 1910 Nordau's view had become entrenched among reactionary social critics, lawyers, and politicians who sought to curb the influence of modernist art and certain popular forms of entertainment, especially the cinema.[28] But alongside the reactionary critiques there was a growing discussion among dissenters of a more sophisticated kind, some of them close to modernist circles and not allied with reactionary forces. Julien Benda, for example, diagnosed the problem of the age—and even the cultural origins of the Great War—in the very idea of physiological aesthetics: the "precepts of modern aesthetics," which "apply exclusively to art that deals with the human soul" and in which "the artist must enter into the inner being of the object . . . and become one with its life principle."[29] The essence of what Benda would later famously call the "treason of the intellectuals" could be found in the widespread embrace of physiological aesthetics and a notion of art for life's sake. Less shrill than Nordau, Benda joined a small but growing chorus of European critics such as

Wilhelm Worringer, José Ortega y Gasset, and Remy de Gourmont in advocating the ordering principle of reason against the physiological and affective modes of modernism.

HISTORIES OF MODERNISM

Throughout *The Pulse of Modernism* I develop a conception of modernism that departs from received notions in significant ways. The first issue concerns periodization: the "early modernism" described in this book extends from the late 1880s to the period of the First World War.[30] My insistence on pushing back the timeline of modernism into fin-de-siècle movements usually described as symbolism, neo-impressionism, and decadence follows from my core arguments concerning the links between physiology and the arts forged from the 1880s to 1914.

Although my use of the term *modernism* jibes with the most general and formulaic notions, such as Clement Greenberg's description of modernist experimentation as driven by a critical, self-reflexive, Kantian spirit, it departs from the specifics of mainline formulations in several respects. While I understand that modernism is not synonymous with the avant-garde, I emphasize the importance of the combative energies of the avant-garde in bringing early modernism into being. The nineteenth-century fin de siècle and twentieth-century aube de siècle were moments when certain practitioners sought to destroy certain formal and institutional structures in the arts and culture, to dissolve the boundaries between art and life, and ultimately, to liquidate all separation of art, life, and politics.

In my account of early modernism, the human body provides the key term for these projects. Until recently, historians of modernism followed the lead of mid-twentieth century critics like Greenberg and Theodor Adorno in viewing the early modernist concern for the cultivation of the body as a symptom of false consciousness, a quasi-Taylorist discipline masquerading as social liberation. Even Jonathan Crary, whose work has many parallels with mine, comes down on this side of the argument, albeit in a much more nuanced way.[31] By contrast, I prefer to view early modernism from within the assumptions of its time before the First World War—an era with more in common with the long nineteenth century than the 1920s. From this perspective, early modernism appears as the culmination of a long nineteenth-century project of transforming human nature through the cultivation of special skills and the alteration of habits with the aim of discovering new forms of bodily and mental aptitude.

The nineteenth-century attitude emerged from a conjunction of the practical cultures of factories and workshops with the ideological convictions drawn from neo-Lamarckian biology. But by the early twentieth century the project of transforming human nature through the cultivation of skills and altering habits had migrated from industrial settings to emerging middle-class pursuits of physical culture, dance, and various forms of body cultivation. The common cause of many early modernists with body cultures provided a promising repository of corporeal and sensory training through which human plasticity might be explored and, most optimistically, new principles of social order germinated. Although many later modernists managed to break free of the body, it was the human frame that made early modernism possible. Early modernism was by, for, through, and about the body.

In *The Pulse of Modernism* I argue that this bodily focus had much to do with the resources offered by the prestigious network of experimental physiology laboratories. Many readers will notice that I do not entirely share the influential view of Lorraine Daston and Peter Galison that "mechanical objectivity" reigned as a dominant epistemology and moral economy of nineteenth-century experimental science.[32] Their view also has more than a whiff of twentieth-century high modernist asceticism about it. With respect to self-registering graphical instruments and the experimental systems built around them, I have found little evidence for the negative epistemology Daston and Galison stress ("instead of freedom of will, machines offered freedom from will"), except in scientific domains where these instruments were imposed to regulate or substitute for visual observation, such as astronomy and clinical medicine.[33] In experimental physiology, by contrast, these instruments were more commonly treated as extensions of human senses and bodily organs, within experimental setups that had the character of a human-machine or animal-machine assemblage.

Daston and Galison's account of the moral economy of mechanical objectivity supports a strong divergence between science and art of the kind enunciated by Claude Bernard's dictum that "art is I, science is we," which contrasts the unrestrained subjectivity of the artist with the self-discipline of the scientist imposed by the scrutiny of the community of peers. Yet throughout the nineteenth century the attempts to fuse science and art were at least as common as claims to their distinctness. Friedrich Schlegel's remark that "all art should become science, all science should become art," found echoes in the Saint-Simonian notion of the avant-garde described above.[34] Physiological aesthetics marked a similar attempt on the part of scientists, as Herbert Spencer observed in his passages on "aestho-physiology" in *Principles of Psychology*: "It belongs neither to the objective nor the subjective world, but, having features of each, it deals with their correlation."[35] Later proponents of physiological aesthetics lined up more closely with this kind of "psychophysical" (or, often, monist) worldview, whose moral, ethical, and political vision of this worldview was very different from the starchy Victorian liberalism of mechanical objectivity: human autonomy was seen to arise, not through restraint, but through a freedom-in-connection that applied to all things, with effects that reverberated throughout the system. In fin-de-siècle Europe this was the vibratory world, the exploration of thresholds and intensities, the dissolution of boundaries between selves and objects.

The emphasis on psychophysics draws me closer to the views of Friedrich Kittler, another colleague whose work has been a profound stimulus to my own. Yet despite the pathbreaking brilliance of Kittler's writings, I take issue with some of his key assumptions.[36] Briefly, my fundamental departure stems from Kittler's insistence that "media determine our situation" (by serving as material and historical a priori conditioning agencies), a notion that assumes the autonomy of technical media before the human.[37] Kittler was interested in genealogies of the image and of sensation from the perspective of technical media, which if pursued rigorously would start from the quantification of stimuli and reaction in animal bodies and eventually lead to the physics and mathematics of systems in which light and sound do not always bend "on human bodies and eyes."[38] I reject the implicit teleology of this approach, which sees all media tending toward the digital and governed by the Shannon-Weaver model of communication.

While I believe this is a philosophically erroneous assumption, my counterargument is primary historical. In my telling, the nineteenth-century experimental physiology configured the body and senses as having an inherent, not merely accidental, relation with technicity. Bodily functions, organs, and senses were operationalized as machines or technical objects in experimental systems; even the most basic functional living substance—the protoplasm—was treated as a storage medium in a manner directly parallel to graphical recording media. For many of the physiologists, artists, and thinkers described in this book, technical media (including crucial Kittlerian media like the gramophone and cinematograph) appeared as an exteriorization of the living, and human-machine assemblages as a stage of an ongoing evolutionary interrelation. This "technics of the body"—the notion that human bodily capacities have always been technically conditioned—proved an indispensable condition for the fin-de-siècle explorations of the affective, preconscious attunements of the physiological body in the cultural arts. There was, in short, no transcendental or pristine path from the nineteenth century to the digital age. There were, rather, multiple pathways from the physiologists' experimental systems, some of which followed Fourier transforms to the modifiable world of digital software, others which led the kinesthetic pleasures of the gut in early modernist painting and dance or in futurist sound performances. Around 1900 the latter predominated.

My approach veers much closer to that of John Pickstone, whose examination of "ways of knowing and working" of scientists and artists reveals the extent to which the physiology lab provided the tender of early modernism.[39] Pickstone urges us "to speak not of science and art as reifications but of analytic methods in both kinds of work."[40] While we have learned to do this in earlier periods—think, for example, of Michael Baxandall, Samuel Edgerton, and others on the practices of surveyors and mixed mathematicians on Renaissance linear perspective in art and architecture, or Svetlana Alpers and Catherine Wilson on Dutch art and science, respectively—we have more often succumbed to the "reification" of science and art.[41] My contention is that closer attention to the practices of scientists and artists in the fin-de-siècle period shows many to be engaged in similar or convergent projects.

Anatomizing ways of knowing and working often requires very specific, and sometimes technical, detail. But it is also possible to characterize those practices within the wider cultural field that encompasses both technoscience and the arts. Indeed, as Pickstone reminds us, many nineteenth-century practitioners themselves strove to do just that, articulating "principles of practice" operable across a variety of disciplines. In Pickstone's account, the decades around 1800—the Age of Revolution—can be characterized by major additions to the repertoire of "working knowledges" and the associated reconfigurations. In brief, to the practices of "extended natural history" there were then added many new forms of "analysis."

These were the modes of "working knowledge" that arose before and after 1800 that Pickstone calls "analysis." Chemistry provided a model of analytical classifications of structure and function that was repeated in comparative anatomy, in the comparative morphology of languages, in treatises on the elementary parts of machines that served as a comparative anatomy for engineers, in medical fields like histology and nosology, and in many other fields. Aesthetics, too, received its analytical exposition in works, from William Hogarth's *Analysis of Beauty* (1753) to David Pierre Giottino Humbert de Superville's *Essai sur les signes inconditionnels dans l'art* (1827), or Charles Blanc's *Grammaire des arts du dessin* (1867), which proposed classifications of aesthetic signs like color and line.

The ways of knowing and working I describe in this book fall within the broader episteme that Pickstone calls "synthetic technoscience," or simply, "synthesis": a strategy that aims to experimentally produce or invent things that have never before existed in the world.[42] Synthesis emerged largely after 1870, with synthetic chemistry as its paradigmatic example. The practice of experimentally creating new molecules—objects that did not exist in the world—out of basic chemical elements differed critically from the older practice of simply analyzing the molecules and compounds that could be found in the word. Pickstone emphasizes that in synthetic practices typically built upon existing principles and practices of analysis, as in chemistry, analytic practices (and especially the periodic table) greatly enabled chemical synthesis. This approach to making "a new combination from 'the prior art'" swept through most late nineteenth- and early twentieth-century disciplines, from electrotechnical research to synthetic dyes and colors, to Jacques Loeb's experimental biology, and much more besides, including aesthetics and the arts.[43]

Pickstone also shows how the epistemological novelty of synthesis has been largely ignored by historians, philosophers, and sociologists of knowledge practices, presumably because the unique features of synthesis contradict purely cognitive (and especially representational) functions. Synthesis produces objects that *act upon the world*—molecules like nitroglycerin (dynamite, an 1867 invention of emblematic importance for many of the anarchist artists I discuss) or acetylsalicylic acid (aspirin, ca. 1900) profoundly altered productive forces and human ability to endure pain, respectively; new phenomena like radioactivity altered physics, medicine, and much more.[44] Working knowledge of synthetic objects typically involves understanding what they do and how they react in different configurations. Making synthetic novelties invariably involved a quest to "meet aims imagined but never realized" (such as human flight), or even to bring entirely new worlds into being.[45] At the same time, for many, the lure of synthetically produced objects had much to do with the new degree of control that might be gained from adding highly engineered human-made creations to the world.

Both the practices and imaginary of synthetic ways of working and knowing suffuse the science and art discussed in this book and, I contend, are central to the project of early modernism. Much of the scientific work I describe in part 1 involves burgeoning practices of synthesis. Graphic recording systems often featured techniques for the mechanical synthesis of recorded curves. The protoplasmic model of the organism presumed a natural process of synthesizing and recombining the periodic vibrations of the cytoplasmic colloids; by the early twentieth century, attempts to artificially simulate these colloidal reactions underpinned the new field called "synthetic biology." Similarly, the view of language that emerged out of experimental phonetics took spoken language to be a process of storing, combining, and recombining phonetic elements.

Techniques of synthesis became even more explicit in the methods of physiological aestheticians and the artists who adopted their approaches, described in part 2. Charles Henry, Gustave Kahn, and Jean D'Udine each transformed older analytic expositions of aesthetics into new methods for producing art as a synthetic creation, as a kind of *recombinant sensation*. Henry, for example, revamped Charles Blanc's and Humbert de Superville's catalogs of aesthetic signs as psychophysiological units of elemental artistic media—line, color, sound—chosen as measurable units of physiological sensation that might produce specific desired effects on the beholder. Part of the motivation for this kind of art was the hope that greater control over the basic elemental media of art would enable new mobile, fluid, and plastic forms in painting, poetry, and music. But control extended to the effects of their art on the viewing or listening public, altering bodily, mental, or emotional states and even transporting the beholder to a new or unexpected state of feeling or consciousness.[46] Works of art, in short, increasingly came to be seen as something acting upon the world, as things possessing a measure of agency and autonomy, a development that corresponded directly with a turn to abstraction and a preoccupation with the formal properties of art. Synthesis was, therefore, a critical piece of the move to liquidate the boundary between art and life.

For physiologically minded early modernist artists, the route to transforming society passed through the synthetically recreated visual or auditory beholder. While works of painting and poetry acted principally on individuals rather than collectives, the physiological aestheticians assumed that they might alter society as well, either by mass consumption or by the power of emotional contagion or imitation to reshape public sensibilities. Just as the work of art was synthetically engineered, so too might society be designed through art, by the invention of programmable physiological units of sensation.

EXPERIMENTALIZING LIFE

This book is divided into two parts. Part 1, "Experimentalizing Life," concerns the development of the experimental system of physiological recording and its application to problems of human function. Part 2, "Experimentalizing Art," examines the transfer of that experimental system into physiological aesthetics and the arts. Within each part the progression of chapters builds on a similar logic of themes. Part 1 begins with a chapter on experimental systems in physiology; it then turns to chapters on the extension of experimental physiology to basic cellular functions and the physiology of language, respectively. The conceptual order of these chapters follows a progression from *technique* (experimental systems in physiology), to *ontology* (protoplasm theory of life and the notion of the vibratory organism), to *anthropology* (physiological linguistics as a prototypical fin-de-siècle human science). Part 2 repeats this thematic and conceptual formula, beginning with two chapters on the transfer of the physiologists' experimental systems to the arts before turning to chapters on the protoplasm theory and aesthetic doctrines of synesthesia and automatism, with a final chapter exploring empathy, kinesthesia, and the rise of abstraction in early modernist painting and poetry in the years just before the First World War.

Chapter 1 examines experimental systems devised by physiologists in the second half of the nineteenth century as vehicles for materializing key phenomena and questions. The predominant focus concerns the graphical methods based on self-registering instruments used to investigate dynamic physiological phenomena. By 1895, graphical recording instruments had become familiar to the public in the form of such new media technologies as Thomas Edison's phonograph and the cinematographs of Étienne-Jules Marey and the brothers Lumière. But well before that, the sensorium of modern science had already been irrevocably altered by new graphical instruments. Physicians monitored the spiky graphs of the heartbeat, the undulating rhythms of the breath, and later, the electromechanically recorded waveforms of brain activity for signs of the patient's condition of health. Engineers monitored "the pulse of parts remotely situate" within machines and calculated the power of engines with the looped curves traced by the machines themselves. Meteorologists tracked the periodic motions of the tides and the fluctuations of the wind to gauge and predict their alterations. Psychologists judged tremulous emotions on rotating drums and polygraph apparatus. Even spiritualist mediums deciphered messages from the beyond in the graphs traced by the quivers and shakes of séance tables.

Physiological experimentation with graphical recording instruments rendered several different kinds of phenomena and questions in material form. Dynamic flows, continuities and discontinuities of forces, rhythms and periodicities were rendered "under the form in which they were produced,"[47] that is, as lines and traces that could be either read by acts of sensible intuition or subjected to formal analysis. In chapter 1 I examine both the genesis and development of these kinds of experimental systems, also some of the skills and operations used by the physiologists who worked with them, and I consider some of the epistemological consequences of their spread within physiology and beyond.

Chapter 2 argues that the physiologists' experimental system helped bring a new scientific object into being: the fin-de-siècle notion of the vibratory organism, of living process as periodical, undulatory, and rhythmic activity. This was the protoplasm theory of life, the basis of what was called "general physiology" in the later nineteenth century. Despite its many adherents in the last decades of the nineteenth century and persistence well into the new century, the protoplasm theory of life has received scant attention from science historians. It stipulated that the gelatinous medium of the cell proved itself to be uniquely suited to store physical forces and therefore to serve as a substratum of all vital processes. In this chapter I argue that protoplasm in the 1880s and 1890s became an "epistemic thing"—a scientific object fashioned in the image of physiological recording devices—as living matter itself became a medium for registering and storing vibratory pulsations. Protoplasmic theory thereby became a critical feature of prevailing theories of physiological psychology and the cornerstone of physiological aesthetics.

The primary appeal of late nineteenth-century protoplasm biology was its capacity to explain biological *plasticity*—the ability of organisms to change in response to varying conditions and environmental imprints. Its central place in the renewed neo-Lamarckism of the late nineteenth-century biology had everything to do with the notion of protoplasm as a dynamic and temporal medium: alterations of form and function came about through changes in vibratory rhythms.[48] Unlike much twentieth-century hereditary thinking, there was no fatalism in neo-Lamarckian protoplasm doctrines: living matter was taken to be extremely malleable, with no predetermined limits to the radical transformations that might be made by human intervention. The idea of plasticity gave rise to a flurry of experimentation in practical techniques to alter life without causing death: blood transfusion, transplant surgery, hypnosis, and "ectoplasmic" spirit phenomena, to name but a few.[49]

But it was in the laboratory that life would be experimentalized. There, the biologist Jacques Loeb wrote in an 1890 letter to the physicist Ernst Mach that "man himself can act as a creator, even in living nature, forming it eventually according to his will. Man can at least succeed in a technology of living substance."[50] As we will see in part 2, the quest to shape living matter in space and time that Philip Pauly has called "biological modernism" gave rise to a directly related quest among avant-garde artists for highly plastic, fluid, and mobile forms of art based in notions of rhythm, vibration, and periodicity, with a similar intention of altering the bodily sensorium of the beholder.[51]

While chapter 1 concerns the technical aspects of experimental physiology, and chapter 2 the critical theory of the vibratory organism, chapter 3 takes up the possibilities of the social and political extension of the physiological techniques through an examination of late nineteenth-century French linguistics. Historians of linguistics agree that a sea change occurred in the science of language during the late nineteenth century, but they have largely missed the role of the laboratory in that transformation. Chapter 3 examines how, with the help of inscriptive apparatus, linguists rendered fleeting and unseen phenomena of speech as materialized and visible objects. Experimental phonetics, the new subdiscipline that emerged from the physiological study of speech, helped displace the primacy of Indo-European philology in the study of language, replacing the as-read language of texts with the living language of speech. But my concern in this chapter is not so much to explore the implications of experimental phonetics for the science of linguistics as to establish some of the ways physiologists and phoneticians succeeded in dissolving the symbolic codes of language into the medium of self-registered curves and thereby established a physiological model of oral communication. The result was a new kind of human science, a "vibratory anthropology" that identified the social bond in the echoing connections of the movements of human speech and those of the human quick. The story unfolds at the intersection of scientific disciplines (physiology, psychology, and experimental phonetics) and fast-moving innovations in instrumental media.

EXPERIMENTALIZING ART

In part 2 I examine how these basic elements of the experimentalization of *life* gave rise to a similar experimentalization of the human activity of making *art*, through a set of deliberate transfers of the techniques, ontologies, and anthropology developed by experimental physiologists. The four chapters that make up part 2 serve as case studies, yet they build cumulatively to show temporal and disciplinary movement across the French and European artistic landscape. The case studies in the artist's adoption of physiological aesthetics expand and bring new detail to the themes introduced in part 1. Yet they also show how the artworks of early modernism realized those themes: how the paintings of Georges Seurat or verse of Gustave Kahn instantiated the temporalities of the physiological experimental system, for example; or how the new protoplasm doctrine played a central role in shaping avant-garde artists' quest for highly plastic, fluid, and mobile forms of art based in notions of rhythm, vibration, and periodicity; or how new painting and poetry were built on notions of a spectator or auditor described in terms of physiological functions such as muscle sense or kinesthetic empathy.

Chapter 4 takes up the "invasion of the region of aesthetics by natural science" in the case of the French polymath Charles Henry, who exerted singular influence over a generation of painters, poets, critics, scientists. I contend that Henry's impact hinged largely on his ability to render the experimental system used in scientific physiology laboratories in ways amenable to the existing practices of working artists. Henry's system packaged or black-boxed the skilled expertise of experimental physiology into a system of aesthetic knowledge engineering that was ready-made for artists eager to dissolve many of their key traditional practical and symbolic codes into scientific algorithms. Specifically, Henry's instruments rendered all aesthetic phenomena, all basic media of the arts—movements, color, musical and articulated sound—in the form of graphic inscriptions: as lines and curves, as recordings of sonorous waveforms, lengths of luminous undulations, or other curvilinear inscriptions. Through Henry's aesthetic expert system, the practice of several artists began to take on elements of the physiologists' experimental setup. The experimentalization of art is supremely exemplified by Georges Seurat, whose late paintings rendered the experimental system on canvas as precisely timed and coordinated interfaces between heterogeneous bodily, mechanical, energetic, and semiotic elements.

In chapter 5 the scenography moves from the studios of painters to those of poets who similarly adapted the physiologists' experimental systems to their art, creating the foundation of modernist poetry in French *vers libre* (free verse). The story revolves around Gustave Kahn, friend of Henry and Seurat and the generally recognized inventor of the new verse form, who developed a method of applying the aesthetic expert system to the practice of versification. Kahn's method hinged on the graphical recording of speech examined in chapter 2. By treating verse as speech rather than as-read text, and speech as recorded graphical inscriptions, Kahn replaced conventional syllabic meter with the "free" rhythms of voice and the periodicities of the poet's physiology. The new rhythmic poetry was conceived in close relation to the Wagnerian ideas of complex music built up around simple rhythmic melodic motifs, which enabled a new fluidity built around complex temporal continuities and ruptures. By the turn of the century, the experimental study of verse became a staple of the leading Parisian laboratory of experimental phonetics, establishing what Ezra Pound later called "hidden strata" of research into the rhythms of "spoken reality" in a network of circulation between elite scientific institutions, artistic go-betweens, and the vernacular culture of the urban cabaret and café concert.

Chapter 6 returns to the vibratory organism as a substrate for psychophysiological aesthetics. One of the most auspicious points of contact between evolutionary psychophysiology and the arts could be found in questions of sensory modalities, especially synesthesia, the sensory pathology à la mode around 1890. This chapter examines a confluence of physiological and artistic investigations of sensory fusion that hinged on the reigning protoplasm theory of synesthesia. Because colored hearing and related pathologies appear to have a hereditary component, some scientists attributed them to an abnormal differentiation of function in the protoplasm. This explanation did not, however, cast any light on the larger animating question around synesthesia: did it present a sign of regression or evolutionary advance? This chapter examines this question through the work of artists Edvard Munch and August Strindberg, who applied physiological aesthetics in a quest to create a new form of art that would accelerate the evolutionary transformation of human physiology in individual spectators and, by principle of aesthetic contagion, create a new form of public sensibility.

Chapter 7 concerns the consolidation of a pan-European modernism in the visual and vocal arts that emerged around 1910 amid growing links between the aesthetics of line, color, and sound in the psychophysiology of the motor function of gesture. On the visual side I consider how the push to abstraction brought together several of the key themes of physiological aesthetics—the quest to unify the senses in protoplasmic vibration, the turn toward robust theories of embodied kinesthetic and empathetic spectatorship, and alliances between artists and the new body cultures—in a common project of human transformation. The second part of the chapter picks up a parallel story of the vocal arts, focusing on futurist ringleader F. T. Marinetti's efforts to surpass *verslibrisme* with a pure phonetic poetry aimed at directly transmitting the rhythmic transformation of auditors. I finish with the Zurich Dadaists, notably Hugo Ball and Tristan Tzara, who took up Marinetti's onomatopoeic art as part of the general drive toward abstraction in the arts, in Ball's words, "to discard language as painting has discarded the object."[52]

THE PULSE OF MODERNISM

PART 1

EXPERIMENTALIZING LIFE

1

REPRESENTATION ON THE LINE

Graphic Method as Experimental System

In principle it would not be difficult to take stock of our entire knowledge by using self-recording machines and other automatic devices.

Otto Wiener, Die Erweiterung unserer Sinne (1900)

WRITING FROM BERLIN IN 1879, THE AMERICAN PSYCHOLOGIST G. Stanley Hall described to readers of *The Nation* back home a nearly completed revolution in scientific communication. In Europe, Hall wrote, "the graphic method is fast becoming the international language of science." In Germany, he added, "it has revolutionized certain sciences by its unique logical method, and in one or two cases at least has converted the lecture-room into a sort of theatre, where graphic charts are the scenery, changed daily with the theme, and where the lecturer is mainly occupied in describing his curves and instruments, and signaling assistants, who darken the room, explode gases, throw electric lights or sunbeams, simple or colored, upon mirrors or lenses, or strike up harmonic overtones, as the case may be."[1]

Such choreography dominated the scientific education of an entire generation of Europeans. Many of them articulated it further, both as a scientific method and imaginary. The introduction of the graphic method into nineteenth-century science reflected the parceling of the world into distinct disciplinary fields. In each of the relevant fields, analysts or experts learned and memorized a mental library of curves, the mastery of which defined their specific competence in their field. Specialists delivered their harvest of graphic representations not only to the marts of disciplinary exchange—journals, conferences, texts—but also to the broader public domain, what French physiologist Étienne-Jules Marey called the commonweal (*oeuvre commun*) of science. In these accounts, the graphic method served to implement a fantasy in which automatic recording instruments would generate a vast heterotopic space of inscription that would push out speech altogether and replace it with mechanized forms of thinking and communication. Graphic data from laboratories, factories, machines, hospitals, tidal analyzers, and demographic surveys would pour into this space, generating a smooth disciplinary exchange of experimental results across institutional, international, and ultimately, disciplinary boundaries. "It would not be difficult to take stock of our entire knowledge by using self-recording machines and other automatic devices," affirmed the German physicist Otto Wiener in 1900.[2]

For Marey and other proponents of the graphic method, the principal enemy of scientific communication had a name: language. "Born before science," Marey wrote, "and not being made for it, language is frequently improper to express exact measures and well-defined relations." A scientific age had rendered language obsolete, Marey argued. Hence, "it is not doubtful that the graphic form of expression will not soon substitute itself for all others, each time it acts to define a movement or a change of state, in a word a phenomenon of any sort." In place of verbal or written discussion, Marey imagined scientific and technical communication as a mute exchange in which the inflections of mechanically registered curves compelled assent or dissent in a similarly automatic fashion. "Let us keep for other needs the insinuations of eloquence and the flowers of language," Marey asserted. "Let us trace the curves of phenomena that we want to know and compare with one another; let us proceed in the manner of geometers among whom demonstrations are not discussed."[3]

For Marey the condition for the possibility of the graphic method as a simple, clear, and universal medium of scientific exchange derived not just from its logical clarity but rather from its capacity to inscribe, and thereby represent, time. Of all of the physical dimensions that determine phenomena, time took precedence in the nineteenth century: omnipresent, but also elusive, enigmatic, and nonobservable. All notions of variation or the variability of phenomena assume time, whether in meteorology, economics, or physiology—the scientific challenge was to measure it in comprehensible form. Time, Marey insisted, takes "form" in the shape of curves that one can see. From this perspective, graphical recording redefined the very notion of phenomena: previously imperceptible events became instrumentally available to the eye and cognitive operations. At the same time, it introduced a new form of image, a new mode into the field of visual representations: one that made time its primary determinant and the condition for its apprehension by a human observer.

ONTOLOGY OF THE GRAPHIC IMAGE

The graphic method emerged around 1800, when a new species of scientific instrument appeared in the cabinets of natural philosophers, betokened by a new semantic marker. Apart from established suffixes for experimental apparatus (*-scope* and *-meter*, for example), *-graph* designated instruments that, as the Greek etymology suggests, could "write" or "draw."[4] The *-graphs* facilitated mechanical forms of writing or image making, generally with little or no intervention of the human hand and, in many cases, the capacity to produce multiple copies from an original.[5] These mechanical instruments for drawing, tracing, and inscribing entered the armamentarium of natural philosophy at the moment when the measuring apparatus acquired a new-found role, use, and representation among experimentalists.[6] Where eighteenth-century natural philosophers had relied on stringent rules of social organization, bodily regulation, and literary reportage to control experimental evidence, the turbulence of the revolutionary epoch made them look to transfer the burden of credible testimony to the scientific instrument or machine. Rigorous attention was devoted to making the instrument a foolproof relay of natural processes, which were then communicated to the disembodied mind of the experimenter.[7] In some versions, the resulting inscriptions functioned as images of nature's ciphers, revealed to the philosophical adept.[8] What was new was that the measure was an image. And not just any image, but one of a special hybrid kind, with elements taken from different sorts of representations: diagrams, graphs of mathematical functions or relative quantities, and traces produced by mechanical devices.

The nineteenth-century graphical image had emerged among the victors of what John Bender and Michael Marrinan call "a kind of warfare among systems of diagram for explanatory power" that had been waged in last half of the eighteenth century.[9] Diagrams had been used for centuries, of course, but Enlightenment thinkers made visual correlation of data a form of knowledge all its own. There were several sources for this epistemological opening. The established power of the array of diagrammatic methods associated with the *costruzione legittima* of Renaissance perspective came under sharp critique, especially the system's positioning of a physical viewer.[10] Late eighteenth-century representational strategies emancipated themselves from the fixed and stable world of Albertian perspective representation, turning space into a series of mobile grids without a center that might be apprehended as a series or from several vantage points. This was a philosophical break with a hierarchical world picture, to be sure; but it was also occasioned by the demands of practices that involved handling and manipulating things in many different ways. The Enlightenment diagram dispensed with the absolutism of the Albertian scheme—its coercive limitation of the user of the diagram to the geometry of sight and the unique perspective of the peephole—and offered users different avenues of organizing visual data.[11]

Diagrammatic practice brought together several different modalities of eighteenth-century visual practice used in philosophical, scientific, and artistic disciplines. Distinctive eighteenth-century diagrams like the plates of Diderot and D'Alembert's *Encylopédie* or Gaspard Monge's system of descriptive geometry emphasized the imagined, tactile manipulation of things as a mode of correlation. New modes of apprehension became possible, including temporal and dynamic processes and the visualization of things that were not present to the eye of the viewer. There was no universal key to reading or deciphering these images, but a mixed set of visual, cognitive, and bodily skills that were acquired through practical use. Marrinan and Bender show how the diagram user's synthetic skills dovetailed with accounts of spectatorship in the writings of Denis Diderot on theater and on painting, which detailed how viewers' immersion in the gestural mechanics of the stage or tableau "literally complete" the work of the playwright or painter.[12] The parallels between stage and tableau and Monge's gestural epistemology of diagrams point to a converging visual language that would allow graphical representation to be described as a theater of operations and eighteenth-century painting and theater to be called diagrammatic.[13]

The graphically recorded images that developed in the nineteenth century were less open-ended than some of these Enlightenment-era diagrams. But they codified a certain number of hybrid elements, especially the new possibilities for rendering mobility and process. The statistical and graphical analysis pioneered by William Playfair and Johannes Lambert established what became the standard mode of representing data in graphs of functions using rectangular coordinates: by its width (abscissa) and height (ordinate), the surface of the rectangle was proportional to the represented quantity.[14] Graphical representations of this kind, often called "the method of curves" in the nineteenth century, permitted a visual comparison of relative quantities.[15]

Around the same time as Playfair's graphical representations, several different European scientists introduced similar methods of self-recording mechanical instruments that produced traces in the form of curves against a coordinate grid. These were apparatus in which the mechanism drove both the inscriptive stylus and a recording surface, producing an image without human intervention. The new instruments of experimental inscription drew heavily upon the methods of manufacture, above all the indispensable techniques of copying, or mechanical reproduction. Copying, of course, had formed the basis for artisanal and industrial processes since the dawn of human history.[16] Casting, molding, stamping, punching, die casting, turning, and printing from surfaces or cavities all comprised a family of traditional procedures that became the focus for an explosion of industrial innovation. Many of the great advantages of steam-driven machinofacture derived from the clever mechanization of these kinds of processes. Their principle "pervades a very large portion of all manufactures," wrote Charles Babbage in *The Economy of Machinery and Manufactures*, "and is one upon which the cheapness of the articles produced seems greatly to depend."[17] The principle was simple: great pains could be lavished upon the original, from which a potentially unlimited series could be reproduced, thus making possible unprecedented new economies.

The newfound and systematic attention to the processes of copying renewed an interest in their philosophical implications. In the industrial age, manufacturers spoke of copying in two registers, practical and theological. In the first instance, proper copying technique preserved metric relations within the object through the transmission, a virtue for standardizing machine components, but it also vouchsafed verisimilitude between original and copy. For many British industrialists, the notion of copying underpinned the theological rationale for a manufacturing society. Traditionally, the arts of copying had been enshrouded with an aura of magic or theological mystery. The logic of the negative—wax to seal, cast to form, stone to print—carried with it the enigma of parentage, of the transmission of physical and, usually, optical resemblance to another object, upon which the imprint remained stored as memory.[18]

Late medieval Christians, as Katharine Park demonstrates, regarded impressed images as a "fundamental type of physical causation, linking processes as apparently dissimilar as visual cognition and the generation of fossils."[19] In some instances that causation occurred as a sort of "action at a distance," as in the famous *acheiropoietoi* images, "true images not made by human hand," of which the Holy Faces served as the paragon.[20]

Copying therefore referred not to a merely material process but to a meeting of sensible surfaces, a matrix where internal properties and external regimes coincided. Hence, whether in its secular or theological formulations, copying or mechanical inscription signified an ontological relay, or in André Bazin's characterization of the photographic image, as a "transference of reality from the thing to its reproduction."[21] Yet, if we follow the provocative description of "cultural techniques" by German media theorists, the idea or thematization of reality transference would have arisen only after a longer history of practice in these sorts of operations—in this case one that stretches deep into Paleolithic antiquity.[22] The first practices of inscription, or resemblance by touch—say, tracking animal prints, of making hand prints or shadow paintings of the kind found in Lascaux or other Stone Age caves— begat further analogous techniques such as death masks and, down through the centuries, myriad cultural practices, from seals, coinage, and heraldry to handwriting analysis and the eighteenth- and nineteenth-century science of physiognomy. Thomas Macho emphasizes that these techniques involve a "pragmatics of recursion," or "self-referentiality": the capacity of painting to depict painting, or writing to deal with writing, extends across different technical media, so that a writing person can be pictured, a picture or mathematical operation can be written about, and so on.[23] It was this principle that was thematized by Babbage and operationalized for industrial purposes, giving the transference of the reality of things prominence in the romance of manufactured things and mass production.[24] And it was the avatars of graphical recording methods, from Poncelet and Morin to Marey, who similarly invoked the power of the graphical recording instruments as a means of allowing nature's manufactory to produce its own images and reveal its mysterious hidden language (*langue inconnue*).

GRAPHICAL INSCRIPTIONS AS WORKING OBJECTS

Mechanically produced graphical inscriptions occupied an unusual epistemological space that aligned functionally with what Lorraine Daston and Peter Galison have termed the "working objects" used by scientists in the late eighteenth and early nineteenth centuries. "If working objects are not raw nature," they write, "they are not yet concepts, much less conjectures or theories; they are the materials from which concepts are formed and to which they are applied."[25] Before they became the staples of experimental science, graphical inscriptions were used by engineers in a variety of critical operations on steam engines and contrivances. By the 1830s they became the critical working tool in the formulation of concepts of mechanical work, or energy, and indispensable means of introducing a temporal axis to phenomena that had previously been gauged by static measures alone.

Perhaps the best example of using graphical inscriptions as working objects originated in the workshop of James Watt and then evolved into a staple practice of practical physics and physiology.[26] Looking to find a foolproof means of measuring the duty, or work performed, of his steam engines, Watt tried several techniques before settling upon the ingenious little technique developed by his assistant John Southern of mechanically tracing the movements of the piston inside the cylinder of engine. The Watt Indicator Diagram, as the instrument became known, consisted of a cylinder in communication with the motor, which contained a piston balanced between the steam pressure and a spring coil. Affixed to the piston rod was a pencil and a registering apparatus made from a piece of paper affixed to a small board, whose displacements were proportional to the volumes created by the piston.[27] The loop-shaped line traced out by the stylus was set against two coordinates that plotted a graph showing the relation between the pressure in the cylinder and displacement of the piston.

The Watt apparatus thus became one of the first devices to rely on a graphic copying process to record on one surface the memory of the actions of another. The most important use was to determine, at any instant of time, and under any given circumstances, the actual power of the engine, gauged as a work-integral. By measuring the area under the curve geometrically, the engineer obtained a figure directly proportional to the work developed by the engine when the indication was taken. Provided that the engine ran continuously at a constant speed and the number of revolutions and length of stroke were known, a remarkably precise determination of "laboring force," later called "work" and eventually "energy," could be achieved.

The second use of the indicator diagram enabled engineers to examine the shape of the curve to determine any perturbations or disturbances, any pathological deviations, in the normal functioning of the engine. It allowed the engineer to discover, for example, whether there were any defects in those parts of the machinery by which the steam is admitted to the piston. By inspecting the trace for irregularities it could be determined, for example, whether the slides were properly set or whether the steam-ports were large enough, a defect that might even suggest that a different arrangement of the working parts of the machinery would be advisable. This was the observational function of the device, its capacity to render visible remote regions within the machine or occurrences too fleeting for unaided inspection. It inevitably evoked a comparison with medical inspection of the body. Already in 1795, Watt's friend George Lee corresponded with a Leeds millowner named Benjamin Gott, who complained, "You inquire after ye Steam Engine—you know a physin can give no good account of ye state of his Patient's health without feelg his Pulse & I have no Indicator."[28]

When the Watt Indicator Diagram became public in the 1820s, after decades of remaining a closely guarded industrial secret, several French engineers seized upon it fervently as the solution to several recalcitrant problems. For restoration engineers trained at the École polytechnique, the prevailing problems were defined within the framework of the system of practical mechanics and descriptive geometry of Gaspard Monge. Throughout the revolutionary epoch, Monge promoted descriptive geometry as a universal language of industry, linking artisans and engineering elites, articulating the boundary area between theory and practice, and enabling the mechanization of operations performed within specific trades.[29] For engineers increasingly concerned with representing dynamic phenomena, Monge's descriptive geometry offered helpful techniques but ultimately fell short of the precision required for the new steam-powered industrial systems.[30]

Throughout the 1820s French engineers struggled with, in the words of one of the most influential treatises on power engineering, "the necessity to establish a type of mechanical currency [*monnaie mécanique*], if one can

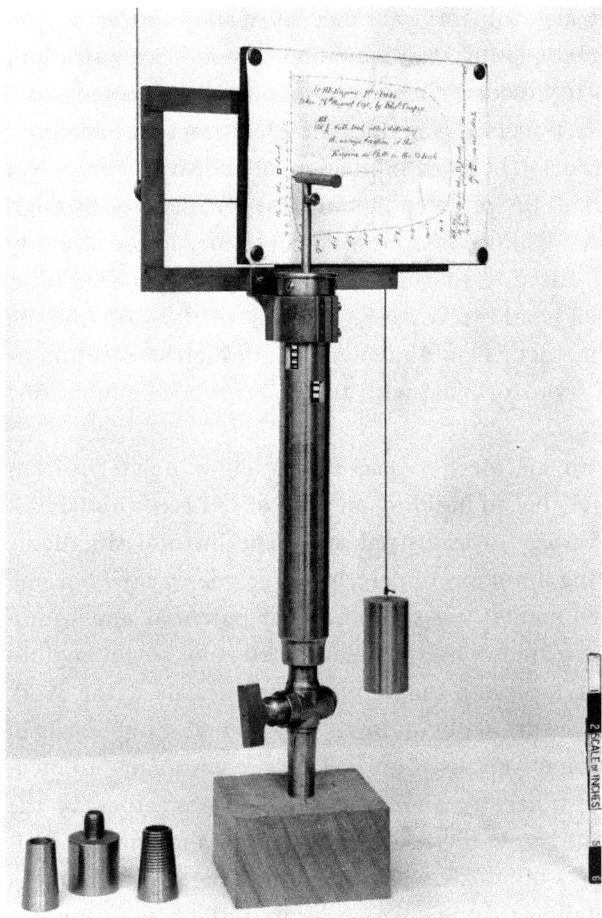

James Watt Indicator Diagram apparatus. Courtesy of the London Science Museum, Science and Society Picture Library, Science Museum Group Enterprises Ltd.

speak thus, with which one can establish the quantity of work employed in executing all sorts of manufacture."[31] The term *mechanical currency* simultaneously invoked the physical and economic resonances of the notion of work, or labor value, positing a kind of universal equivalent that might serve as a medium of exchange between "the businessman and the capitalist" and the engineers in gauging the power of engines.[32] Jean-Victor Poncelet, illustrious student of Monge and professor at the United Artillery Engineering School in Metz, reckoned this measure in terms of the vertical elevation of a heavy body: "This definition and this measure of mechanical work conforms with the way in which, in the arts, all works are paid in relation to the vertical elevation of loads."[33] Contemplating Watt's method of graphic registration, Poncelet recognized that it provided a means to graphically represent time in terms of graphical space traversed—a critical desideratum that had vexed French engineers for decades. The most immediate benefit was a graphical means of measuring work as the product of effort and the distance through which it is exerted: force(*x*)distance instead of force(*x*)time. This was easily achieved by plotting the curve of movement against a coordinate grid in which the spaces traversed would serve as the abscissa, the flow of time the ordinate. The instrument, then, would involve combining the continuous uniform movement of a stylus or plate with the object whose motion one wished to measure.

Poncelet, together with his Metz colleague and fellow polytechnician Arthur Morin, immediately began building all sorts of self-recording dynamometers for use in a variety of industrial and experimental situations. Much of the universalizing ambition of descriptive geometry now became materialized in the instruments, whose domain of potential application would prove as broad as mechanics itself. Dynamometers for steam engines improved upon the Watt Indicator Diagram; others measured the work expended with contrivances drawn by animals or locomotives on roads of different constructions; some were used for ballistics experiments, to measure air resistance or the trajectory and penetration of projectiles, or the recoil of cannons; some measured the relative elasticity of materials of various kinds.[34] These problems of practical physics formed the constellation of problems that would find their theoretical expression in the new sciences of energy.[35]

With their temporalized graphical indications, the self-recording dynamometers, chronographs, and related instruments invented by Poncelet and Morin marked a critical methodological and symbolic transition from late Enlightenment–era balance instruments to the instrumental culture of the new steam-powered world. The older instruments—lever, balanced clock, chemical balance, spring dynamometer, and so on—measured only a quantity of heat, weight, or motion in terms of inputs and outputs that canceled or counterbalanced variations over time in static or steady-state descriptions.[36] The new graphical recording instruments implemented in myriad concrete measures the primacy of linear time in a new cosmos of irreversible forces, conversions, history, activity, progress, energy, and eventually, entropy associated with the steam-powered world. In nearly every science—thermodynamics, astronomy, political economy, philology, archaeology, evolutionary biology, and soon, physiology—linear temporality became the critical variable. Many sciences therefore took their key evidence from artifacts that bore the imprint of time—documents, remains, survivals, fossils, ruins and edifices—while more experimentally oriented sciences turned to graphical recording methods as the means of producing inscriptions of temporalized events. The fanfare that often accompanied these instruments resulted from their simultaneous capacity to further practical tasks, construct new objects of knowledge, and assist in framing the new, progressive image of the world.[37]

Poncelet and Morin proselytized far and wide for the new instruments. Demonstration devices displaying graphic recording of the law of falling bodies placed in French lycées would inculcate the principle of mechanical work as a "self-evident axiom" for every schoolboy. At the same time, Poncelet and Morin campaigned (unsuccessfully) to have the graphical measure of mechanical work adopted as a legislative measure. Noting just how much confusion reigned among legislators deliberating on the values of roads, bridges, canals, and railways, or among agriculturalists considering investments in equipment, Morin suggested that the new measure of work, "founded on well-established experimental bases," might clarify calculations of the utility of public-works projects and enable industrialists to trade in the currency of labor value.[38] The engineer observed that although the measure of horsepower found widespread service as a conventional unit of measure, it "has no legal value, and it would be great to desire that a legislative measure that could give that character, since it is the currency of industrial work [*la monnaie du travail industriel*]."[39] The French engineers developed this "currency" at the very moment when political economists, Karl Marx more thoroughly than anyone, delineated the way in which time had become the measure of value in capitalist societies.[40] The value of commodities was gauged in terms of the objectification of abstract human labor, a disembodied and departicularized form of labor that had become comparable with any other form of labor. Abstract labor was without quality and measurable exclusively by its duration. This entailed an inevitable slippage whereby time itself became a form of value, a currency of exchange.

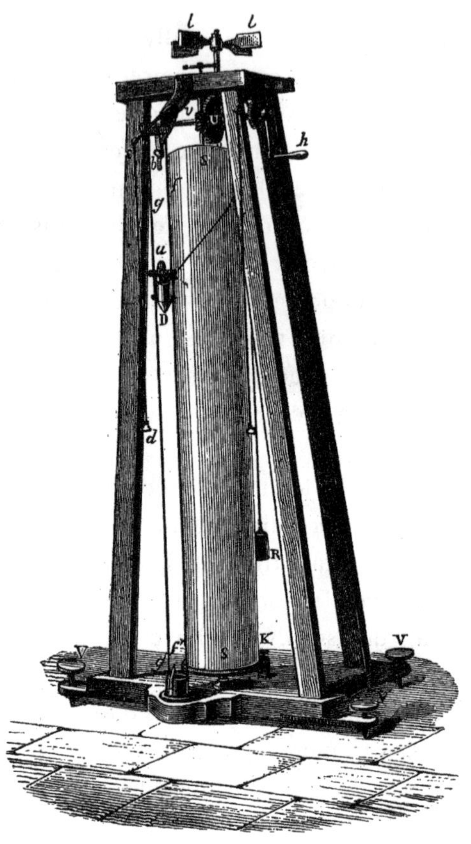

Morin Self-Registering Falling Bodies Demonstration apparatus. From Étienne-Jules Marey, *La Méthode graphique dans le sciences expérimentales et principalement en physiologie et en médicine* (Paris: G. Masson, 1878).

The efforts of Morin and Poncelet to establish the graphical measurement of mechanical work as a staple working object of physicists and engineers soon led to its creative adoption in foreign countries as well as new disciplines.[41] In Prussia, where the instruments were widely discussed, a young medical doctor and member of the Berlin Physical Society named Hermann Helmholtz adapted the instruments for an ingenious set of experiments that displayed the "mechanical work" expended in the muscle contraction of frog legs in the "time-spaces" of the graphically recorded curve.[42] When the physiologist Emil Du Bois-Reymond succeeded in repeating the experiments, he exclaimed that it was "a spectacle for the gods, to see the muscle working like the cylinder of a steam engine."[43] The theatrical metaphor went to the well-established heart of the graphical epistemology, of course, as the movement relations were rendered on the two-dimensional surface of the inscription. But much of Du Bois-Reymond's excitement revolved around the successful introduction of this graphical working object—a thing that belonged neither to the world of nature nor to artifice but that constituted knowledge—into the theater of his physiology laboratory. Du Bois-Reymond would frequently speak of the "aesthetics of experimentation" throughout his long career, referring to the effects produced by different arrangements of components in experimental setups.[44] Over the next half century, physiologists would elaborate graphical self-recording methods into a complex and adaptable experimental system, extending the choreography of graphical representation across laboratories around the world.

FROM INSCRIPTIONS TO EXPERIMENTAL SYSTEMS

Starting in the 1840s many scientists began to think about graphical recording instruments in more complex ways than simply as devices for producing inscriptions. Once a critical number of ingenious apparatus had been built to investigate different phenomena, clever experimenters began to devise ever-new arrangements to tackle new questions. In an important sense the rearranged experimental setups *were* the questions themselves: more than simply a means to capture this or that natural phenomenon, the experiment sought to test the behavior of a specific arrangement of partial objects that comprised the setup. This is part of what we mean when we say, with Hans-Jörg Rheinberger, that experimental systems are "vehicles for materializing questions" as well as "machines for making the future."[45]

It is easy to think of experimental systems, or the instrumental complexes that comprise them, as standard packages. Yet, as Ruth Benshop observes, scientific "instrument making is partially continuous with the functioning of the instrument and thus with the practice of experimentation—that is, with experiment making."[46] The experimental systems based on graphical recording methods in physiology and allied fields evolved out an array of apparatus that were part of a dispute in the French Academy of Sciences during the 1840s. The dispute was centrally concerned with different experimental approaches to a set of common problems in ballistics, and it effectively brought to light several instances of military-industrial espionage. But the participants were alert to the multiple uses of these instruments for a range of scientific and practical problems, including the measurement of small velocities of time, improved measures of mechanical work, materials testing, and several applications in the burgeoning telegraph industry. At this point "the graphic method" had yet to acquire its full definition and had yet to assume a clear place among experimental methods—that would be one of the outcomes of the dispute.

This dispute would turn out to be about more than just the machines themselves: it was also about the very idea of experimental systems that prevailed in nineteenth-century physiology.[47] What initially seemed most striking about the apparatus in question was their remarkable precision in measuring small intervals of time. But what emerged from the dispute was that these instruments constituted an entirely new class of machines: ones that arranged different, in Henning Schmidgen's words, "time-based syntheses of diverse and distinct partial objects opening paths from materiality to semiotics."[48] Each experimental setup entrained a set of coordinated material flows and interruptions that resulted in a semiotic output that was itself a material record of the experimental events. Several critical features of a new experimental practice emerged.

First, there was no ontological distinction between living and nonliving elements of the system—component parts made of metal, wood, India rubber, animal tissues, and even whole organisms (including humans) functioned equally as "component parts." Schmidgen quotes the Dutch physiologist Franciscus Cornelis Donders, who programmatically insisted on this point in his textbook on human physiology. "We hope to have made evident," Donders wrote, "the mutual connections between the parts and the phenomena of the body . . . in the same way as in our artificial products (*Kunstprodukten*), and we transfer the terminology from the latter to the former."[49] There was no natural or logical connection between these components, only their contingent coupling for the purpose at hand.

Second, there was no fundamental difference between material and semiotic objects—this distinction only arose as a function of the configuration. James Clerk Maxwell, in an analysis of scientific apparatus written for the catalog of the exhibition of the Special Loan Collection of Scientific Apparatus, held at the South Kensington Museum in 1876, noted that the components of scientific apparatus were mostly like those found in working machines (sources of energy and means of transporting energy), with the exception of the final action, which in scientific apparatus was the production of an inscription, indication, or measure, and in working machines a modifying action on the object of labor.[50] The semiotic product of the experiment did of course continue to exert agency upon the world, as it found its way into data sheets and publications, shaped future experiments, et cetera.

Finally, while each semiotic marker provided a measure of time, what was critical in this context was that time did not simply mean duration or change but, as Schmidgen observes, was taken to be the *milieu intérieur* of the experimental machines themselves. These experimental setups operated on the assumption of theoretical reversibility: this was inherent in their common French designation as "instruments of continuous indication" (*appareils à l'inscription continue*), which implied that the minute units of movement within the system could be resynthesized into continuous movement. Yet, paradoxically, it was the interruptions of the continuous flows—material, organic, energetic, semiotic—that marked the curvilinear inscriptions and defined their points of interest. In every system it was critical to define the starting point (or multiple starting points) for the event sequences, to gauge the reaction time of the system itself to the stimuli, the transmission time of the signal (air pressure, for example, was very slow), and the inertia of various components (the stylus, for example). The guiding assumption here was that it was only by gauging and resynthesizing these discontinuities that the ideal of a continuous inscription was achievable. Time, as Charles Sanders Peirce would put it, is "the continuum par excellence, through the spectacles of which we envisage every other continuum," thus it provided the necessary frame for representing fluctuant sensations and discontinuities in the pulsatile system.[51] Against the background of continuity what stood out were discontinuities, rhythmic alterations, and points of inflection in the inscribed curve.

The manuals and overviews of these self-recording instruments would be rewritten many times. But few would exceed the lucidity of the overview provided by Emil Du Bois-Reymond in a letter to Alexander von Humboldt, written around 1850, that sought to bring the elder statesman of European science up to date with the new research.[52] Du Bois-Reymond divided his document, entitled "Overview of Methods for Measuring Small Time-Spaces That Have Recently Come to Be Applied," into six parts. Humboldt in turn reduced it to simpler terms, scribbling at the top: "an introduction, 1) measurement of small parts of time, 2) and self-registering apparatus." The time-measuring apparatus grew largely out of ballistics experiments and used electromagnetism to set a clockwork in motion and stop it at the beginning and end of a time-space to be recorded by a galvanometer needle. The third part of Du Bois-Reymond's letter to Humboldt concerned the principle of self-registration, as described by Werner Siemens in a report to the Berlin Physical Society. This included the principle of a rotating disc or cylinder, developed by Thomas Young; marks that were mechanically produced, as in the Morin instruments; marks produced through an electromagnetic mechanism, as developed by Charles Wheatstone, Louis Breguet, the Russian artillery engineer Constantinoff, and Siemens. Du Bois-Reymond added that the self registering apparatus had yielded a variety of graphic methods: "[François] Arago and [Heinrich Wilhelm] Dove's experiments on the duration and discontinuity of lightning, respectively; inscriptions of fugitive movements rendered as curved or oscillating lines on rotating cylinders or discs, as in Watt's steam-engine indicator; [Guillaume] Wertheim's experiments on the elasticity of materials; [Carl] Ludwig's kymograph; Helmholtz's studies of muscle contraction; and Wheatstone's self-registering barometer and thermometer." Du Bois-Reymond further added that the "parabola described by a horizontally thrown stone, is the simplest realization of this always same sensible path—the horizontal projected force replaces the rapidly moving disk in its plane."

The two broad categories of instrumentation described here—galvanometric or chronoscopic time-measuring apparatus and self-registering machines—became the basis of many of the experimental systems of scientific physiology and its disciplinary offshoots (especially experimental psychology) in the second half of the nineteenth century.[53] Many experimental physiologists in the 1850s and 1860s, as Henning Schmidgen has shown of Helmholtz and F. C. Donders, alternated between the two classes of apparatus in attempts to materialize different kinds of questions. But by the 1870s the two instrumental approaches had generated increasingly divergent instrumental phyla, each with their own distinct research questions.

Over the course of the nineteenth century, specialists expanded the elements of the experimental system in discipline-specific ways. Physiologists vastly expanded the tools of research and training, including an armory of recording instruments to investigate different physiological functions. Many teaching laboratories featured little more than the rudimentary elements of laboratory tables, recording apparatus, and stimulating apparatus. But with each decade of expanding laboratories and a growing instrument-making industry, there appeared more sophisticated motors to drive rotating drums, variously operating by gas, water, or electricity; clockwork and weight-drive systems; and pulley systems to connect to the drums.[54] The drums themselves were sometimes replaced with nondrum mechanisms (especially for studies of muscle), such as a stationary swinging pendulum or horizontally displaced plates. Laboratory practitioners—physiologists and medical students alike—spent much time checking settings, preparing the smoked drum, and monitoring the setup for a given experiment. These efforts stabilized the experimental system based on graphic recording instruments, fixing it as a rubric in catalogs and training manuals. By the late decades of the nineteenth century, this kind of experimental setup was a staple of virtually all physiology manuals and textbooks, as well as the topic of dedicated treatises like Marey's *La Méthode graphique dans le sciences expérimentales et principalement en physiologie et en médicine* (1878) or Oskar Langendorff's *Physiologische Graphik* (1891). These works were basically compendia of experimental setups, different arrangements of flows of material and semiotic stuff in physiology and other experimental sciences. But the core process of experimentation with self-recording systems in physiology can be described as a practical means of deterritorializing the body, of transforming dynamic function into a surface of inscription.

For the avatars of experimental systems based on graphical recording, the term *inscription* carried an enormous epistemological burden. Marey famously described graphical recording in metaphors of writing: "natural writing" (*écriture naturelle*) and "the language of the phenomena themselves," for example.[55] In *La Méthode graphique* he even shored up this metaphor with a Rousseau-esque potted genealogy of graphical inscription. "In the first ages of humanity," Marey wrote, "the exchange of ideas could only be achieved by signs," by certain "gestures or certain sounds" to which "conventional meanings were attributed." This began with animals and evolved among human populations into languages "more or less clear and more or less expressive." With a "more advanced degree of civilization," writing emerged, first in the "natural graphics" of hieroglyphs seen in Egyptian stelae, which constituted a "veritable universal language." Finally, the mode of

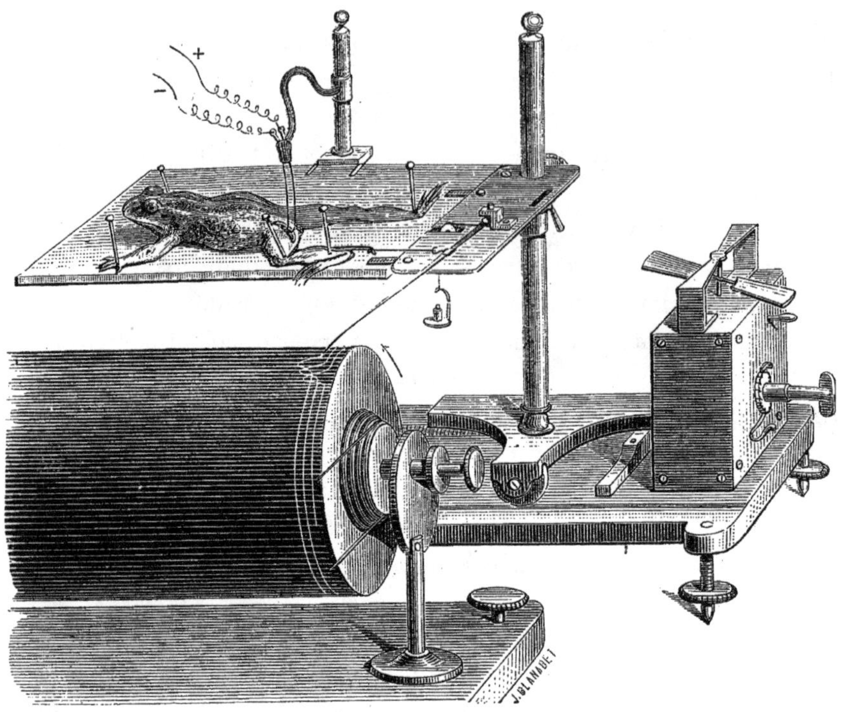

Myograph apparatus, for measuring muscle contraction in a frog gastrocnemius muscle. From Étienne-Jules Marey, *La Méthode graphique dans le sciences expérimentales et principalement en physiologie et en médicine* (Paris: G. Masson, 1878).

graphical expression introduced by Descartes's geometry was combined with inscriptive apparatus to make the perfect mode of scientific expression that overcomes confusion and obscurity.[56]

More than a century later this familiar Rousseau-derived narrative evokes the well-known critique made in the early work of Jacques Derrida, in his account of the logic of the supplement, and similar figures employed by Bruno Latour to describe scientific practices. Writing, in this narrative, "holds [an absent presence] present at a distance and masters it."[57] Derrida suggests that each inscription, each act of writing, must cede authority to earlier items on the chain—the utility of each inscription depends on its ability to be exchanged for another. One might find in this chain of signification, with Derrida, a "mirage"; or it might be viewed more positively, with

Latour, as "circulating reference," the "Ariadne's thread" through the "seeming chaos and confusion" of scientific practice.[58] Either way, the notion of "inscription" in our examples brings us back to the indexicality of the chain of inscriptions. The succession of inscriptions must remain (in principle) reversible, allowing a restaging of the conditions in which each inscription was produced. Every graphical inscription, in other words, furnished a read-out on the experimental setup than produced it.

What Marey found virtuous in this kind of experimental system—the refusal to distinguish between bench work and the writing of papers, or between the collating of results and the design of an experiment, or even between the work of the machine and the work of the scientist—others found disturbing. "You want, they say, to substitute machines for human intelligence; scratched curves on paper for the lucidity of reasoning and the power of arguments," Marey sighed, defiantly insisting that the "flowers of language" had no place in science.[59] Yet this was rhetoric, too, insofar as it insisted on the automaticity of interpretation that graphical inscriptions allowed. The problem was that inscriptions functioned both as indexes and as representations, which meant that there was another level of epistemological operation, another set of techniques of observation, in graphical recording systems.

TECHNIQUES OF OBSERVATION: THE DOUBLE READING OF THE GRAPH

Physiologists erected a model of the observer that was predicated on a continuum of sensibility joining the human organism with the experimental system. Most nineteenth-century physiologists were medical doctors by education, trained in the highly skilled system of traditional sensory mediation known as *tactus eruditus*, the physician's "learned touch." Accustomed to this kind of sensory discipline, the physiologists developed their own protocols for reading and evaluating instrumental inscriptions.

Marey suggested that graphical inscriptions demanded a double reading.[60] First, they demanded a formal, cerebral, and intellectual calculation: the scale of the coordinates, the time frame, the peaks and valleys, continuities and ruptures, analysis of a function in two variables. This reading enacted a mental reconstruction of the event or process inscribed. At the same time, the observer perceived a sensible intuition of the tracing, a direct perception of the qualities of the line: its rising or falling, the rhythms of its changes of direction, repetition, form, or physiognomy traced out by lines themselves without reference to anything beyond themselves. These two different readings of the graphic curve could be and frequently were carried out separately, without reference to the other. But much of the rhetoric of the graphic method blurred or conflated the formal and analytical with the sensible and intuitive—both reflected the remediated content of earlier media—and therein lay much of its appeal as a universal language of science.

The formal analytical tools available to the graph reflected its origin as a hybrid of several different representational techniques: diagrams and graphical representations of data; mathematical graphs of functions in two variables; and the recorded traces used in physics and precision mechanics. Diagrams and graphical statistics had come into being during the late eighteenth century, most often to represent the data of political economy as graphs of functions in two variables.[61] They emerged as a side effect of the increasing propensity among Enlightenment mathematicians to treat the analytical calculus as a language of function, even though the mathematician's preference for algebraic virtuosity led to scorn for the graphic representation of these functions.[62] Although the mathematician's advances in the calculus of functions provided an aura of rigor for the experimentally recorded graphic curves, the mathematics remained little explored by physicists and still less by physiologists, who often traded in curves that described highly irregular functions that pushed the boundaries of nineteenth-century mathematics. Yet even when the mathematics of particular graphic inscriptions remained beyond the capacity of users of the graphical method, the inherent mathematical quality of the curves conferred a special scientific legitimacy upon them.

The graphic curves were more important as measuring devices, as instruments of ordinary quantification, rendering displacements by the amplitudes of movements. In order to obtain a graphic representation of a phenomenon it was necessary to render it as a displacement (increase in temperature, blood pressure, nerve impulse), which would then be transcribed as an image. This capacity to measure displacement was something novel and important in measuring mechanical work or energy as the product of effort and the distance through which it is exerted. In its emphasis on dynamic

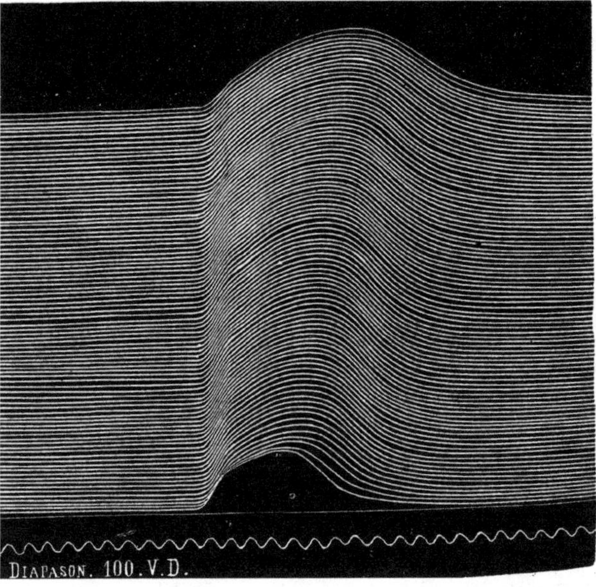

Myograph curves. From Étienne-Jules Marey, *La Méthode graphique dans le sciences expérimentales et principalement en physiologie et en médicine* (Paris: G. Masson, 1878).

process it set graphic recording measures apart from optical instruments, which produced images of stationary phenomena, but also from the static quantities registered by balance instruments, like the spring dynamometer, which measured only the quantity of motion or effect of the work done. The convexities and concavities of the recorded curves captured the unfolding of energy relations "under the form in which they were produced."[63]

The second reading of the graphic curve, what I am here calling the sensible-intuitive reading, presumed the instrumentalized bodily relation between the observer and the instrument. In his quest to overcome the "defectiveness of human senses," Marey imagined graphic recording instruments and their components as analogs of human sentience, models of the ways in which functional activity cut channels deep into the organism. The scientific observer followed and understood the movements of the recording apparatus through an act of implicit recognition of the sense of the instrument as an externalization of human physiology.

The sense externalized by the recording instrument was, paradoxically, the very one it supplanted: touch. Impulses were rendered as what Charles Sanders Peirce called *indexicals*. The term refers to touch as the point of contact between an image and what it represents: the indexical acts as a temporal trace of that contact, taking "holding of our eyes, as it were, and forcibly directing them to particular object."[64] Peirce offered a pointing finger as the "type of the class" but also proposed a number of other examples: a footprint, a weathercock, demonstrative pronouns such as *this, here, now,* and certain kinds of images, like photographs. Indexicality demands a particular form of inferential reasoning, which begins with the acknowledgment that the inscription is before anything else a record of its own having been made. With many indexicals, especially the subcategory of traces to which graphic inscriptions belong, the image is contiguous with its cause, but it does not have to resemble its cause (think of a skilled tracker inferring from footprints a vivid and accurate picture of the person who made them and the circumstances in which they were made).

When the self-recorded inscription was formatted within the coordinate grid, it became further transformed into an *image of a trace.* The graphical inscription thereby acquired a new authority by enabling apprehension to shift from tactile to visual. Touch is local (we can only touch things at the size they are). Visuality, to speak with Bruno Latour, becomes universal when it participates in the classical technologies of the image. Inserting the trace into a coordinate grid allowed it to be subject to numerous mathematical operations, including the simple translation to different scales, which allowed users to see the same thing as the same thing over a wide range of sizes or magnitudes.[65] Such operations enabled graphic images to function as what Latour has called "immutable mobiles" in an exchange economy of inscriptions.[66]

In medicine and physiology the dominant model of indexical inference (emphasis on palpation and observation of signs on the patient's body) gave way to the skilled reading of the graphic signposts of disease. The epistemological frame remained indexical, of course, but it allowed the shift from tactile to visual inspection. Much more could be said about this, of course; but for our purposes the key point is that it promoted a new form of indexical inference that emphasized disease process, which was understood (by analogy to energy systems in physics) as dynamic and temporal. It allowed the scientific physician to observe normal and pathological functions from the standpoint of an alignment with a moving system.[67]

This observational position made possible a new kind of formalist observation in the biomedical sciences, in which complex dynamic processes were reduced to relatively simple visual and quantitative relations. Here the key

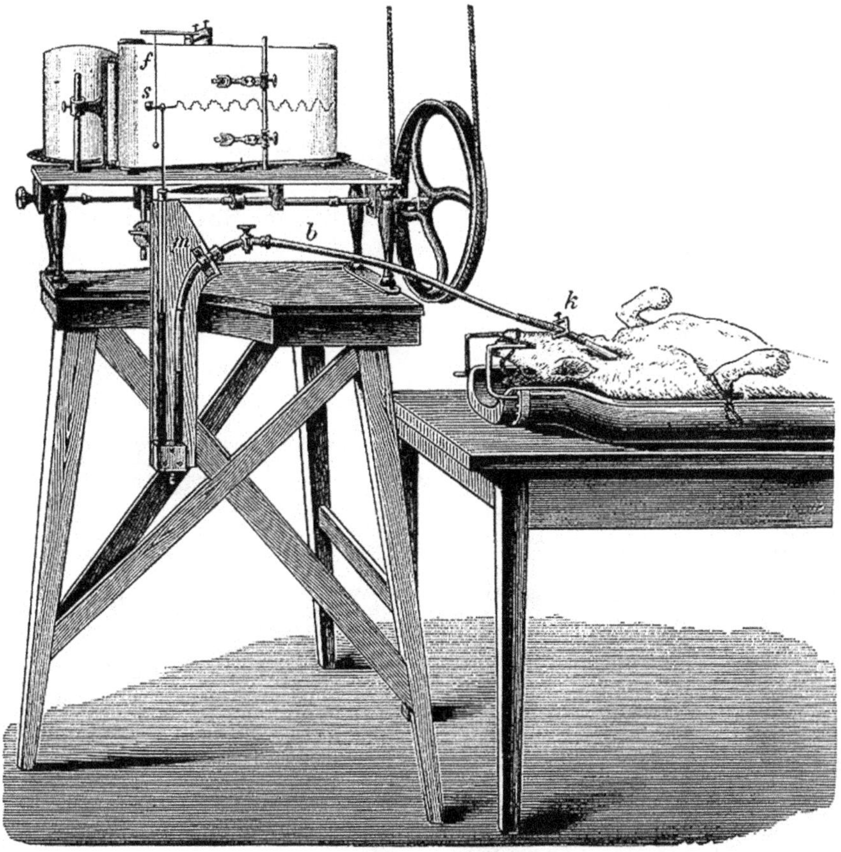

Carl Ludwig, blood-pressure experiment / machine-driven kymograph with endless paper. From Oskar Langendorff, *Physiologische Graphik: Ein Leitfaden in der Physiologie gebräuchlichen Registrirmethoden* (Leipzig: Deuticke, 1891).

analogy was to musical notation, which Marey, Ernst Mach, and others compared to physiological graphics: "There has long been a mode of graphical expression for very fleeting, very subtle, and very complex movements that cannot be expression in any language. This admirable language is read in all countries, and is a universal language in the proper sense. I speak of musical notation."[68]

Traditional medical pulse lore was filled with attempts to escape from the tactile to the visual by rendering the evanescent perception of pulse in the form of musical notation.[69] It was at least as old as Galen, who used the Greek notion of *rhythmoi* (positions of the body in dance) to account for the felt movements of movement and rest in arterial pulse.[70] The various medieval and early modern attempts to render tactile perception in the visual notation of music were primarily concerned with representing rhythm, the patterns of motion and stillness, continuity and discontinuity, as they unfolded in time.

With nineteenth-century graphical representation the pulse (and indeed, all pulsatile physiological phenomena) finally gained a formalism of its own—one still close to musical script, with its horizontal coordinate representing time, divided into measured units, and its vertical axis used to show variations in intensity. Marey illustrated the parallel between music and graphical representation with a fever chart of a cholera patient. With the vertical lines representing equal time intervals in the form of daily entries, the curves represent heterogeneous but simultaneous processes in relation to one another—like a musical score in which the different parts of the orchestra and the choir are represented synchronously.[71] The representa-

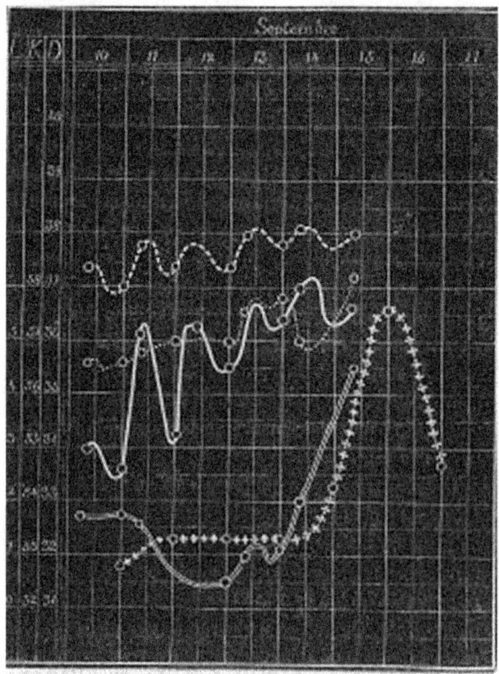

Graphic representation of a case of cholera observed at Saint-Antoine Hospital by Dr. Lorain. From Étienne-Jules Marey, *Du mouvement dans les fonctions de la vie: Leçons faites au Collège de France* (Paris: Germer Baillière, 1868).

tional analogy to music allowed the physiologist to think about reciprocal temporalities, multiple rhythms, unfolding at the same time, converging or diverging on the legible surface of the image.

Marey's antilinguistic, antihermeneutic stance established a principle of formalism in science that laid the basis of several formalist modernisms in the arts. Yet this very antihermeneutic formalism entailed a rich repertoire of skilled interpretation. It hinged on the notion that the graphical image created a mental impression, a trace on the sensorium of the observer, which had its own psychological and physiological time. So the answer to the questions posed with the experimental system ultimately came in this form: as an interplay of reciprocal temporalities, between the experiment and its resulting inscription and the reading sensation on the part of the observer; between the physical, measured time of the apparatus and the psychophysiological time of the human beholder who engaged in the act of scanning the image.

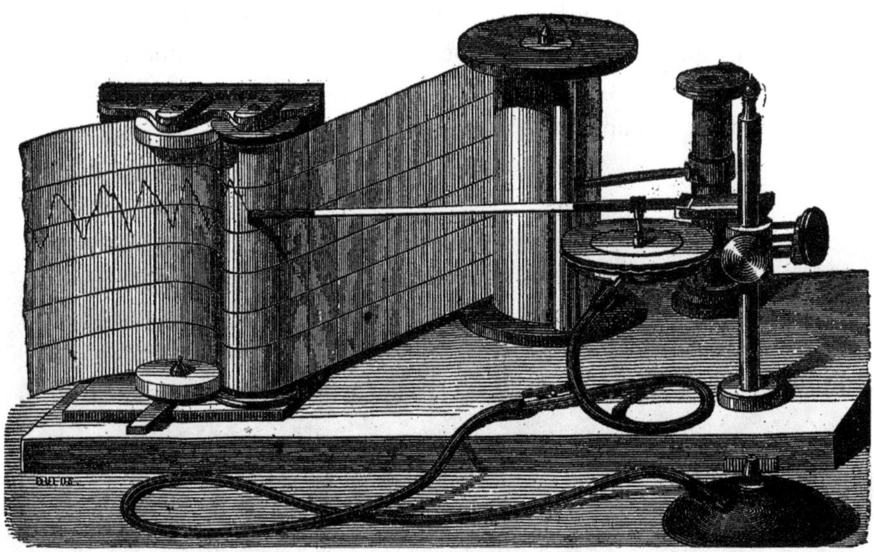

Marey polygraph, a versatile, multiuse apparatus illustrating the key components of graphic recording instruments: pneumatic tubes for transmitting the signals, the Marey tambour (circular drumlike surface), stylus, and rotating drums with graph paper. From Étienne-Jules Marey, *La Méthode graphique dans le sciences expérimentales et principalement en physiologie et en médicine* (Paris: G. Masson, 1878).

As we will see in later chapters, modernist artists would devise ways to capture all of these rhythms and temporalities of these lines and traces within the different media of the arts, incorporating them into artworks that would provoke awareness of those inner and outer rhythms in the beholder. Yet well before these developments, no less an artist than the great French photographer Nadar (a.k.a. Gaspard-Félix Tournachon) recounted the "absorbing attraction" of the play of abstract lines he encountered through his friend Marey: "these sheaves upon which white lines on funerary black unfold paintings of the infinite variations of the hymn of life . . . they are just waves, curves, jumps, vibrations, whims, jerks, abrupt ascents and sudden or gradual descents, rebounding similarly to the jagged summits of some chain of volcanoes. In the diversity of the stigmatic symptoms of our existence, in the rhythms of all human sufferings, each disease, each poison, has its personal scale."[72] Nadar's description straddled the mechanical and objective character of the graphic inscriptions and the observer's bodily and emotionally felt sense of the phenomena that was intrinsic to their fascination and indispensable to their practical interpretation. And it opened a third possibility: the rises and falls, rhythms and rebounds, described neither the phenomena themselves nor the material curves, but an interior sensation or emotion unfolding as a variation in time and apprehended through the mimetic faculty.

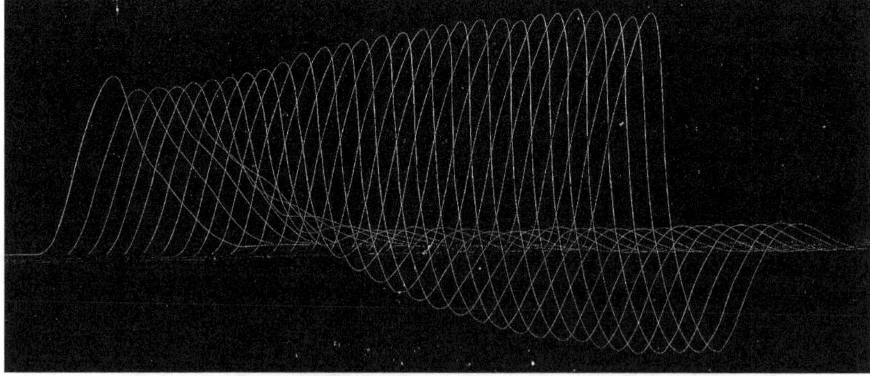

Myograph trace of a gradually stimulated frog muscle.
From Étienne-Jules Marey, *La Méthode graphique dans le sciences expérimentales et principalement en physiologie et en médicine* (Paris: G. Masson, 1878).

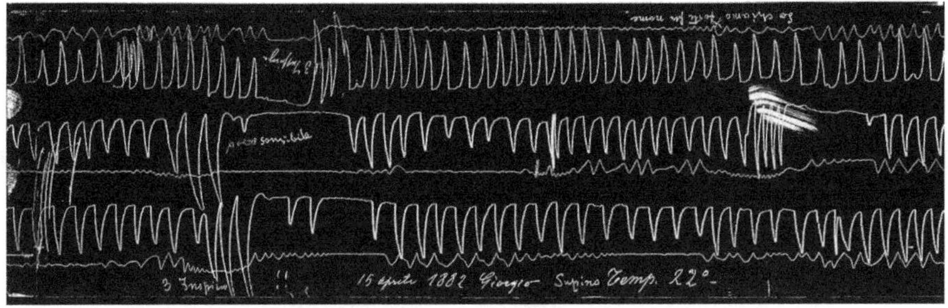

Angelo Mosso, graphical recordings of arterial pulse, 1882.
Courtesy of the Biblioteca Angelo Mosso, University of Turin, Italy.

Nadar's remarks on the graphical method appeared as part of a description of a visit to the laboratory of Marey in the 1860s, where he encountered all manner of organisms ("pigeons, buzzards, frogs, turtles, and adders") mingling with the recording apparatus that "reproduced life outside of life."[73] In this formulation the sensible-intuitive reading of the graphic trace gained suasion from the physiologist's view that many components of recording instruments effectively turned the body inside out, producing a freestanding, functional double of human or animal functions. Marey's physiological recording devices, for example, duplicated the body's own arterial structure in the tube used to transmit the pulse signal. Similarly, the receptive components of the apparatus, first the Marey tambour (the skin), then the elastic pneumatic tubes (here acting as nerves), and the smoked drum or paper (memory), could all be said to stand in for different components of the sensory functions of the observer. With these comparisons in mind, many experimentalists referred to the recording instruments as prosthetic devices, as amplifications of sense in the manner of the microscope, telescope, and stethoscope.

There was nothing new in scientists' treatment of instruments as prostheses to overcome frail and imperfect human senses. At least since Francis Bacon scientific instruments had often been presented as such, a means to overcome the frailty of sense resulting from the Fall. But late nineteenth-century descriptions of scientific instruments as sensory extensions appealed not to biblical but to evolutionary narratives for justification. These evolutionary accounts derived less from Darwinian than neo-Lamarckian theories about the emergence of tools and techniques among prehistoric human ancestors. At some point in human evolution, so the theory went, the long process of the physiological division of labor reached its limit and took shape in beyond-the-skin tools and artifacts. The flint ax, the hammer, and other primitive tools extended the gestures of the hand; more advanced machines, including the steam engine, externalized general functions of movement; and scientific instruments extended the functions of human sentience. Scientific instruments, like the other tools of civilization, referred to human beings as their source.

This anthropomorphic account of scientific instruments remained widespread throughout the late nineteenth century. But alongside the received accounts of prosthetic instrumentation, Marey offered an even more radical interpretation of the ontology of recording instruments as autonomous sensory agents. They were not simply the extensions of sense. Rather, they acted "like new senses," possessing "their own domain," standing over and against the human observer and constituting "their own field of investigation."[74] Instruments—or at least this special class of instruments—had in Marey's view acquired a degree of autonomy analogous to self-acting machines capable of doing the bidding of humans with little or no reference to their progenitors.

It was this autonomy that vouchsafed "life outside of life," the deterritorialization of physiological function. Later chapters of this book consider several examples of process, from the physiology of speech and its reterritorialization in the sciences of language, to the physiology of motor functions and their externalization in the visual and auditory arts.

BERGSON'S CRITIQUE: DURATION AND THE "CINEMATOGRAPHICAL ILLUSION"

While experimental physiologists viewed most problems of time measurement as technical issues, there remained a host of thorny epistemological problems that lurked around the project of measuring an entangled multiplicity of reciprocal temporalities. It is hardly surprising that fin-de-siècle philosophers rushed in to sort them out, beginning with Henri Bergson, whose complex philosophy of duration can be read as building on a critique of scientists' assumptions, with several lessons drawn from experimental physiology. In this section and another at the end of chapter 2, I offer a brief examination of Bergson's key concepts in relation to my discussion of the physiologists' experimental system. Here I am concerned with Bergson's critique of the experimental system as it pertained to the physiological measurement of time and his concept of duration; at the end of chapter 2, I will take up the way he engaged the literature on protoplasm and living substance to expand his notion of duration into the *élan vital*.

In numerous key philosophical passages, Bergson appeared to speak of the kinds of images and experimental techniques explored in this chapter—he was well acquainted with graphical recording methods and wrote about them in minor writings. Yet he refrained from doing so explicitly or from naming those whose work appeared at the center of his concerns.[75] Still, after about 1890, the philosophy of Bergson and the experimentation of Marey and others formed two poles, two ways of approaching what many philosophers, artists, and scientists experienced as a common discourse about movement, time and space, memory, and life.

But Bergson also had philosophical reasons for thinking outside the experimental system. In *Creative Evolution* (1907) he insisted that the challenge of philosophy is to overcome the inherent preference of thought for a "logic of solids"—for taking material things as its reference and point of departure. "We shall see," Bergson wrote, "that the human intellect feels at home among inanimate objects, more especially among solids, where our action finds its fulcrum and our industry its tools; that our logic is, pre-eminently, the logic of solids; that, consequently, our intellect triumphs in geometry, wherein is revealed the kinship of logical thought with unorganized matter, and where the intellect has only to follow its natural movement, after the lightest possible contact with experience, in order to go from discovery to discovery, sure that experience is following behind it and will justify it invariably."[76]

It was just this propensity to think through material tools and the immaterial features of lived experience that marked the critical edge of Bergson's first major work, *Essai sur les données immédiates de la conscience* (*Time and Free Will*) (1889), where he drove a wedge into the epistemological conundrum of physiological time measurement.[77] At issue was the core problem of the relation between the physical magnitudes of measured time and the felt or experienced intensities of physiological phenomena such as muscle action or affective states. Bergson argued that the psychological experience of intensities could not be reduced to measured time for the simple reason that time was always and only measured through extension, that is, through some kind of spatial reference, while intensity was "inextensive" and resistant to spatial reduction. While the physiologist's experimental system placed these different measures within an overarching continuum of temporal relations, Bergson insisted that they were different in kind and therefore incommensurable.

To make his argument, Bergson developed an alternative methodology based on what he called "intuition," which involved an even more fundamental notion of "duration" (*durée*)—the idea for which Bergson is most famous. Much can (and has) been said about these concepts in Bergson's philosophy, of course, but for our purposes we can say that Bergson amplified the sensible-intuitive dimension of the experimental system (embodied by the reader/experimenter), which he pitted against the metrological elements of the system. In the act of intuition, which was usually overlooked or factored out of experimental reckoning, Bergson uncovered a world marked by a "lived" sense of time that was irreducible, multiple, and anchored in the perspective of a particular location.

In a critique of the "experimental method" (here associated with the iconic figure Claude Bernard, but perhaps more accurately describing the methods of Marey), Bergson insisted that measurement is but an artificial and spatial juxtaposition of two separate things that are brought into relation by a recognizable (and spatial) scale.[78] In later writings Bergson insisted that the spatial dimension of measurement and the fact that all laboratory measurements had to be read were systematically ignored by scientists.[79] Time measurements did not capture time but only distracted attention away from its intensive character, the condition for the possibility of any genuine comprehension of movement. Our instruments push us always toward thinking of time as a "necklace of pearls"—the metaphor again evoked the "logic of solids," treating time as a series of solids (pearls) lined up along another solid (string). Bergson's metaphor generalized away from the more proximate one: the graphical inscription, with fixed points along a traced line. Within this scientific grid, time never escapes reduction to space; movement becomes a summing of points, or intervals, which in turn become the mysterious entities to be explored.

The epitome of this was what Bergson called the "cinematographical illusion of thought." The philosopher's notion of the cinematograph appears to have derived less from the burgeoning industry of films by the brothers Lumière or George Meliès than from the cinematographic apparatus based on Marey's chronophotography, which decomposed movement into high-speed moments or intervals and reconstructed them into a single immobile image.[80]

Bergson strikingly insisted that *the mechanism of our ordinary knowledge is of a cinematographical kind*," inasmuch as our thought consists in setting forth a "kind of cinematograph inside us": "We take snapshots, as it were of the passing reality, and, as these are characteristics of the reality, we have only to string them on a becoming, abstract, uniform, and invisible, situated at the back of the apparatus of knowledge, in order to imitate what there is that is characteristic in this becoming itself. Perception, intellection, language so proceed in general."[81]

Our habits of ordinary and philosophical thinking found confirmation in cinematography or graphical "readouts" of the physiologists' experimental systems.[82] Yet the instrumental modes of perception showed the paradoxical nature of this mode: it is impossible to reconstruct movement by juxtaposing one immobility with another immobility. "There must be movement somewhere," Bergson suggested, before then answering where: "it is in the apparatus."[83] There, inside the cinematographic black box, a multitude of parts whirled in a mobility that was effaced in the sequential image. Bergson thus blew the whistle on the central dilemma that the physiologists had grappled with all along: the multiple effects of time within the apparatus were not reducible to the inscriptions produced as the end state of the experimental process.

Bergson's critique of the "cinematographic illusion" appeared in his *Creative Evolution* and was closely tied to his ideas of *élan vital* and the mobility of life, which he pitted against ideas of evolution that reified life into serialized structures and static entities. As we will see in the next chapter, Bergson correctly perceived that the life sciences of his time had produced an image of life that corresponded with the experimental system's features and assumptions. His alternative conceptions of life, which extended the psychological experience of duration to a notion of duration rooted in biology, a physiological time all its own, built on the foundation of his critique of the experimental system. And as we will see in later chapters, Bergson's physiological time entailed an aesthetics in which every expressive medium of art would be understood as the end of a process whereby life would become spatialized and knowable.

2

THE VIBRATORY ORGANISM

Protoplasm and General Physiology

LIFE the popular name for the activity peculiar to protoplasm. This conception has been extended by analogy to phenomena different in kind, such as the activities of masses of water or of air, or of machinery, or by another analogy, to the duration of a composite structure, and by imagination to real or supposed phenomena such as the manifestations of incorporeal entities. From the point of view of exact science life is associated with matter, is displayed only by living bodies, by all living bodies, and is what distinguishes living bodies from bodies that are not alive.

Encyclopedia Britannica (1910–11)

HISTORIANS OF THE LIFE SCIENCES HAVE LONG CONSIDERED THE productive role of models and analogies in conceptualizing living organisms as objects of research.[1] We have seen how, since the late 1840s, physiologists conceived of organisms using models drawn from the sciences of energy. After 1870 many physiologists sought to join the sciences of energy and life together, proposing that the unified forces of the physical world fused in a nitrogenous, semifluid, elastic substance that could be found in the cells of all organisms: *protoplasm*. They reckoned that the gelatinous medium would prove itself to be uniquely suited to store physical forces and therefore to serve as a substratum of all vital processes. In this sense protoplasm was conceptualized by analogy to self-recording instruments, as a living apparatus in the cell for capturing and recording energetic traces from the milieu.

For many biologists protoplasm became, in the words of the young Spanish scientist Santiago Ramon y Cajal, "the battlefield of the forthcoming science," where the "discovery of the laws that this matter obeys . . . will be the greatest conquest of humanity."[2] Ramon y Cajal's prediction hinged on the assumption that the protoplasmic "theater of cell organization" would become the primary site of attempts to explore the parameters of *biological plasticity*, the shaping of living matter in space and time. Biological plasticity, as Hannah Landecker observes, "is an idea of living matter that is also a practical approach to it."[3] In this chapter I argue that what historian of biology Philip J. Pauly calls "biological modernism"—the drive to create technologies of living substance—had its beginnings in these late nineteenth-century experiments on the plasticity of protoplasm.[4] Late nineteenth-century biologists conceptualized protoplasm as a site for doing physiology at the subcellular level, using versions of the familiar self-recording experimental system described in the previous chapter to configure living substance as a pulsatile medium capable of storing manifold temporalities within it. In this chapter I argue that the protoplasm theory provided ontological support for an important domain of physiologists' experimental practices based on graphical recording instruments. This argument will set the stage for the material transfer of biological modernism to the modernisms of painters and poets. By the 1890s scientists and their publics (including many artists, as we will see in chapters 6 and 7) had begun to anticipate the creation of new technologically mediated life-forms and new interventions in human nature. This expectation prepared the ground for artists to adopt refashioned elements of the physiologists' experimental systems in their own practice, as a means of turning art into a medium for experiments in living substance and human nature.

The anticipation of new technologies of living matter reverberated well beyond biology, with protoplasm serving as a muse to thinkers as different as Charles Sanders Peirce, Sigmund Freud, Friedrich Nietzsche, and Henri Bergson. The uses of protoplasm by these thinkers, we will see, also provided context for the experiments of artists and poets. For Freud protoplasmic bridges explained the nerve junction, while for Nietzsche the predatory behavior of protoplasmic beings served as a model for the will to power.[5] For many late nineteenth-century this "protoplasmania" gained momentum from the crucial role that cell plasm played in monist philosophies.[6] Protoplasm furnished the evolutionary and diachronic conditions for a parallelism between the vibratory universe described by physicists and the "vibratory organism" favored in psychophysical worldviews; notions of the unity of life joined with the unity of forces in the physical world.[7] For Peirce, among others, the epistemological quest to track all signs of force should properly begin with the protoplasm, since "physical events are but degraded or undeveloped forms of psychical events."[8] Perhaps most consequentially for both science and art, protoplasm theories underwrote critical arguments in Henri Bergson's *Creative Evolution* (1907), giving them new life in the nascent forms of modernism on the eve of the First World War.

"THE PHYSICAL BASIS OF LIFE"

"Great is Protoplasm. There is no life but protoplasm, and Huxley is its prophet," intoned Samuel Butler, inflecting the protoplasmic creed with echoes of the Qur'anic *shahada*.[9] Although he was preceded by several decades of protoplasm research, English biologist Thomas Henry Huxley (1825–95) was indeed the first in the prophetic line, as his 1869 lecture "The Physical Basis of Life," launched the fascination with protoplasm as the primordial medium of life. Another Darwinian lieutenant, German naturalist Ernst Haeckel (1834–1919), soon followed with an elaboration of Huxley's hypothesis in his 1875 treatise *Über die Wellenzeugung der Lebensteilchen oder die Perigenesis der Plastidule*. In this work Haeckel provided a comprehensive biological vision of the cell plasm, challenging the reigning molecular theory of heredity proposed by Darwin with a "theory of the transmission of force" as the basis of heredity and indeed of all the phenomena of living organisms.[10] The historiography of science has favored Darwin's theory, but many late nineteenth-century scientists found the protoplasm theory more promising.[11] As an answer to the question "what lives?" it located fundamental problems of the life sciences at the subcellular level, pushing questions of heredity more deeply into the terrain of general biology.[12]

Huxley's proclamation of protoplasm as the "physical basis of life" came with high drama in a controversial Sunday-evening lecture in Edinburgh.[13] Showing bottles of smelling salts and carbonic acid—the constituents of protoplasm—to his rapt audience, Huxley argued that all living things, algal mats and humans alike, are unified in sharing one basic kind of matter. The primary evidence for the protoplasm as the physical basis of life could be found in its chemical constitution: basically proteinaceous and subject to heat coagulation, with a cellular "catholicity of assimilation" that made it uniquely suited to store vital forces.[14] Protoplasm's suitability as a sub-

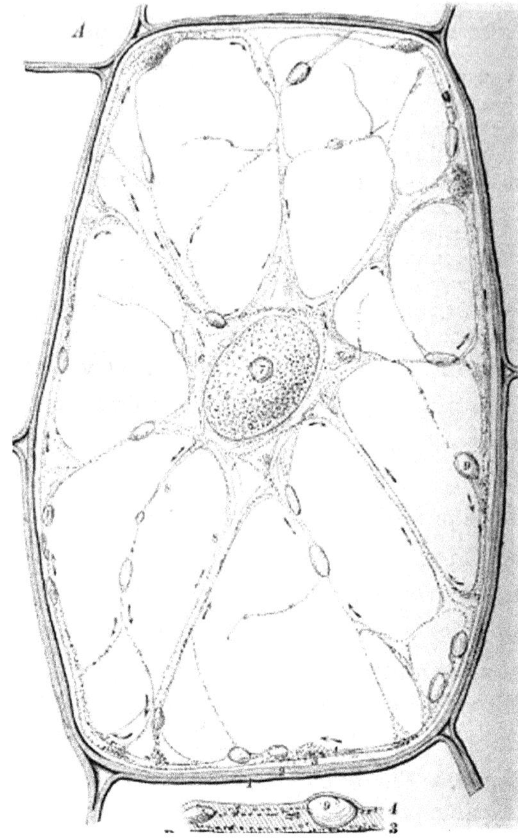

Protoplasm, ca. 1880. A cell enlarged one thousand times, showing the morphology of the nucleus and protoplasmic streams. From Johannes von Hanstein, *Das Protoplasma als Träger der pflanzlichen und tierlichen Lebensvorrichtungen* (Heidelberg: Winter, 1880).

stratum for living processes was manifest in its contractility, evident in the "unceasing activity" that characterized the protoplasmic layer of nettle hair, in which "local contractions of the whole thickness of its substance pass slowly and gradually from point to point, and give rise to the appearance of progressive waves."[15] Huxley did not spell out what he thought the physical relations of these waves might be, but as with nineteenth-century wave theories of light that postulated a very thin elastic solid or "jelly" stretching across space, the protoplasm seemed to provide a medium both rigid enough to transmit rapid vibrations and fluid enough for ordinary matter to move through it.[16]

But more than a substratum for vital forces, Huxley boldly asserted that protoplasm showed the way to a physiological theory of heredity. Sensitive to external forces such as heat, light, pressure, and very possibly, the ether, the material structure of the protoplasm appeared uniquely suited to carry the imprint of recurring actions. The granules became driven "through channels in the protoplasm which seem to have a considerable amount of persistence," though they sometimes coursed in new directions when "opposite streams come into direct collision, and, after a longer or shorter struggle, one predominates."[17] Huxley contended that in complex organisms, the differentiation of function was accompanied by greater specialization of the protoplasm.[18] Protoplasm, in other words, should be seen as the seat of the famous principle of the division of physiological labor postulated by French physiologist Henri Milne-Edwards: one and the same portion of protoplasm could successfully take on the function of feeding, moving, or reproducing apparatus, while in more advanced organisms these functions were carried out by specialized organs as a result of evolutionary differentiation.

Thanks to Huxley, protoplasm became a household word, especially in Britain. Huxley's thesis found immediate supporters and detractors, both philosophical and scientific. "Mr. Huxley changed the glory of God into—Protoplasm!," exclaimed one Presbyterian minister, contending that the protoplasm was the new Baal of materialism and atheism, with Huxley its high priest.[19]

Others took a wholly positive view, finding "science almost sublimated into poetry" in protoplasm's "rushing and roaring" maelstroms within the cell.[20] Protoplasm even reverberated in Parliament, when Benjamin Disraeli remarked in a speech, "This is essentially a material age. We live in an age when young men prattle about Protoplasm, and when young ladies in gilded saloons unconsciously talk atheism."[21]

A more scientific objection to Huxley's proposal came from Scottish philosopher James Hutchison Stirling, who challenged the universal identity that Huxley imputed to protoplasm. Stirling understood that Huxley's account of protoplasm buttressed Darwin's theory, even if Huxley did not say so explicitly in his essay. The contractility of protoplasm provided what Stirling called an "auto-plastic living matter that, produced by ordinary chemical processes, is yet capable of continuing and developing itself into new and higher forms." This "would fairly enable Mr. Darwin, supplemented by such a life-stuff, to account by natural means for everything like an idea or thought that appears in creation."[22] In fact, this kind of materialist evolution—or any definitive position on the boundary between the organic and inorganic—was probably not of much concern to Darwin. But it was of importance to Huxley and Haeckel, the chief lieutenants of Darwin's battalion. Haeckel's attraction to protoplasm derived in part from the notion that the simplest and therefore phylogenetically most primitive known animals, the moners, appeared to consist of nothing more than a nonnucleate globule of protoplasm, yet displayed properties of sensibility normally attributed only to organisms with a nervous system.[23]

PERIGENESIS DER PLASTIDULE AND THE PROBLEM OF HEREDITY

Haeckel's theory of protoplasmic heredity and function drew upon several decades of German and French research that began with the pioneering descriptive studies in the 1830s and 1840s of Eduard Dujardin, Hugo von Mohl, and Jan Purkyně, who coined the elevated term *protoplasm* to designate what German biologists colloquially called *Urschleim* and French scientists called the *sarcode*.[24] By the mid-nineteenth century biologists took mounting interest in the seemingly homogenous ground substance preponderant in the cell. The fascination began with Ferdinand Cohn's identification of the identity between plant and animal protoplasm in 1850, which was followed by a welter of investigations of the vital properties of cell mass. The tide crested with Max Schultze's investigation into the contractility of lower marine animals, which led in 1860 to the acknowledgment that living cells could be found in a "primitive membraneless condition," in which the cells appeared as merely a naked clump of protoplasm with a nucleus.[25] In a series of studies on the contractile properties of protoplasm, Schultze claimed that this single substance made up the substratum of vital activity in the tissues of all living organisms. This claim was soon echoed by numerous prominent biologists. Ernst Brücke endorsed it, with the qualification that protoplasm must have a more complex structure and organization to sustain the phenomena of life. Haeckel, too, called the protoplasm "the original active substratum of all vital phenomena" and provided empirical support, especially in his monograph *Die Radiolaren*.

The close similarity between cellular protoplasm and the morphology of protozoa convinced Haeckel of a necessary connection between cytology and evolutionary development.[26] With his biogenetic law (ontogeny recapitulates phylogeny) in mind, Haeckel observed that even humans, placed at the apex of creation, exhibited a cell stage during ontogenetic development that united them with the lowest of all forms, the moners. Protoplasm therefore seemed to provide the royal road to "a mechanical explanation of vital phenomena, and especially for a truly monistic, i.e., mechano-causal knowledge of organic nature."[27]

Haeckel's proposal challenged the heredity theory of his scientific idol, Charles Darwin. Darwin's "provisional hypothesis of pangenesis" held that cells shed small particles, called gemmules, which collect in the reproductive organs prior to fertilization, conferring a role for every cell in the organism in the constitution of offspring. Although Darwin emphasized the genetic role of the gemmules, he nevertheless treated them as constitutive units of the cell. Haeckel found Darwin's hypothesis unsatisfying—"the only part of Darwin's theory with which I disagree," he wrote—both because of its vagueness and implausibility, and because it ignored important research in cell theory, physiology, and morphology, the laboratory sciences in which Germans excelled. Both Darwin's pangenesis and Haeckel's perigenesis relied on Lamarckian notions of acquired characteristics, but Haeckel thought his own approach more in line with the evidence of experimental biology.

Haeckel proposed instead that the colloidal substances comprising the non-nucleate preponderance of the cell had the ability to receive and maintain the waveform vibrations of the external world and to pass these on to all cellular offspring. For the next two or three decades the two theories of heredity stood, in the words of the British biologist Ray Lankester, in "the same relation as the emission and undulatory theories of light": competing ontologies of corpuscles and waves, to be sure, but also theories whose contentions were fought not simply on the grounds of evidence but on their larger implications.[28]

Haeckel argued that the appeal of his waveforce theory of evolution rested in its broad compatibility with the mechanical and thermodynamic worldview predominate among nineteenth-century physical scientists. Haeckel sought to join his vision of waveforce theory and evolution with the mechanical and thermodynamic worldview of experimental physiology pioneered by German physiologists during the late 1840s. It postulated a periodic or waveform model of movement in the cell that was consistent with the physiologists' graphical inscriptions of macroscopic functions in the body. As physiologists became accustomed to working with these images, they began to see all movements of life as a play of undulating lines. The innovation of Haeckel's perigenesis theory rested in the suggestion that the waveforces of complex organisms originated in the most primitive manifestations of life. The varied functions of complex organisms, each with their specific rhythms and periodicity, came about through the differentiation of function in the division of physiological labor.

But Haeckel's wave theory did rather more than simply posit an energetic basis of life. In his account, the protoplasm itself acted as a kind of graphical recording device, receiving impulses from the milieu and storing them as active vibrations in its colloidal structures. It was a prime case of turning an "epistemic thing"—an object that is brought into existence by the experimental setup, in this case the physiological graphic—into a feature of the natural world itself.[29] Sensations or impulses thus inscribed themselves on organic tissues in a form similar to the physiological graphics produced in laboratory instruments.[30]

Haeckel's was not the only attempt to describe organic tissues as a recording device—numerous neo-Lamarckian experimentalists sought the imprints of the environment in plant or animal anatomy and morphology.[31] Étienne-Jules Marey, for example, in a classic statement on neo-Lamarckian physiology, described how functional movements inscribe themselves as traces on different organs. "The bone sustains, like soft wax, all of the deformations of the exterior forces imprinted upon it," Marey wrote, concluding that tissues and surfaces served as so many internal recording cylinders, each capturing the imprints of organic movements.[32] Marey argued that this was the mechanism that underwrote the transformist slogan "function makes the organ," thus making *movement* the chief determinant of morphological change.

Haeckel's approach to the mechanism of evolutionary heredity also mingled evolutionary assumptions with a reading of the physiologist Ewald Hering's much discussed essay *Über das Gedächtnis als eine allgemeine Funktion der Organisierten Materie*.[33] Hering suggested that there are close connections between the conscious memory of ordinary life and the phylogenetic "memory" transmitted through the inheritance of acquired characteristics.[34] Both were attributable to the effect of vibrations imparted to the organism from external objects: vibrations that were repeated often enough passed from conscious memory to the unconscious inheritance of the organism. Although largely speculative, Hering's idea unleashed several decades of attempts to fix a theory of heredity and memory as the effect of traces or vibrations on organic tissues.[35]

In spite of his enthusiasm for Hering's idea, Haeckel found the physical properties of Hering's "organized matter" too vague. Haeckel set out to improve upon Hering's account, declaring his agreement with the physiologists who "justifiably rule out all vitalism and teleology . . . who jettison all mystical and supernatural actions of the type of 'vital force' (*Lebenskraft*) and limit themselves to 'physical-chemical'—or in a broader sense 'mechanical'—forces."[36] Haeckel referred to Kant's insistence on mechanical explanations as the necessary condition for any natural science and suggested that an account of the physical basis of life needed a better physics if it were to be plausible.

But Haeckel appeared to contradict himself with a hearty embrace of Goethe's scientific ideas, displaying what Jane Bennett identifies as the "naive ambition" of vital materialists from Lucretius to Kafka, namely, the use of the art of philosophical contemplation to "linger in those moments during which they find themselves fascinated by objects, taking them as clues to the material vitality they share with them."[37] For Haeckel all matter "possesses an inherent sum of force" as part of its nature, and this force should be seen as a spiritualizing principle.[38] Hence, the cell, like the atom, is ensouled (*beseelt*). Similarly, Haeckel argued,

> without the hypothesis of the soul of the atom, the most vulgar and most general phenomena of chemistry explain nothing. Pleasure and displeasure, desire and aversion, attraction and repulsion should be common to all atoms. . . . Otherwise, what would the basis of the chemical doctrine of elected affinities rest upon, if not on the unconscious supposition that in reality atoms, which attract and repel, are endowed with certain tendencies, and that by following these sensations or impulses also possess the will and the capacity to reconcile or to distance themselves from one another.[39]

Haeckel appears to have believed that the new synthetic chemistry, despite its uncompromising opposition to vitalism, presupposed Goethean anthropomorphic principles—above all, the special chemical and physical properties of carbon, especially in the semifluidity and instability of carbon albuminoid compounds that appeared to be where one should look for the mechanical causes of particular movements through which life and nonlife differentiate themselves.

In Haeckel's formulation, every "plastidule" (minute structures within the protoplasm) had a characteristic wave pattern as a result of its history and environment, which constituted memory for the organism and heredity for the species. "Heredity is the memory of the plastidules," Haeckel wrote, "and variability their power of comprehension."[40] Where Darwin argued that the modification of characters suggests the discrete particulate character of hereditary materials, Haeckel argued that the possibility of widely variable waveforms entailed a broad spectrum of potential modifications to the organism. "Adaptation," Haeckel explained, "is a modification of the plastidule's movement pattern, through which it acquires new characters."[41] These wave patterns are passed along by both the sperm and the egg, which

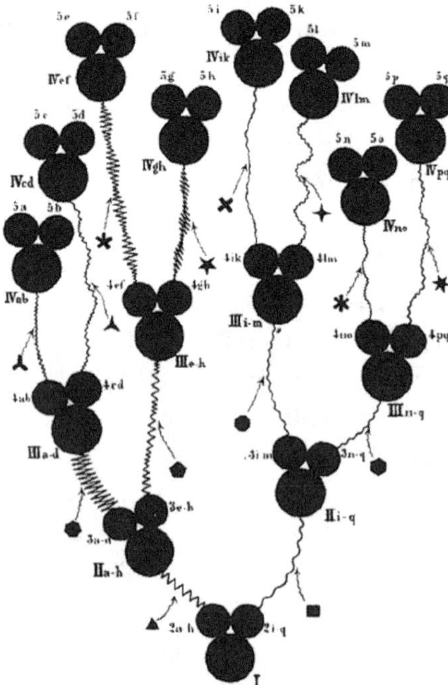

Haeckel's schematic diagram of the actions of the plastidules, that is, of the inheritance of different wave motions, with inherited wave motions represented by divergent undulations emanating from each of the pair of smaller spheres in each generation. The small geometric figures intersecting the wave patterns represent different environments working their influence on each generation and modifying the wave motions inherited by the next generation. From Ernst Haeckel, *Über die Wellenzeugung der Lebensteilchen oder die Perigenesis der Plastidule* (1875), in *Gemeinverständliche Vorträge und Abhandlungen aus dem Gebiete der Entwicklungslehre*, 2nd ed. (Berlin: Henschel; Leipzig: Kröner, 1924).

combine at conception to produce a new wave pattern in the new organism's plastidules, which became further transmitted mechanically by cell division through the progressive differentiation of tissues and more complex organic forms.

Haeckel illustrated his concept with a schematic diagram of the actions of the plastidules. In this diagram, each simple cell is represented by a larger ball. The two-cell offspring, the results of cell division, are shown by the two smaller balls. The wave lines signify the vibrations of each individual cell with their unique plastidule movement. The small bodies in various shapes represent the sum of the external conditions of existence, which influence the nutrition of the cell and alter the original plastidule movement through adaptation. Thus the original plastidule movement, transferred through heredity, is modified by the plastidule movements contributed by each parent. In its unique periodicity, the wave movement transfers the inheritance of its most immediate ancestor, but indirectly also the inherited characteristics of its earlier ancestors as well as their conditions of existence.

THE GREAT THROB OF LIFE

Haeckel argued that at a broader level, branching waveform movement could explain the divergence of characters that Darwin saw as the mark of evolution. The individuality of each cell or unicellular organism was signaled by its own unique waveform, which then reproduced itself in its own hereditary line. The unbroken continuity connected all persons, all living organisms, with the great pattern that could be traced back to the beginning of life, a wave pattern that the organism recapitulated in individual development. Haeckel maintained that since the number of possible waveforms was incalculably large, this mechanism of heredity could generate an enormous amount of variation without trading in the assumption of continuity for discrete entities or any recourse to jumps or discontinuities. But the possible amount of variation was not unlimited. The length of the waves themselves was bounded, and their existence was confined to a specific place and location in the protoplasm.

Haeckel's description of the *Wellenzeugung* of protoplasm formed a complement to his well-known Descent Tree. In his *Generelle Morphologie der Organismen* (1866), Haeckel presented a tree depicting the evolution of plants, protists, and animals, which could be read to support either the hypothesis of one moner (Haeckel's term for the simplest existing organism) as the source of all life, or the hypothesis that three (or as many as nineteen) different monera gave rise to the various phyla.[42]

In his *Wellenzeugung* essay Haeckel reminded the reader that the grand movement depicted in the "tree of life" was primarily a story of protoplasm—the only organic substance shared (and preponderantly so) by all living forms. Haeckel intended his perigenesis theory to apply equally to cells conjoined with other cells in organisms of all levels of complexity and to single-celled organisms composed mostly of protoplasm. He elaborated: "The evolutionary movement presented by this series of our ancestors can be depicted simply by an undulating line in which the life of each individual corresponds to one wave. But we do not limit our view to the series of our direct ancestors: let us extend our vision and embrace the ensemble of our near relatives; we can express their relations very well in the form of a Descent Tree. . . . The genealogical tree as a whole presents the image of *one ramified waveform movement*."[43]

Viewed through the lens of the perigenesis theory, the Descent Tree depicted organic development as a summing of periodic waveforms, which stabilized at intervals into specific physiological functions, each with their own characteristic periodicity. The vibrations in the protoplasm of unicellular creatures congealed into functional motions, modified gradually by use or disuse, and in complex organisms differentiated themselves into more specialized organs and functions, following the principle of the division of physiological labor.

The principle of the division of physiological labor played an important role in Haeckel's theory and was critical to the extensions of the protoplasm doctrine examined below.[44] Introduced by the French physiologist Henri Milne-Edwards in various texts beginning in the 1820s, the notion of the physiological division of labor allowed biologists to "compare and study living things as if they were machines created by the industry of man."[45] Adopting Adam Smith's famous metaphor wholeheartedly, Milne-Edwards wrote that the "body of all living beings, whether animal or plant, resembles a factory . . . where the organs, comparable to workers, work incessantly to produce the phenomena that constitute the life of the individual."[46] Single-celled, protoplasmic organisms, by contrast, could be compared to "workers

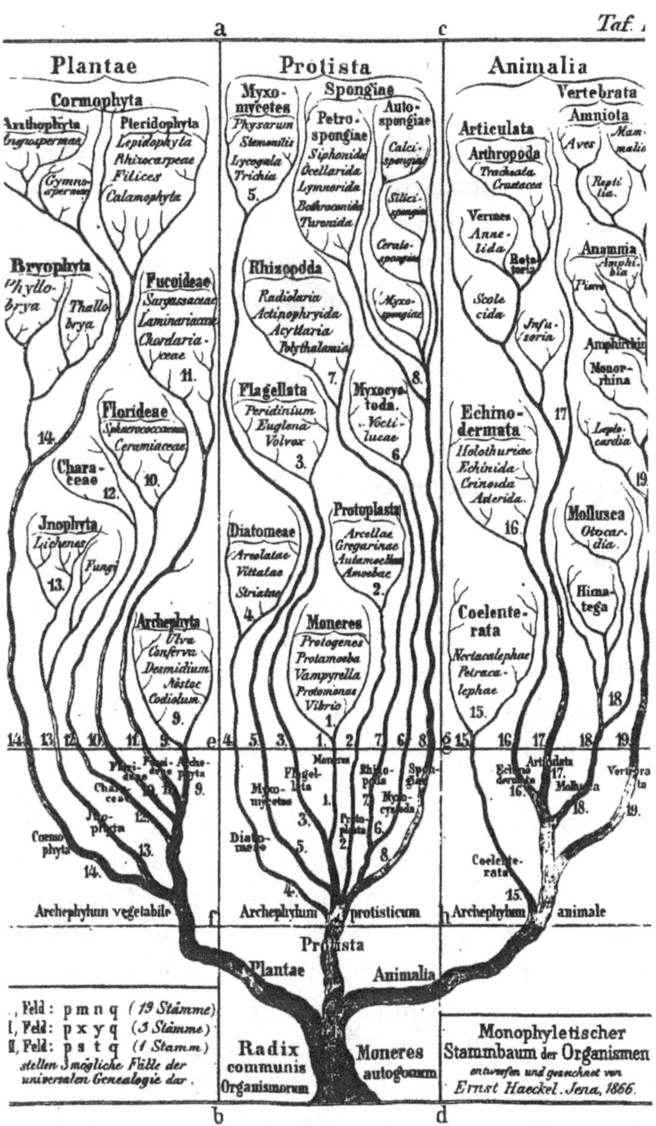

Haeckel's Descent Tree of Organisms, with *pstq* representing the hypothesis of one moneron as the source of all life; *pxyq* representing the hypothesis of three monera as the origin, respectively, of plants, protists, and animals; and *pmnq* representing the hypothesis that some nineteen different monera gave rise to various phyla of plants, protists, and animals. From Ernst Haeckel, *Generelle Morphologie* (Berlin: Reimer, 1866).

without tools," trying to perform functions without the necessary organs to accomplish them. Other primitive organisms, Milne-Edwards wrote, "are like one of those poorly managed factories where each worker is charged with the entire series of operations necessary for the confection of the manufactured object."[47] In more differentiated organisms the functional labor was apportioned between different instruments (*appareils*) or systems, such as circulation, sensibility, movement, nutrition, et cetera. This labor, moreover, could in principle be studied with the methods of the engineer, using graphical recording instruments to measure the "magnitudes of the forces put in play, and the manner in which these forces are applied."[48] Two features of Milne-Edwards's principle should be underlined here: its purely functional nature and the sense that it implied that function could be described in the engineer's graphical method of measurement.[49]

Both of these features were critical to Haeckel's perigenesis theory. In higher organisms the branching wave movement therefore produced the rhythmic, periodic characteristics of specific functions like circulation, respiration, and locomotion. Transferring Milne-Edwards's factory metaphor to the time-honored image of the genealogical tree, Haeckel ingeniously combined the idea of entwining and branching waveforms, which represented in miniature "the development of every human family, the genealogy of every dynasty."[50]

Haeckel thus ingeniously combined the idea of entwining and branching waveforms with the time-honored image of the genealogical tree, which represented in miniature "the development of every human family, the genealogy of every dynasty."[51] The tree diagram had many biblical and secular antecedents, as Mary Bouquet has shown, and many of whose features found their way into the trees or branching diagrams constructed by mid-nineteenth-century biologists to illustrate relationships between species.[52] Robert J. Richards argues convincingly that well before Haeckel, Martin Barry's "Tree of Animal Development" (1837) placed at its roots the germ, which was morphologically similar in all animals; and from this common ancestral monad the invertebrates branched off on one side, vertebrates on the other, with fishes, mammals, and finally man ramifying through progressively higher branches of the tree.[53]

Haeckel's iconic tree of the ancestral lineage of humans offered the trunk as the *Ur* form, which gradually diversifies and ramifies through vast spans

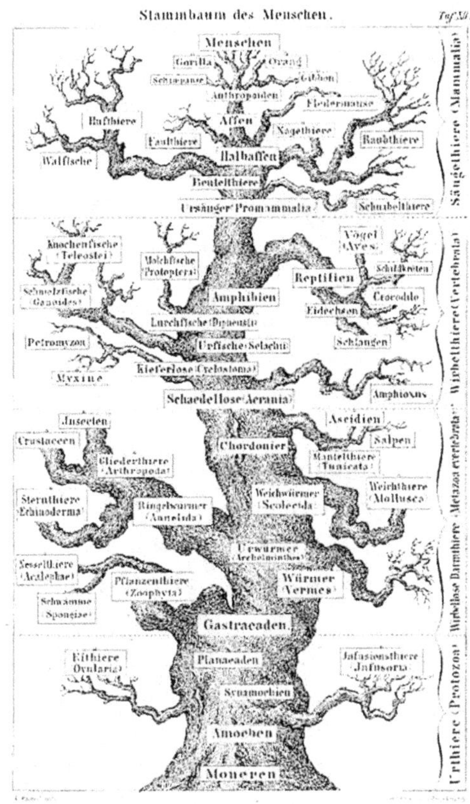

Haeckel's Human Descent Tree (*Stammbaum*), depicting the developmental line from single-celled monera to humans. From Ernst Haeckel, *Anthropogenie* (Leipzig: W. Engelman, 1874).

of time. Yet, in Haeckel's Descent Tree time's arrow persists across vast shifts of scale, from the microscopic protoplasmic movements to the macroscopic directionality of phylogenic evolution. Haeckel's vision of life unified by protoplasmic substance captured the scientific imagination of a generation of biologists and provided an indispensable pillar of biological monism. The young Santiago Ramon y Cajal, who would later oppose the theory, gave elegant expression of it in the 1880s. "There are no progenitors and no progeny," he wrote. "There are no separate and independent individuals, alive or dead, but only one single substance, protoplasm, which fills the world with its creations, which grows, which ramifies, which (temporarily) individuates, but which never dies. In our own being there still moves that ancient protoplasm of the *archiplasson*, the starting point, perhaps, of organic evolution."[54]

Because it spanned the entirety of biological time in its memory capacity, Haeckel's protoplasmic continuity could also be seen as the bearer of certain timelessness or immortality. In this sense it directly corresponded with theories of the ether, whose rhythmic and oscillatory motions also bore the stamp of eternity. In the well-known account put forth in 1875 by British physicists Balfour Stewart and Peter Guthrie Tait's *Unseen Universe*, for example, ether was interpreted "as a way in which the universe conserves a memory of the past": every event, every experience and every sensation endures as if recorded, impressed on the light waves of matter, because "photographs are continually produced and conserved of every event."[55] Already in the 1870s some scientists and philosophers began to speculate on the presence of an organ receptive to ether waves in humans and other animals.[56] Many fin-de-siècle monists speculated that protoplasm might fit the bill.

Across Europe, several young experimental physiologists such as Michael Foster, Max Verworn, and Alfred Binet adopted Haeckel's schema as a model of what came to be called "general physiology," a unified science of life based on the actions of the cell. The key assumption hinged on the parallel between the cell protoplasm in complex organisms and the actions of unicellular organisms that were uniquely composed of protoplasm.[57] In Foster's physiology laboratory at Cambridge University, for example, students were led through a curriculum of animal physiology that emphasized that "the whole animal body is modified protoplasm."[58] Foster, who had served as Huxley's demonstrator for two summer courses at the South Kensington Museum before taking the new physiology chair at Cambridge, opened with the automatisms of protoplasm, then progressed through stages of functional development in various organisms, culminating in studies of the rhythmicity of the higher functions such as the human heartbeat. Foster's general aim was to convey "the essential unity of the rhythmic beat of the heart and the amoeboid movement of protoplasm"; the challenge was to show how ramifying wave movements became altered through the evolution of function, how the "slow, irregular, crawling movements of the primordial protoplasm are gradually transformed and gathered up into the sharp short stroke of the heart's beat."[59]

Foster insisted that the heart's beat—or any other automatic function of higher organisms—occurred through a harmony of cells acting in a mimetic manner, "as if each cell felt by its primeval protoplasmic sensibility the throb of its neighbor cells, and as if that throb were the keynote by which all its own molecular processes were pitched."[60] Repeating the lesson of Haeckel's tree of life, Foster noted that "our whole life [is] one throb, the sequence of our fathers', forerunners of our children's."[61] In Foster's ringing phrase, protoplasm served as the site of mimetic forms of memory, closely akin to the principle of "inner imitation" or "aesthetic empathy" (*Einfühlung*) that later psychophysiologists and aestheticians would make a cardinal principle of early modernist aesthetics (see chapter 7).

Foster's insistence of the interplay of evolutionary and physiological scales of time served as the outline of a general physiology that accumulated many key practitioners over the next several decades. É.-J. Marey's investigations of manifold systems of physiological time were of course a primary model and parallel, while Max Verworn's general physiology emphasized the task of doing physiology at the subcellular level. While these early investigations were explicitly tinged with Lamarckian evolutionary concerns for plasticity, the arc of laboratory experimentalism increasingly anticipated the creation of new life-forms under experimental and technologically mediated conditions. Several versions of this new biological modernism—cellular and subcellular experimentation conducted in vitro—centered on protoplasmic plasticity and problems of physiological time, with the aim of controlled intervention and manipulation of the conditions of life itself.[62]

FROM PROTOPLASM TO CELL PSYCHOLOGY

From the 1870s, scientific and philosophical interest in the invisible realm of the mind began to grow, and for certain thinkers Haeckel's developing theory of "cell psychology" was of particular interest. In several essays written during the late 1870s, Haeckel argued that the perigenetic movements indicated not only physiological functions but the presence of psychological functions (*Seelenleben*), with their seat in the protoplasm. This held, moreover, for unicellular organisms as well as for cells that lived in "states" or organized social communities governed by the division of labor and mutual interdependence.[63] "This perspective is based on the study of infusoria, amoebae, and other unicellular organisms," Haeckel insisted, adding that "among these single-cells, living in isolation, we find the same manifestations of psychic life—sensation, representation (*Vorstellung*), will, movement—as in higher animals composed of a large number of cells."[64]

Asking rhetorically, "What is the Soul or Psyche?," Haeckel replied that "soul is the sum of a number of special cellular activities, among which feeling and will, sensation and involuntary movement are the most important and the most generally distributed."[65] Both cells and protozoa were "ensouled" and therefore amenable to psychophysiological investigation using "mechanical" methods. Such an approach would, Haeckel insisted, overcome the shortcomings of the fledgling field of "psychophysics" by placing its questions within the evolutionary history of psychological functions. One would find that while every living cell possessed a "cell psyche" (*Zellseele*), only higher animals and humans possess "psyche cells" (*Seelenzellen*), found in structures like the ganglia of the brain, which governed higher functions such as thought, representation, and consciousness.[66]

Haeckel's conjectures about the ensouled protoplasm kicked off a wave of experimental and speculative attempts to specify the elementary features of psychological life in both cellular protoplasm and the movements of unicellular organisms. Judy Johns Schloegel and Henning Schmidgen have shown how Haeckel's description of the cell psyche inspired many talented young scientists internationally to conduct experimental investigations of the psychology of unicellular organisms, or "protists."[67] Max Verworn, for example, found unconscious processes of reflexive, automatic, and impulsive movements, as well as elementary sensations and representations, which led him to conclude that "every elementary part of the protoplasm has its own autonomous psyche"[68] Verworn's studies largely agreed with similar studies on the "psychic life of microorganisms" conducted two years earlier by the French psychophysiologist Alfred Binet.[69] Binet's studies showing the presence of primitive psychological functions in protozoa were explicitly directed to refute British evolutionist George Romanes's claims that mental and psychological functions were a relatively late development in evolution.

In France, Binet aimed to refute claims that mental and psychological functions were a relatively late development in evolution.[70] Binet's studies joined protoplasm investigations with a broader wave of French interests in the burgeoning field of psychophysiology. Binet published his results in the *Revue philosophique*, a periodical edited by Théodule Ribot, one of France's leading exponents of the "psychology of movements," investigations of how "movements enter into the majority of our states of consciousness as a constitutive element."[71]

Movements included involuntary motions like those studied by evolutionary physiologists, as well as voluntary actions and gestures in higher animals and humans. For Ribot and followers like Charles Richet, Charles Féré, Frédéric Paulhan, and Binet, feelings, thoughts, and ideas were generated by virtual movements set in motion from outside the organism (stimuli and sensation) and from real movements on the inside (ideas and internal sensations).[72] These studies probed the way in which sensations, often sound or light, but also the perception of movement, cause a corresponding movement in the viewer's breathing, vascular system, eye muscles, or an "inner imitation" of the movement in the musculature of the body or even the cellular protoplasm. The great fascination for this work rested in the ubiquity of imitation in the formation of human nature and the uncertain boundary between normal degrees of imitation and the pathological extremes of imitation found in somnambulists (hypnotized subjects) and hysterics.

Binet's research on the psychology of microorganisms sought to frame these questions of human psychophysiology within a broader program of evolutionary development. One could show the essential unity of the psychological vibrations in the protoplasm of simple organisms with the rhythmicity of ideas and affects in the muscular sensations of humans. Binet's vision of a functional psychophysiology spanning unicellular organisms, at one end, and the human brain, at the other, paralleled the root and treetop of Haeckel's Descent Tree. A photograph of Binet's laboratory schematized this conception: between the two poles set by images hanging on the wall, of unicellular infusoria and the human brain, stood the psychophysiologists and their trusty graphical recording apparatus for investigating functional movements as the key to human psychology.

Others explored the analogy in the opposite direction. Thomas Edison, for example, suggested that his phonograph be understood as a sensory prosthesis by appending Huxley's essay, "On the Hypothesis that Animals Are Automata," to his first publication about the instrument. In an 1880 essay, "Memory and the Phonograph," the French philosopher Jean-Marie Guyau rooted Edison's analogy still further in the protoplasm-to-brain schema of functional evolution: "Lines are incessantly carved into brain cells, which

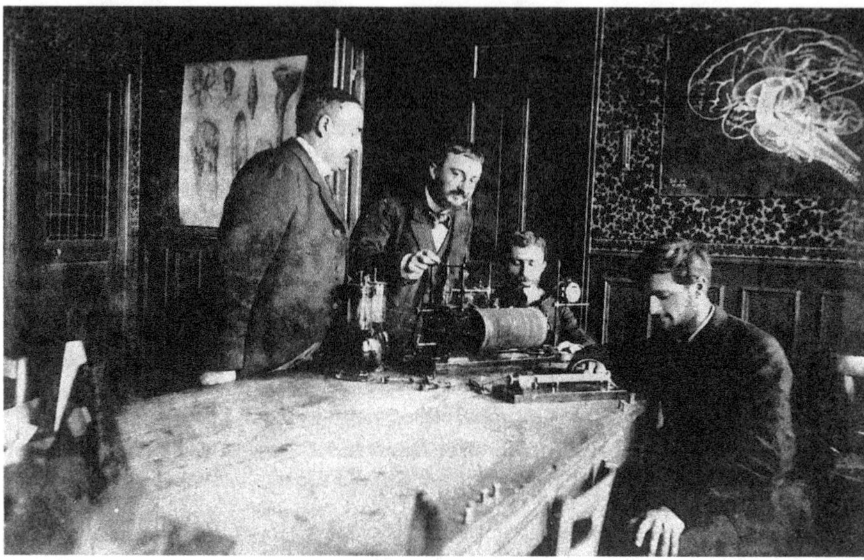

Alfred Binet and students in a Sorbonne laboratory in the 1880s, using a Marey recording device and flanked by a unicellular infusoria (left) and the human brain (right). From Alfred Binet, *La Suggestibilité* (Paris: Schleicher Frères, 1900).

provide a channel for nerve streams. If, after some time, the stream encounters a channel it has already passed through, it will once again proceed along the same path. The cells vibrate in the same way they vibrated the first time: psychologically, these similar vibrations correspond to an emotion or a thought analogous to the forgotten emotion or thought."[73] Guyau's meditation on the phonograph as prosthesis pinpointed pulsatile life as the very medium of exteriorization.

Binet was not alone among French physiologists in linking protozoa to the psychology of movements. Jules Soury, a neurophysiologist whose French edition of Haeckel's essays on cellular psychology had galvanized enormous interest in France, reiterated Claude Bernard's remark that "protoplasmic beings . . . of which one cannot say whether they are animal or vegetable . . . show life in a naked condition." Life in its bareness appeared as incessant movement. In complex beings, where the protoplasm has been subjected to a higher degree of specialization, functions of the nervous system are nothing but a form of energy, in short, psychological phenomena have a chemical, thermic, and mechanical equivalent.[74]

Movement, expressed in these force equivalents, yielded systems of signs that formed the basis of all knowledge. "Outside of movement," Soury observed, "observation and experience teach us nothing. All of the symbols under which we represent the world to ourselves are in the last analysis nothing but signs of movement."[75] Protoplasmic forces thus figured as the baseline of all signification, the *fons et origo* of all semiosis.

The American philosopher C. S. Peirce similarly looked to protoplasm as the source of signification. With a deep commitment to a universe of absolute chance, Peirce used mathematician Arthur Cayley's mathematical theory of tree diagrams to reject the assumption that there is but one kind of protoplasm. Rather, Peirce insisted, one might anticipate that "enough different chemical substance having protoplasmic characters might be formed to account, not only for the differences between nerve-slime and muscle-slime, between the whale-slime and lion-slime, but also for those minuter pervasive variations which characterize different breeds and single individuals."[76] Yet out of the near infinity of possible kinds of protoplasm, its unique ability to "take habits" (i.e., "the course which the spread of liquefaction has taken in the past is rendered thereby more likely to be taken in the future") made it "the only bridge that can span the chasm between the chance-medley of chaos and the cosmos of order and law."[77] Peirce suggested that the persistence of protoplasmic movements provided the basis for all stability of feeling and cognition, including both the solidity of love attachments as well as of logic and scientific law.

BERGSON AND THE VIBRATORY ORGANISM

But the philosopher who most fruitfully engaged the protoplasm discourse was Henri Bergson. As already noted, Bergson acknowledged that he was no exception to the propensity of the human intellect to use material objects as the springboard to philosophical reflection. If Bergson's early concept of duration owed something to the graphic and chronophotographic methods, the notion of *élan vital* developed in his *Creative Evolution* (1907) grew from an immersion in the biological literature.[78] The task of that work, he explained, was a reform of philosophy through the insights of the science of life, and vice versa, a reform of the sciences of life through the spirit of philosophy.[79] In the remainder of this chapter, I would like to sketch the role of protoplasm in *Creative Evolution* with an eye to how it grew out of—and then modified—the core concepts in Bergson's early writings (duration, memory, and intuition). My purpose here is not to provide a complete analysis of Bergson's relation to the life sciences, nor even the protoplasm doctrine, but simply to suggest how his work tracked the themes of this book.

Bergson's notion of his philosophy as an attempt to overcome the entrenched "logic of solids" presented a particular problem in the attempt to come to grips with life, or the "evolutionary movement," whose essence lies in process rather than things. The emblem of this tendency for Bergson was the "false evolutionism" of Herbert Spencer, "which consists in cutting up present reality, already evolved, into little bits no less evolved, and then recomposing with these fragments."[80] But the same tendency could be found elsewhere, including among leading Darwinian and neo-Lamarckian thinkers, who similarly worked backward from individuals to the system, which was pieced together on the basis of a given mechanism.[81]

The challenge was to shift the focus from *organization* to *mobility*; the way to achieve this was to think *duration*. "Evolution implies a real persistence of the past in the present," Bergson insisted, "a duration which is, as it were, a hyphen, a connecting link."[82] Bergson here framed the question of life as directly related to the problem of conscious activity he had dealt with in previous works. There was empirical support for this, he noted, in the latest studies that found evidence of consciousness among protoplasmic organisms.[83] Here he repeated a line of reasoning he had taken up in previous works, where he found precedent for thinking about the interval in psycho-physiological experiments in the perceptual functions of "the various prolongations of the protozoa," the "ambulacra of the echinodermata," and "the stinging apparatus of the coelenterata."[84] The interval between stimulus and response in these simple organisms was the evolutionary forebear of the gap between physiological stimulus and response in humans—the very span out of which he would elaborate his philosophy of duration. The point was that duration could be found in protoplasm, the most rudimentary manifestation of life, as a symptom of consciousness and of the functions of life itself. The presence of duration precluded a mechanistic explanation for either consciousness or life more generally. "The more duration marks the living being with its imprint, the more the organism differs from a mere mechanism, over which duration glides without penetrating. And the demonstration has most force when it applies to the evolution of life as a whole . . . inasmuch as this evolution constitutes, through the unity and continuity of the animated matter which supports it, a single indivisible history."[85]

Bergson offered the image of "a single indivisible history" in strikingly familiar terms: in none other than Haeckel's notion of the genealogical tree as a ramified wave coursing through the protoplasm from monera to humans.

> Where, then, does the vital principle of the individual begin or end? Gradually we shall be carried further and farther back, up to the individual's remotest ancestors: we shall find him solidary with each of them, solidary with that little mass of protoplasmic jelly which is doubtlessly at the root of the genealogical tree of life. Being, to a certain extent, one with this primitive ancestor, he is also solidary with all that descends from the ancestor in divergent directions. In this sense each individual may be said to remain united with the totality of living beings by invisible bonds. So it is of no use to try to restrict finality to the individuality of the living being. If there is finality in the world of life, it includes the whole of life in a single indivisible embrace.[86]

This description of Haeckel's famous image, offered without citing Haeckel, underscored Bergson's point that life must be seen as an indivisible and continuous totality. But here Bergson also offered an original reading of the Haeckel Descent Tree in terms that resembled his account of graphical and chronophotographical images considered in the previous chapter. The apparent discontinuity of the genealogical tree (when viewed as a series of relatively static species and genera) was the direct analogy in the life sciences to the propensity of psychical life to focus on a series of separate acts— as in the chronophotographic measurement of time—and thereby obscure the continuous flow that underlay them. Time, once again, was irreducible to space. By the same token, the spatial distance between different forms of life—between monera and humans—remained nonexistent with respect to the critical feature of life: consciousness. Throughout these passages Bergson took care to maintain an identical vocabulary for describing the history of life and psychological experience.

Bergson's reading of the Descent Tree radicalized Haeckel's account. This sense of fluidity, of undulation or the "throb" behind the consolidation of structures—functions, species, genera, and so on—as transient states of life had always been part of the Haeckelian picture, as we saw above. But Bergson shifted figure and ground, giving primary reality to the differentiating movement or impulsion—the *élan vital*— and diminishing the importance of the material substrate in the making of the ramified series. "This élan," he emphasized, "conserves itself between the lines of evolution and is the deep cause of variations, at least in the cells that transmit it and through summing create new species." Nor did it matter if the mechanism of heredity was seen to pass through the Weissmanian germ plasm, since "it might therefore be said that though the germ-plasm is not continuous, there is at least continuity of genetic energy, this energy being expended only at certain instants." Regarded from this point of view, Bergson emphasized, *life is like a current passing from germ to germ through the medium of a developed organism.*[87]

With his account of the "protoplasmic jelly" at "the root of the genealogical tree," Bergson took refuge in the authority of Claude Bernard, who had insisted on the protoplasm as life "so to speak in a state of nudity," amorphous and "without definition," a "kind of vital chaos that has not yet been modeled and where everything finds itself confused."[88] By taking up Bernard's view, Bergson hoped to head off the objections of the biologists who regarded protoplasm as substrate, through which the mechanisms of life derived. Bergson rejected all reductionist accounts of protoplasm as a physical-chemical medium out of which life is formed, arguing that despite the great gains in organic synthetic biology, "we are still far from compounding protoplasm chemically."[89] Much more promising, he suggested, were the experiments of Otto Bütschli on emulsions of olive oil and sugar or table salt, which produced movements that appeared decidedly like protoplasmic circulation.[90] Although these were hardly conclusive findings, they furnished Bergson with what he needed to make some form of generative movement— a transmission of force or "genetic energy"—the primary condition of life, independent of the chemical or physical substrate through which it worked.[91] Echoing the long-standing French neo-Lamarckian mantra that the "function makes the organ," Bergson made the barest functional movement in protoplasm the condition for the possibility of its rudimentary morphology.

Bergson's reversal of the figure/ground relation of impulsion and protoplasmic substrate would clear the way to treating life as duration and as memory. "Whenever anything lives," he asserted, "there is, open somewhere, a register in which time is being inscribed."[92] Life should be understood as the necessity to prolong a stimulus through a reaction, through a voluntary capacity to store energy instead of immediately expending it. At the simplest extreme of life, in protoplasmic organisms, the relation between stimulus and response are nearly automatic, the organs of perception and the organs of movement are one and the same. Yet even among protozoa, Bergson insisted, there existed a measure of freedom in its contractile possibilities, in a capacity to choose when to contract or expand, for example. In more complex organisms the interval between perceptual reaction and motor response widened, until the range of possible responses expanded and became more unpredictable—a delay or gap that we associate with freedom and greater consciousness. The widened gap was defined by memory—by the pressing of the past into the present as a range of options to be activated in the present. Unlike the narrow lost time of protozoan stimulus-response, among humans it opened out to the dimensions explored by Bergson's friend Marcel Proust in *À la recherche du temps perdu*.

It is well known that Bergson rejected any notion of memory as a "reservoir" or storehouse in the brain, a position that similarly denied any organic or protoplasmic memory that would be described as a repository in the cellular substratum. But Bergson's account of memory did locate a point of origin in the activity of protoplasm, a pattern that became further defined through the "progress of living matter" in the "differentiation of function which leads first to the production and then to the increasing complication of a nervous system capable of canalizing excitations and organizing actions."[93] The web of differentiated functions in complex organisms produced a complex system of interlocking durations, with critical points (like the brain, among others) where matter (in the form of images) becomes capable of mobilizing actions.

This picture of the organic body arguably reproduced the general features of the experimental systems described in the previous chapter, in which material and semiotic relays were canalized and framed in specific sequences. The close linkage of experimental system and a philosophical biology based on the notion of duration proved attractive to many physiologists for at least a generation, including Alexis Carrel, Constantin Monakow, and Pierre Lecomte du Noüy.[94] Carrel's lifelong pursuit of rhythms of duration in living cells led him to expand the experimental system to include microcinematography as a means of examining physiological time in the cell and, more consequentially, to invent in vitro tissue culture in order to visualize physiological duration.[95] At a more general level Carrel conjectured in Bergsonian fashion that "physiological duration depends entirely on the presence in the universe of organized living matter" and appeared "as a soon as a portion of space containing metabolizing things becomes relatively isolated from the surrounding world."[96] Each tissue, each organ, each physiological system has its own periodicity, and even this unique chronotype changes over the course of the life of the organism. The task of Carrel's "biological modernism" was to stage controlled interventions in order to observe, operationalize, and manipulate physiological periodicities for the improvement of health, longevity, perhaps even mortality. This was, Hannah Landecker notes, "the most hands-on interpretation Bergson's work has ever received; it was a science of duration complete with its own glassware, instrumentation, choreography, outfits, lighting, and atmosphere."[97]

Yet for Bergson, this kind of operationalized scientific work still inevitably fell short of what could be accomplished by the right kind of philosophical intuition. "Scientific intelligence," he wrote, provides accounts of life's operations from all perspectives, without penetrating inside, going "all round life, drawing it into itself instead of entering into it."[98] There is a difference between knowing the world intellectually and living bodily within it. Metaphysics—and art or aesthetics—follows the path of sympathy or intuition, an alignment with the generative force itself. "The intention of life," Bergson wrote, "the simple movement that runs through the lines, that binds them together and gives them significance, escapes it."[99] Bergson thus elevated the mimetic throb that Foster and others identified as the sign of life itself to the principle of aesthetic creation and reception: every expressive medium of art is the end of a process whereby life in its interiority becomes spatialized through the process of self-representation. The process of artistic creation occurs when an artist aligns him or herself, "placing himself back within the object by a kind of sympathy . . . by an effort of intuition" with the movement of life.[100]

As we will see later (especially in chapter 7), this "sympathy" (what Germans called *Einfühlung*, or empathy) formed a crucial part of artists' reception of Bergsonism in the years before the First World War. Many artists and aestheticians located sympathy in the muscle sense or other visceral modes of perception, functions that bore the imprint of undifferentiated protoplasm. There, too, they would find the seat of rhythm and periodicity in vibratory organisms. Like the Bergsonian biological modernists exploring the multiplicities of duration in experimental systems, artistic modernists explored fluctuant sensations and memories in the rhythmic and spatial disjunctions of plastic or sonic arts.

These themes—and indeed many of those of Bergson considered here—built upon a nascent vibratory anthropology developed in fin-de-siècle France on the basis of the physiological techniques and protoplasmic conception of life thus far considered. In the next chapter, we will examine how the new approach to human nature both shaped and refracted critical social and political tendencies of the French Third Republic. Together these elements—instrumental techniques, models of life, and anthropology—would furnish the avant-garde with the means to attempt to remake art, life, and society.

3

VISIBLE SPEECH

Experimental Phonetics and the Physiology of Vocalization

> Speech is a movement, it is the air that leaves the mouth or nose vibrating under the impulsion of the organs of phonation.
>
> Abbé Rousselot, *Les Modifications phonétique du langage* (1891)

LIKE SO MANY OTHER MODERN INSTITUTIONS, THE WEB OF LANGUAGE was at least partially spun in laboratories, with the aid of precision measurement and media technologies. From 1875, when the French Société de linguistique joined forces with Étienne-Jules Marey, important networks of collaboration between physiologists and linguists were developed to investigate speech acts using graphic inscription devices. When this collaboration resulted in the founding of a permanent laboratory for experimental phonetics at the Collège de France in 1897, the doyen of French linguistics, and one of the principal sponsors of the new laboratory, proclaimed that the new laboratory ensured the demise of German speculative philology and the consolidation of a science of language. Linguistics would, Michel Bréal wrote, "finally be in a position to record the facts instead of asserting a priori principles. There will be no more phonetics in vacuo, aided by technical terms that, while no doubt extremely learned, convey only misleading or vague ideas. . . . Thanks to the instruments of Edison and Marey, we will be able to write sounds—or rather they will write themselves, so that what the ear perceives in a necessarily confused and fleeting way will be able to be examined minutely and at length by sight."[1]

Bréal's remarks call attention to a remarkable conjuncture: the coterminal construction of the modern laboratory as a "system of literary inscriptions" and the new studies of forms of signification.[2] Both developments

have been the focus of much study, but their points of interaction have been almost entirely overlooked. Historians of linguistics, for example, agree that a sea change occurred in the science of language during the late nineteenth century, but they have largely missed the role of the laboratory in that transformation. Historians of the scientific laboratory, on the other hand, have described inscription devices and graphic methods only rarely considering the late nineteenth-century battles over the status of the sign.[3] This chapter describes the pivotal interaction between the two disciplines in and around Marey's laboratory, which turned experimental phonetics into a key element of the emerging disciplinary identity of French linguistics. As Bréal's remarks suggest, experimental phonetics helped displace the primacy of Indo-European philology in the study of language, replacing the as-read language of texts with the living language of speech.[4]

With the help of inscriptive apparatus, linguists rendered fleeting and unseen phenomena of speech as materialized and visible objects. The *image vocale* or *image acoustique*, to use the terms of Bréal and Ferdinand de Saussure, respectively, served to codify the concept of the *phonème*, which Sylvain Auroux has called "the key notion for the constitution of the science of linguistics."[5] The material signifier or acoustic image became transformed into a circuit model of communication in which words or verbal messages are exchanged, put across, got over, sent, passed on, received, and taken in. Articulate sounds—elementary phonemes or entire words—thereby became analogies to the dots and dashes transmitted by cable throughout the French empire. "Words . . . are like telegraph signals," wrote Bréal, "with preassigned values to be transacted."[6]

Bréal used a metaphor to describe what the new Collège de France laboratory's director, Abbé Pierre-Jean Rousselot, cast in terms of physiological mechanics. Rousselot's declaration that "speech is a movement" pushed aside cherished notions of language as an expression of the soul or as the marker separating humans from animals. Other aspects of language—semantics, grammar, and psychology—were similarly downplayed in favor of the physiology of verbal expression. Rousselot's formulation reflected a methodological choice that has not been retained in the grand tradition of linguistics that runs through Saussure and Chomsky. But it reflected important problems and possibilities of the fin-de-siècle science of language that derived from the physiologists' experimental system.

My primary concern in this chapter is not to explore the full implications of experimental phonetics for the late nineteenth-century science of linguistics but to establish some of the ways the physiologists and phoneticians succeeded in dissolving the symbolic codes of language into the medium of self-registered curves, and thereby managed to set down the basic physiological conditions of this circuit model of oral communication. My larger aim is to show how Rousselot's methodology also aligned his linguistics with a burgeoning common project of the Collège de France faculty in the 1890s to develop a new and modernizing philosophical anthropology based on the physiology of movement. Besides Marey and Bréal, the psychophysiology of movement stood at the center of Bergson's work on "motor mechanisms," Théodule Ribot's lectures on the psychology of motor physiology, Pierre Janet's studies of the psychophysiology of behavior, and Gabriel Tarde's treatise on the psychophysiological laws of imitation as the basis of society.[7] Taken together these projects comprised a cohesive epistemological nexus for a new approach to the human sciences derived from the physiology of movement. Each of these projects, moreover, aimed to extend the new vision to one or more extramural domains as a means of social modernizing. Taking Rousselot's approach as our focus, we will therefore learn much about the possibilities that first arose with the social and political extension of the physiological system.

VISIBLE SPEECH

In 1874 the French Société de linguistique signaled its turn to the in vivo study of language by electing deaf-mutism expert Léon Vaïsse as its president.[8] Vaïsse, a former colleague of Maria Montessori and author of *De la parole considerée au double point de vue de la physiologie et de la grammaire* (1853), took his election as a "testimony of [the linguists'] interest in my lifelong professional work," since in the education of deaf-mutes some of the most interesting questions of the science of language arise. The approach of the French experts on deaf-mutism, Vaïsse assured, offered "a sureness of method, which the philologists of another time could not have suspected." French linguists, he noted, possessed the intellectual maturity to "abandon the path of rash speculations" favored by German scholars. "To the studied patience of the erudites from across the Rhine," Vaïsse wrote, "you, French linguists, know how to unite the practical sense from across the Channel, and among you delicate critique is never a foreign importation."[9]

Vaïsse's exhortation to scientific nationalism in linguistics responded directly to German philology, which had fashioned itself as a crucible of national identity.[10] In this regard, Vaïsse followed the lead of France's leading linguist, Michel Bréal, who held the chair in comparative grammar at the Collège de France and was perpetual secretary of the Société de linguistique. Bréal diagnosed a dangerous pathology in the tradition of Indo-Germanic philology.[11] In his introduction to Franz Bopp's *Vergleichende Grammatik*, he relentlessly attacked German philology at its source in the Sanskrit studies of Friedrich Schlegel, which prompted a generation of Germans to embark on an intellectual quest for the South Asian subcontinent.[12] At the bottom of Schlegel's conception lay notions of language as an organism informing the very spirit of the people. Sanskrit represented the original perfection of the languages that Schlegel and his countrymen termed Indo-Germanic or Indo-European, which were marked by similar vocalic roots and analogous systems of grammar and internal structure. Although Bréal credited Bopp with resisting the more mystified impulses of this tradition, his German master remained beholden to its core epistemological assumptions. Bopp's analytical morphology could only make sense of languages whose orthography or transcription system could plausibly conform to their pronunciation, because it only dealt with letters and not with sounds.[13]

Bréal insisted that any claims about the status of phonetic laws based solely on the regularities of letters could not be deemed reliable. Bopp's approach assumed that the very being of language resided in written texts outside any human agency, individual or collective.[14] The neogrammarians (*Junggrammatiker*) who followed Bopp codified this assumption with their insistence on blind and inalterable sound laws. Bréal countered that language had to be seen as a social fact, as a set of conventions determined by whim, calculation, and not least, fashion.[15] The study of language, he insisted, had to privilege speech rather than written texts.

Vaïsse echoed Bréal's critique of *outre-Rhin* notions of overarching sound laws derived from the written, textual history of languages. As an expert in deaf-oral instruction, Vaïsse specialized in teaching the deaf and mute to speak as if he or she could hear. Hence, Vaïsse's approach to language favored the individual speaking subject and its volitional capacity to alter its manner of articulation. Vaïsse's program thus dovetailed with Bréal's attack on the German notion of language as an *abstrait imaginaire*: there must be physical and psychological determinants of the act of speaking. In his presidential address to the Société de linguistique, Vaïsse unveiled a new physicalist research program that would unite the diverse interests of the organization.

> Language, considered in its physical elements, is that which forms the raw material of our common research. A bit of air is released from the lungs and strikes the ear, after having been agitated, broken, and deflected in various ways against the walls and the surfaces of the mouth and by the diverse dispositions of the tongue—this is the matter out of which articulated language is composed . . . but in its workings, speech, the last and most important manifestation of the human soul, transports thought on these molecules of air, the infinitely small is reconciled with the infinite large, the atom carries the world![16]

Vaïsse maintained that the new doctrines of energy conservation enabled linguistics to treat the act of speaking as a matter of force and movement. The long tradition of building speaking machines and automata—from the famous talking machine of Wolfgang von Kempelen to Johannes Faber's chattering automaton—was ripe for renewal in an age of improved technologies.[17]

To this end Vaïsse led a delegation of members from the Société de linguistique that approached Étienne-Jules Marey about the possibility of collaborating on studies of speech phenomena using the kinds of inscriptive apparatus for which the physiologist had become famous in his work in cardiology, respiration, and other bodily functions. Vaïsse thought that Marey's graphic methods could provide a system of transcription similar to that used by the Scottish professor of articulation Alexander Melville Bell, father of the inventor of the telephone. In his system of "visible speech," Bell traced out the characters of a glossographic alphabet that offered "invariable marks for every appreciable variety of vocal and articulate sound . . . with a natural analogy and consistency that would explain to the eye their organic relations."[18] Bell's work had quickly gained international renown among experts on elocution and deaf-mute education. But Vaïsse thought Bell's approach could be improved upon with help from experimental physiology.[19]

Only a few years earlier, Marey had stirred the Paris medical community by using graphic methods to show the succession, duration, and intensity of the movements of the inner cavities of the heart. After this initial success, Marey committed himself to extending techniques of graphic inscription to as many physiological functions as possible, advocating nothing less than a transformation of the signifying scene of the experimental laboratory. Not surprisingly, he jumped at the proposal to bring linguistic phenomena under the purview of graphic methods, with the intention of replacing the "flowers of language" in science with the precision of machines, the "language of the phenomena themselves."[20] The collaboration between Marey and the deaf-oral experts would launch a fruitful, decades-long trajectory of research linking the inscription of speech and melioration of deaf oral pedagogy.[21]

For the linguists, tailored investigatory methods in a well-tooled laboratory would confirm the autonomy of their discipline. So would a unique category of phenomena: speech. Although the laboratory did not enable linguistics to completely sever its ties to traditional philology, it definitively called into question the traditional primacy of the written word in the sciences of language. In the guise of speech, language once more became a source of communication, a theme almost entirely absent from philology. But the communicative turn in linguistics, which would eventually become part of sociological investigations of the social bond, rested on a firmly physiological or physical basis in the scenario of articulation and audition.

Out of these considerations the new experimental phonetics research group was formed, consisting of Marey, the linguist Louis Havet (secretary of the Société de linguistique), and the physician and deaf-mute expert Charles Rosapelly. Their primary endeavor was to capture the simultaneous interaction of physiological functions connected with the acts of speech: the thoracic cage, the larynx, the lips, and the air pressure within the nasal passages. Although problems of deaf-mutism remained among their concerns, Havet directed their arsenal of physiological instruments at one of the canonical texts of German Sanskrit philology, the *Pratisakhya*, a Vedic text reckoned to be more than two thousand years old that had been a focus of Sanskrit philology for more than two decades.[22] The *Pratisakhya* occupied a special place among the Vedas, for it furnished an exhaustive description of the vicissitudes of Sanskrit pronunciation: enunciation, tone, duration, pitch, evenness, and compounding. Brahmanic tradition held that the

Vedas were a mere transcription of an oral tradition practiced by the *rishis* in heightened states (*dhyana*), so that the phonetics of the mantras found within them could not be easily reproduced on the basis of conventional orthography. Moreover, defective pronunciation of sacred texts was regarded as a profanation.[23] To ensure a more perfect state of pronunciation, then, the *Pratisakhya* described the parts of the body from which certain syllable sounds originate and through what kind of effort they are brought forth. Many of the sounds described were without representation in writing. Some sounds, for example, were intercalated in pronunciation, within couplings such as *kn, km, tn, tm, pn, pm,* and so on. The ancient Hindus called this pairing of a "mute" consonant with a nasal consonant a *yama,* or twin.[24] Despite exhaustive attempts at self-experimentation, however, the Hindu sages proved unable to decide which sound was the "twin" of the other. During the formation of the mute consonant that commenced the pair, the soft palate remained closed. It opened, however, at the moment of the formation of the nasal consonant.

The French savants set out first to resolve this dilemma of Vedic linguistics. But the stakes were higher: if successful they would show the limits of phonetic self-experiment in general and thereby render invalid the greater part of the conclusions of German philology.[25] Rosapelly indicated the intention of the physiologists' intervention to overcome "organic analysis" in matters philological: "Modern phoneticists have preciously assimilated these rather minute, but entirely exact analyses (in the *Pratisakhya*), of the different inflections of language; physiological experimentation sheds still more light on the different acts of the lips, the tongue, and the soft palate in the formation of consonants." Rosapelly's experimental methods were guided by the "principle of least action," in which "all human acts tend to be executed with the least possible effort."[26] German physiologists had used the principle with great success to describe the way in which persons learn to calibrate the muscular movements of the eye when learning to see. Marey and Rosapelly invoked the principle to ascertain the analogous processes involved in learning to articulate the sounds of language.

Here is how the experiments were done. Under Marey's direction, Rosapelly and Havet set out to test Hindu phonetic wisdom by constructing an apparatus that would simultaneously inscribe the movements of pressure within the nasal passages, the vibrations of the larynx, and the movements of the lips. The first apparatus consisted of an inscriptive manometer, which traced a horizontal line when there was no nasal emission and elevations in the curve in cases where articulated phonemes exerted pressure. The second instrument consisted of an electromagnetic stylus (modeled after a Deprez galvanometer), which made a trembling line tracing the vibrations of the larynx and a straight line when there were no reverberations. The third inscription device traced the movements of the lips, dropping when they parted and making a straight line when they were together. Finally, a Marey pneumograph was used to inscribe the rise and fall of the chest during respiration.[27]

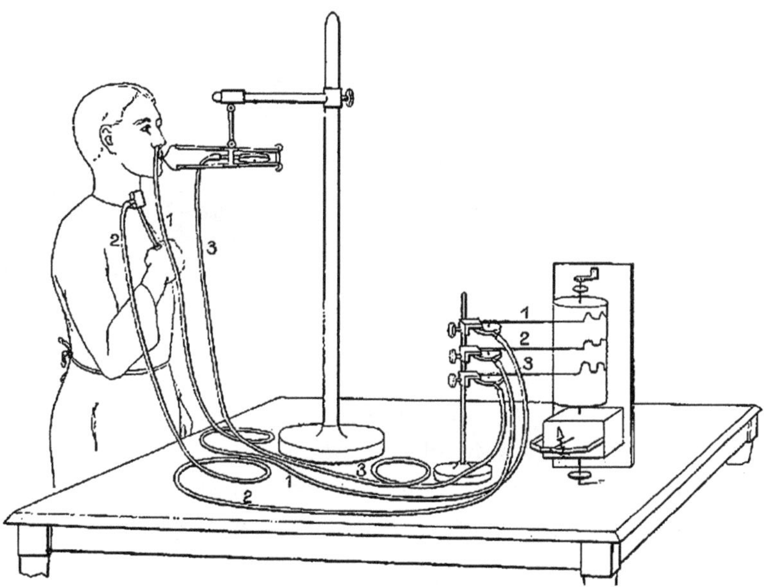

Marey-Rosapelly vocal polygraph for simultaneously recording the different acts of speech: (1) emission of air by the nares; (2) vibrations of the larynx; and (3) movements of the lips. All were received by Marey tambours and recorded on a rotating drum in three superposed curves indicating the order of succession, duration, and intensity of the movements. From Charles Rosapelly, "Inscription de mouvements phonétiques," *Physiologie expérimentale: Travaux du laboratoire de M. Marey* (Paris: G. Masson) 2 (1875).

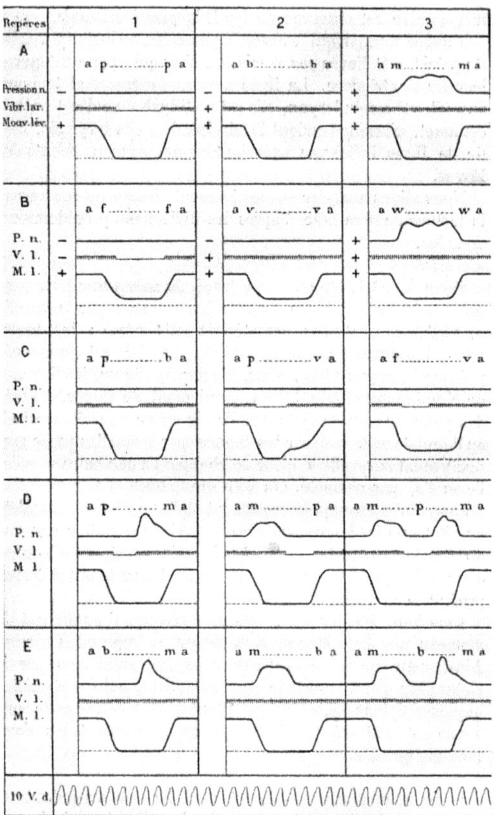

Vocal polygraph inscriptions of nasal, laryngeal, and labial movements in the pronunciation of Sanskrit phonemes called *yamas*. From Charles Rosapelly, "Inscription des mouvement phonétiques," in *Travaux du laboratoire de M. Marey* (Paris: G. Masson, 1875).

The results signaled the triumph of physiological methods over organic self-experiment.[28] For the physiologists, the separate bodily indications of the phonemes revealed that the sound was a twin of the mute consonant and not, as the Hindus believed, of the nasal sound, since the simultaneous traces showed (most clearly for *apma*) that the soft palate opened before the labial act, which signaled the emission of the consonant *m*. For Havet and the linguists, the studies suggested the importance for comparative linguistics of sounds not represented in writing. Traditional philology was shown to be too exclusively focused on the sounds of written consonants, rather than on the nuances of living speech.

The physiologists' critique of "organic" phonetic self-experiment centered on the limits of human hearing capacities. Experimental physiology claimed advantage over the unaided auditory sense by virtue of its ability to render phonetic phenomena to other modalities of sense, especially to vision. "Our aim in the experiments," wrote Rosapelly, "was to replace the auditory sensation with an objective expression of the acts of phonation."[29] By "objective" Rosapelly meant ocular, more specifically the well-known "acoustics of the eyes" developed by the physicists Rudolph Koenig and Jules Lissajous, who had produced different graphic representations of sound phenomena.[30] The aim of these techniques, following the pioneering work of Hermann Helmholtz, was to present a visual analog of the exact form of the acoustic phenomena. The primacy of the visual sense derived from the capacity to fix it in an immobile image, which could be examined and perhaps subjected to Fourier analysis.

For the linguists, the inscription of sound made it possible to render the hitherto fleeting phenomena of speech into a materialized scientific object: the phoneme. Although the term first appeared innocuously in a lecture by A. Dufriche-Desgenettes to the Société de linguistique, it soon became directly associated with the laboratory experiments of Havet, who also introduced the term into the international vocabulary through the International Phonetic Association.[31] Thus the phoneme, which, in Sylvain Auroux's words, became the "key notion for the constitution of the science of linguistics," grew as a direct product of the signifying apparatus of the laboratory. Much of the rest of this chapter will chart the phoneme's biography, from Marey's laboratory through its role in French linguistic surveys to its deployment as *image vocale* or *image acoustique* in the respective systems of Bréal and Saussure.

FROM VISUALIZING VOWELS TO PHONOGRAPHIC PLAYBACK

Focus on the unwritten aspects of speech led to studies of vowels, which even traditional philology regarded as problematic, since some phonetic scripts such as Arabic and Hebrew often neglected to indicate them at all.[32] Reverberating vowel sounds had been at the center of several attempts to graphically inscribe the human voice in the 1850s and 1860s. The impetus had come from the British researcher Robert Willis, who criticized phoneticians for considering vowel sounds only with regard to "the form and actions of the organs of speech themselves."[33] In the 1860s Helmholtz took up Willis's claim that the qualities of vowel sounds are independent of a particular sound source. For several decades the question of vowels thus contained within it the implicit secondary question of whether speech could be exhaustively investigated as a purely physiological or mechanical process of articulation (with the listener effectively replaceable by a deaf person), or whether it was more properly a matter of acoustics and the physiology of hearing.[34] From the late 1850s a series of new instrumental media were devised to resolve the question, which was finally put to rest after the invention of the phonograph in 1878.[35]

One of the most notable machines was the handiwork of an ambitious young French stenographer named Léon Scott de Martinville. Scott designed his phonautograph as an attempt to elevate stenography (also called "phonography" until the end of the century) to an automatic and universal pasigraphy, by forcing "nature to constitute by herself a general written language of all her sounds."[36] The pure voice would supersede the myriad systems of notation based in mere convention, which Scott had recounted in his *Histoire de la sténographie* (1849).[37] In order to accomplish the direct inscription of the voice, Scott constructed an analog model of the anatomy of the human ear. His subject spoke into the wide end of a bell. A mobile membrane attached to the bell's interior registered the vibrations, which were inscribed by a stylus in a revolving drum covered with smoked paper. The resulting curves were highly irregular and without much immediate use for scientific study of phonation. Despite its technical insufficiencies, Scott's phonautograph circulated widely in Europe and North America, an object of rapture to masses and monarchs.

Nevertheless, Scott's phonautograph occupies a critical position in nineteenth-century instrumental media of sound. Jonathan Sterne places it at the beginning of what he calls "tympanic" sound-reproduction technologies, taking the term from the eardrum, or tympanum, in its capacity to receive sonorous vibrations from the air and transduce them into something else, such as tracings on a cylinder, flames, or electric currents.[38] Although Scott's focus on stenography or writing distracted from this critical feature of the phonautograph, his apparatus departed from the phonetician's methods because "it rendered speech visible through a representation of the waveforms produced by speech, rather than through a representation of positions of the mouth."[39] It was a hearing machine, rather than a talking one.

At about the time that Scott's phonautograph was beginning to make the rounds, the instrument took a prominent role in a debate that erupted among physiologists over the nature of vowels and consonants. In a groundbreaking study on the physiology of speech for linguists and deaf-oral instructors, physiologist Ernst Brücke made a firm distinction between vowels and consonants, insisting that "in all consonants there is either a closure somewhere in the mouth channel . . . or a narrowness that provokes a clearly audible, autonomous noise that is independent of the sound of the voice," while in vowels this was not the case.[40] Vowels, Brücke maintained, were pure sounds, while consonants were mixtures of sounds and noises. F. C. Donders wrote an open reply to Brücke on this question, arguing that the timbre of different vowels was formed in the cavity of the mouth after originating in the larynx.[41] The best evidence for this was provided by the vowels uttered in a whisper, without any involvement of the larynx. This theory suggested that vocalization could be studied as a purely acoustic phenomenon, without any involvement of the organs of articulation.[42] This claim found critical support in Helmholtz's pathbreaking studies of the *Klangfarbe*, or timbre, of vowels, which produced a surprising result: the vocal cords alone were responsible for pitch, while the buccal cavity alone produced timbre.[43]

Two decades later Helmholtz's theories were put to rigorous testing by Rudolph Koenig, a German acoustician and instrument maker based in Paris. Where Helmholtz's instruments sought to simulate the ear's ability to synthesize sinusoidal sound waves, Koenig built a splendid instrument that would display sound to the eye, the so-called *flamme manométrique*—which used gas flames to produce the dogtoothed patterns of graphic inscriptions.[44] The apparatus was as ingenious as it was dramatic. At the extremity of a gas pipe, Koenig placed a small reservoir of metal carrying a thin burner to light the gas. A thin rubber membrane formed an inside wall of this reservoir. When a series of vibrations were transmitted to this membrane, the gas of the small reservoir became alternately compressed and dilated, thereby submitting the flame to rapid rises and falls too quick for the eye to directly perceive. With a four-sided mirror turned by a crank, however, each flame gave the image of a long luminous ribbon with a pattern of dogtoothed indentations. These images remained too fleeting for analysis, however, until Koenig managed to devise a method for recording them photographically. The temporal appearance of the flame images was gauged with a simultaneous

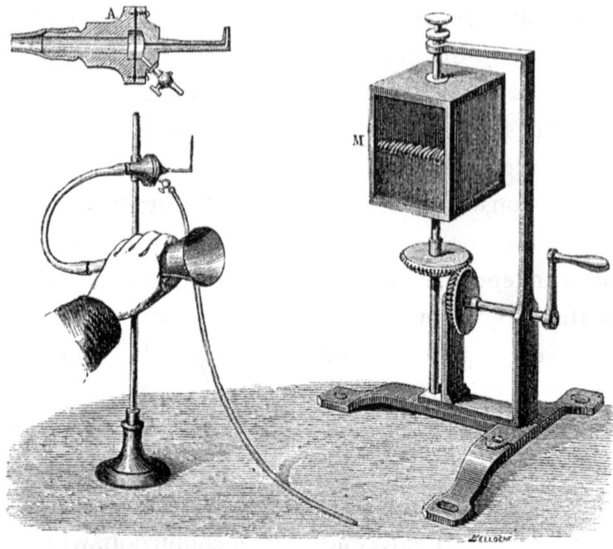

Koenig manometric flame apparatus. From *Popular Science Monthly* 14 (1878).

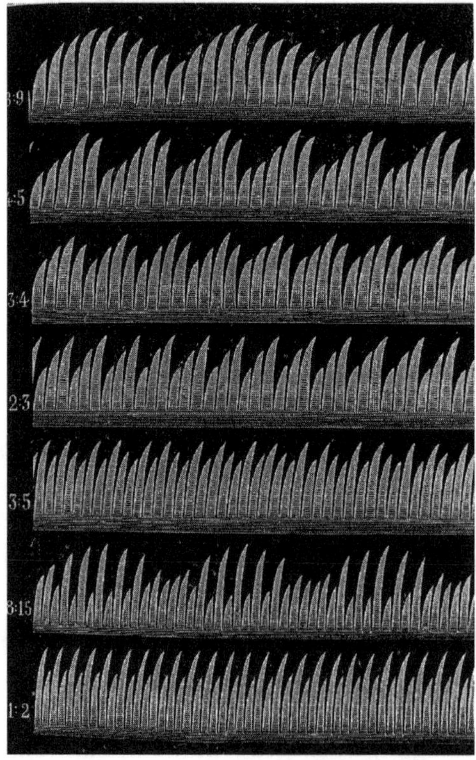

Photograph of manometric flames. From *Popular Science Monthly* 14 (1878).

flame vibrating, not to the sound of the voice, but to the action of a tuning fork with known periodicity.

Despite its dramatic appeal, Koenig's manometric flame apparatus proved incapable of resolving Helmholtz's claim that the timbre of vowels depended on the relative intensities of different harmonies. That awaited the invention of the Edison phonograph, unveiled in 1877 to the astonishment of scientists and laymen alike. In the early years after its invention, the phonograph served many interests and functions, from avatar of a new mode of mechanical reproduction, or muse to new philosophies of automata, to the progenitor of a new entertainment industry. But, as Julia Kursell has shown, the Edison phonograph also became a scientific instrument of the first order, with critical employment in the ongoing debate over vowels.[45]

Already famous for his recent work on the telegraph, Thomas Alva Edison intervened in an increasingly busy and expectant field of researchers concerned with recording and reproducing sound. The British civil engineer W. H. Barlow fired the imagination of the English-speaking world in 1874 with an instrument he called the logograph. Barlow's instrument refined the bell and membrane setup, with a spring attached to the membrane to keep it in a state of tension and also being connected to a pointer with a sable-brush stylus.[46] Several other British and American experimenters stepped quickly into the breach opened by Barlow. Alexander Graham Bell, son of the abovementioned Scottish phonetician, working on problems that would result in his invention of the telephone, consulted Boston ear specialist Clarence John Blake about the structure and function of the human ear. Bell reported his astonishment that "such a thin and delicate membrane" as the eardrum "could move bones that were, relatively to it, very massive indeed."[47] With this thought in mind, Bell and Blake set out to improve upon the Scott and Barlow instruments by taking a real human middle ear, suitably lubricated with glycerin and water, and adjoining it to a large bell, at one end, and a piece of hay to act as a stylus.[48]

Edison entered this field on the heels of his continuing work on the telephone, and his interest revolved around problems of storage, reproduction, and transmission of the sound waves rather than perfecting the conditions of visual analysis.[49] Perhaps more pressing were rumors that the French poet and inventor Charles Cros had in April 1877 submitted a complete description of a talking machine to the Paris Academy of Sciences. But Edison was probably spurred to publish and patent his phonograph research after the appearance of a notice in *Scientific American* describing the Marey-Rosapelly vocal polygraph experiments. The editor emphasized the difference between the Edison and Marey-Rosapelly arrangements, which had been systematically compared, with a more detailed article concerning the latter presented in the very same issue. Where Marey and Rosapelly achieved a remarkable visual representation of vocalization, Edison's innovation consisted in making an indent of the waveforms of sound in an amorphous substance so that the process could be a means of playing back the sound.

Over the next twenty years the phonograph found constant use in deaf-mute instruction, particularly in the work of H. Marichelle, who showed, in Marey's words, "that the phonographic trace is the only expression which perfectly defines the nature of a vowel."[50] Marichelle used the phonograph not in the customary way, but as a graphic inscription device, whose traces he examined through a corneal microscope and measured with an ocular micrometer. He also became adept at the procedure perfected by L. Hermann in 1889 of photographically reproducing the phonograph records and analyzing the sinuous curves whenever possible with the harmonic principles of Fourier's theorem and Ohm's law.[51] Marichelle used this method to produce a complete series of drawings of the phonographic grooves for French vowels.

An additional advantage of this approach over customary physiological methods, Marichelle claimed, was that a single phonographic instrument could be used to capture most of the multiple inscriptions taken in earlier studies by different devices. The deaf-mute instructor reckoned that all phonemes, vowels and consonants alike, took their characteristics from the region in the vocal apparatus from which they emanate. They became vowels or consonants only by virtue of a further modification, the degree of openness or closure in the "generative orifice."[52] Marichelle insisted that it was useless to teach vocal sounds in isolation, not as they are used within words, where minute differentiations occur depending on the articulative conjunction. During the 1890s Georges-René-Marie Marage worked imaginatively between different media, building analog models of the organs of articulation to synthesize vowels. Using tuning forks for the larynx and resonators for the supra-laryngeal cavities crafted in the exact shape and size of the human mouth, Marage artificially calibrated the synthesized sounds with precision measurements drawn from graphical recordings and manometric flames.[53]

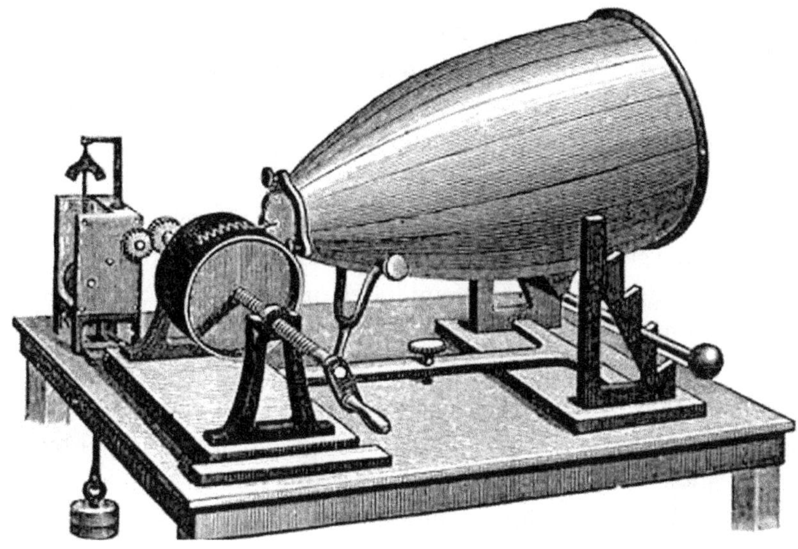

Scott phonautograph. From Étienne-Jules Marey, "L'Inscription des phénomènes phonétiques," pt. 1, "Méthodes directes." *Revue générale des sciences* 9 (1898).

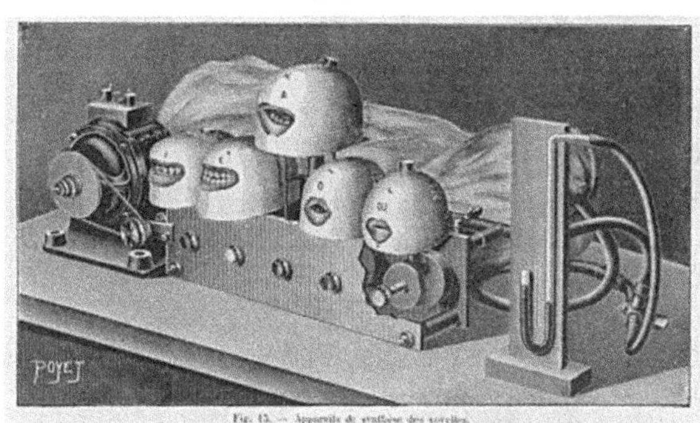

Marage's apparatus for synthesizing vowels. From Anonymous, "La Machine à synthèse des voyelles du docteur Marage," *La Nature* 2, no. 7 (1908).

After 1891 Marichelle worked together with Marey's *préparateur*, Georges Demeny, to produce an "optical equivalent of the phonograph" to invigilate speech.[54] Demeny produced numerous close-up chronophotographs of a subject, usually himself, producing short phrases at rates of fifteen to twenty-four images per second. Demeny synthesized the images with an instrument of his design, the "photophone," a peep-show device that combined a zootrope or a Plateau phenakistoscope with a light source to produce a moving image of vocalization. Images of Demeny mouthing "Vive la France" and "Je vous aime" quickly spread far and wide, as an improved version of the instrument, the phonoscope, competed with Edison's kinetoscope for popularity in parlors and exhibitions around the world.[55]

Contemporaries exclaimed that Marichelle's use of media technologies—phonograph and chronophotograph—had finally wrenched phonetics "away from the acousticians" and "profoundly changed the theory of speech."[56] These in turn gave rise to a veritable explosion of technologies designed to produce transparent and efficient communication using phonetic inscriptions and algebras. Instruments such as Edison's Graphophone flooded the burgeoning market for technologies of stenography and internal business communications.[57] At the macroscopic level, the Danish linguist Otto Jespersen worked together with an international committee, which included Wilhelm Ostwald and the French logician Louis Couturat, to develop an "algebra for speech sounds" as the basis for an international auxiliary language for use in commerce, science, and diplomacy.[58]

THE MOTHER TONGUE

During the 1880s French linguists turned fervently away from Paris to the provinces, implanting the phonetics laboratory in the byways of the countryside as a means of making visible the elusive and prolific patois that thrived there. "The present state of linguistics," announced one linguist, "imperiously demands a more profound study of the patois which have succeeded in surviving the ever more dangerous attacks of the written language."[59] "Imperious" referred to the politics of the situation, where government-sponsored education had, a century after the revolutionary surveys, begun to succeed in eradicating some patois, while other dialects remained stubbornly intact. Continuity of purpose, if not of method, reigned in surveys of French patois throughout the nineteenth century. Yet by the 1880s, these studies, while still devoted to the implantation of French and the eradication of patois, had taken on the added curatorial function of detailed description and, when possible, of phonographic archiving of vanishing tongues.[60] The linguistic anthropologist Lucien Adam, for example, requested that his correspondents gather folktales and provide a careful phonetic transcription as well as grammatical characteristics and lists of words.[61]

By the late 1880s, field studies of patois had become dominated by the extramural implantation of the phonetics laboratory. Previewing the "triple alliance" between physics, physiology, and philology—which would define the linguistics of the future—Eduard Koschwitz wrote that "linguists had for too long forgotten . . . that languages are composed of sounds, which by their acoustic effect belong to physics, by their formation to physiology, and that the letters of the alphabet are nothing but the very imperfect signs of living sounds of the present and the past. The study of the real value of these past or present letters can only be determined by a scientist who knows how to recognize the emissions of the voice hidden under the letters."[62]

These remarks served as a tribute to the work of the Abbé Rousselot, the first person to take the work of the phonetics laboratory out to the French countryside where he was born and bred. After coming to the French capital to study with Gaston Paris and Michel Bréal amid the rising tide of patois studies, Rousselot worked in the laboratory of É.-J. Marey and Charles Rosapelly and, together with France's foremost linguistic geographer, Jules Gillieron, cofounded a journal devoted to the dialects of France, *Revue des patois gallo-romanes.* This twofold training effectively bridged the gap between the laboratory and field linguistics, disciplines that had hitherto exchanged work but not really merged. "What was still lacking . . . and what one found in Rousselot," stated an obituary notice after his death in 1924, "was a linguist doubling as an experimenter, a savant knowledgeable about problems of phonetics and capable of resolving them by perfecting the procedures of the graphic method."[63]

Rousselot's dual interests grew from a life marked by the rapid modernization of rural France in the Third Republic. Born in the southwestern French village of Saint-Claud, in the department of Charente, he spoke patois at home and French in school. He reflected this divide in his career, vacillating between geographical and genealogical studies of patois and efforts to promote standard French pronunciation. This pairing formed the core of his brilliant dissertation, a study of the village patois spoken by his own family in Charente, which he rendered in the cosmopolitan idiom of the graphic method, using instruments partially of his own design. He published the work in two monographs, one devoted to his findings, the other devoted to the technical arsenal used in his investigation.[64]

Through an ingenious combination of methods, Rousselot depicted the development and character of his native patois, in contrast to his acquired standard French. Beginning with a preamble entitled "Why I Studied My Patois and How I Studied It," Rousselot remarked that he had been impressed by the recent work of linguistic geographers, especially Charles de Tourtoulon's *L'Étude géographique sur la limite de la langue d'oc et de la langue d'oïl.*[65] But he found himself "shocked" to see that the work "was concerned with the letters rather than the sounds of which the letter is the symbol." For that reason Rousselot decided that "instead of studying the dead letter" he would study "living speech."[66] Tourtoulon's emphasis on geographic boundaries led Rousselot to see the importance of his own native dialect, which marked the limits of the idioms of the north of France and those of the Midi. He began with a general reconnaissance of the region, traveling with the help of local priests who were native to it.

Rousselot's first move sought to enframe his mother('s) tongue within the compass of larger geographical patterns of dialect, from Charente to the Allier and Loire. Then he turned to a more detailed study of the phonetics, morphology, syntax, and lexicology of the patois of Cellefrouin; then to language spoken within his own family; and finally to a detailed study of his own mother's speech, which he compared with his own. Arguing that "speech is composed of a multitude of sounds and noises of which only the principal ones are represented in alphabets," Rousselot based his study on field samples taken with graphic inscription devices.[67] Variations of sonority, spirographic measures of the breath expended in speech, and the duration and musical pitch of the sounds comprised the principal phenomena under investigation.

Vowels served as a focus of Rousselot's study. In fact, the association of vowels with dialects and patois was an idea of ancient provenance, reiterated over and again in metropolitan studies of provincial speech, including the revolution-era surveys of the Abbé Gregoire.[68] In contrast to the stable, form-giving, and maintaining function of consonants—the only true letters of the written alphabet—vowels were taken to define the mutability of oral culture and thus became virtually synonymous with patois itself.[69] "Patois is variation, and the vowel designs its nature": these two convictions went virtually unchallenged in the traditional conception.[70] To fix the nature of the vowel would thus be to capture the very essence of patois and, in a sense, language in its most natural state. Largely unfettered by literature, teachers, dictionaries, grammars, and state policies, patois, "on the contrary, is uniquely transmitted by oral tradition. Almost nothing disrupts its natural evolution."[71] Hence Rousselot's scientific credo: "With regard to cultivated languages, I would frankly side with the preference of the botanist who accords the plants of the field over the plants of our gardens."[72]

Rousselot thus configured patois as an element of the natural landscape, ripe for conquest, civilizing, and policing through technologies of writing. To Cellefrouin he brought along an astonishing arsenal of linguistic surveillance equipment. The mobile laboratory contained about a dozen apparatus, all built by the renowned Paris instrument maker Charles Verdin, with supervision by Marey and Rosapelly.[73] The core of the inscriptive apparatus consisted of a recording cylinder with a Foucault regulator, a Deprez electric signal, and a Marey *tambour à levier*. The latter device consisted of a rubber membrane with a lever inscriptor that could be easily affixed to diverse organs of the body—the lips and tongue, the thorax, larynx, teeth, or nasal passages—with the help of several supplementary appliances. Rousselot's kit contained several simple inscriptive devices of his own invention, such as the "larynx explorer" and the "speech inscriptor." The latter was an attempt to synthesize the principal advantages of Koenig's manometric flames and the Edison Graphophone and phonograph. Rousselot used a Verdin microphone with an embouchure borrowed from the Edison Graphophone, which enabled one to speak without having to touch the lips to the material. The signal-transmitting apparatus featured strong electromagnets and a powerful battery to overcome resistance and to give all phases of the current without interruptions.[74]

Rousselot correlated the traces of speech with their sources in specific bodily organs of articulation. The aim was to determine the exact locations of the palate, larynx, thorax, et cetera, from which sprung the articulation of phonetic utterances. These anatomical "regions of articulation" were then arranged spatially on the map of Cellefrouin, showing the parallel distributions of phonetic variation across the entire region. Rousselot's linguistic geography paralleled a common practice among anthropometers, ethnographers, and demographers to produce maps charting geographical distribu-

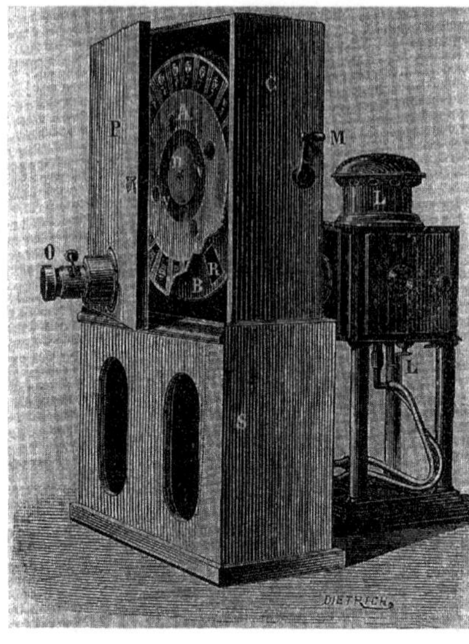

Demeny photophone. From Étienne-Jules Marey, "L'Inscription des phénomènes phonétiques," pt. 1, "Méthodes directes." *Revue générale des sciences* 9 (1898).

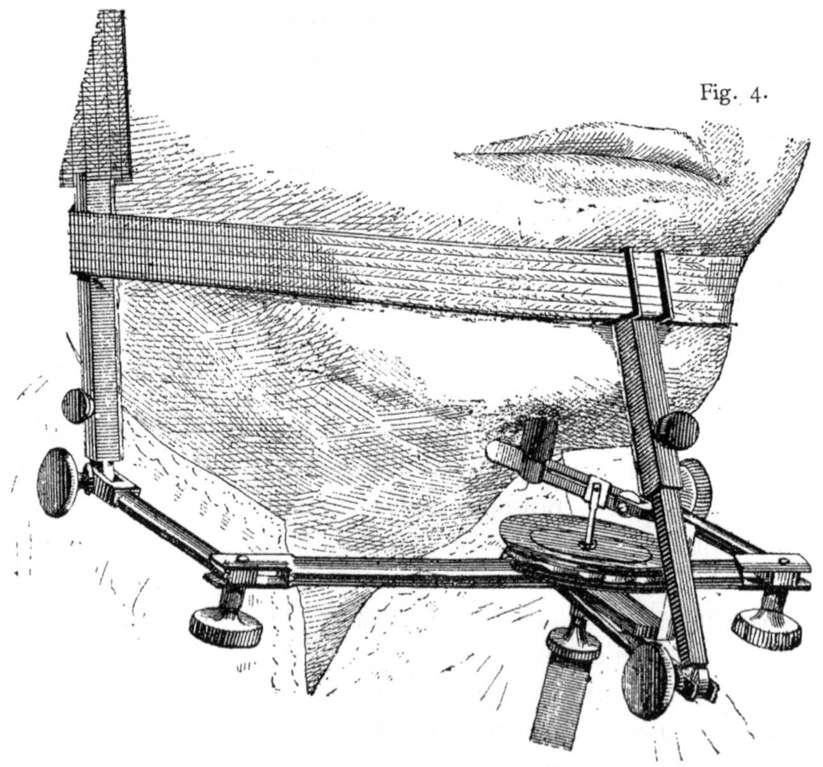

Rousselot speech inscriptor. From Abbé Rousselot, *La Méthode graphique appliquée à la phonétique* (Paris: Macon, 1890).

tions of characteristics ranging from stature, cephalic index, hair or eye color to occurrences of epilepsy and color blindness. Rousselot never published such a map, but he delineated the very same portrait of Cellefrouin in prose. He supplemented his measures with a historical ethnography of the region drawn from municipal and parish records, oral history, and his own family history. The aim of this exercise was to give as complete as possible a diachronic picture of the evolution of the dialects in the region, with emphasis on the "outside influences"—natural or human—that may have affected the development of dialectological differences.[75] With this movement between linguistic anthropometry and cultural history, Rousselot distinguished "the laws which have their raison d'être in our physical nature and those which have their raison d'être in the generative faculty of our spirit."[76]

Rousselot made efforts to gauge the effects of the French state's attempts to subdue patois and instill standard French in the region. The results were surprising. Standard French had utterly failed to influence the vocalism of *la France profonde*. When it came to relating the vowels of Cellefrouin and common French, Rousselot wrote that "French has still not succeeded in imposing its vocalic system. In adopting the language of Paris, the province has been able to recast its consonants . . . but its vowels have not been affected one bit."[77] Once again patois had remained impervious to the advances of the civilizing mission.[78] Rousselot diagnosed this failure as the constant tendency to privilege the written over the oral language: "It is not spoken French that is spreading; it is the French of books; and this is still more accommodating. Each person only reads the vowels in his own manner of speaking. Education is coming to rectify certain points, but these are few, and our indulgence on these matters is large. In addition, the instructors frequently share the defects of the region where they teach, if they are not even worse. More than one barbaric sound can invoke his paternity."[79]

During the 1900s, Rousselot's experimental phonetics even took root in key bastions of German philology. In 1893 he spent the summer semester at the University of Greifswald, where he lectured and demonstrated his apparatus and sent well-equipped Germans into the bush to study *Volksmundarten* from a fresh standpoint. In 1897 the Leipzig linguist Hermann Breymann published a survey of the phonetic literature that effectively took Rousselot as its hero for abandoning the "subjective" methods of the philologists and "placing phonetics on a purely experimental basis" by using "methods of self-registration long known in other sciences."[80] Many Germans argued that Rousselot's enthnographic phonetic would transform the traditional approach to historical syntax. "Without a more profound study of the different patois," wrote Eduard Koschwitz, "there will be no historical grammar and, as a consequence, no comparative grammar."[81]

The French Société d'anthropologie echoed this view when, on May 3, 1900, it moved to support the creation of a Musée glossophonographique des langues, dialectes, et patois to order and classify the full range of speech patterns not only in France but throughout the world. The museum, explained its promoters L. Azoulay and Vinson, would create a phonic parallel to recent attempts to found a national photographic museum, on the grounds that phonography is to hearing what photography is to sight, and attempts to found photographic museums were underway throughout the world.[82] Azoulay argued that both inscriptive media should be taken as forms of writing. He quoted the promoter of the photography museum, the astronomer Pierre Janssen, to underscore this point: "Photography registers the chain of phenomena during time, just as writing registers the thoughts of men during the ages. Photography is to sight what writing is to thought. If there is any difference, it is to the advantage of photography. Writing is subject to conventionalities from which photography is free."[83]

The Société de l'anthropologie enthusiastically endorsed the proposal on the grounds that such a glossophonographic archive would extend the important work of Rousselot. One member suggested that its compilers might follow the example of the anthropometric surveys conducted on military conscripts. Fresh recruits would provide a full and accurate picture of the "extreme diversity, in one epoch, of the pronunciation and the intonation of a single language according to the social classes and the regions of the country."[84] Echoing Rousselot's simultaneous attempt to inscribe and eradicate his mother('s) tongue, without any sense of irony or perversity, this society member remarked that mechanical reproduction could preserve for civilization what it had itself exterminated. "Thus," he concluded, "one could save from death the voice of peoples who are themselves dead."[85] Within weeks Azoulay had secured the assistance of Sir Robert Hart, customs officer for the Chinese colonies, and produced a series of phonographic recordings of the sixteen principal dialects of China. International interest in the project mounted immediately after the French voted to support the museum. The

Vienna Academy of Sciences quickly passed a resolution to support a similar institution in Vienna, and similar phonographic archives were soon established in many cities around the world.

"SPEECH IS A MOVEMENT"

Rousselot summed up his foundational assumptions in his definition of speech. "Speech is a movement," he wrote. "It is the air that leaves the mouth or nose vibrating under the impulsion of the organs of phonation."[86] This definition also served as a methodological credo for experimental phonetics as a discipline: movement is the basis of language, and language itself is merely a means of expressing corporeal movement, a simple epiphenomenon. Rousselot's credo thus inverted the assumptions of traditional philology (along with those of the Saussurean linguistics tradition that continued them), which assumed that language was primary and the organs of phonation a mere means to produce it. The insistence on considering movements the primary essentials of speech also challenged a tendency among phoneticians in Rousselot's own time to use recording apparatus to favor the study of sound alone, and to equate tones and noises produced with speech rather than as the means whereby the movements of speech are made audible.

Yet what seemed stripped-down, positivist, even impoverished in Rousselot's notion of language gained scope by its implicit connection to the new epistemologies rooted in the psychophysiology of movement. It was Rousselot's great technical skill in the design and use of graphical recording instruments that conferred stunning precision to this project, making it possible to show that the fine distinctions in the sounds of patois revealed extremely delicate nervous and muscular mechanisms involved in perceiving and reproducing language. Rousselot's student Hubert Pernot recounted an episode during fieldwork in the Pyrenees, in which attempts to measure the speech of a local peasant demonstrated this point.[87] Attempts to measure a vowel—the *a fermé*—of a speaker of a local dialect had proved impossible. Closer investigation revealed that the instrument was calibrated to the *a fermé* of the experimenter at fifteen vibrations per second; the instrument was adjusted to take in still more vibrations per second, and the Pyrenean vowel was successfully captured. The extreme precision of the instrumentation revealed the still greater finesse of human muscular control, which

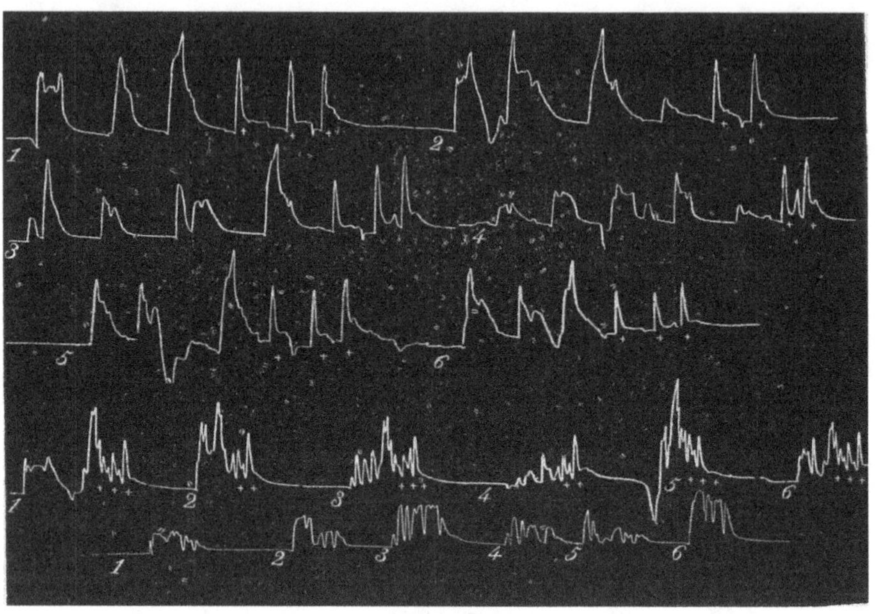

Graphic recordings of patois. From Abbé Rousselot, *Les Modifications phonétiques du langage étudiée dans le patois d'une famille de Cellefrouin* (Paris: H. Welter, 1891).

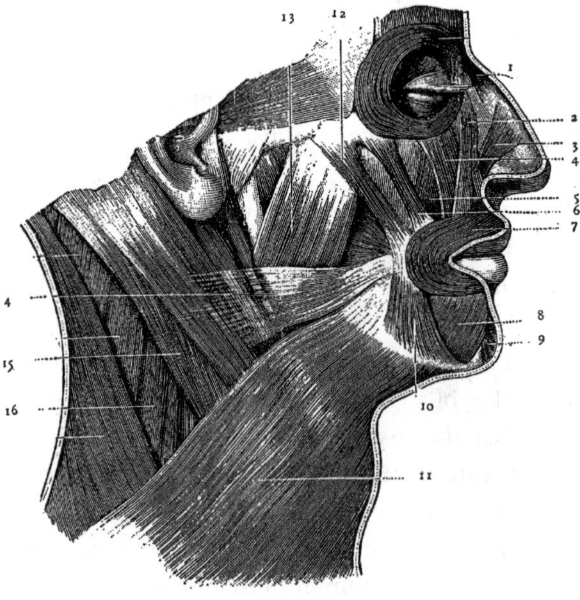

Muscles of the face, superficial view. From L'Abbé P.-J. Rousselot, *Principes de phonétiques expérimentale*, 2nd ed. (Paris: H. Didier, 1924).

allowed the rustic and illiterate speaker to act as such a precise recording instrument of his parents and grandparents that it took the most sophisticated instrument makers of Paris to make a device to match him. Every inhabitant of his village possessed the same precision, moreover, emitting an *a fermé* close to, but distinct from, all others. Every villager could be said to act—empathically—as a neuromuscular metrologist, calibrating phonic imprints and laryngo-buccal gestures with a standardized precision that enabled unerring recognition by fellow villagers. Yet Rousselot's instruments also revealed a small margin of error, a personal equation, that provided the opening for individuality, innovation, and change. In this sense the instruments extended what we saw in chapter 1 as the experimental system's sensitivity to gaps, to relations of continuity and discontinuity, to the structuring principle of society itself. In later chapters (5 and 7), we will consider how this interplay in Rousselot's research between the social calibration of speech and individual personal equation would attract the collaboration of poets interested in innovative modes of versification.

Rousselot's broad structural picture of the living dialect aimed at demonstrating a larger truth: the dynamic, evolving character of patois. His animating question concerned how his own speech differed from that of the mother who taught him to speak, and how this and other modifications like

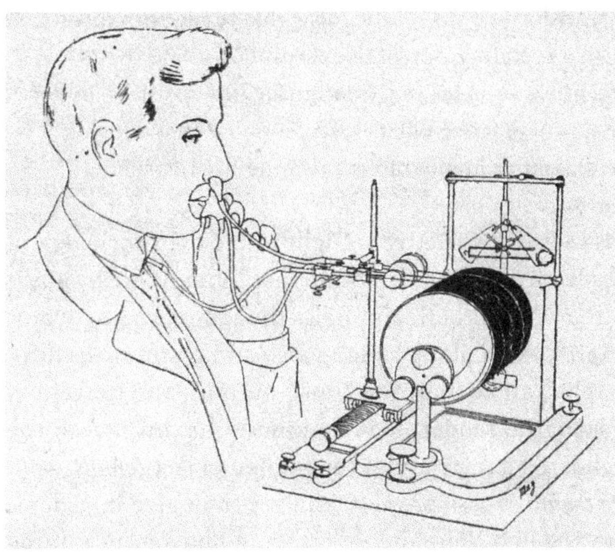

Recording speech, ca. 1897. From L'Abbé Pierre-Jean Rousselot and Fauste Laclotte, *Précis de prononciation française* (Paris: H. Welter, 1902).

it gave living speech a constantly changing character. Innovation was Rousselot's broad theme: how linguistic gestures and habits are modified and transformed in larger groups through small individual innovations. Gabriel Tarde, after 1900 a Collège de France colleague of Rousselot, and one of his keenest readers, proposed that Rousselot's methods be adopted by social scientists on a grand scale.

> If one wants to make sociology into a truly experimental science and to imprint it with the most profound seal of precision, it is necessary, I believe, to generalize in its essentials the method of the Abbé Rousselot with the collaboration of a large number of observers. Suppose the twenty, thirty, fifty sociologists, born in different regions of France or other countries, carefully and minutely as possible write up the series of small transformations in the political order, the economic order, et cetera that they have observed in their town or native village and in their immediate social circles. Suppose that instead of limiting themselves to generalities, they take note of individual manifestations of an increase or decrease of the religious faith or political faith, of morality or immorality, of luxury, of comfort, of a modification of political or religious belief, suppose that they make efforts, like distinguished linguists, to return to the individual source of the small diminutions or augmentations, or transformations, of the ideas that tendencies have been propagated within a certain group of people and translate themselves through imperceptible changes in the language, the gestures, in the grooming, in any sort of practice whatsoever, suppose that and you will see the ensemble of similar monographs as eminently instructive.[88]

Tarde's embrace of Rousselot is instructive in light of his own sociology of innovation. Tarde proceeded from the assumption that humans are by physical necessity gesticulating and mimetic animals; thoughts exist as vibratory cerebral states that are passed along by language and gesture. To think and communicate is to relive an action in its broad outlines and to recite it through gesture, a physiological rendering of Aquinas's maxim that in the knowing subject is engendered a mimicry of the known object (*omnis cognitio fit secundum similitude cogniti in cognoscente*).[89] Since people live in groups, they are given to mimicking and therefore to knowing one another. Tarde called the quanta of mimetic transition "imitative rays" (*rayons imitative*), small rhythmic patterns archived in the bodies of individuals but defining the links that make up social collectivities. While most rhythm patterns were calibrated to the stable norms of behavior, small innovations sometimes became imitative rays rippling through the social fabric.

While Rousselot portrayed mimetic gestures of speech in rural France, Tarde drew prime examples from urban settings like the cabaret and café concert: the bourgeois gent who imitates the slang and strut of a proletarian, or the *femme du monde* who reproduces the intonations of a singer. These geographies were obliquely linked, of course; the working-class population of Parisian nightspots was drawn heavily from migrants from rural France, who were now becoming Parisians by immersion in vibrant popular culture. Tarde's sociology self-consciously mirrored the vital exchange of energies in these settings, which he viewed as the principal source of innovation, the wellspring of the new and modern. Writing of the innovations in verse, for example, he argued that the rules of prosody should not be seen "simply as the play of the physiological functions of the individual, but also and especially as the play of social functions that consist fundamentally as undulatory propagations."[90] Mimetic physiology, in other words, could not be confined to the individual body, when by definition it required a social body for its realization.

Although influential in its day, Tarde's sociology soon became eclipsed by that of his rival Émile Durkheim, just as Rousselot's linguistics faded behind the overweening prestige of Ferdinand de Saussure's approach. Both Durkheimian sociology and Saussurean linguistics notably severed their links with physiology at their respective points of departure. Durkheim launched his *Division of Labor in Society* (1893) with a critique of Henri Milne-Edwards's principle of the physiological division of labor, arguing that the partition of labor had its sole origin in the *conscience collective* of autonomous society. In his *Course in General Linguistics* (published posthumously in 1916, from lectures given between 1906 and 1911), Saussure similarly rendered the phonological elements of language (*parole*) a mere substratum conditioned and constrained by the thoroughly social language system (*langue*). The twin pillars of twentieth-century French social science thus forged their autonomy at the expense of the physiological, vibratory anthropology considered in this chapter.

Yet this development obscures our historical vision of the epistemological nexus around the physiology of movement that linked Rousselot and Tarde with Marey, Ribot, Bergson, and others. These men's projects, arrayed in the epicenter of the French academic establishment, took the physiologists' experimental system as the springboard for a new philosophy of life, of organism, of speech and thought, and even for a new anthropology and sociology. Moreover, together they comprised an ambitious modernizing project that would fulfill many of the ambitions of the early Third Republic. In part 2, "Experimentalizing Art," we will examine some of the modalities through which these projects propagated themselves into the body of French and European society through the cultural arts of painting and poetry. In these stories the question will concern how, in the hands of nonscientific users and publics, experimental systems and epistemic things become refashioned—or deformed—into expert systems adapted to disciplines, with their own habits, practices, and traditions.

PART 2
EXPERIMENTALIZING ART

4

ALGORITHMS OF PLEASURE

Art as Expert System

HENRY, Charles.— . . . Measures with a dynamograph the value of a metaphor of Mallarmé, comments on a black canvass the verses of Jules Laforgue, traces the graphs of diseases, reduces to equations the paintings of Degas. Will prove that rigorous relations link the solubility of lead nitrate to the revolt of the Taipings.

Félix Fénéon, *Petit bottin des lettres et des arts* (1886)

BY THE LATE 1870S NUMEROUS EUROPEAN COMMENTATORS SPOKE of an "invasion of the region of aesthetics by natural science."[1] The new field went by different names, reflecting differences in approach or simply national or linguistic variation. Besides physiological aesthetics, there was "aestho-physiology" (a Spencerian approach), *Kunstphysiologie* (German approaches derived from Helmholtz, Brücke, and others), and *esthétique scientifique* (or *esthétique critique*) in France.[2] Although these approaches enjoyed much discussion, often great academic acclaim, their reach remained largely philosophical and discursive, without much impact on working artists. Among the varieties of physiological aesthetics in play in the late nineteenth century, it was Charles Henry's "scientific aesthetic" (*esthétique scientifique*) that shaped the vanguard art world, altering the practices of painters, poets, and even some musicians, and helping to recast the very idea of art itself.[3]

Some of Henry's great influence might be chalked up to his social position among the absinthe-sipping bohemians who launched the Parisian avant-garde explosion of the 1880s. He knew the right people—the neo-impressionist painters, symbolist poets, and numerous allied critics, scientists, and flâneurs—to bring about real change in the arts. He also knew and understood the ideological and institutional crisis that these artists experienced, producing an aesthetic system that addressed their concerns in tangible ways. Yet my contention is that Charles Henry's singular influence hinged largely on the reception of his scientific aesthetic as a deliberate method to transfer the experimental system used in scientific physiology laboratories to the practices of artists' ateliers.

Among the many authors who joined physiology, psychology, and the arts, Henry, a Sorbonne librarian, was the only one who successfully translated the new physiology into tools, techniques, and concepts that corresponded with existing practices of artists. While some artists may have had enough scientific education to comprehend what they read, few had experience with the tools and methods of the laboratory. Henry's combination of personal friendships with painters and poets and his experience as a laboratory *préparateur* for physiologists Claude Bernard and Paul Bert gave him intimate working knowledge of the everyday techniques of artists and scientists alike. Although Henry's physiological aesthetics proposed a radical break with the established foundations of art theory and practice, his practical knowledge allowed him to render it in terms and techniques that corresponded with what artists already knew how to do.

In this chapter I characterize Henry's scientific aesthetic as a proto–expert system designed to make experimental physiology applicable to the arts with a minimum of conceptual understanding on the part of artists. Expert systems, as Harry Collins reminds us, should be seen as links in a chain between experts and end users.[4] Henry's system packaged, or black-boxed, the expertise of experimental physiology into a system of aesthetic knowledge-engineering that was ready-made for artists eager to dissolve many of their key traditional practical and symbolic codes into scientific algorithms. "It is not a matter of talent, but of techniques," wrote the artist Paul Signac in describing the scientific aesthetic.[5] In this sense the aesthetic expert system aimed to store knowledge of a sort that could enhance the skills of the artist, or to serve as master to an unskilled apprentice. By a similar logic, moreover, proponents of artistic knowledge-engineering hoped that it could turn an ever greater number of consumers of art into active participants in the production system.

Charles Henry's aesthetic expert system hinged entirely on the properties of the experimental system of graphical recording methods. Its task was to dissolve the traditional codes of aesthetics and artists' practices into the experimental system's relays of bodily and machine elements that opened pathways to semiotic events. In practical terms this meant, for example, recasting traditional aesthetics' philosophical treatment of sensation in the terms of physiology, where recording instruments now showed sensation to be "the totality of modifications imprinted on the movements of diverse organs."[6] The new technical aesthesis opened the media of the arts to an entirely novel form of analysis by dissolving traditional forms of sensation into the currency of curves. "One could not study the subjective impression of movements, of colors, of musical and articulated sounds," Henry wrote, "when natural philosophy had not yet distinguished, classified, and formulated its objects, when nothing was known about the composition of forces, the decomposition of the spectrum, the nature of musical intervals, of consonants and vowels, when the physiology of the nerves was not yet anticipated, when the sense of the evolution of language was absolutely lacking. . . . It seems that the problem is ripe."[7]

All aesthetic phenomena, all basic media of the arts—movements, color, musical and articulated sound—were in principle translatable to graphic inscriptions: to lines and curves, either as sonorous waveforms, the lengths of luminous undulations, or other curvilinear inscriptions. "By the graphic method," Henry intoned, "all phenomena are translatable by the changes of direction automatically registered . . . this is the course to be followed if one wants to know the aesthetics of things, and it is probable that the results will go beyond the scope of aesthetics . . . with the use of more and more delicate apparatus and more precise media of observation."[8] The scientifically minded artist, then, would work not with nature and the human senses but would manipulate the aesthetic phenomena at their source in the technical sensorium. Through Henry's aesthetic expert system, artistic practice began to take on elements of the physiologists' experimental setup, with the direction of time-based flows between bodily and machinic element toward the creation of semiotic events, namely, the production of lines or curves according to the graphic method. These curves then became the basis for a new set of artistic practices or formalisms, the new "language" of artistic modernism.

Artworks produced with the new aesthetic expert system were presumed to compel their effects because the psychophysiologically determined formalisms had been calibrated to produce their responses automatically in the normal human spectator. The creation of art through an experimentalized physiological method was therefore only one-half of a twofold arc of projection and reception. Henry and the artists who followed him proposed a radical reconfiguration of the beholder or spectator of art, on the basis of an assumption that worked—had always worked—through a largely automatic process. Physiological aesthetics offered the chance for artists to seize this critical fact of art in their quest for intensified effects upon spectators. While heightened aesthetic intensities had intrinsic appeal, the vanguard artists in Henry's circle also embraced this proposal as a means of control over consumers in their budding independent or secessionist art market outside the salon system. Experimentalized art thus responded to the perceived crisis of the art system in 1880s France.

Yet before long, several of the most ardent proponents of the scientific aesthetic came to view this "machinic" conception of art as the source of profound and unsettling aporias. Georges Seurat, whose experiments with Henry's system drew charges that his paintings relied exclusively on mere technique and not training or creative genius, turned the question into profound explorations of the public function of art and its relation to the division of labor and the broader social effects of machinery. Seurat developed a unique form of art that translated the experimental system into a personal method in painting. Like any good experimental system, Seurat's method served as a vehicle for generating questions about every dimension of the medium, from the formal and material aspects of painting, to the physiological conditions of perception, and not least, to the social and political conditions of his art.

MECHANIZATION OF LINE

It all hinged on line. Henry's scientific aesthetic, including his work on color and sound, turned on the notion that all aesthetic perception relied on the principle of the line. In art and aesthetics, of course, the problem of line was antediluvian. Line formed the basis of composition in all of the visual arts. It also served as the bearer of emotion or affect and the carrier of the artist's unique personal signature. With the advent of graphic recording instruments, moreover, it had also become the trace of unseen forces, the diagram of energy relations in both the organic and inorganic. Although some scientists, like Gustav Theodor Fechner, had proposed to integrate the aesthetic uses of line with the mathematical or physical interpretation, this move had been roundly rejected by the leading exponents of graphic recording, from Hermann Helmholtz to Étienne-Jules Marey. Henry took it up anew, adopting the new resources of laboratory science to a twofold task. First, he set out to empirically establish the graphically recorded line as a mechanism of the kind commonly understood to be aesthetic. His second objective sought to ground this finding in an original psychophysical theory of perception, based on an ingenious farrago of physiology, mathematics, and neo-Pythagorean conjecture.

For centuries artists and aestheticians had formulated the problem of line in the language of physiognomy, the broad term for traditional doctrines of proportion. The ancient postulation of an analogy between inner character and external facial or bodily characteristics enjoyed a remarkable revival in the nineteenth century, both as a popular science of character and as a means of literary and artistic representation. For artists, physiognomy provided stock-in-trade knowledge about bodily gesture, proportion, and expression. Artists, as Judith Wechsler points out, read the conventional physiognomic codes, but in the opposite direction. "Where physiognomics," Wechsler writes, "from pseudo-Aristotle through Lavater, starts from the outward sign and teaches how to interpret it in terms of inward character, the treatises for painters start from an emotion or disposition and teach the signs that will express it; and in this they are paralleled by guides to gesture for actors and orators."[9] French art education had accumulated a highly articulated corpus of physiognomic rules of thumb, derived not only from Johann Kaspar Lavater but from a long tradition, including the ancient Greeks, Leonardo da Vinci, Jean-Phillipe Rameau, and above all the works of the seventeenth-century author Charles Le Brun, who represented the emotions described in Descartes's *Traité sur les passions de l'âme* (1649) as they were manifested in each movement of facial features.[10] For Henry, the project of a scientific aesthetic required the translation of these rules of thumb into a systematic doctrine of explicit and infallible psychophysical algorithms. His approach built upon the assumption of the abstractability of physiognomic signs, as well as the notion that they were implicitly gestural, both for the artist and for the active viewer.

Henry took his approach to physiognomy primarily from Charles Blanc, professor at the Collège de France and author of *Grammaire des arts du dessin*

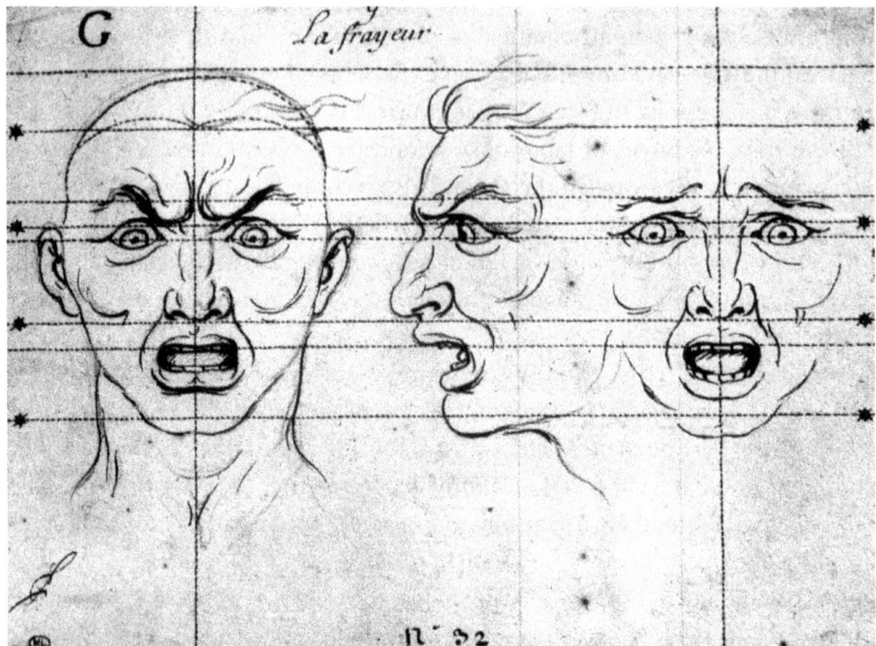

"La Frayeur." From Charles Le Brun, *Conférence sur l'expression générale et particulière* (Paris, 1698).

(1867), the canonical textbook in late nineteenth-century French art education.[11] Blanc promulgated a view of physiognomy distinctly at odds with those expressed by Guillaume-Benjamin-Amand Duchenne de Boulogne, Pierre Gratiolet, or Charles Bell, all of whom grounded physiognomic signs exclusively in the body; Blanc pursued the idea of physiognomy as a science of absolute signs. This was the doctrine of an early nineteenth-century Belgian named David Pierre Giottino Humbert de Superville, who in his *Essai sur les signes inconditionnels dans l'art* (1827) presented a theory of "unconditional" or universal signs whose significance is not attached to the organs of the face or any other physical object but to a grammar of lines and color.[12] Through Blanc's lectures and writing, an entire generation of French artists absorbed Humbert's theories, albeit in a bowdlerized form.

For aestheticians, the appeal of Humbert's theory of linear expression lay in its direct relation to the traditional doctrines of proportion. His leading idea held that one of the universal absolutes is the vertical line, rising from

Diagrams of linear directions and of the human face. From David Pierre Giottino Humbert de Superville, *Essai sur les signes inconditionnels dans l'art* (Leyden: Hoek, 1827–32).

the center of the earth and passing through the axis of the standing human to reach the heavens. The other absolute is its opposite, the horizontal direction. Together these two form a cross, modulated by the only other essential directions (left and right). These last, Humbert maintained, are not absolute; their movement relative to the two unvarying axes is the basis of their expression. He famously illustrated this principle with three schematic faces, with features represented by lines of equal length. Humbert argued that differences in expression manifested by these faces—gaiety, calmness, and sadness—must be explained by changes in direction. Direction alone, therefore, underpinning representation but independent of it, is to be regarded as the universal sign of human emotion. These three great lines, the horizontal one and the two oblique ones, apart from their mathematical value, have a moral signification; that is to say they have a secret relationship with feeling. The vertical, which exactly divides the human body in two parts, equally divides the head in two. On each side of the axis the double organs are symmetrically placed: the eyes, the nostrils, the ears, and the two corners of the mouth, since the mouth is an organ at once simple and double.[13]

For the artist, Blanc continued, what distinguished his approach to physiognomy was its capacity to represent values *in abstracto*, without any necessary reference to the human frame, but only to the universal coordinates of vertical and horizontal. Thus, in the theory of linear directions "we find the code of all proportions, the repertoire of all measures, the example and the law of all movements, the trace of all curves, the prototype of all the arts of design."[14] Linear values could be used to give precise emotional expression in nonanthropomorphic systems of representation, including architecture, landscape, and ornament.[15]

Once emotional expression could be specified as linear direction, it became amenable to precise quantification and measurement. This was the insight of Henry, avid auditor at Blanc's lectures and attentive reader of Humbert. Since physiognomic codes always implied an x, y coordinate system (the absolute vertical and horizontal axes), there was no reason why they should not be treated with the rigor of the graphic method.

Where these researchers looked to dramatic personal responses to conditions of extreme fright or distress, Henry and his allies suggested that the specific character of aesthetic phenomena—measurable properties of form, color, and sound—provoked similarly measurable reactions in the human subject.[16]

The line itself, in other words, not only recorded or represented emotional phenomena, but might also be shown to generate affective reactions.

To explain how different forms of stimulation excited or suppressed physiological function, Henry turned to the novel and celebrated concepts of dynamogeny and inhibition advanced by the physiologist Charles-Édouard Brown-Séquard as basic modes of regulation in the animal body.[17] *Dynamogeny* referred to "those excitations, more or less instantaneous, in the nervous or contractile parts more or less distant from the site of irritation, which exaggerate a power or a function."[18] *Inhibition*, by contrast, derived from those stimulants that, in analogous conditions, make a power or function diminish or disappear.[19] Brown-Séquard had amassed a large archive of experiments that pointed in this direction. One of the most celebrated concerned the dynamogenic influence of a liquid obtained from crushed testicles, a laboratory derivative of what the half-American physiologist knew as a delicacy of the American West known as "prairie oysters" or "Rocky mountain oysters," reputed to be responsible for the legendary virility of cowboys. Together with France's leading electrophysiologist, Arsène d'Arsonval, Brown-Séquard took dynamometric measures of muscular strength as well as precision assessments of the force and distance of the urinary streams of experimental subjects, before and after they were injected with the "vaccine" drawn from mammalian testicles.[20]

Much younger and insouciant about matters of virility, Henry applied Brown-Séquard's principles to art and aesthetics. In a paper written by Henry and read by Brown-Séquard to the French Academy of Sciences, Henry proposed that dynamogeny and inhibition refer to the mechanisms through which the psychic apparatus reacts to sensory impressions. Relatively complex sensory phenomena are to be considered dynamogenic when they require minimal internal work (*travail intérieur*) to be apprehended by the subject; or inhibitory when they demand a considerable amount of the same psychological effort or work.[21] Thus, beautiful forms bring a maximum amount of complexity with a minimum burden; ugly forms require greater amount of work for less return in perceived complexity.

With one more step Henry made the Brown-Séquard theory viable for aesthetics. With his typical conceptual ingenuity, the young savant proposed that dynamogeny bring on an experience of pleasure, while inhibitory conditions are felt as pain. This proposition squared with the widely discussed evolutionary viewpoint, most famously advanced by Herbert Spencer, that held that pleasure derived from a sense of usefulness, pain from a sense of futility. On this view, moreover, "all pleasure increases vital function, all pain diminishes it."[22] Pleasant sounds "nourish" the auditory nerve, beautiful pictures improve the visual organs. It followed that all arts were life enhancing, valuable elements of human evolution.

Pleasure and pain had become a theme in several Paris laboratories. Charles Richet, a friend of Henry, had conducted experiments on pain in Marey's Collège de France laboratory as part of investigations concerning Helmholtz's studies of muscle contraction and nerve impulse velocity in frogs.[23] Richet sought to establish pain as a variety of intelligence that manifests in different forms—hunger, thirst, fatigue, disgust, as well as in reactions to discordant sounds, fetid odors, bitter tastes, and dazzling light—all of which were more acute in more intelligent organisms, for whom these serve a "salutary function, by constraining us through cruel alerts, to manage our organism and to avoid brusque changes of condition."[24] Richet used graphic registration devices to measure reaction times to painful stimuli. Following Helmholtz he compared the excitation in the nerve to an electric current passing through a metal wire; the excitation in the center provoked a shaking analogous to a bell that continues to resonate long after it has been struck. Memory, Richet contended, was nothing more than the persistence of the vibration provoked by a sensory impression conducted by the nerve.

Charles Henry embraced Richet's findings. Where Richet made careful distinctions delimiting the relation between pain and inhibition, Henry took the physiologist's experiments to indicate that all painful stimuli provoked inhibitory responses.[25] And he adopted Richet's model of the nervous system, where perceptual stimuli set off a vibratory displacement in the normal tension of the system. These tenets enabled Henry to set down his own methodological principles, stipulating that for aesthetic experiments it was necessary to choose "stimuli with well-defined properties: linear measures, sonorous vibrations, lengths of luminous waves, et cetera."[26] Physiological reactions to these stimulants were to be measured, wherever possible, with the graphic method, since all perceptions were accompanied by a manifestation of force and therefore a movement or displacement of muscles or other organs. When measurement was not possible—say, for lack of adequate instruments for capturing certain organic movements—it would be possible to analyze the measurable properties of aesthetic media in relation to judgments of agreeable or disagreeable sensations.

Several experimental psychologists set out to investigate Henry's ideas. Charles Féré, a young medical doctor and intern under the celebrated neurologist Jean-Martin Charcot, conducted a series of studies on patients from the wards of the Salpetrière psychiatric hospital. Féré acknowledged that he undertook the experiments "at the behest of M. Charles Henry," but the aims of his studies followed the general direction of research at the Salpetrière.[27] Charcot, art aficionado and self-described "visuel," had long encouraged patients to draw or paint their interior states.[28] Féré, by contrast, introduced graphic methods as a means of introducing "objective" methods into neuropsychiatry. For his first series of experiments, Féré used a dynamograph— a hand dynamometer designed by Duchenne de Boulogne and adapted by Charles Verdin to include a self-registering function—to measure what he called "ideomotor induction," or the variations in force impelled by sensory stimuli. Féré maintained that these studies established the principle of his method, that "the energy of a movement is related to the intensity of the mental representation of the same movement."[29] This was, of course, a basic tenet of psychophysical research. But Féré contended that the introduction of the graphic inscription apparatus made possible new forms of precision measurement of psychological actions. Inasmuch as "the sensations furnished by the diverse organs of sense have a common measure furnished by the dynamometer," they "immediately determine a production of force, and one can therefore legitimately deduce that the psychophysiological functions, like physical forces, reduce to mechanical work."[30] Féré's studies, in other words, brought psychophysics within the broader compass of Mareysian physiology: a mechanical mind to accompany the mechanical body.

Studies of sound and of color bore this out. With a special tuning fork made for him by Rudolph Koenig, Féré sounded a series of pure notes, comprising a full octave, to hysterical subjects with a dynamometer in hand. The results proved remarkable: with each ascending note, dynamometric force increased, only to diminish again as the tones descended the scale. To control for the influence of the experimenter, Féré used a plethysmograph to measure the rise and fall of blood circulation in the forearm. When Féré superposed the two curves—dynamograph and plethysmograph—he found them nearly identical.[31]

Experiments with color yielded similarly astonishing results. Together with Albert Londe, Féré projected the colors of the spectrum, obtained through a special prism, to normal and hysterical subjects, who were again equipped with dynamographs and plethysmographs. Under the influence of blue, violet, and a pseudo-yellow color (they were unable to get a pure yellow), the subjects' contractions remained relatively unmodified, while red and orange produced stronger reactions. Hence, Féré concluded, the dynamogenic effect of colors appears to be proportional to the length of the electromagnetic wave that comprises them. Since the intensity of perception, for hearing as well as sight, corresponds to the number and amplitude of vibrations of the air or the ether, Féré observed, "it seems that the vibration should be considered as the standard [*unité*] of excitation for hearing and for sight."[32]

Commenting on Féré's experiments, Henry also underscored the point that psychophysiology was now in a position to determine natural standards for both "objective" and "subjective" phenomena. He sought to draw the full implications of Marey's physiology, as he understood them, for psychophysiology. To this end he furnished his own version of the "ideomotor" theory, in which "the sensation corresponds to a real movement, which leads to a virtual movement; the idea to a virtual movement, which leads to a real movement."[33] Henry insisted that this theory would extend Mareysian physiology and "singularly augment the reach of the graphic method" by allowing us to "consider the sensation or the idea as virtual exercises of our natural mechanics."[34] Previously inaccessible and private psychological functions, including the formation of complex ideas, would now be rendered in the public currency of the graphic method. But for Henry, it meant still more: the theory of virtual psychological movements ensured a common medium of exchange between the individual senses themselves and the psychological apparatus, thereby establishing a basis for the analogies between artistic media.

THE MATHEMATICAL ORGANISM

From this point Henry set off in his own theoretical direction. The Sorbonne librarian put forth original, yet sometimes obscure, lines of argumentation, in support of an imaginative, neo-Pythagorean conception of mathematics. Only a few of Henry's scientific readers (and still fewer of his artist comrades) seem to have been able to follow him confidently down this argumentative path; most readers simply had to trust that the erudite historian of mathematics and author of mathematical textbooks knew whereof he spoke when he made abundant references to contemporary mathematicians, usually without a careful explanation of their work.[35] This section is an attempt to reconstruct the theory behind the texts.

Where other physiologists regarded the experimental method of graphic recording simply as an effective means for gaining an indication of physiological actions, Henry interpreted the inscribed curves as a window onto the inherent mathematics of the soul. In his view, Marey's studies had already revealed the mathematical character of animal movement: adaptive, efficient motions showed an intrinsic mathematical sense in the organism. Henry regarded his contribution as a formulation of the basic mathematics of psychophysiological mechanics.

Just as important in Henry's account was recent German research demonstrating that visual perception involves substantial unconscious mathematical calculation.[36] Helmholtz, in particular, had shown that in the mechanics of eye movements, the ocular muscles operate according to the principle of least effort, or as Helmholtz preferred to say, easiest orientation.[37] Helmholtz's investigations served as emendations to the account given by Wilhelm Wundt, who had brilliantly shown that the eye muscles follow Carl Friedrich Gauss's theory of least constraint; this theory stated that each mass in any system of masses, connected to one another through any sort of external constraints, moves at every instant in the closest agreement possible with free movement, that is, under the least possible constraint. Since Gauss had observed that with this principle, motions occur in nature in the same manner in which a mathematician would prescribe them, Gauss's theory entailed the remarkable inference that the eye functions as a mathematician, implementing the probability calculus to achieve maximum efficiency.

For Henry, this principle suggested a means to reasonably calculate the amount of effort required to perceive a given aesthetic form. Since the movements of the eye muscles or other organs could, in principle, be considered as linear trajectories, one could use these to measure the variations of interior work by measuring the shape of the external form. The aesthetics of form could finally be stated in terms of Henry's psychophysics: "The problem of the aesthetic of forms thus comes down to this: which lines are the most agreeable? But a small bit of reflection quickly shows us that line is an abstraction: it is the synthesis of two parallel senses and contraries in which they can be described: the reality is direction. . . . The problem thus reduces to a new statement: which are the most agreeable directions? In other words, which directions do we associate with pleasure and with pain?"[38]

Virtual movements, like real movements, could be deduced from linear form. Moreover, since all sensations could be reduced to the curvilinear properties of the graphic image, their reception and processing were governed by a similar unconscious mathematics. "The method therefore consists of comparing the deductions of calculation with experience," Henry explained. "Among normal organisms, in which the physiological state is correlated with ideal unexpressed states, there should be agreement between experience and the calculations: among the others [the abnormal], one must discern the reversals or breaks that need to be moderated or reduced."[39]

But how could one go about defining the conditions of unconscious mathematical calculations, where no real, organic motions were involved? In one of the most curious assumptions of the scientific aesthetic, Henry proposed that the seemingly complex problems of perception could be greatly simplified by reducing them to the mathematics of the circle. Some commentators, following José Argüelles, have claimed that Henry chose the circle for mystical reasons.[40] While it is true that later in life Henry rhapsodized mystically about the circle, finding historical precedents for his view in figures such as Leonardo da Vinci, his initial reasons for choosing the circle followed from his principal scientific sources. Helmholtz's theory of visual orientation posited that the eye moves along its own coordinate system, which he called "directional circles," any deviation from which would constitute an "error" for the eye.[41] Circles similarly played a fundamental role in Marey's biomechanics, where complex bodily movements typically reduced to the problem of the simple lever, which, the physiologist wrote, "can only be described in terms of complete or partial cycles."[42] Finally, Henry found useful the definitions of several geometers, especially the professor of mathematics at the Collège de France, M. E. Laguerre, who argued that all motions could be regarded as "cyclical," that is, reducible to a description in terms of their direction.

Henry offered a somewhat plausible postulation that virtual movements proceeded in a parallel fashion to the schematic picture of the bodily organism. In his view, psychological organization consists of a mechanism composed of a center (which he sometimes called the "I"), similarly equipped with four appendices, which orient themselves through symbolic representations of the radiating cycles. This being, in other words, could move from the center in all directions, "from low to high and right to left in a plane and in planes perpendicular to that one, from front to back and from back to front."[43] Moreover, just as the human members move in exclusively circular fashion, the human being unconsciously gauges these movements in imaginary circles. "I note," explained Henry," that from the point of view of the conscience the form of expressive movements is circular. I remark that the living element is from this point of view like a compass, which not being able to describe continuously anything but small cycles and, more or less discontinuously, grand cycles, must express more or less changes in the direction of force, the variations of stimulation and the physiological work that corresponds to it."[44]

These arguments led Henry to the cornerstone of his scientific aesthetic: the theory of directions. Each of these fundamental rectilinear motions, when described continuously, produces either dynamogeny or inhibition (and thus, pleasure or pain), as observation and experience allegedly showed in a variety of vital phenomena, from reflex actions to heliotropisms. Movements from low to high are dynamogenic; from high to low, inhibitory. Movements from back to front are dynamogenic; front to back, inhibitory. Movements from left to right are dynamogenic; those from right to left produce inhibition. Continuous circular movements produce similar effects: when the tangents are directed upward to the right and downward to the left, as in the hands of the clock ("cycle dextrorsum"), it is more agreeable to the eye than when the tangents move upward to the left and downward to the right ("cycle sinistrorsum").

With this theory, Henry believed he had placed Humbert's doctrine of the physiognomy of line on the solid ground of psychophysics. Humbert's metaphysical catalog of voluntary gestures—prostration or concentration for pain, exultation and radiating for pleasure– assumed new life in the vocabulary of science. Moreover, Henry claimed, these conformed to a broader conception, the "law of gesture in the physiognomy of expression," which he defined as follows:

> It is evident that the goal of these movements is, in the case of pain, a tendency to place the body in the situation that demands the least work to produce; for the case of pleasure, in the situation that demands the most work to produce. Pleasure, which is an effort of perception tending toward the minimum, thus expresses itself by the tendency to realize the maximum of work and finally by a maximum of work; pain, which is an effort of perception tending toward the maximum, expresses itself by a tendency to realize the minimum of work and finally the minimum of that is zero.[45]

This "law," then, defined the transition from the affective to the cognitive features of Henry's aesthetic: emotions became conceivable in terms of psychophysical algorithms describing the properties of aesthetic forms.

The theory of directions could also be expressed as a matter of continuity and discontinuity. Since dynamogeny corresponds to mechanical work executed in the shortest possible amount of time, continuous lines increase that function, while discontinuous lines bring about inhibition. The aesthetic question similarly became a matter of these kinds of energy relations considered in their virtual manifestations: "What is the form of expressive movements that can be described continuously, that is, with the production of work, and what is the form of those that can be described discontinuously, that is, with impediments at each instant."[46] In practical terms, this problem could be approached with the familiar methods developed to analyze graphic representations, with special attention to the points of inflection in the curve, which marked breaks or changes of direction.

At this point, Henry confronted the principal limitation of the theory of linear directions inherited from Humbert. Complex forms, such as graphic inscriptions, typically contain many different "directions," some of which can even cross each other. For these cases, the problem demanded redefinition—and the introduction of a second key term: the *angle*. "Each change of direction is an angle," wrote Henry, "which each angle is measurable by the arc of the circle intercepted by its sides, the center of the circle being the summit of the angle."[47] Angles thus served as further markers of energy relations where directional movements changed: "All variations of physiological work represent themselves by the changes of real or virtual directions of force."[48] By this Henry meant to include not only the real angles that

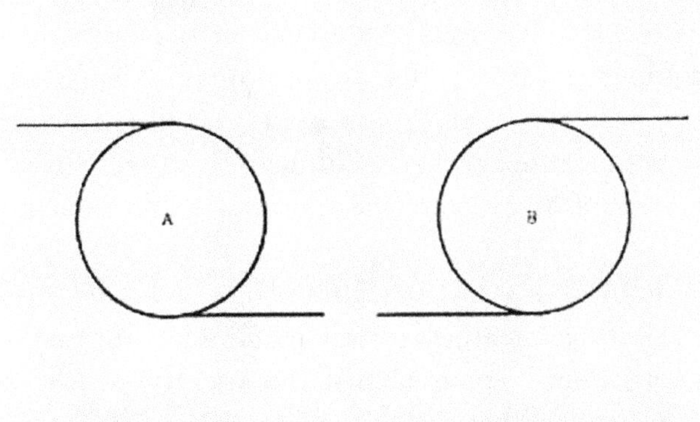

Inhibitory cycle (left) and dynamogenic cycle. From Charles Henry, "Le Contraste, le rythme, la mesure," *Revue philosophique* 28 (October 1889).

might be measured in graphic form but also imperceptible, virtual changes of direction, each modification of consciousness, that occurred within the "ideal mechanism of the living organism" in the act of perception.[49]

Once again, the ever resourceful Henry took up suggestions made by Marey and reworked them in unexpected ways. Henry applied the terms of recent mathematical and aesthetic theories of music. *Rhythm* signified the character of continuous representations, while *measure* designated a regular discontinuity or caesura within rhythm. Henry emphasized that when speaking of rhythm, continuity specified a subjective, psychological link between two objectively given stimuli. Measure, on the other hand, referred to a break in continuity that repeated itself at identical intervals. "What essentially distinguishes rhythm," Henry wrote, "is periodicity; measure is distinguished by regularity."[50]

Measure suggested division into segments along a horizontal axis, as in music. But for Henry's theory of the circular basis of organic movements, this approach would not be possible. Instead, he posited (following Marey's geometric chronophotographs of locomotion) that the segments be represented as rays emanating from a central point. In the process of perception, then, concrete forms are decomposed into circular segments, which correspond to the psychological operations, conceived as decomposed in segments of straight lines. With each change of direction, we pass from one cycle to another, and this passage appears as the moment of an "inflection" (*arrêt*) in the progression. All forms, for Henry, are decomposed against the intrinsic background of these sections of the circle, which taken as a whole define the circumference of a circle. Our internal, unconscious mathematics thus operates as a graphic recording device, or better, an apparatus of integration, where curves are evaluated against the background of a circle rather than an x, y coordinate grid. "Since we cannot realize rectilinear direction," Henry explained, the question became, "which are the rhythmic sections of the circumference?"[51]

The answer would come from Gauss. Henry, like Wundt and Helmholtz before him, turned to the Göttingen mathematician to illuminate the mathematics of the unconscious. Henry proposed that the scientific aesthetician would be able to determine rhythm and measure by following Gauss's theorem concerning regular polygons: "rhythmic numbers" would be those whose value is equivalent to the interior angles of the regular polygons. Gauss's theorem provided this by furnishing a rule for inscribing the polygons within the circle: $x = 2n + 1$, where x is the number of the sides of the polygon and n any whole number, provided that x is a prime number. Henry contended that human beings, consisting themselves of a circular disposition, deploy this theorem intuitively in perceptual acts that demand the evaluation of the interior angles of the polygon. "I will prove," he wrote, "that Gauss, in establishing this magnificent theory, has at the same time founded the whole science of rhythm and indirectly that of measure."[52]

With this formula, the rhythmic or harmonious divisions of the circle could be compiled and expressed either as angles or as divisions of the circle. These divisions, moreover, could also be represented through the reciprocals of these numbers, expressed as fractions (i.e., 1/2, 1/3, 1/4, 1/5, 1/6, 1/8, 1/10, etc.). To facilitate the calculation of angles between the radii dividing the circle, these fractions could be expressed as degrees; one-quarter of the circle, for example, equals 90 degrees; one-eighth equals 45 degrees; one-tenth equals 36 degrees, and so on.

Henry's theory of rhythm and measure drew a fundamental analogy between the perception of visual and musical form. Both forms of representation took place in three dimensions, with the difference that visual form unfolded in space, musical form in time. Both linear perspective and temporal representation, moreover, assumed a purely ideal notion of the present, from which space appeared continuous and time discontinuous. For spatial representation, dynamogeny arose from continuity in the cycle; from the

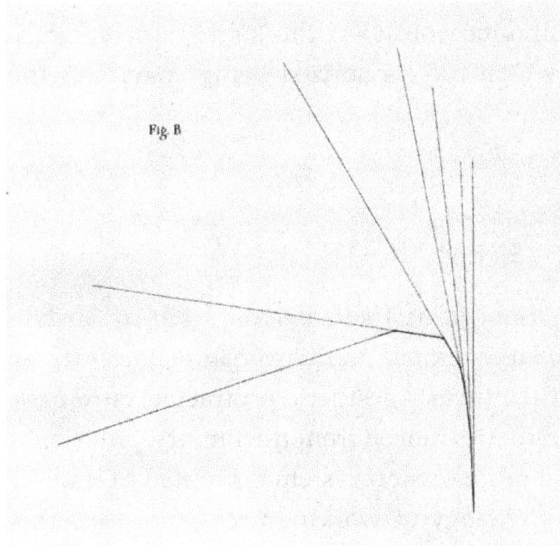

Inhibitory angle. Charles Henry, *Rapporteur esthétique: Notice sur ses applications à l'art industriel, à l'histoire de l'art, à l'interpretation de méthode graphique* (Paris: G. Séguin, 1888). Courtesy of Indiana University Libraries.

point of view of time, it depended on the possibility of transforming the considered number of breaks (*arrêts*) into continuities.

In both cases dynamogeny arose from the Fechnerian psychophysical law of the least effort of perception. In the case of musical perception, however, the perceptual operation functioned differently. Proportions of measure, Henry argued, became agreeable when the numerator and the denominator do not differ from each other except in terms of the value of the unit or of a very small rhythmic number. Henry illustrated this supposition by comparing the segments of a line on the sides of an angle. He assumed that our perceptual mechanism evaluates the relations of magnitude by taking in the largest segment first, in the dynamogenic directions of left to right, and then the first eye movement suffices to determine the relations of magnitude. A second movement would be unnecessary and wasteful, and would not enhance the perception. The comprehension of these different proportions demanded, in effect, different types of intuitive mathematical operations, what Henry called "algorithms," following the theory of the Polish mathematician, neo-Kantian philosopher, and messianist Josef Hoëné de Wronski.[53] Since all representations took form in time and space, these could be described as successive or simultaneous, continuous or discontinuous, concordant or antagonist, which Henry characteristically described as both mathematical operations and, simultaneously, as the largely unconscious, psychophysical states through which the "organized being" navigates the world.

"WORKERS OF THE LINE": THE AESTHETIC EXPERT SYSTEM

The real importance of Henry's scientific aesthetic derived from the instruments, both in practice and, to a larger extent, in their imagined uses in the arts. It was through Henry's instruments—aesthetic protractor, chromatic circle, and olfactometer—that aesthetics moved from the literary-philosophical domain to become a material proto–expert system calibrated to transfer the practices of experimental physiology to working artists in terms that were familiar and practicable.[54] The need for this system stemmed simply from the fact that all artists already had many general and highly specific skills related to their craft, but few had the time or opportunity to acquire the working knowledge and skills of experimental physiology.

Perhaps because of his intimacy with working painters and poets, Henry understood this limitation, as well as the sincere desire on the part of the artists to profit from physiological expertise. Henry appears to have understood the extreme limitations of language as a means of communicating the workaday knowledge of scientists and artists alike. Hence a question emerged at the heart of his scientific aesthetic: what can come to be known through language, and what can come to be known through practice? His answer, demonstrated through his aesthetic instruments and his explanations of them, probed into territories associated in the later twentieth century with expert systems, that is, with methods for codifying expert knowledge into algorithms that can be turned into machines or machinelike behaviors on the part of end users.

This is a topic that has been richly explored in recent science studies, notably by Harry Collins and his associates. One of Collins's critical points of departure concerns the transmission of different forms of knowledge. He has challenged the notion that scientific knowledge can be transmitted adequately through information channels such as scientific journals and textbooks. Much of science demands both broad and specific skills, including tacit knowledge of specific machines and procedures that resemble knowledge in craft traditions. Collins and Robert Evans have assembled several varieties of these skills in an illuminating "periodic table of expertise," which classifies the different kinds of knowledge one might possess.[55] Especially relevant for our discussion of the fin-de-siècle avant-garde are the categories of "specialist expertises," which Collins and Evans further subdivide into "ubiquitous tacit knowledge" and "specialist tacit knowledge." Under "ubiquitous tacit knowledge," the authors place what they call "beer-mat knowledge," "popular understanding," and "primary source knowledge"; under "specialist tacit knowledge," they place "interactional expertise" and "contributory expertise." These latter two categories are particularly relevant for our discussion. "Contributory expertise" is the most comprehensive expertise and the kind to which the term *expert* is usually ascribed. It allows individuals to contribute to their domain of specialist knowledge because they have internalized certain physical, craft skills, which they combine with mastery of the language of the field.

The concept of "interactional expertise," by contrast, is a novel category proposed by Collins and Evans to describe the possession of linguistic skills in the absence of "practical competence," by which they mean embodied expertise in research work. It is expertise in the insider language appropriate to the reporting of science (or, for that matter, art). Anyone who can participate in scientific discussions without being able to do the actual benchtop experimental work would fit in this category. Interactional expertise is still immersion in a culture of participants, but not in a practical sense. As Collins and Evans explain, the interactional expert "may be able to understand scientific things, and to discuss scientific things, but is still not able to do scientific things."[56] Interactional experts, they contend, can command a fluency in the language of a domain as those who are fully immersed in the domain. The notion of interactional expertise also brings out the exact opposite notion—in this case proposed by science studies scholar Monika Cwiartka—accommodating those who have practical, embodied, expertise in the absence of discursive competence in the domain, or "the ability to do benchtop work only."[57]

These categories provide a useful framework for describing the configurations of scientific and artistic expertise in the cultural sphere of fin-de-siècle art worlds. We find certain actors who perfectly embody one or another "element" in the periodic table, and others who combine more than one to varying degrees. Besides those who might be called pure "contributory experts"—scientists like Marey, Richet, or Féré; painters like Seurat, Pissarro, and Signac; or poets like Jules Laforgue, Stéphane Mallarmé, or Gustave Kahn—there were many critics, philosophers, and flâneurs who possessed interactional expertise in the arts and/or sciences. The most important of these in the avant-garde was the critic Félix Fénéon, whose witty and incisive art criticism provided public explanations of the scientific theories of Henry and others in relation to the work of avant-garde painters and poets, a feature memorialized in the title and composition Signac's famous portrait.[58]

Henry himself might be difficult to classify here, since he clearly possessed some contributory expertise in the sciences and interactional exper-

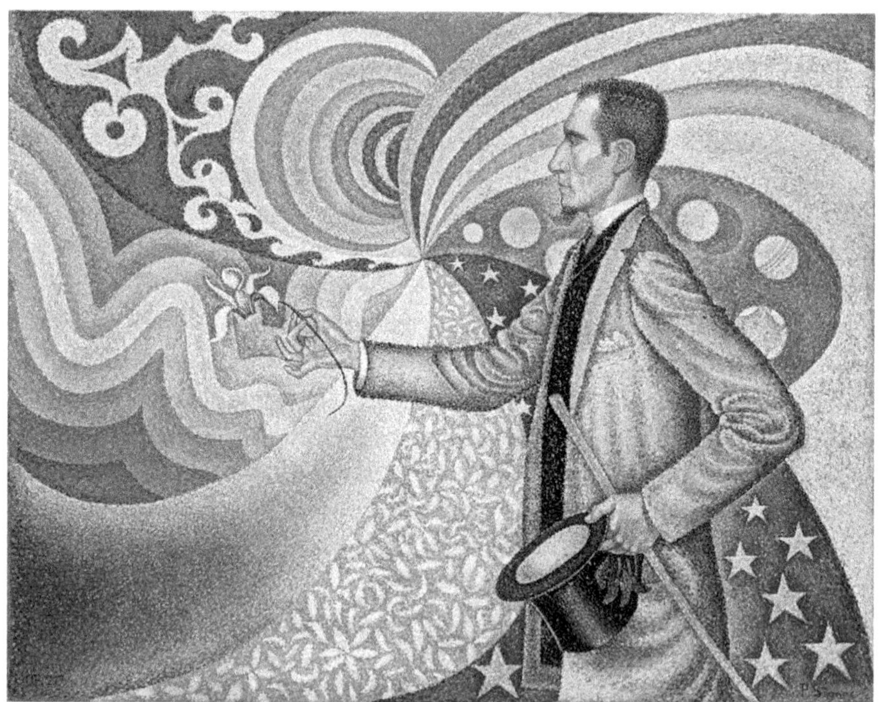

Paul Signac, *Opus 217. Against the Enamel of a Background Rhythmic with Beats and Angles, Tones, and Tints, Portrait of M. Félix Fénéon in 1890*. 1890. Oil on canvas, 29 x 36 1/2 in. (73.5 x 92.5 cm). Museum of Modern Art, New York. Fractional gift of Mr. and Mrs. David Rockefeller. © 2014 Artists Rights Society (ARS), New York

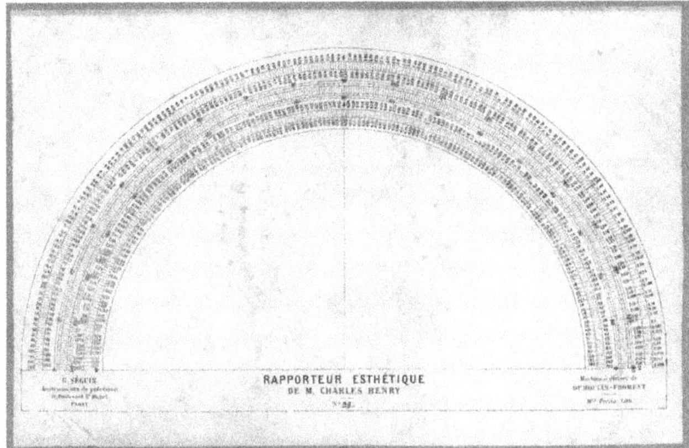

Aesthetic protractor. From Charles Henry, *Rapporteur esthétique* (Paris: G. Séguin, 1888). Courtesy of Indiana University Libraries.

tise in the arts. But the essence of his scientific aesthetic consisted in its capacity to deliver practical expertise in physiological aesthetics, whether or not artists acquired fluency in the theoretical discourse. As Henry conceived them, these instruments followed the principle articulated a few years later by Frederick Taylor for the use of the slide rule, in what Taylor called "the art of cutting metals" on the scientifically managed shop floor. "By means of these slide rules," Taylor wrote, intricate mathematical problems "can be solved in less than half a minute by any good mechanic, whether he understands anything about mathematics or not."[59] What held for scientific management also obtained, in principle, for scientific aesthetics: with the aesthetic protractor, any good artist or artisan could deploy the intricacies of Gaussian mathematics or Mareysian physiology, whether he understood them or not. For that reason, Henry dedicated his first instrument, the aesthetic protractor (*rapporteur esthétique*), "not only to scientists, engineers, and medical doctors, but also to art critics and archaeologists, architects, and all those workers of the line: designers of industrial art, tailors and fashion designers, typographers, furniture makers, carpet designers."[60]

Like the slide rule, the aesthetic protractor was an instrument of remarkable simplicity. Produced by the instrument maker Georges Séguin, it consisted of a protractor printed on translucent fabric, which came with an accompanying handbook of theory and practice. Like an ordinary protractor, it was shaped in a half circle and was marked off in degrees from 0 to 180. On an adjoining scale was placed another series of numbers, the reciprocals corresponding to the fractional divisions of the circle. With this latter

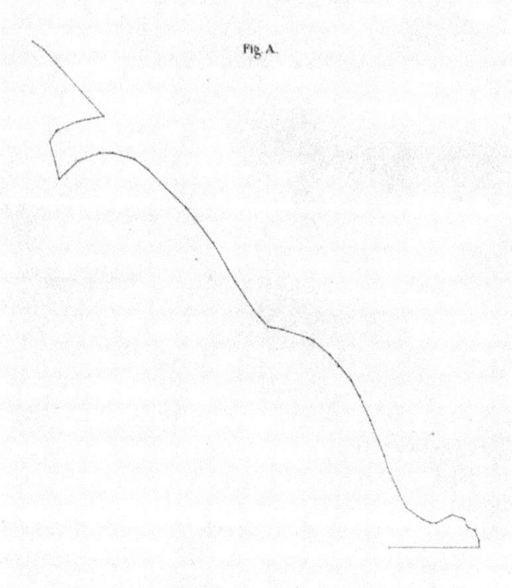

Sample lines for measurement with the aesthetic protractor. From Charles Henry, *Rapporteur esthétique* (Paris: G. Séguin, 1888). Courtesy of Indiana University Libraries.

scale and a set of accompanying tables provided by Henry, the user could locate rhythmical numbers "at a glance" and convert them into degrees. This enabled two kinds of operation. First, rhythmical angles could thus be located directly on the protractor, without any mathematical calculations. In this way, the working artist could determine whether the angular distances between lines radiating in different directions from a single point were harmonious and thus would produce pleasure in the onlooker. Second, with these algorithms in hand, it was a simple matter to create, or to analyze, rhythmical changes of direction in linear forms and thus assess the effects of an artistic composition.[61]

To illustrate how the instrument would bridge the gap between the theory and practice of scientific aesthetics, Henry looked to medicine, itself similarly bedeviled by an analogous divide between the laboratory and the clinic. In its dependence on the rigorous training of the senses—the sensitivity of the hand to the pulse, for example, or the eye to color gradations in urinoscopy— the clinical art had long been recognized to have affinities with the fine arts.[62] Nineteenth-century medical instruments, especially the thermometer and graphic registration devices, had begun to replace much of the medical doctor's tacit knowledge with machines and quantifiable measures.[63]

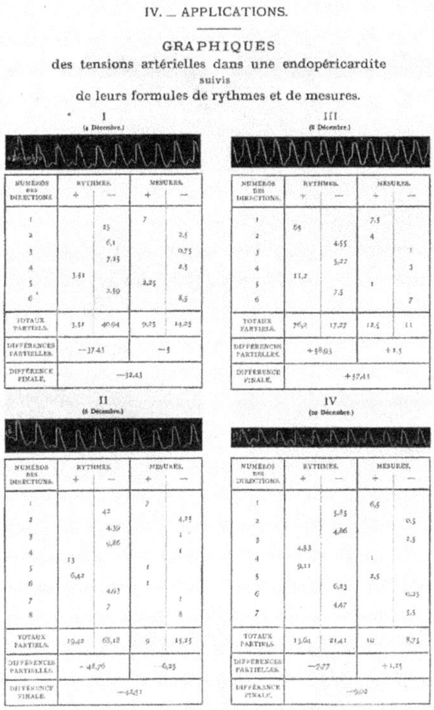

IV. _ APPLICATIONS.

GRAPHIQUES

des tensions artérielles dans une endopéricardite
suivis
de leurs formules de rythmes et de mesures.

Analysis of sphygmographic recordings of arterial tension in endopericarditis. From Charles Henry, *Rapporteur esthétique* (Paris: G. Séguin, 1888). Courtesy of Indiana University Libraries.

But, as Henry observed, the graphic recording still left the physician with the task of interpreting the curves, a skill as much a matter of learning and enculturation as the traditional pulse reading. The aesthetic protractor could be used to eliminate the residual empiricism plaguing even the most instrument-driven practice of medicine, such as that described in Paul Lorain's textbook, *Études de medicine cliniques faites avec l'aide de la méthode graphiques et des appareils enregistreurs* (1877).[64] Henry reproduced Lorain's textbook case of endopericarditis, with the aim of showing "how laborious and uncertain" the clinical application of the sphygmograph could be, "even in the hands of an eminent physician."[65]

Henry reappraised Lorain's case history in light of his own instrument. Lorain began recounting the clinical history and results of auscultation, and then he described the pulse curves: "The sphygmographic traces clearly indicate the disturbance of the circulation. When the tension is extremely weak, the dicrotism delays so much that one only finds it on the vertical line

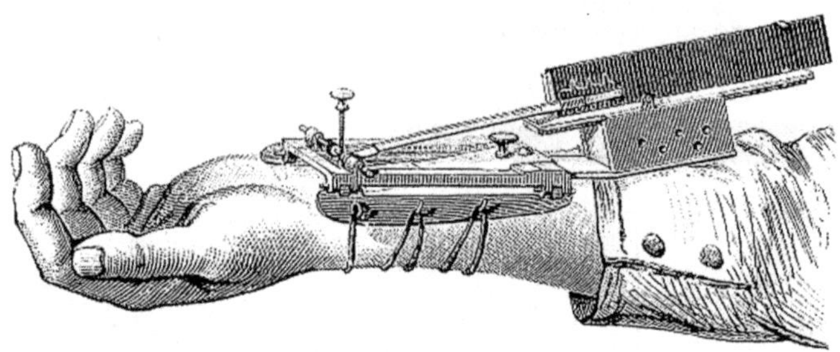

Marey sphygmograph, as used by Paul Lorain in the curves analyzed by Charles Henry. From Étienne-Jules Marey, *La Méthode graphique dans le sciences expérimentales et principalement en physiologie et en médecine* (Paris: G. Masson, 1878).

ascension of the following pulsation (traces of December 6, 8, 14, 20). The intermediate traces follow, day by day, the course and delay of this dicrotism: they explain it."[66]

Using the aesthetic protractor, Henry explained, the same visual evidence could be given a new precision. If one took the contours marked by two small bars over the figures and prolonged their directions, he reported, the unequal aesthetic value emerged in a striking manner. When the "measures and rhythms" were taken—that is, when the tangents of the curves and the angles they formed between them were analyzed and compared—the initial pathology and the progressive return to normal health revealed itself in the transition from nonrhythmic numbers to rhythmic numbers.[67] This heightened precision could facilitate, supplement, or clarify clinical judgment. With the aesthetic protractor, clinical medicine would move one step closer to automation, the mechanization of mechanization, pushing back the last intentional act in clinical diagnosis.

But mechanize creativity? To mechanize diagnostic judgment was one thing—the senses had increasingly come to be seen as being like machines: the eye an optical instrument, the ear a harmonic analyzer, and so on. Yet the artistic imagination still appeared to most as the unmechanizable bas-

III. — TABLE DES NOMBRES RYTHMIQUES

compris de 1 jusqu'à 8,589,034,590, calculée par M. Bronislas Zebrowski.

Nombres rythmiques	FACTEURS.	Nombres rythmiques	FACTEURS.	Nombres rythmiques	FACTEURS.	Nombres rythmiques	FACTEURS.
[illegible]	[illegible]	[illegible]	[illegible]	[illegible]	[illegible]	[illegible]	[illegible]

Table of rhythmic numbers. From Charles Henry, *Rapporteur esthétique* (Paris: Verdin, 1888). Courtesy of Indiana University Libraries.

tion of the autonomous spirit. Anticipating this challenge, Henry emphasized that recourse to standard instruments for certain kinds of artistic judgments should not be confused with "substituting the mechanism of an instrument for the creativity of the artist." Genius, he emphasized, is inimitable, "since it expresses itself not only through the visible rhythms but by an infinity of more or less invisible rhythms." The artist, moreover, "is but an eye, an ear, a nervous system normally organized and developed" who senses the rhythm, realizes it virtually as an idea, and produces it externally.[68]

But these senses require education and training. Until now this education had required countless hours of apprenticeship, of instructing the eye, of memorizing and internalizing physiognomic rules of thumb and the officially sanctioned canons of taste. With the aesthetic protractor, much of that painstaking labor could be simplified, as artists learned to use the instruments or to calibrate their perceptions to the standards of the instruments.

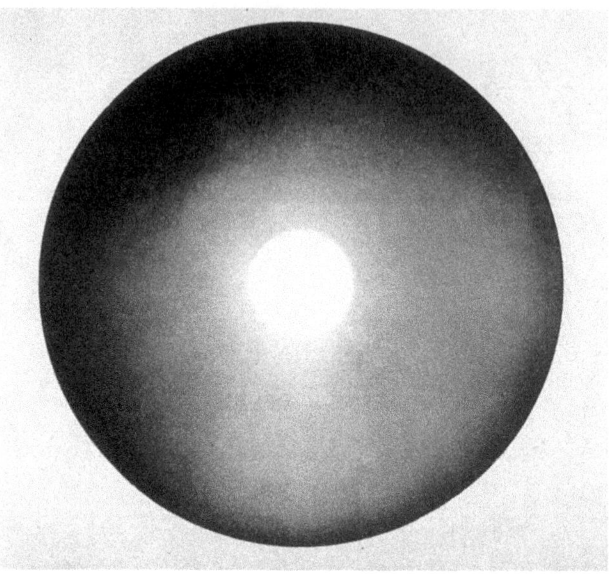

Cercle chromatique. From Charles Henry, *Cercle chromatique, presentant tous les compléments et toutes les harmonies de couleurs* (Paris: Charles Verdin, 1888).

What Henry claimed to do for line with his aesthetic protractor, he did for color with a similar instrument, the chromatic circle (*cercle chromatique*).[69] Many nineteenth-century scientists—David Brewster, James Clerk Maxwell, Hermann Helmholtz, Michel-Eugène Chevreul—produced chromatic circles with differing conclusions about what the fundamental colors were. But Henry tackled the problem in a unique way. Having connected the psychological functions with directions, and having further shown that perception could be reduced to certain numerical formulae, he proceeded to analyze the visual sensation, and then he constructed his chromatic circle as a deduction from his theory. Finally, he showed that the results of his theory accorded with the results of experience and even brought a range of disordered optical phenomena into coherence: the differences between colored lights and colored pigments, irradiation and the means of avoiding its effects, the illuminating power of the different parts of the spectrum, binocular vision, the salient and indented appearances of stained-glass windowpanes, the different laws that govern mixtures of colored lights and mixtures of colored pigments, the relations between light and vegetation, and much more.

The use of color among neo-impressionist painters is a complex topic, largely beyond the scope of this book. Seurat and Signac devised their methods of applying the dots and dabs of paint to the canvas from several different sources, including Henry's theory of color directions, but also Michel-Eugène Chevreul's theory of color mixing in pigments and a clever, ambiguous reconciliation of the Young-Helmholtz theory of optical mixture and the Hering opponent-color theory.

This technique was dubbed *pointillist* by some critics in the 1880s, but the painters sternly rejected that term, insisting on *divisionism*, which referred to a method of splitting and recombining color sensations on the canvas as a means of producing both local and all-over effects. As Floyd Ratliff shows, the neo-impressionists grasped that the synthesis of color in the eye varies with distance and other circumstances, hence their eclectic approach to the use of color theories.[70] The role of Henry's chromatic circle appears to have been primarily directed toward all-over effects, in which the application of color sensations was given angular and directional value, or composed in harmonious proportions, in keeping with the oft-quoted remark of Eugène Delacroix that "the art of the colorist is obviously similar in some ways to mathematics and music."[71] This is evidenced in Signac's lithograph playbill advertising both the anarchist Théâtre libre and Henry's *Cercle chromatique*, which Robert Herbert has shown to illustrate some aspects of Henry's instrument and theory.[72]

Around 1890, Henry turned his attention to odors and the olfactory sense, developing an instrument to accompany those used in line and color. Olfaction had been central to the decadent imagination at least since Joris-Karl Huysmans's character Des Esseintes, in *À Rebours* (1884), described a dazzling fantasy of a perfume symphony.[73] In practice, however, the problem of olfaction proved somewhat more difficult, both because of the anatomy of the olfactory apparatus and the complex chemistry of odorific vapors. Unlike sight and hearing, which were accomplished by registering the vibrations transmitted by a medium, sensations of smell occurred by contact between membranes in the nasal passages. Henry's instrument, the olfactometer, was designed to bypass some of this complexity and measure the aggregate psychophysiological effects. Built by the instrument maker G. Berlemont, the Henry olfactometer determined the weights of odors passing successively through a cubic centimeter affair, in an attempt to determine the minimum perceptible quantity of each odor by the experimental subject. The apparatus consisted of a glass reservoir traversed by two tubes that slid one into the other. The first was blocked by paper at the bottom. Inside of this was a

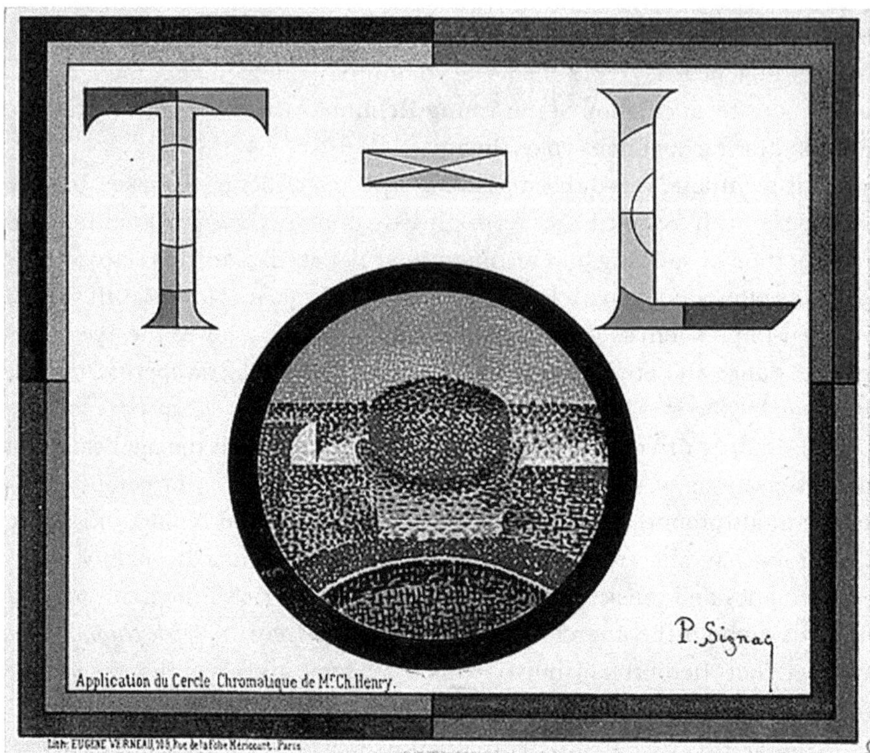

Paul Signac, application of Charles Henry's chromatic circle, Théâtre libre playbill of January 31, 1889. Color lithograph on heavy-wove paper, 6 1/8 x 7 1/16 in. (15.5 x 18 cm). Collection of the Museum of Fine Arts, Boston, gift of Peter A. Wick. © 2014 Artists Rights Society (ARS), New York The image illustrates aspects of Henry's color circle and some principles of the contrast of colors. The *T* and *L* appear as sections cut out of Henry's color wheel--right side up in the *T* and upside down in the *L*. The hyphen between the *T* and the *L* is composed of the two pairs of opponent colors: red versus green, yellow versus blue. The tondo is filled with contrasting colors; and at the top, the orange-red of the stage is opposed by the bluish-green of the spectator's hair; in the middle, the yellow of the footlights sets off the purple hair, and so on.

glass tube graduated in millimeters, which was introduced into the nostrils. When the tube was raised, a portion of the vapor, measured by a stylus and recording cylinder, flowed into the nose of the subject, who inhaled the vapor according to a specific expansion of the thoracic cavity, as determined by a Marey pneumograph. Together with Gustave Robin, Henry carried out experiments using a variety of different essences: wintergreen, ether, ylang-ylang, lavender, rosemary, bergamot, and English mint. In papers presented to the French Academy of Sciences, Henry demonstrated that the intensity of the effects of scents made a rapid succession of sensations almost impossible, since consecutive odors caused a rapid anesthesia of sense. On the other hand, he observed, if the times separating two successive sensations were too long, it became impossible to combine them, and the anticipated effect was disturbed by strange feelings. In short, he concluded, "smell is rather the complement of other excitations than an artistic excitation like a melody or a picture."[74]

This observation prompted a discussion at the Academy of Sciences around whether Henry's olfactometer would provide a promising vehicle for researching the famous gap, or "lost time," in the transmission of sensation through the nervous system.[75] Like the *temps perdu* in Helmholtz's curves of the nerve transmission of muscle contraction in frogs, or the intermittencies of cardiac rhythm registered with Marey's sphygmograph, the *temps perdu d'olfaction* provided a special kind of access to the latencies of sense perception and, bearing in mind that similar responses had been found in protozoa, to organic memory. It is very possible that Marcel Proust, author of the three-volume *À la recherche du temps perdu*, read this report in the *Revue philosophique*, perhaps while munching a madeleine biscuit.[76] What we do know is this: Proust reflected on the work of art as the bearer of a "hidden rhythm—still more vital that we perceive it ourselves—of our soul, similar to those sphygmographic traces that automatically inscribe the pulsations of our blood."[77] The thought jibes closely with Henry's aesthetic and signals an approach to sensation, time, memory that suffuses Proust's masterpiece.

For his part, Henry promoted his olfactometer not just as an aid to art but as an earnest instrument of social meliorism. He insisted that through his aesthetic instruments the artist's métier would expand to a position of great social responsibility, analogous to that of the doctor, engineer, or scientist. Artists would, in short, be bearers of the algorithms of normality in all things visual, the guarantors of the role of beauty in the healthy functioning of society. It is the artist, Henry wrote, who "best senses and ensures that the milieu is most normal, most harmonic."[78] Specifically, the norm would serve as a means of intervening in the built world by calibrating it to promote optimal health and development—a public-works program for psychophysical well-being. This suggested enormous possibilities for engineering the environment in the interests of human betterment or transformation. Simple graphic representations might be placed in schools, for example, to suffuse the milieu surrounding the child with an atmosphere of lines and colors that served the unconscious education of the senses.[79]

When his theories and inventions were put in place, Henry prophesied, the world would see the appearance of, "not schools, but brilliant social states like life in Greece or the Renaissance, which produced the great periods of art." Furthermore, he wrote, "reciprocally, to aid the normal development of art is to lend a greater hand to the realization of our still far-off destiny: the creation of universal harmony."[80] This vision of art in a regenerated society became a regular feature in accounts of neo-impressionism in the anarchist press. In the coming days of harmony, Charles Albert wrote, neo-impressionism would be employed "for our railway stations and our factories, for our schools and hospitals, for our meeting halls and our playhouses, for our baths and gymnasiums, as well as for the beauty of our streets and our towns."[81]

ANARCHISTS AND ART MARKETS

Charles Henry developed his aesthetic theories and instruments while circulating among a remarkable array of young bohemians representing a variety of disciplines and points of view, but at this point in their lives, all with sensibilities shaped by anarchism, science, and the prospect of a new art. Jules Christophe's lively account of the nightly crowd at a Left Bank café placed Henry squarely with his milieu:

> At number five of that sweet and odéonesque Avenue de Medicis, carved right into the Luxembourg Gardens, is the unknown, elm-shaded Brasserie Gambrinus. There, from 1884 to the autumn of 1886, . . . one would see, every night, this "budding" literature: Messieurs Gustave Kahn, finely Semitic; Papadiamantopoulous, blue-bearded Athenian (pseudonym Jean Moréas); Joseph Carageul, a red-bearded Narbonnais; Félix Fénéon, a Burgundian with Yankee manners, born at Turin; Charles Vigner, the elegant Swiss; Paul Adam, the Parisian with

the extremely white and stiff collars; and others: Edouard Dujardin, creator of *La Revue wagnérienne*; Fédor Fédororowitch de Wyzewa, the "Oblomovist of Montmartre"; Marius Pouget, brilliantly metalized into d'Orfer Morhardt, the Swiss critic; Charles Morice, Verlainesque poet; Jules Laforgue, the lunar Gerson, who unfortunately died last August 20; Charles Henry, the dynamist of art, future author of a "mathematical and experimental aesthetic"; Gastor Dubreuil, who expressed ideas about music in the newspapers; Maurice Barrès, the Boulangist prose writer. There were also those Parisian painters of an independent style: Dubois-Pillet, Georges Seurat, Paul Signac, with Alexis Boudrot and David Estoppey, simply Impressionist "painters-drawers"; Maurice Raymond, of polychrome statuary; and Barbavara, an Italian doctor, a student of Charcot.[82]

This was a remarkable collection of figures at a "budding" moment. Henry's aesthetic projects brought many of the interests of these figures together in a common set of ideas and tools. A new art was the aim, of course, but it was pointless to create new modes of painting without an accompanying field in which they could be inserted. For this reason, Henry and the neo-impressionists promoted the scientific aesthetic as a strategic element in the burgeoning independent art market of fin-de-siècle France.[83] After the struggles of Manet and the impressionists to establish a market system outside the state-run salons, the younger neo-impressionist generation championed their scientific approach as an alternative form of authority. Since the 1860s, the challengers to the salon system had increasingly presented paintings as propositions within a theory of art. Scientific approaches to art were a version of this tendency, raising the banner of innovation in the positivist climate of the early Third Republic. Scientific approaches to art, moreover, extended the compass of Kropotkinist anarchism, an ideology that described itself as scientific and counted some of France's leading scientists among its adherents.

Yet, for all of the useful "branding" that the scientific aesthetic provided, artists' embrace of Henry's methods rested primarily on the control these methods might offer within the insecure conditions of the fledgling art market. By promising artworks in which content was indissolubly linked to form and color, so that every tone, gesture, and hue contributed to the desired effect on the "normal" viewer, Henry's physiological aesthetics suggested that success in the market could be calculated and ensured in advance. In this ambition Henry and his associates aligned themselves with a pan-European tendency to theorize economics and aesthetics on similarly physiological terms. Since the 1860s, French artists, dealers, and critics associated with the fledgling Salon des indépendants had looked to their more commercially minded counterparts in the British art world.[84] The French discovered that, alongside the market-based institutions of art, the British had also begun to theorize what John Ruskin called "the political economy of art," which included numerous theories that placed political economy itself on a foundation of physiological aesthetics, that is, of psychophysiological conditions of pleasure and pain.[85]

From around 1890, Henry and Signac embarked on a project using their aesthetic instruments to reform the mode of production in a second art market, that of the industrial and decorative arts. Although Signac regarded himself as a fine artist, and did not himself make decorative art, his anarchist ideology convinced him that it was his avant-garde duty to bring his expert knowledge to his comrades in the industrial arts.[86] With the aesthetic protractor, Henry and Signac sought to link their expert system with end-users in the arts industries; the instrument would enable artisans to calibrate their sensory perceptions with those held in an archive of dynamogenic and inhibitory measures drawn from the long history of decorative arts.

The aims of this project were not merely aesthetic, but political and social, aiming at a thorough reform of the very constitution of the burgeoning consumer society. The bridge between fine arts and decorative arts had already been institutionalized by the reforms of the early Third Republic.[87] In the republican view, which the anarchists shared, the things created by a society embodied the character of social relations: the division of labor, harmony, efficiency, and moral properties all found direct expression in the aesthetics of things.[88] Consumption therefore carried both possibility and risk, as Leora Auslander observes, being "understood as potentially and profoundly disruptive of the libidinal economy, capable of either deregulating and destabilizing, or of making, the family and society."[89]

Or as Signac scribbled in his notebooks: "Justice in sociology, harmony in art."[90] Justice and aesthetic harmony shared a common logic of proportion. Both spring from a notion of symmetry, since, as Elaine Scarry points

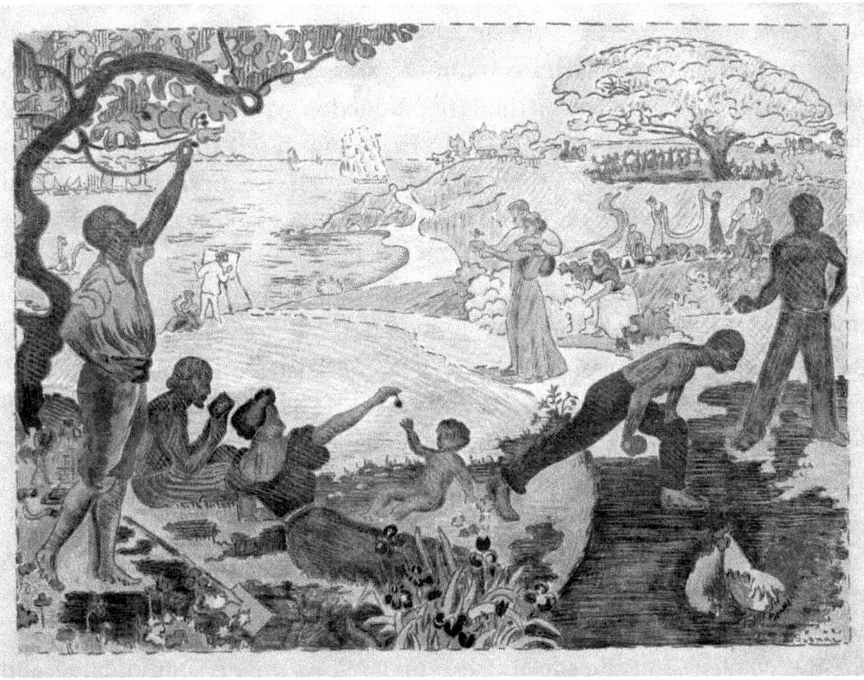

Paul Signac, *In the Time of Harmony: The Golden Age Is Not in the Past, It Is in the Future*, 1895. Colored lithograph on paper, 37.47 x 50.17 cm. Sterling and Francine Clark Art Institute. © 2014 Artists Rights Society (ARS), New York

out, one can intelligibly speak of "the symmetry of everyone's relation to one another" when speaking of justice.[91] In the vocabulary of Henry and Signac, "harmony" bespoke the relations of aesthetic and social elements, both of which had become severely perverted in modern societies by the conditions of large-scale capitalism. "Harmony" could also serve as code for "anarchy"—as in the Signac's 1895 mural originally called *In the Time of Anarchy: The Golden Age Is Not in the Past, It Is in the Future* (a saying from anarchist leader Charles Malato's *Philosophie de l'anarchie*), but changed to *In the Time of Harmony.*

By 1890, broad agreement had emerged across the political spectrum that the French decorative-arts industry had fallen into acute crisis, with sweatshop conditions in the ateliers and a corresponding degradation in the quality of art that emerged from them, as evidenced by the dramatic decline of the international market share held by the traditionally dominant French industry.[92] From the anarcho-communist perspective, it came down to the corrosive alterations in the methods of production wrought by the rise of the department stores, which compelled artisans to forfeit their already meager sovereignty, leaving a condition that the Le Playist sociologist Pierre Du Maroussem described as a monstrous "bastard system of small and large industry."[93]

Within this context, Henry and Signac understood the question of aesthetics as one concerned not merely with art and artworks but with what French philosopher Jacques Rancière calls the "distribution of the sensible" in society. Social inequality, Rancière argues, is accompanied by "a way of mapping the visible, . . . the intelligible, and also of the possible." Aesthetics attempts a "redistribution of experience," a realignment of the embodied inequalities in the constitution of the sensible world."[94] Signac's invocation of justice and harmony in sociology and art pointed to this ideological purpose, with Henry's aesthetic expert system as the vehicle for redistributing experience. The republican ideologues liked to speak of the work of art as restoring the wholeness of the social body sundered by the division of labor and its attendant inequalities. For anarchists this was not good enough: social injustice would produce inharmonious art, which would only contribute to further injustice. What Henry's scientific aesthetic purported to offer was a means to rectify and normalize the initial act of projection—making art—as a means of directing the changes wrought by the act of recovery. Then, as Henry told an audience at the artisanal-workers library, the Bibliothèque Forney, "normal passions, the joyous cry of happy organisms, will replace the struggle for existence of abnormal ages with the concerts in which the laws will be science and the production of a new art."[95]

With this in mind, Henry and Signac sought to restore harmonious proportions to things and productive relations in one fell swoop. Harmony might be achieved, they thought, by introducing the new algorithmic methods of the scientific aesthetic to artisans, which would not only beautify objects but help equalize relations between small and large producers. Signac characterized the project in a letter to Vincent van Gogh: using the aesthetic protractor, he said, we "are going to teach the workmen, apprentices, etc., to see the correctness and beauty of things, for till now they have only received aesthetic education by means of empirical formulae couched in misleading or fatuous device."[96] The aim was to enable workers to become self-calibrating, training their senses against the standard of the instrument as a means of increasing their autonomy from the monopolies of the department stores as well as the state schools.[97]

Henry and Signac sought to help artisans cope with their increasingly limited time to spend on specific designs. Fin-de-siècle taste in decorative arts and luxury goods favored historical pastiche, imitations of Greek, Roman, Renaissance, Louis XIV, or Louis XVI styles.[98] Unlike fine artists, for whom originality was critical, artisans needed to make pleasing copies of a vast catalog of historical forms. Henry and Signac set out to produce an inventory of historical forms, tested with the aesthetic instruments. They aimed to establish the "normal" law through comparative studies ranging over a wide variety of historical periods and classes of objects, from Persian vases, Louis V swords, and Neufforge stools to modern objects, including the typesetting for the masthead of the Paris daily, *Le Figaro*. Rhythmic forms were juxtaposed with nonrhythmic forms (such as the *Figaro* typeface) to show the norm, manners of deviation, and the possible means of rectification.[99] Compiled in the album format, these studies provided studious artisans with a valuable repository of forms. Translated into designs—furniture, upholstery, clothing, carpets, utensils, and the like—they would serve the dominant taste for historicist pastiche, allowing consumers to cruise the libidinal archive of past civilizations, to appreciate their particular form of life, their virility or feminine allure.[100]

The comrades-in-arts began their investigations with artifacts of ancient Greece that were highly prized in antiquity, played significant roles in the commercial relations of the Hellenic city-states, and were thought to reveal important ethnological characteristics of their producers.[101] Three intact amphoras, from Cnide, Thasos, and Rhodes, formed the basis of Henry and Signac's first study. All three ancient jugs had been examined extensively by the eminent archeologist Albert Dumont, who explained their aesthetic qualities in relation to their milieu of origin.[102] Dumont deemed the amphora from Cnide unsurpassed in its elegance. Rhodes produced amphoras that in Dumont's estimation were "very cultivated" and inferior only to those of Cnide. By contrast, the amphoras of Thasos, the capital of a northern island that filled the jugs with white wine to trade for cargos of wheat, featured "handles with uncultivated form" and were "heavy, thick, and large."[103] All

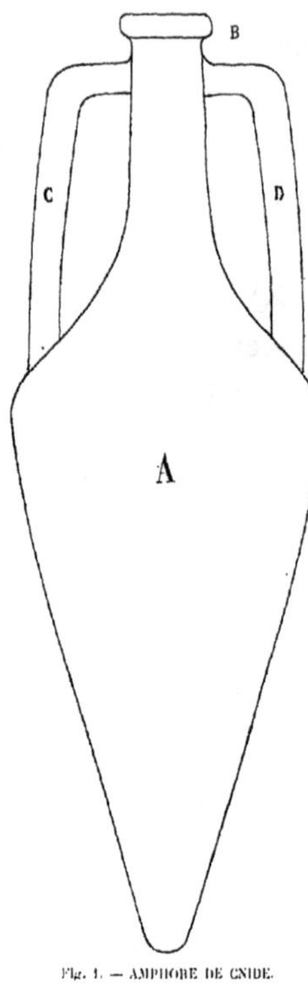

Study of a Cnide vase, by Charles Henry and Paul Signac. From Charles Henry, *Application de nouveaux instruments de précision (cercle chromatique, rapporteur et triple décimetre esthétique) à l'archéologie* (Paris: E. Leroux, 1890).

of Dumont's judgments were borne out remarkably by the measurements taken by Henry and Signac, using the aesthetic protractor, on enlarged photographic reproductions of the amphoras. The Cnide and Rhodes amphoras exhibited multiple rhythmic angles and very few nonrhythmic angles, which when summed revealed rhythmic coefficients. The Thasos amphora featured several nonrhythmic angles, which yielded a nonrhythmical coefficient for the object as a whole.

What might these measures reveal about the ethnological characteristics of the ancient Greeks? Setting aside the practical lessons for artisans, Henry presented these amphoras as examples of the historical, evolutionary character of psychophysiology. Writing against the grain of materialist accounts of ornamental arts dominated by Gottfried Semper (and just before the publication of Franz Wickhoff's and Alois Riegl's great works on the genesis of style in the ornamental arts of antiquity), Henry considered Greek aesthetic forms as conditioned by the particular milieu from which they originated, and therefore capable of revealing the psychophysiological characteristics of their makers.[104] He proposed a model that joined assessment of technical standards with the psychophysical sensibilities of the cultural epoch in question. In Henry's telling, the technical standard found in historical artifacts could be used as an indicator of anterior conditions of psychophysiology and, by a Cuvierian logic, of reconstructing wholes from fragmentary parts. "As to the law of evolution," Henry wrote, "there exists only one method to know in what way sensations such as those of color and form have evolved, and that is to rigorously compare forms and polychromatic objects from the aesthetic point of view. This cannot be done without precision instruments capable of exact documentation of the laws that one could consider normal for the harmony of forms and colors."[105]

Henry's attempts to delineate a linear, developmental history of psychophysiological aesthetics through the history of artifacts inspired his collaborator to produce a similarly linear and formalist genealogy of modernist art. Signac's *D'Eugène Delacroix aux néo-impressionnisme* presented a model of historical succession based on a series of "firsts"—formal innovations that culminated in the art of the neo-impressionists, "the definitive masters" who nevertheless "are still in the period of research, and understand just how is left for them to do."[106] Signac's account strikingly suggested an experimental model of art in which painting appeared as a material system to be explored, altered, and probed. As a literary genre, Signac's treatise itself marked the first instance of a kind that would be repeated in formalist histories of modern art and, more broadly, by the German tradition of *Kunstwissenschaft* from Heinrich Wölfflin forward. The experimental system thus became an implicit feature of narratives of modernist art.

SEURAT'S METHOD

Georges Seurat featured as the greatest of Signac's neo-impressionist masters and the best example of the experimental technique whose genealogy Signac delineated in his manifesto. Signac had long promoted Seurat as the standard-bearer of what he thought of as the techniques collectively owned and employed by the neo-impressionists, also known as the Neos. Seurat became unhappy with being associated with a generalized scientific technique, complaining to Signac that it would diminish the individuality of each artist. "I have always thought," he wrote, that "the more of us there are, the less originality we will have, and the day when everyone practices this technique, it will no longer have any value and people will look for something new, as is already happening."[107] Seurat added defiantly that it was his "right to think this and to say it, since I have only painted to find something new, to find my own mode of painting."[108] Despite this insistence on what he called "my method," there is plenty of evidence that he continued to experiment with the techniques and ideas shared by his fellow Neos, as well as those of his friends, the poets Jules Laforgue and Gustave Kahn.

Beginning with the work of John Rewald and William Innes Homer, art historians have uncovered much about Seurat's engagement with science, including that of Charles Henry. Other scholars have pushed back, questioning the extent to which Seurat and his colleagues really understood these ideas.[109] Seurat thus emerges either as a beneficiary of the scientific theory, or as a victim of (pseudo) scientific Svengalis. Both of these arguments depend on an outmoded and inadequate concept of science. In this section I argue that the "science" in Seurat's method was not a matter of following some theories and perhaps taking a few measurements to guide composition. We have seen how Charles Henry's system did not require "contributory" scientific expertise, but a simpler end user's competence. Still, I argue, Seurat was able to construct a method that functioned as painter's analog to the kind of experimental system that informed Henry's psychophysical aesthetics. Like the physiological experimental systems considered above, Seurat's method involved precisely timed and tuned coordination of interfaces between heterogeneous bodily, mechanical, energetic, and semiotic elements. And like any good experimental system, Seurat's was less a method for producing effects (although it was also that) than a vehicle for generating questions—questions of the very kind that emerged with the experimental systems of physiological aesthetics.

Let us first recount the encounters of the scientists and artists. Seurat met Henry in 1885, probably through their common friends, the poets Gustave Kahn and Jules Laforgue.[110] The painter had already absorbed the light and color theories of Helmholtz, Ogden Rood, and Chevreul and had found them a key resource in the composition of his early masterpiece, *A Sunday Afternoon on the Island of the Grande Jatte* (*Un Dimanche après-midi à l'Île de la Grande Jatte*), the "manifesto painting" for the new *impressionnisme scientifique*. But meeting Henry opened Seurat to the resources of science in a new and direct way. The painter acquired a scientific tutor in the eccentric librarian, who brought an implementable aesthetic expert system that reverberated with the central aesthetic and social preoccupations of the avant-garde. It must be borne in mind that Seurat's connection with Henry took place at an important moment in the development of the neo-impressionist and symbolist avant-gardes, just when a broader network of friendships and alliances among painters, poets, and critics was being consolidated. But Seurat's relation to Henry's artists' expert system evolved more rapidly than that of his friends: in around four years, Seurat traversed several stages of response to the expert system. After an initial triumphal sense of advantage conferred by the system, Seurat perceived a sense of overreach, as the system increasingly appeared as a rote technique. In his last paintings Seurat probed the limits of the system, without giving it up, developing a synthesis between the new expert technique and aspects of the older, intuitive ways of working.

After 1886, several avant-garde artists attended Henry's evening lectures at the Sorbonne and, presumably, the Saturday-morning laboratory exercises that accompanied them. The artists listened—some with comprehension, others without—as the young savant presented his system, filling blackboards with diagrams and equations and using props to illustrate differences in color perceptions. In September of that year, Félix Fénéon announced that painters had expanded their scientific resources beyond Rood and Helmholtz and that "soon the general theory of contrast, rhythm, and measure of Charles Henry will provide them new and very certain information."[111]

Seurat's first experiments with Henry's scientific aesthetic came with *The Models* (*Les Poseuses*), first shown at the 1888 Salon des indépendants. Fénéon gingerly announced that Henry's technique had inspired, but not determined, the painter's technique, pointing out that "all of the happy curves of the back, of the belly, to the nape of the neck, the other slips on the bottoms," had been executed by "a pseudo-scientific fantasy." Similarly, the

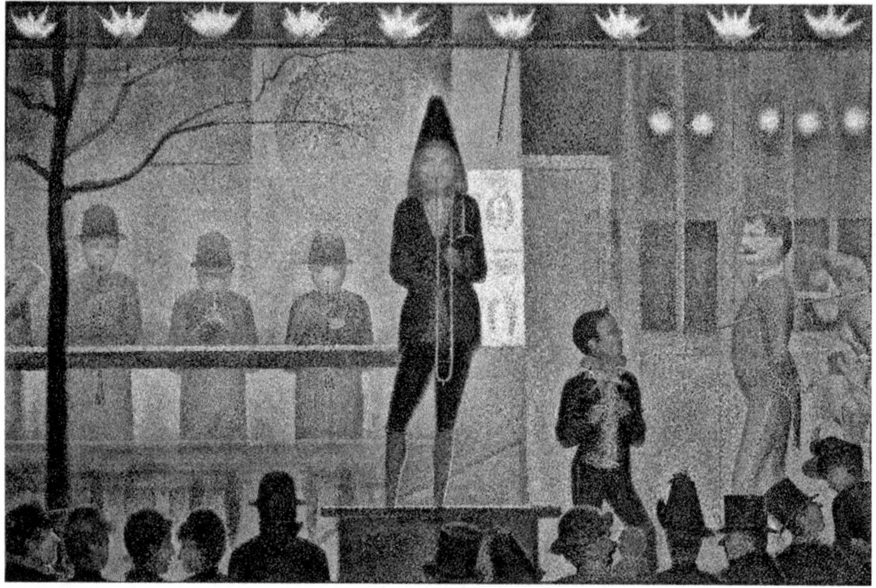

Georges Seurat, *Circus Sideshow* (*Parade de cirque*), 1887–88. Oil on canvas, 39 1/4 x 59 in. (99.7 x 149.9 cm). Metropolitan Museum of Art, New York.

critic Fénéon noted, "a red umbrella, a straw umbrella and the green bottom orients itself according to the direction that has red, yellow, and green according to the chromatic circle of Henry. The swell of a glorious rhythm and calm vivifying forms and colorations, and this work humiliates the memory of the nudes of galleries and of legends."[112]

Whatever its exact degree of conformity with the measures of the psychophysical aesthetic, *Les Poseuses* exemplified for its public the integral values that set apart the Neos' technique from that of the impressionists. In what Fénéon called the painting's "uniform and nearly abstract execution," its rhythmic small touches of paint, it defied the "trails of impasto" and the "dexterity of touch" associated with impressionism.[113] Against the impressionists' celebrated voluntarism, enshrined in the spontaneity of the eye and hand, in the ability to "make Nature grimace" (in Fénéon's immortal phrase), in the foregrounding and valorizing the hitherto concealed structural supports of painterly representation, Seurat offered an updated version of his geometrical style that rendered "the old Impressionists . . . more and more out of date.["114] Fénéon put a fine point on the new direction. "M. Seurat," he wrote, "well knows that a line, independently of its topographical role, possesses a measurable abstract value."[115]

It was in the second painting exhibited at the Salon des indépendants in 1888, *Circus Sideshow* (*Parade de cirque*), that Seurat put Henry's scientific aesthetic into practice. We know this from several sketches and notes concerning the execution of the canvas that Seurat left behind.[116] In one of his notebooks, Seurat sketched four high and narrow windows (one more than on the canvas) in the upper right-hand corner of the sheet. Below that Seurat wrote "$1/3$," a harmonious proportion in Henry's table and the one with which Seurat built the painting. Seurat composed the *Parade* around this and other regular mathematical rhythms, where certain groupings of specific distance are repeated several times. Around the sheet Seurat made several direct citations from Henry's "Introduction à une esthétique scientifique." On the right, Seurat wrote the word "rhythm" twice, as well as the formula "rhythm is order in time, or measure" (*le rhythme est l'ordre dans le temps ou la mesure*). Beside these words are four large circles, with polygons inscribed within them, probably indicating harmonious geometric angles of rhythm and measure. In the upper left-hand corner, Seurat drew the three faces devised by Humbert, with ears superadded. Near these he wrote

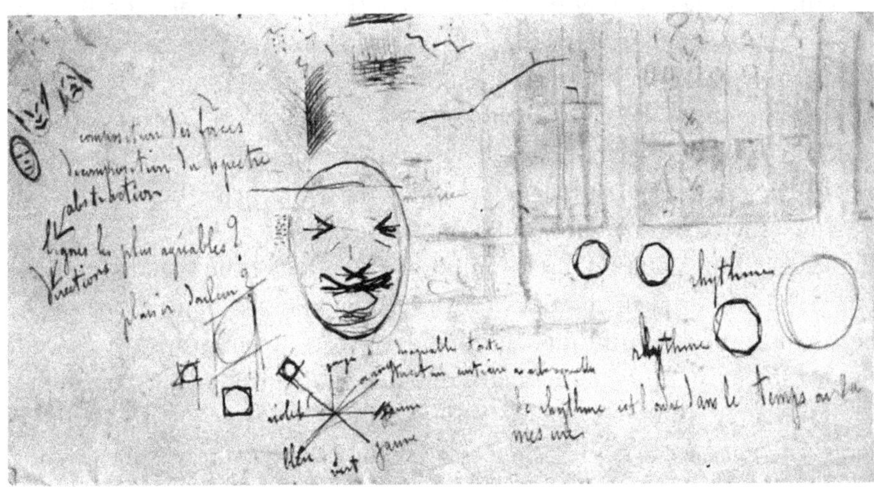

Georges Seurat, notebook sketches, 1887. Private collection.

the phrase "composition des forces" and "décomposition du spectre." In the center of the sheet, the three faces (without ears) are superposed into one, alongside the words "tête de musicien." To the left of this face Seurat noted the phrases "lignes les plus agréables" and drew arrows between the words "abstraction," "direction," and "lignes." He also inscribed the words "plaisir" and "douleur," referring to the dynamogeny/inhibition opposition.

His sketchbook reveals, moreover, that Seurat organized the painting around the golden section, the ancient Pythagorean formula for beauty of form and proportion and the *Urprinzip* behind Henry's aesthetic. In Seurat's sketch, as Robert Herbert points out, the hexagon inscribed in a circle, repeated two times, correctly articulates the famous relation, since the side of each polygon inscribed in a circle is within the proportion of the golden section in relation to the section of the circumference that it engenders. As the classic link between theories of form in art, architecture, and music, Seurat's use of the golden section to underscore and unify the themes of *Parade de cirque* rendered an architectural space of music, a reunification of the arts, following the Wagnerian imperative.

The Wagnerism of the painting emerges more clearly in the unity of artistic form and content. In this painting, like Seurat's other "entertainment" paintings (*Chahut, Le Cirque*), the composition featured a *repoussoir* figure, or *Rückenfigur*, whose back-to orientation worked like a viewer who has stepped into the painting. Such figures, from a long tradition of what Leon Battista Alberti called "figures who point," classically enabled artists to include versions of themselves or of plausible spectators in order to impel the imagination into the scene. Traditional painters often placed them to observe things we cannot see, because they were beyond the frame of the scene.[117] Seurat's placement produces a similar effect, allowing us to hear the concert and thus to experience something like the Wagnerian *Gesamtkunstwerk* within the frame of the painting. By assuming the position of the spectators, all of our senses are awakened, at first in their habitual condition of separation, but then in their reunification through the effect of synesthesia: we begin to hear the music and see the colors and lines in their totality, their unity.

But Seurat accomplishes still more with the *repoussoir* figure. He summons the very scene of perceiving or consuming art—thereby raising the aesthetic problem and evoking the corresponding mixture of imagination and anxiety about how we respond to works of art. Was this not yet another way of stating the problematic of the scientific aesthetic? After all, what end did Henry's scientific synthesis serve but to heighten our romantic hopes and our fearful jitters about what pictures and visual images can and cannot do?

Psychophysics was but an entrainment in what the anarchists called mechanical solidarity, a means to fuse sensory and social physiology. The *Gazette des Beaux-Arts* reacted to Seurat's painting as yet another exercise in naturalism, dismissing it with a complaint about the prevalence of social art: "Today we dedicate as much canvas to the evocation of physiological, social, and moral misery as the Veronese did to the celebration of Venetian festivals. . . . That, one might say, is a sign of the times."[118] Misery perhaps, but there is also a sense in Seurat's canvas in which, like the reunification of once divided senses, the separate social classes all come together in this sort of mass entertainment. The canvas, as Herbert observes, offered a cross-section of Parisian society: "the worker in his cap, three bare-headed *fille du peuple*, bowler-hatted petit bourgeois, and middle-class gentlemen in their top hats accompanying elegant women wearing fashionable bonnets."[119] As if to underline the taxonomic character of these types, Seurat divided his classes, placing them at the left and right of the canvas. As Herbert points out, the social hierarchy ascends in tandem with Henry's linear directions. The movement to the lower left of the *Parade*—the bannister with the cheap seats for the proletarian audience—is painted with the inhibitory or sad tones of blue-violet, blue, and blue-green. The lines moving upward and to the right, where the bourgeois queue for the box office, are rendered with the dynamogenic or happy colors red, orange, and yellow. Seurat would use this technique even more strikingly in his last works, exploiting the occasion of the social encounter of different members of society to create an interplay between active performance and passive voyeurism.

But it was in Seurat's penultimate and last entertainment paintings, *High Kick* (*Chahut*) and *The Circus* (*Le Cirque*), respectively, that his use of Henry's techniques came into its own. The artists in Seurat's circles knew, or had good grounds to suspect, that Seurat's canvasses were composed with Henry's methods. In a thoughtful essay on *Chahut*, the young Belgian Henry van de Velde, who had entered the Neo circles, explained, "The intention, through a sustained direction of lines, is to create a feeling of gaiety. Hence all these lines rising from the right toward the left, shooting forth from one corner of the frame and bursting into fireworks on the other side. For soon the meaning of lines will be revealed to us. Seurat indicates the gay ones, fixed for all time, according to him. Straight ones—austere, because devoid of rhythm. Can one not also see heartbroken ones, letting themselves slip below the ground plane; and insinuating ones."[120] Signac, characteristically, argued rhetorically that "if Seurat's *Chahut* and *Le Cirque* were not composed of dynamogenic lines, hues, and values, they would not be, in spite of their titles, paintings of movement and joy."[121]

Seurat initially embraced this view of his "scientific" techniques. But there is also evidence that he became increasingly sensitive about the status of his authorial voice, irritated by criticism that diminished both his "paternity rights" as the one who introduced scientific techniques to the Neos, and, almost paradoxically, the overemphasis given to technique in discussions of his work. Late nineteenth-century French painters, as Richard Schiff has shown, spoke of their own originality uneasily and with uncertainty.[122] Most settled upon Charles Blanc's notion of "style" in design, which emphasized the "imprint of humanity upon nature," the manner of imaging, or the style of representation.[123] Technique defined style, which in turn designated authorship or individual imprint. But the ideal remained the artist who "speaks a universal artistic language, paints with a style that mediates with immediacy; and this eternal language does not evolve through any mediating process, whether academic training, emulative imitation," or, one might add, scientific instruments.[124] The artistic language, in this account, arose through the artist's personal experience of nature, as well as from his own nature or self, a condition that would make the painter's work inimitable, not capable of being copied by others. For Seurat, then, to be successfully copied by his own circle meant losing his place at the center, to experience a *mise en abyme*, by resembling those who resembled him. The problem lay in the perception of the scientific aesthetic as a rote technique, capable of being appropriated with relative ease by others, and thus not eligible for consideration as an authentically original artistic idiom. It was a sign of overreach. To be taken as a mere style, mannerism, or rote technique would remove any advantage that had originally been gained from the artists' expert system. Imitators rushed in, or worse, technique became a distortion of the very notion of art.

The presence of this anxiety remained evident in Fénéon's frequent need to fend off this charge, often fiercely. To assume that neo-impressionist works could be easily copied, Fénéon argued, would be to "mistake calligraphy for style." Moreover, "A recent Pissarro, a Seurat, a Signac, all look alike, proclaim the critics. Critics have always made, with pride, the most embarrassing confessions. Finally, these painters are accused of subordinating art to science. But they are simply using scientific data to direct and perfect the education of their eye and to control the accuracy of their vision. . . . Mr. X can read treatises on optics for all eternity, but he will never paint *La Grande Jatte*. . . . This kind of painting is only for painters. The studio jugglers will have to go back to card tricks and their cup-and-balls."[125]

In another counteroffensive Fénéon sharply distinguished the Neos from the hordes of common artists who "believed in the reality of things, adored the mannequin of truth, and prided themselves on their photographic realism." "Among the mobs of mechanical copyists of externals," he wrote, "these four or five artists impose the sensation of life itself. For them objective reality is simply a theme for the creation of a higher, sublimated reality, suffused with their own personality."[126] Once again copying—here named in its quintessential form of photography—is decried both for its narrow-band conception of reality and, especially, for its absence of authorial imprint. Fénéon, perhaps deliberately, here recapitulated contemporary debates over the legal status of the photographic image.[127]

Around 1890, the problem of originality began to trouble Seurat to the point of spoiling his personal ties with members of his circle. Relations became especially strained after Fénéon published a biography of Signac featuring a scintillating synopsis of that painter's technique, without a single mention of Seurat, who took a proprietary view of the scientific approach to painting. In a tortured exchange of letters, filled with clarifications and apologies, the wounded Seurat complimented Fénéon on his discussion of (Signac's) technique. But in his next letter to Fénéon, he remarked that he no longer wanted critics to stress technique in discussing his work, adding, "Signac must be suffering as much as me from technical popularization. He was of the opinion two months ago."[128] Despite these misgivings, or perhaps because of them, Seurat not only carried on with his highly technical method of painting but even elevated the question of technique to a primary theme, now with all of the contradictions it raised placed front and center.[129]

It is clear that the lesson many avant-garde artists took from Charles Henry's work was the machinelike character of all art, whether or not it was acknowledged. Paul Valéry's 1889 manifesto, "On Literary Technique," written under the spell of Henry's aesthetic, described literature as "the art of playing on the soul of others. It is with this scientific brutality that the problem of the aesthetics of the Word . . . has been set for our age."[130] Depicting art as the "methodical excitation of nervous and psychical activity," Valéry analogized the work of art to an expressive machine: "The work of art takes on the character of the machine to impress a public; to arouse emotions of the corresponding images."[131] Metaphors of art-as-machine permeated Valéry's writings: the composer as an emotional mechanic, the medium as the machine, and the reader as the raw material shaped by the poet mechanism. Valéry understood this as a revelation of the truth of art itself, rather than a particular mode of modern art. He underscored this message in his "Introduction à la méthode de Léonardo de Vinci" (1894), where the artist/mechanic maximized his effect by rendering his materials effectively:

> What is called in art a realization, is in fact a problem of rendering—one in which the private meaning . . . plays no part, and in which the principal factors are the nature of those materials and the mentality of the public. . . . On the basis of psychology and probable effects . . . every combination of elements made to be perceived and judged depends on a few general laws and on a particular adaptation, defined in advance for a foreseen category of minds to which the whole is specially addressed; and the work of art becomes a machine designed to arouse and assemble the individual formations of those minds.[132]

Valéry similarly imagined a future where pictures would be made in a "picture making laboratory, specialists officially clad in white, rubber-gloved, keeping to a precise schedule, armed with strictly appropriate apparatus and instruments, each with its appointed place and exact function."[133] Something similar pertained to Valéry's own art, literature, as he wrote in later reflections on Leonardo: "To write should mean to construct, as precisely and solidly as possible, a machine of language in which the released energy of the mind is used in overcoming real obstacles."[134] Valéry emphasized that art understood this way functioned not as representation in the traditional sense but as a kind of direct material action on the sensory-motor organization of the beholder. The "scientific brutality" of art derived from its hidden yet violent coercive power.

If Seurat was similarly gripped by this notion of art, he appears to have viewed it more ambivalently. The aporias of creative originality and mechanism may have been the artist's entry into a larger debate in anarchist circles about the meaning of technique and technology, of machines and their place in the labor question. Anarchist opinion on the machinery question was far from uniform. While core theorists like Peter Kropotkin and Élisée Réclus regarded technology as a central figure of evolutionary progress, the rank and file still found resonance in Friedrich Engels's skewering charge that with all political authority annihilated, everyone would be subject to the naked rule of technology.[135] Hence, in articles on machinery in the anarchist press, anarchist opinion makers typically acceded to this received view, only to reverse the argument near the end and restore the primacy of technology in the coming days of harmony.[136] Such unresolved questions hardly proved damning, however; the hallmark of anarchism was its politics of irreconcilables. Readers of the anarchist press were accustomed to this kind of dialectical reasoning on a variety of themes——individualism versus communism, freedom versus order, quietism versus terrorism, lofty aristocracy versus ordinariness and lumpenproletarianism, voluntarism versus determinism—the machinery question took its place within a long list of anarchist aporias.

T. J. Clark has argued compellingly that Seurat's affinity for anarchism (or the affinity of anarchists for Seurat) had much to do with his remarkable ability to maintain, incorporate, and display such contradictions in his art.[137] Nowhere was this more true, I submit, than in his attitude toward technique in *High Kick (Chahut)*. To contemporary viewers *Chahut* signified, apart from its associations with the sexual license of the café concert, a dance of extreme difficulty, performed only by highly skilled dancers. As Richard Thomson reports, a contemporary dictionary defined *chahut* as the "can-can pushed to its ultimate limits, dance taken to the point of hysteria."[138] In Seurat's painting, the dance takes on a machinelike appearance, due in part to the representation of several dancers' legs in alignment. The painting, moreover, appeared as high-speed photograph, a capture of a moment in time, which eliminated the sense of the artist's touch, the expressive character of the hand, giving the work the character of a mechanical reproduction.

Indeed, contemporary reports confirm that when neo-impressionist paintings were exhibited during the late nineteenth century, they often struck viewers as mechanical. As an 1894 review of a neo-impressionist exhibition noted, "Since members of the public have free entrance to the gallery, it is not unusual to overhear someone ask, after several moments of close inspection, 'It's done mechanically?'—only to defer respectfully to the reply, 'No, Monsieur, it's by hand.'"[139] This vignette, somewhat facetious and probably a little embellished, may or may not have referred to Seurat in particular. But it called attention to the ways in which neo-impressionist canvasses produced effects, at least in the some viewers, resembling those of the reigning standard of mechanical reproduction.

Thus the machinery question sprung directly from the paintings. Ever since the early days of photography, promoters and marketers of equipment hailed it as, in Henry Fox Talbot's words, a "method which dispenses with all [the] trouble," arguing that the invention enabled people without manual facility, patience, or special training to achieve its refined uniformity of surface and precision of rendering.[140] This was the positive anarchist view of the machine—accessible, democratic, and above all, positioned to free the individual to pursue the "higher"—intellectual, cognitive, and visionary—aspects of art. Fénéon, in fact, rushed to give this spin to Seurat's technique, deflecting the charge that Seurat's paintings might be achieved by almost anybody: "Skills of the hand become a negligible question because every material difficulty in facture is avoided. It's enough for the maker to have an artistic vision, to be a painter and not a prestidigitator."[141]

In his late paintings Seurat pitted hand and machine, eye and photographic apparatus, against one another—painting "done mechanically by hand," as Schiff has described Seurat's way of using freehand to simulate the look of mechanical reproduction.[142] The hand still remained everywhere in evidence, breaking through, sometimes imitating, sometimes outflanking mechanical reproduction. With the dabs of paint in divided complementary colors following Chevreul's theory, or with the measured angles and directions, Seurat called attention to the gradient from dexterous hand movements to machinelike operations, mechanisms that were indifferent to their surroundings, programmed by predetermined instructions or algorithms. Working this way, the painter functioned to all intents and purposes like a machine; put the other way around, the workings of the machine

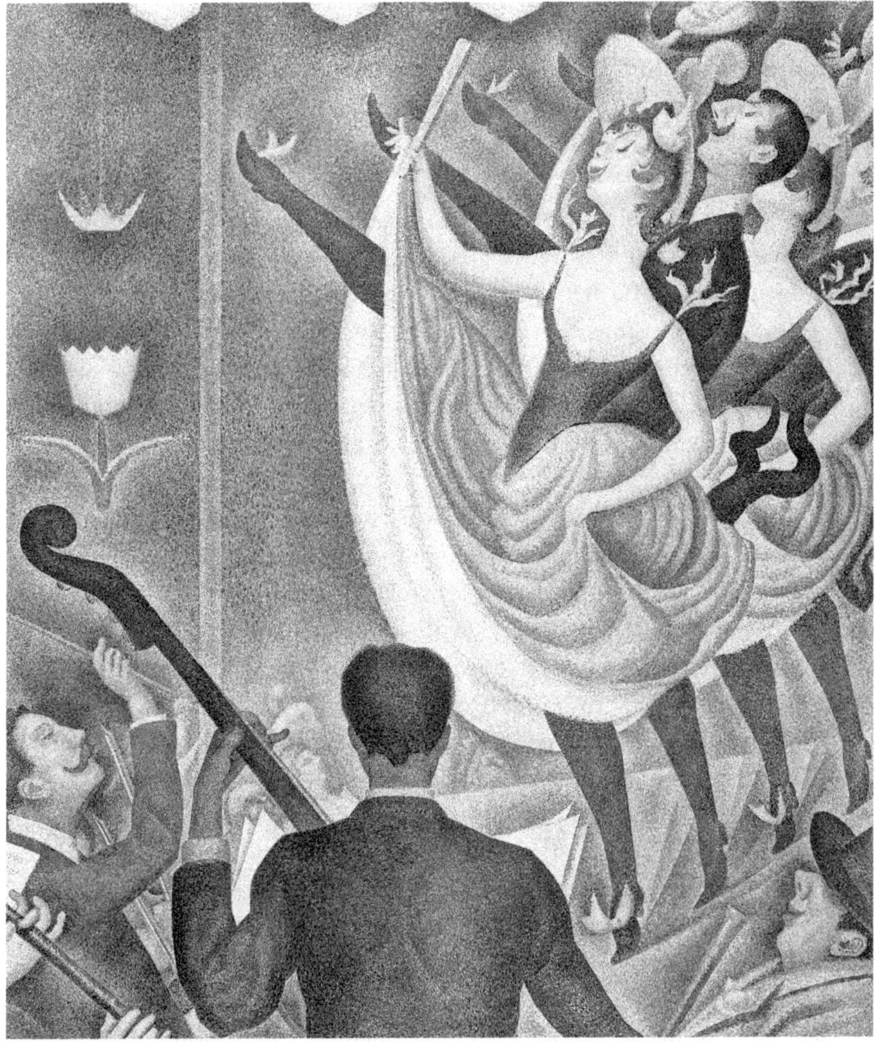

Georges Seurat, *Chahut*, ca. 1889–90. Canvas, 171.5 x 140 cm. Otterlo, Kroeller-Mueller Museum.

(or machinelike algorithms) effectively mimicked those of the living body, of which it served as an improved artificial copy. With these innovations Seurat effectively changed the question from one of demonstrating what *could be done* with the artists' expert system to what *could and could not be done* with it. Seurat recognized that the solution to this question required both a heightening of the "machinery question" and a partial return to those old-fashioned ways of working that the expert system had displaced. The way forward required a synthesis of the new technical system and the old painter's skills.

Part of Seurat's point was surely political, calling attention to the sense in which the fundamental human tendency to be dominated by its technology was amplified and naturalized by the domination of labor by capital. In the *Chahut* the female dancer served as the emblem of this predicament. The cancan dancer was not a machine, of course; her dance, like Seurat's painting, was done mechanically through her bodily skill, highlighting the topical issue of gender and machinery. The question of women's labor had appeared in Seurat's work before, in *Les Poseuses*, for example, which evokes the labor of the recently unionized artist's models.[143] Joan Wallach Scott has shown that the question of the woman worker featured prominently in nineteenth-century French discussions of the social order and the effects of industrialization.[144] Machinery, Scott observes, stood at the heart of the dilemmas surrounding *l'ouvrière*: "when mechanical power could be substituted for human strength, at least one of the marks of difference between men's and women's work could be erased."[145] Among many anarchists, for whom the replacement of muscular strength by machines marked a key characteristic of the coming age, a new equality between the sexes would follow inexorably, along with the other elements of social transformation. One anarchist *ouvrière*, writing in *Le Révolté*, forcefully argued that for too long inferior muscular strength had been used to impose upon woman "a veritable servitude." But now, she informed her male comrades, "I find my faculties just as noble as yours, just as useful for general human evolution." In fact, she pointed out, "one greatly exaggerates the muscular inferiority of woman." Woman had always been, and still was, "the first worker of humanity" and the "first beast of burden," who performed much of the most toilsome work and who, in ordinary life, expended a sum of physical force "not only equal but often superior to that of man."[146] Such claims would not fall happily upon all ears, of course. Many workers felt that machines would simply feminize work, by, in Scott's words, "dissociating production from human physical effort, from the value-creating activity recognized by the wage and associated in political economy with masculinity."[147]

These remarks suggest a richer reading of Henry's "law of physiognomic gesture" built into the scene of *Chahut*. The action of the dancer requires a maximum expenditure of energy, and this is responsible for the great pleasure afforded to the spectator. Seurat's rendering brought out the implicit version of the labor theory of value in Henry's psychophysical "law." But the value produced by the dancer's work here failed to translate into the usual signifier, the wage.[148] Instead, it translated into the pleasure of the spectator, members of the proprietary class, with the implication that the wage fell well short of compensating the work performed.

Seurat thus presented a supremely ambiguous image. We are left wondering whether the dancer is enslaved by the imitation of machines—whether she has become the "machine of the machines" or whether, perhaps like Seurat, she might be said to have bettered the machine at its own work. In this case the machine might be viewed positively as an aid to work, as a standard to be emulated, or simply as a muse. And the status of the machine highlighted the ambiguity around the class relations depicted in the "naturalist" aspect of the painting. We are unclear whether the dancer is a *machine à plaisir* for the prurient, pig-faced bourgeois spectators or whether her machine-like prowess has somehow turned the tables on them, as their lowly position on the canvas might suggest. With Seurat's late work, as T. J. Clark observes, it is hard to know whether the artist sought to deliver anarchist paintings or paintings that would be the "other" to anarchism, its exterminating angel, just as anarchism sometimes was to socialism and socialism always was to the bourgeoisie.[149] One has the sense that all of this troubled Signac, leading him to intervene stridently in the critical fray, in an article entitled "Impressionnistes et révolutionnaires," published in *La Révolte* shortly after the early death of Seurat at the age of thirty-one. Seeking to dispel the ironizing ambiguity of the *Chahut*, Signac vouched for his late friend's anarchist credentials. "The synthetic representations of the pleasures of decadence, dance halls, *chahuts*, circuses as the painter Seurat did them, he who had such a vivid awareness of the depravity of our epoch of transition," Signac wrote, "bear witness to the great social trial that is taking place between workers and Capital."[150] Signac's remarks strained to reign in the paradoxes, to reduce the painting's multiple messages to the reassurances of the party line. Seurat's irony seems to have set off anxiety in his more dogmatic and literal-minded colleague. Perhaps Signac could not see that Seurat had changed the question; or maybe he understood that very well and that was the problem.

All of this would suggest that we view Seurat's painting as what W. J. T. Mitchell calls a "hypericon" or "metapicture"—a picture that is about the act of making and responding to art.[151] In the traditional idiom of painting, such painting typically referred to the hidden and the means whereby it might be revealed, as in the anamorphisms of the Dutch painters. Here the question is posed anew in the language of machines and psychophysiology. Just as machines are our fate in productive labor, so too there can be no notion of vision, no way of conceiving making and responding to art, apart from the new standard brought by modern technologies of vision. Seurat's work stressed that technical media structure the data of our experience, "as if nature were nowhere to be found."[152] From this perspective, the image, paradoxically, became more natural than it had been, under various forms of realism and naturalism, because it cleaved to the primary data of human physiology.

Staying close to physiology meant, somewhat paradoxically, emphasizing the materiality of the painting. Seurat's method of applying paint produced a constant oscillation between what Henry called rhythm and measure, or what we might call analog continuity and discrete discontinuity. Seurat is famous for his use of "divided touch" brushstrokes, sometimes referred to as "pointillist," which create an image out of countless digital fragments. Yet these discrete strokes interact to form larger analog wholes: they congeal into continuous lines flowing throughout the canvas, eventually taking shape as the overall gestalt of the image, but containing within them an infinity of breaks, interruptions, and ruptures. Signac emphasized the problems of internal scale and external viewing distance in the neo-impressionist technique, and Seurat exemplifies this very well. The oscillations between analog and digital vary constantly with changes in position, giving the image a sense of being unfinished or still being formed.

The poet Gustave Kahn reported conversations with Seurat that seemed to confirm his sense that the painter's method "offered precise points of similarity with our theories of verse and the phrase." More specifically, Kahn pointed to the "kinship" of his "theory of discontinuity" with Seurat's optical mixing.[153] Kahn's theory of discontinuity, as we will see in chapter 5, referred specifically to an aesthetics of oscillation between analog flows and punctuated stops or interruptions, as in his compositional method of his

Chansons d'amant (1891). "Having been inspired by the beauties of the ara-besque," he explained, "I've tried to translate the idea in conformity with my system, not by narrating and deducing in turn, but by translating in turn, as independent parts, all of the facets of all the moments of the sensation."[154] Kahn described the dynamic curved line as series of moments of sensation—time-ordered perceptual shards interacting to produce a redirection of atten-tion, a complex montage of stillness and motion. Kahn was clearly rendering in his own medium of poetry Henry's dictum that "rhythm is order in time, or measure"—the very idea Seurat inscribed in his sketchbook. Prosody is a more explicitly temporal art than painting, of course; and Kahn's account of the interplay between continuous flow and discrete cuts brings time to the fore in a way that tends to elude talk about painting. Yet it points us to the sense in which, as Schiff observes, Seurat's "touch-by-touch system—like a digitally ticking analogue clock—seemed to keep every variety of temporal-ity alive within it."[155] One is reminded here of the lesson that Proust may have taken from Henry's olfactometer. The task of translating all moments of sensations exposes gaps, shards of "lost time," displacements that might be researched and explored. The painter, like the novelist, sought to produce a work of art that contained all the temporalities within it.

Containing temporalities between multiple parts and interfaces was pre-cisely one of the features I have attributed to the physiologist's experimental systems. What was psychophysical aesthetics—or Seurat's method—if not a temporal chaining of heterogeneous elements? Part of the remarkable effect of Seurat's paintings is to entrain the spectator to a complex and open-ended system of material energies and semiotic events. Seurat's quest to "find some-thing new" in his painting led him to a method that materialized questions related to every dimension of the painting: material, conceptual, perceptual, social, and political. Unlike Signac, who turned both artistic technique and anarchist ideology into static doctrines, Seurat rendered them as dynamic operations that would produce an unexpected result or an indeterminate future. The most general aesthetic effect of this method was a new kind of fluidity or plasticity. In the next chapter we will consider further the paral-lels with kindred movements in poetry and music—Kahn's method of versi-fication out of discrete "organic cells" of rhythm and measure and Debussy's use of the melodic-rhythmic cell—that generated a similar mode of fluidity in their media, using analogous techniques.

5

LIBERATING VERSE

Rhythm and Measure in Poetry

> I do indeed bring news. The most surprising news. Such a case has never
> been seen. Verse has been dealt a blow. Governments change: prosody
> always remains intact: whether because during revolutions no one notices
> it or because the coup does not impose itself with the opinion that such a
> dogma can change.
>
> Stéphane Mallarmé, "La Musique et les lettres" (1894)

STéPHANE MALLARMÉ'S TIDING TO HIS BRITISH AUDIENCE IN 1894 told of events already well-known in France: a revolution had finally arrived in verse, against all expectations and, as the remarks allude, with inspiration from revolutionary anarchist doctrines.[1] While anarchist prophets like Peter Kropotkin and Jean Grave preached the dismantling of threadbare political and social institutions, like the senate and the stock exchange, and less patient anarchist foot soldiers dynamited public opera houses and cafés, several comrade-poets made their contribution by delivering a bomb to the frayed institution in their charge: the rules of prosody. This meant, more precisely, demolishing the classic form of French poetry—the alexandrine—in favor of a freer and more harmonic verse form. French prosody, since its painstaking codification by François de Malherbe in the early seventeenth century, had indeed shown greater staying power than most French institutions. The alexandrine—a twelve-syllable line divided into two halves (the hemistichs) by a pause (the caesura)—had changed little from the classical period until the Romantics. Even the poets of *vers libéré*, such as Baudelaire, Verlaine, and Rimbaud, left the core of alexandrine syllabism intact while loosening the form with rhyme and end-of-line accentuation.[2] Like political revolutions before it, the revolution in verse began in France, under specifically French conditions, but it soon traversed national and linguistic borders, bringing its liberating spirit to English, German, and Slavic languages, and others besides, making modernist poetry a genuinely international enterprise.[3]

The revolution in verse came through the events described in a statement by Paul Valéry. He referred to the efforts of Mallarmé's younger colleagues, especially Gustave Kahn and Jules Laforgue, whose innovations made established luminaries like Mallarmé into followers as much as leaders. Kahn and Laforgue frequented the same circles as the neo-impressionist painters: *vers libre* and *impressionnisme scientifique* were artistic siblings, the Castor and Pollux of vanguard painting and poetry. Like the neo-impressionist painters, Kahn and Laforgue developed their conception of vers libre with the help of the so-called scientific aesthetics of Charles Henry.[4] Vers libre, Kahn announced in "Réponse des symbolistes," derives from "an adherence in literature to the scientific theories constructed by induction and controlled by the experimentation of M. Charles Henry" and "analogous reflections [that] have created the multitonal tone of Wagner and the latest techniques of the [neo-]impressionists."[5] Kahn's famous definition of symbolism as a quest to "objectify the subjective" referred directly to Henry's notion of the artist as a nervous system that senses the rhythm, realizes it virtually as an idea, and produces it externally.[6] Kahn's theory of vers libre aimed to render this a practicable idea for versification.

Poets were not painters, of course; their art was made of different materials, their craft drew from its own traditions. Yet, as this chapter will show, Kahn and Henry found the critical resources for translating the scientific aesthetic into verse in the fledgling field of experimental phonetics, a budding disciplinary offshoot of experimental physiology and linguistics. Building upon the literature on the physiology of speech, they sought to build poetry on vocal gestures in much the same way that the neo-impressionist brushstrokes were visibly gestural. The utopian ambitions of the vers libre aesthetic also paralleled those of the painters: alterations in the physiological effects of verse would transform poets and auditors alike, and even the life-world they inhabited.

VERS LIBRE AND THE SYMBOLIST MOMENT

Vers libre was launched in 1886, the *annus mirabilis* of the fin-de-siècle French avant-garde.[7] It was the year of several symbolist literary manifestos and even more reviews devoted to symbolist, neo-impressionist, and other avant-garde movements.[8] The 1886 literary manifestos—Kahn's "Réponse des symbolistes," Jean Moréas's, "Le Symbolisme," and René Ghil's *Traité du verbe*—superficially bore much in common, and were easily lumped together, but before long their fundamental differences emerged.[9] Under the big tent of "symbolism" they shared a common intention to make music their artistic model and inspiration, seeking, in Paul Valéry's description, "to draw from language almost the same effects as purely sonorous causes produced in nervous beings."[10] But the various symbolist camps took divergent approaches to this objective. Moréas's treatise, which garnered the most public attention and made him the public figurehead of the symbolist movement, called for a new rhythmic fluidity, for example, but his precepts did not go beyond received *vers libéré*.[11] Ghil proposed *la méthode évolutive-instrumentiste*, appealing to psychophysiology for a science of phonetic associations that would establish stable correspondences between vowel sounds and colors, and between vowel sounds and instruments of the orchestra.

In 1886 the *verslibristes* initiative began with the launching of key journals, like *La Vogue* and *Revue indépendante*, to promote their art. Founded by Léo d'Orfer, Gustave Kahn, and Félix Fénéon, *La Vogue* opened with an editorial statement that "the social revolution will come; all the coalitions [against it] will only serve to bring it about."[12] *La Vogue*'s table of contents over its first year of publication gives some idea of how poetry was thought to contribute to the revolution: it featured new vers libre poems by Kahn, Laforgue, Moréas, Francis Vielé-Griffin, and even Charles Henry; unpublished poems by Rimbaud and other precursors of vers libre, including translations of Walt Whitman by Laforgue; and critical theoretical works by Henry and Kahn that positioned the new art of verse in the ideological, scientific, and aesthetic field.

Vers libre eludes easy definition.[13] It designates a form of poetry liberated from the laws of rhyme, meter, and especially, syllabism (the division of the sounds of language by syllables, rather than by the alphabet or by signs), essentially relying instead on rhythmic units. By establishing a distinction between meter and rhythm as the difference between that which is measured and the factor which measures, two kinds of verse arrangements are found possible, rhythmic and metrical. The technical innovation that opened a radical new approach to poetry, a kind of "free verse," as the term was translated into English, is the key concern of this chapter.[14] But the technical distinction between rhythmic *vers libre* and traditional metrical poetry also opened an oppositional space within the institution of poetry, a counterworld for artist-revolutionaries who sought new spaces of freedom in the secessionist art salons and, especially, in the unregulated demimonde of café concerts and cabarets.[15]

The *verslibriste* poets viewed the poet's vocation in *anarchisante* terms, as an artisanal craft—they too were "workers of the line"—and they sought to join their innovations to the popular chansons performed in the Parisian venues frequented by the artisan classes. Much more than painting (and like music and dance), poetry was both a high and a low art. It was also a performing art, at least some of the time. Hence, the vers libre aesthetic, which later became associated with difficult, formalistic modernism, was born in a quest to connect with the fluid, *insouciant ésprit fumiste* of the cabarets. Either way, its relation to performing arts accompanied the extension of physiological aesthetics beyond the lecture halls and literary salons, deeper into vernacular culture.

LANGUAGE IN LINES

Letters between Kahn and the poet Jules Laforgue suggest that Charles Henry's aesthetic ideas were developed in close dialogue with Kahn and that poetry had been central to the scientific aesthetic from the beginning.[16] Laforgue had been introduced to Kahn by Henry, and letters between the poets typically contained affectionate and jocose references to their common friend "the scientist," "the phalansteric," "the utopian," et cetera. But Laforgue departed from this tone in a letter, intervening with uncharacteristic sternness over Kahn's allegation that Henry had stolen his ideas on the aesthetics of poetry. Laforgue's scolding seems to have worked, as Kahn dropped the matter. In later years, his own reputation intact, Kahn repeatedly referred to the critical role of Henry's ideas in the development of vers libre and proudly reported that he had helped Henry design the aesthetic protractor.

Kahn's ideas clearly had their roots in Henry's scientific aesthetic, but they were developed with an intimate grasp of the poet's craft.[17] Kahn began with the recognition that prosody was, after all, nothing other than the poet's method of controlling the reader's temporal experience of the poem. Rhythm in poetry had traditionally been something that occurred as an effect of the temporality of prosodic organization. Kahn's innovation consisted in his attempt to think of poetic rhythm largely outside the rules of prosody, as the temporal distribution of elements of language, especially spoken language, such as timbre (in recurrences such as alliteration, assonance, and rhyme), duration, pitch or intonation, and intensity or volume.[18]

Physiologists in the 1870s, as we will see below, had begun to use inscription devices to visualize the temporal array of these elements of speech in graphic form. Charles Henry's insight was that these inscriptions would enable the poet to reimagine prosodic effects as "shapes of energy," just as the painter would view visual form.[19] "The remarkable graphic method of tracing vowels and consonants," Henry claimed, would enable poets to apply the theory of rhythm to these perfectible graphics" and to "gauge scientifically the natural rhythm of language and . . . measure precisely the agents of phonetic transformation."[20]

It was, however, comparatively easy to reconfigure painting and design in the language of physiological curves, since visual arts contained linear elements that comprised an essential part of the artist's training, skill, and everyday work. To apply the theory to verse, it would similarly have to be regarded as language in lines—an assumption akin to Jeremy Bentham's practical definition that when the lines run all the way to the right margin, it is prose; when they fail to do, that it is verse.[21] Lineation made it possible to render verse in the periodicities of graphically recorded curves. Thus, Henry argued, the scientific aesthetic would serve poetry by undertaking a classification of rhythms, or what Henry called "the science of possible metaphors," where metaphor was defined as "the relation that links two more or less similar changes of direction: the more subtle and profound the changes, the more complex the formula, and the more beautiful the metaphor."[22]

Kahn rendered Henry's somewhat bizarre notion as a powerful idea. Graphical recordings of spoken verse could replace traditional scansion, the method of dividing verse into its metrical feet. Instead of scanning syllables, poets might record and examine the rhythms and caesuras that appeared "naturally" in the graphical recordings of the verse. The basic operations of the scientific aesthetic might be further applied to poetry, in a manner similar to painting, providing a radical new foundation for the craft of versification.

This idea was not entirely new. The fledgling science of experimental phonetics, which centered on graphically recording the vowels and consonants of ordinary phonation, had recently begun to take on the analysis of verse. Henry and Kahn had encountered the graphic recording of human phonation in the Collège de France lectures of Étienne-Jules Marey, as well as those of Michel Bréal and Gaston Paris. It was probably these lectures that alerted Henry and Kahn to the pioneering work of Ernst Brücke on the physiology of high German verse, as well as that of Paul Passy, a student of both Paris and Brücke, on French prose.[23] Brücke's experiments in the physiology of verse followed close on the heels of his colleague Hermann Helmholtz's experimental investigations into the physiology of music in his monumental *On the Sensations of Tone as a Physiological Basis for the Theory of Music* (1863).[24] But where Helmholtz had shown that the European musical tradition had effectively advanced by exploring its own physiological conditions (by corroborating the physiology of hearing in its distinctions between major and minor, consonance and dissonance, etc.), Brücke noted how odd it was that the rules of German prosody and meter were so skillfully taught and employed even though their underlying principles remained highly contested.[25] Some of this had to do with the clarity and elegance of ancient Greek and Latin models from which German prosody was derived, even when the classical models failed to correspond to the "verse that the living mouth speaks and the living ear hears."[26] Brücke declared that these classical prosodic models were of as little interest to him as Galenic anatomy: the laboratory, not texts, would be his guide to verse.[27] Brücke used a kymograph to record the mathematical time relations of anapests, spondees, caesuras, and accents, demonstrating that the natural laws of meter for the German tongue make certain verse forms borrowed from the classics logically unusable, and others, hitherto unknown, possible. Moreover, Brücke argued, the experiments showed that there were natural subrhythms emanating from the muscles of the chest, larynx, and other organs that offered rich possible effects in the art of verse declamation.

Brücke's work diagnosed the problem of prosody, but for Kahn and Henry his studies pointed the way to a revolution in verse. Brücke's contention that classical verse models were unsuited to the character of spoken German could extend to the "artificial" French alexandrine as well. Even though French was a Latin-derived language, alexandrine-based versification remained, in the words of the linguist Gaston Paris, "petrified" in the pronunciation of the sixteenth century.[28] French poets remained timorously stifled by this gap between the living tongue and the official poetic language, which constrained them arbitrarily like an antiquated legislature. Vers libre would follow the linguists' turn to living language for its material, finding its voice in oral and primitive poetry, disregarding the arbitrary laws imposed on classic verse, rejecting Greco-Latin vowel-consonant syllabism for Indo-Sanskrit distinctions of sonority and muteness. Where traditional scansion relied on the different lengths of vowels and the armature of consonants in the as-read verse form, Kahn suggested that verse be conceived primarily as spoken, "in accord with phonetics or with current French pronunciation in Paris," that is, with the graphical features of recorded speech—rhythm, measure, duration—taking the place of scansion in the measurement of prose.[29]

A BLOW OF THE PICK TO THE ALEXANDRINE

Kahn framed his theoretical argument for vers libre within a historical and evolutionary consideration of early poetic schools that sought liberation from the alexandrine. They missed the point, he argued, by clutching at a few innovations—like the caesura, enjambment, and the French mute *e* (*e muet*)—instead of developing a definite idea of the nature of verse. Verse is an organism, Kahn contended, and as such it has an organic unit, *la cellule métrique*. It is an error to think, he argued, that the alexandrine is just a verse composed of twelve syllables, with a pause at number six and a rhyme at number twelve. The anatomy of verse is different, so much so that the great poets did not make the caesura the pivot of their prosody. These poets felt, more or less instinctively, the organic composition of the verse and applied empirically the principles adequate to its true nature. In Racine, La Fontaine, and Molière, the caesura became a stressed syllable without a pause, and sometimes a syllable of secondary importance.

To illustrate this Kahn analyzed the opening couplet of Racine's "Athalie."[30] According to the traditional metric, these lines are each scanned as two hemistichs of six syllables each:

Oui, je viens / dans son temple / adorer / l'Éternel,
Je viens, / selon l'usage / antique / et solonnel

Kahn argued that this demonstrates that these lines were formed with four blank verses, thus:

Oui, je viens dans son temple
adorer l'Éternel
je viens selon l'usage
antique et solonnel

"If one pushes this investigation further," Kahn wrote, "one discovers that these verses are scanned thus":

Oui, je viens—dans son temple—adorer—l'Éternel
Je viens—selon l'usage—antique—et solonnel.

Kahn described this as a "first verse composed of four ternary organic cells and a second verse composed of two binary organic cells alternating with two quaternary organic cells."[31]

Kahn argued that this proved that the caesura was a creation of the prosodic legislator (Nicholas Boileau)—"pure arbitrariness, . . . the will of a spoiled critic," Kahn wrote—and had no part in the poet's composition of the verse.[32] Racine composed with a great artist's instinct for the "cellule organique" of verse—or perhaps by lucky accident. Either way, the reliance of traditional scansion on the different lengths of vowels and the armature of consonants in as-read form thus appears as an arbitrary imposition upon the real working methods of the classic poets. They intuitively understood composition as a number of vowels and consonants that possess a unity for the ear and a unity of sense, or in Kahn's borrowing Henry's language of graphical representation, "the smallest possible fragment, tracing an arrest of voice and an arrest of sense."[33] In other words, this is a rhythmic impulse, "housed in the individual measure, the 'cellule organique' et 'indépendante' whose terminal boundary is marked by the coincidence of a juncture in meaning with a rhythmic juncture."[34]

Kahn dismantled the tyranny of syllables (and their principle of number) and of rhyme. Without the artificial mechanisms of rhyme and the fixed metrical perspective of line, phonic elements might freely associate on the basis of new principles derived from acoustic kinship or affinity. Assonance and alliteration were among the qualities that would invite associations in verses such as "Des mirages / de leur visage / garde / le lac / de mes yeux."[35] Here Kahn's emphasis on verse music found its voice in an analogy to the Wagnerian injunction against pre-fabricated music and for allowing music to build organically out of its simple element, such as a chord or arpeggio, combining "not as masses knitted together, but allying naturally like parent atoms."[36] Kahn used a similar parental metaphor. "To assemble these unities and to give a sense of cohesion to the verse they form," he wrote, "they must be married in. These items are called alliterations, either a union of parented consonants or assonances by similar vowels."[37] Acousticity should determine rhythmicity. Sound patterns had always been important in verse, of course; but they had rarely been determinants of rhythm.

Once the rhythmic autonomy of the measure was restored, it became necessary to consider the relation between the measure and the stanza (*strophe*), and the grouping of verses more generally. The stanza cannot remain a closed grid, Kahn insisted; no one form can express the all the diverse sentiments, emotions, and thoughts. The stanza thus requires a liberty equal to that of the verse, elastic and flexible. In fact, there should be no need to codify verse in stanzas at all—the verse should take the form of the accent and its intensities, the duration of the sentiment evoked, or the sensation rendered. Following such a conception, Kahn observed elsewhere, one finds "in the graphic representation of a stanza the schema of a sensation. . . . The tendency is towards a poem in prose that is very mobile and patterned rhythmically according to the velocities, the oscillations, the contortions and the simplicities of the Idea."[38]

We have no extant graphic recordings of verses made by Kahn or Henry. It is therefore impossible to point to experimental evidence for the composition of poems (unlike the followers of Kahn discussed below, or painters like Seurat and Signac, for whom such evidence does exist).[39] But there can be little doubt that graphical recording served as a heuristic model for recovering the primary oral and aural nature of verse from the written and eye-read text. To define the ways in which voice inhabits and impels text and produces emotion, idea, and sensation Kahn later introduced the concept of *accent d'impulsion*, the enunciatory drive of the poet to inscribe the voice in the poem, "to write his own individual rhythm in place of donning a uniform tailored in advance."[40] The function of lineation in free verse poems is to trace out, or make visible, the momentum, intonation, and tone propelled by the *accent d'impulsion*—in direct analogy to the peaks and valleys of speech curves.

In Kahn's view, the newfound awareness of accentuation, an outgrowth of the discovery of the primacy of the colors of phonation, necessitated free verse, a kind of poetic prose, "rhythmed and numbered with a sort of music."[41] Kahn's mobile poetic prose, in works like his *Les Palais nomades* (1887), led the reader through proto-cinematographic sequences of images, calibrated modules of arrests of rhythm, and sense-conjured fluctuations of reminiscences with varied intensities and durations, driven forth by the poet's inner psychological rhythm.

Kahn's formulation of vers libre suggested a new way to define rhythm outside of the moorings of traditional prosody. Rhythm in vers libre, as Camille Mauclair would describe it, was "entirely physiological: the beat of the arterial blood, the amplitude or the constriction of respiration, according to the emotion, are the natural impulsions."[42] Unlike vague symbolist analogies to music, physiological rhythms rooted the invention and audition of verse in a solid yet open-ended field of possibilities. Executed properly, Mauclair quipped, vers libre was to the alexandrine "what a Schumann *Lied* was to a polka."[43] Physiology, as a science of law-like regularities in the animal body, might have been taken to offer a kind of uniformity to poetry. This was true, up to a point. But the verslibristes, following trends in French physiology, viewed human physiology as a limitless array of personal equations—individual differences—that defined personality, temperament, and quality of thought.[44] Kahn wrote of his attempt to "find in myself a personal rhythm sufficient to render my lyricisms in the pace and the accent that I think they require."[45] Similarly, "there are as many kinds of vers libre as there are poets," Mauclair noted, "and the music of each is unique."[46] Physiology was the generator of rhythm, but in order for verse to be truly free it had to be autonomous: it had to unfold out of the properties of the rhythm itself. "It is the poem that makes itself according to its intimate logic," wrote Mauclair, "and not the poet who sits down with the intention of making a poem and filing down syllables like fingernails. . . . It arrives in what the physiologists call the curve of cardiac rhythm, generator of the transcribed rhythm, which is the state in which the regular or symmetric verse presents itself, before or after, the polymorphic state."[47] In this view, rhythm might be thought to come before the words in the poet's sensorium. But, in this account, rhythm might also be said to stand above the words, too, and persist after them. If verse would gain a newfound autonomy through rhythm, it might have to come at the expense of language itself.

The body would thus be the site of rhythmic innovation. While verslibriste poets would later make use of institutionalized laboratories of experimental phonetics to explore this question, early verslibristes would rely on self-experiment, "demanding no more than their instinct for rhythm and the sensitivity of their ear, the cadences and the musical substance of their verses."[48] Whether deliberately or not, through their efforts modernist poetry began as something of a return to the auto-investigations of the Vedic *rishis* in the psychophysiological powers and possibilities of incantation: the vibratory effects of the different organs of phonation, the lengths and intensities of tones, the rhythms and caesuras of the breath, the accelerations and decelerations of pulse rates. Poetry became another vehicle for the experimentalization of life.

"A MORE COMPLEX MUSIC"

Critics have sometimes taken Kahn's doctrine as a purely negative one, a blow of the pick to the alexandrine that opened a space for a generation or more of fervent experimentation with rhythmic expression. But Kahn, like Henry and most symbolist contemporaries, viewed the innovations in verse as a historical necessity, an evolutionary step in the development of poetry. The positive vision of vers libre linked the newfound possibility of rhythmic expression with music. Kahn's insistence that he sought "in an emancipation of verse . . . a more complex music" was accompanied by an assertion of a historical turn away from painting to music as the primary source of poetic analogy.[49]

But for Kahn and other symbolist poets, the analogies between poetry and music that suffused symbolist verse contained an implicit third term—physiology, especially the function of vocalization—materially registered by an expanding array of experimental media. Physiology mediated the poetry/music analogies in several ways. It was central to evolutionary arguments explaining the origins and historical development of both poetry and music; it explained the aesthetic commonalities and differences between the two arts, and therefore the possibilities and resources they offered; it therefore explained the route to innovation, suggesting the ways to transform the auto-experimentation of the ancient *rishis* into new modes of the experimentalization of life.

Within the broader genus of fin-de-siècle evolutionary aesthetics, literary Darwinism proved a particularly hardy species, partly because it developed on the back of the thriving field of the evolution of language itself. Charles Henry, in an interview for Jules Huret's *Enquête sur l'évolution littéraire*, argued that the new poetry grew from the evolutionary history of language, specifically the tension between the "natural sounds" of vowels and the qualities of voice necessary for the formation of distinct words (i.e., consonants).[50] Henry's explanation veered back to his better developed theory of "the evolution of musical sensation," advanced in 1886, while Kahn publicly defended his verslibriste brand of symbolism against public assaults.[51] In his 1886 article, Henry's exposition began with considerations of using precision psychophysical methods to understand Greek sound, much like those he later used in assessing ancient Hellenic visual form. Sound, he averred, could be precisely defined in terms of direction, as the intensities of sounds stand in relation to the amplitude of vibrations, and the height or acuity stands in relation to the number of those vibrations in a unit of time. While the Greeks regarded their modes (Ionian, Dorian, Phrygian, etc.) as objective phenomena, Charles Féré's recent dynamometric studies in *Sensation et mouvement* (1887) had shown their perception to be "subjective, entirely physiological."[52] Henry adumbrated a series of changes in musical forms from the Greeks to the Christian era, arguing that each change involved adaptive measures on the part of members of each historical society. The psychophysiological significance of this was enormous, he claimed, and also directly related to politics, as Plato indicated with his famous notion that one cannot tamper with the rules of music without shaking the fundamental laws of government.

Rather than deifying Greek art, Henry suggested that we moderns should look to our own social life to define our art, since "each must determine his own personal equation."[53]

This was, in Henry's elliptical way, an intervention in the raging symbolist debates. Henry's argument sought to join his evolutionary psychophysiological aesthetics with key Wagnerian aesthetic doctrines of the symbolist avant-garde. While Wagner's music and aesthetics drew favor from political and aesthetic conservatives in some parts of Europe, in France it found ardent adherents in the avant-garde, promoted especially by the key symbolist journals *La Vogue, Revue indépendante,* and *La Revue wagnérienne.*[54] Henry's law of the evolution of musical sensation echoed the fundamental premises of Wagner's treatise *Art and Revolution,* which postulated an aesthetic evolution from outer to inner formal necessity. Wagner's account similarly began with the ancient Greeks, who through their art mirrored the beauty and strength of their public life, communed with themselves, and feasted their eyes on their own noblest essence. According to Wagner, after the decline of Greek, unified public art, however, the arts—poetry, music, painting, and so on—fell into a condition of separation, mutual isolation, and ultimately, decline, through a false division of labor in society. By the time of the advanced bourgeois world of the nineteenth century, the separation of the arts meant that every organ of sense had come to apprehend a different world. A new revolutionary art—the aesthetic column of the political revolutions of 1789 and 1848—would have to hold up the mirror anew, not to the public life of the state, but to "inner natural necessity," not in "subordination to an outer imagined force," any authority that would keep the arts, and ipso facto, the senses, apart.[55] This would mean, among other things, the reunification of the arts in the *Gesamtkunstwerk,* the total work of art, in which the synthesis of the arts would recover the unity of physical and mental labor, including the unity and harmony of the senses.

French vanguard theorists sought to join this Wagnerian trope with the similar political narrative of Peter Kropotkin and the evolutionary aesthetics of Herbert Spencer, Ernst Haeckel, and Charles Henry. As Émile Hennequin noted in an essay comparing Wagnerian aesthetics and the doctrines of Spencer, the task was made easy by the common evolutionary and physiological assumptions, especially the parallels between the industrial division of labor and the physiological division of labor, which separated the bodily senses and the artistic media, the evolution of an "outer" psychophysiology with an "inner" psychophysiology based on artistic intuition.[56] Wagner and Spencer agreed, moreover, on the primacy of the voice as the first instrument and the basis of all music. Wagner insisted on the poetic voice as the foundation of the total work of art, arguing that composers erred when they looked to dance to replace the primordial dramatic rhythms of the voice. The primacy of the voice followed Wagner's claim that the first human expression was a succession of vowels, a melodic language of emotion, accompanied by gesture, through which it took its rhythm. Vowels, moreover, were essentially the same as one another and gained emotional inflection through the "enclosing consonants," which acted as the "garment of the vowel," defining its limits and giving it a particular color.[57] Spencer similarly described music as "an idealized language of emotion" that arose from the physiological division of labor in the organism. "All feelings, then—painful or pleasurable, sensations or emotions—have this common characteristic, that they are muscular stimuli," Spencer wrote. Music arose specifically from the muscular principle behind all vocal phenomena, namely, that "the muscles that move the chest, larynx, and vocal chords, contracting in proportion to the intensity of the feelings—every different contraction of these muscles involving, as it does, a different adjustment of the vocal organs . . . it follows that variations of the voice are the physiological results of variations of feeling," expressed through "loudness, timbre, pitch, intervals, and rate of variation."[58]

This broad synthesis, variably expressed, underwrote the theoretical doctrines of *verslibriste* symbolism. An influential article by the philosopher Jules de Gaultier, "Essai de physiologie poétique," published in the key avant-garde journal *La Revue blanche*, alongside contributions from Kahn and Henry, set down the mature and most influential version of the doctrine.[59] The recent attempts to renovate poetry by drawing closer to music, Gaultier observed, turned at the same time "toward the mysterious sources of life, toward the original soul of animality."[60] This meant a turn to the origin of language: before the written sign there was the phonetic sign, which was a modulated cry, and before that, a simple cry. "The cry directly expressed the physiological emotion felt by our ancestor under the shock of a sensation or a perception," Gaultier wrote, "and for a long time one cry was distinguished from another only by its degree of intensity in relation to the felt sensation." But over time the "diversity of muscle contractions" gave rise to modulations and, finally, to articulate speech. Articulate speech amounted to a system that codified physiological states and rendered them transmissible between organisms of similar nature. "In this way the most remote ancestor of the word would have been the nervous vibration," which was exteriorized and prolonged and sonorous matter, and ultimately, the word. "This was therefore also the origin of rhythm, the series of sonorous vibrations repercussing the series of nervous vibrations, which themselves constituted the physiological emotion."[61] A slow division of physiological labor followed, in which the great word disaggregated into an ensemble of words connected to one another, linked by sensation, the phrase governed by a rigorous rhythm, the law of number cutting and proportioning the emission of sonorities according to the spurting of blood in the arteries, the play of the lungs, the movements of the diaphragm. Human language, in this epoch, "was a sort of poetry, a rhythmic and living thing, incorporated in the physiological being itself, expressing in an association of sounds a sense and a sensation, fulfilling the demands of nature for the total transmission of the state of the soul, satisfying that passion to attain its maximum expansion that is the law of every force, the need to exteriorize, to communicate itself integrally in order to be integrally understood."[62]

But there was more. Gaultier arrived at an explanation of the divergences between poetry and music that gave an evolutionary underpinning to the judgments of Helmholtz and Brücke on the foundations of the respective media. Poetry and music began similarly in rhythmic vibrations, yet the latter advanced steadily in its forms and concepts, while the former held tight to archaic forms and changed relatively little. Music emancipated itself, Gaultier argued, because it focused solely on the exteriorized sonorous vibrations, detached from the organism, becoming a virtual medium that allowed relentless experimentation and, over time, a diversity of formal structures from which composers chose freely. Poetry, by contrast, followed the evolution of language, which tended in a different direction: toward propositional and analytical language, the contemplation of ideas, thereby "weakening its power to vibrate in unison with others."[63] Poetry itself failed to evolve much and therefore underwent only a regression. Poetry's prosodic rules petrified the primitive physiological conditions and could therefore only express similarly primal thoughts and emotions. "Meter," Gaultier contended, "imposes the repetition of certain sonorities, fixes the voice in certain temporal stops, augments or diminishes its volume, governs the movements of the lungs, and by modifying the flux of blood in the arteries, attenuates or precipitates the heartbeat, creates in the reciter a physiological state, the reproduction of which spontaneously gives birth to the soul of the poet."[64]

Because poetry applied to the organism itself, it could only evolve when human physiology itself was transformed. "Poetry awaits the evolution of the nervous process, attends the transformation of the cerebral lobes into ideas, in notions and verbal signs, and it is that transformed substance, . . . that rhythmic power in order to beautify the obstruction of the word by the recovered contour, by the continual bursting forth [*jaillissement*] of the primitive vibration."[65] The needed spiritual matter could be found in the supple, diverse forms that music had evolved: poetry needed to reconnect with its long-lost artistic sibling. The answer then, consisted in overturning received poetic forms and inventing new forms of free verse, "with its freedom of pacing, its flexibility, its sinuous curves," which "adapts itself marvelously to the sonorous reproduction of these indefinite nervous processes."[66]

Gaultier's essay deepened and extended the philosophical contentions of verslibrisme. The charge of petrified poetic form was now placed within a deep evolutionary narrative that also legitimated the formal innovations of vers libre as a species of physiological aesthetic experimentation.

RHYTHMIC-MELODIC UNITS

The implementation of musical analogy required tools for conceptualizing verse as pure rhythm. According to the theorist and poet Robert de Souza, the verslibristes found inspiration in two key works, Louis Becq de Fouquières's *Traité général de versification française* (1879) and Paul Pierson's *Métrique naturelle du langage* (1884).[67] Unlike Helmholtz, who used musical notation to identify the pitches of the speaking voice, Becq de Fouquières in his well-known handbook used musical notation to render the rhythms of spoken verse. "To compose a verse," he wrote, "is to construct a musical phrase."[68] The proof of this showed in his instructions to musicians for setting a poem to music. While the key or the pitch allows some degrees of freedom, the rhythm of the poem remains unalterable and binds the music to its structure. Becq de Fouquières gave several examples of this, notating verse rhythms in musical rhythms of quarter and eighth notes. But even with the musical notation, Becq de Fouquières's analysis of verse rhythm still rested entirely on syllabism.

This was not the case with the brilliant but lesser-known analyses of Paul Pierson, who followed the counsel of his teacher Gaston Paris and traveled to Vienna to study the physiology of language with Ernst Brücke. Pierson's analysis of the metrical structure of French verse was based entirely on experimental phonetics (i.e., phonation as graphically recorded), but, lacking scientific instruments, he rendered his phonetic analyses in musical notation. The aim of Pierson's work was to build a science of natural rhythm for ordinary spoken (nonpoetic) language. Pierson's investigations of the rhythmicity of natural language confirmed the verslibristes' claim that accent rather than syllables served as the generating pulse of rhythm in French. But Pierson also showed that accent was a very complex thing indeed, made up of a highly variable combination of duration, intensity, and pitch, which gained its specific inflection from the voice of the speaker.

If phonetic analysis provided a model of the rhythms of articulated phrases, Wagner's music offered the model for how these material elements might be composed in verse. In a radical departure from traditional methods of composition, Wagner rejected the use of large prefabricated blocks of music, attempting instead to let the smallest musical units (scales, arpeggios, single intervals, etc., as well as qualities of timbre, etc.) carry the weight of expression.[69] He assembled notes in groups of binary or ternary eighth notes, of double eighth notes and triplets, and then returned to these combinations that he had already presented, modifying them by all sorts of prolongations, retardations, alterations, syncopations, and dissonances. Out of these small units he aimed to produce a new sort of emotional realism that allowed a subtle recording of small nuances and variations from moment to moment, giving a loosened, fluid structure to the music, which allowed the free circulation of motifs and musical fragments, themselves susceptible to metamorphosis through shifting orchestral textures. Robert de Souza explained the sense of the Wagnerian musical model for vers libre: "The new music transforms without destroying the sensation of rhythm, striking the ear with very distinct perceptions of initial creative schemes, brief and simple, repeated to infinity—naturally in an irregular fashion—within the musical tissue. The majority of Wagner's *leitmotiven* are simple rhythmic figures, short, and for that reason, very prominent, fecund matrices of multiple combinations and in an original way, similar."[70]

Wagner's motives were often taken from popular song, of course. The verslibristes similarly found ready-made pulsing fluidity in traditions of French chanson. Nearly all early French vers libre poets took an interest in popular song and produced their own equivalents, whether the medievalizing chansons of Gustave Kahn and Jean Moréas; the rounds and rustic songs of Francis Vielé-Griffin, Maurice Maeterlinck, and Gabriel Vicaise; or the cabaret songs of Jules Laforgue. Especially when unacceptable traces of folkishness were removed, popular song proved, perhaps better than any theory of versification, the claim that the innovations of free verse were founded on tradition and that the rules of classical French prosody were external and artificial. Never having succumbed to the alexandrine discipline, French *chanson populaire* remained essentially rhythmic, with the number of syllables subordinated to rhythm and assonance taking the place of rhyme. Popular song typically treated language as highly malleable, extending, truncating, or yanking it into new shapes at will, achieving impulsively the liberation of rhyme into the half rhyme, repetition, and rhymelessness so arduously mandated by free verse theorists. Viewed through its close alliance with primitive song and music, the otherwise complex and refined art of vers libre revealed a hidden simplicity and spontaneity that sprung from intuition and instinct.[71]

VERSE BACK TO MUSIC

The transfer of musical ideas to poetry occurred almost immediately in the opposite direction. The young Claude Debussy—who in the 1880s also frequented the vanguard cabarets and café concerts; avidly read *La Vogue, Revue indépendante, La Revue wagnérienne,* and other periodicals; and was personally acquainted with many of the Hydropathes avant-garde—tried to put the new aesthetic of versification to work in music.[72] In broad terms, this meant following the *wagnérienne* and impressionist methods of breaking down musical elements into discrete units.[73] With respect to rhythm, Debussy followed the example of the verslibristes in seeking unconventional units, akin to tonic accents in verse, that might generate the rhythmic pulse of a musical piece. Debussy pushed the idea still further, treating these fundamental rhythmic relations as the basis for an exploration of mathematical proportions in music, playing with golden sections, arabesques, and other psychophysical relationships, in the spirit advocated by Charles Henry.[74]

Debussy's experiments in translating vers libre principles into music can be seen clearly in his *Proses lyriques*, four songs based on his own free verse texts composed in 1892–93.[75] Debussy set the text syllabically, with the accompanying musical duration corresponding to its spoken duration and tonic accent.[76] The novelty of the piece rests in his rendering of the poets' small rhythmic units in analogous form of musical syntax, expressed in a recognizable pianistic rhythmic figuration. In these songs Debussy built the composition out of melodic-rhythmic cells, often only a measure long, which were repeated or slightly varied. Like the gestural brushstrokes of impressionist painting or the vocal elements of vers libre, these musical cells are distributed throughout the musical texture, resulting in a mosaic of discrete, juxtaposed units. Out of the detail of layered textures of unconnected sounds there emerges a form well suited to express variations of mood, feeling, and *jaillissement* of inner rhythms in characteristically symbolist themes, such as colors, waves, ennui, dreams, moonlight, nostalgia, and interiority.

In "De rêve," the first song of the *Proses lyriques*, Debussy set his original free verse texts to music syllabically, with only a few exceptions, making the musical duration that each syllable receives reflect its spoken duration and tonic accent. In a detailed analysis of the piece, Sharon Prado confirms and extends Roy Howat's contention (based in part on correspondence between the composer and his publishers) that Debussy was experimenting with the theories of Charles Henry and the verslibristes, substituting proportions for regularities.[77] She demonstrates first that the pattern of durational accents within each stanza follows the proportions of the golden section, which becomes the governing principle for all four songs in the *Proses lyriques*.[78] Prado then shows that this pattern is even more pronounced in the musical-rhythmic cells that define the piano accompaniment: layers of small rhythmic-melodic units establish motifs that are projected into larger structures, or subjected to variations, with the predominant motif following the proportional relationships of the Fibonacci series: 1, 3, 8, 13, 21, and 34.[79] In other songs of the *Proses lyriques*, notably "De soir," Prado discerns Debussy deploying a direct musical counterpart to the verslibriste use of enjamb-

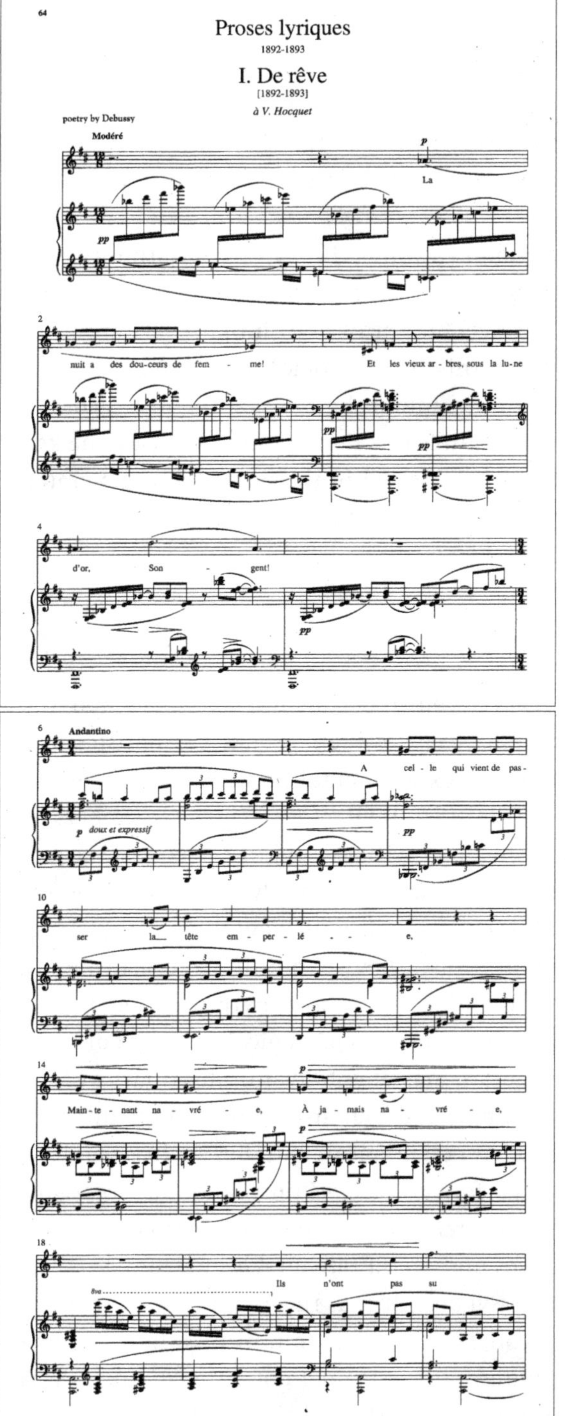

Claude Debussy, "De rêve," from *Proses lyriques* (1892–93), extract from musical score.

ment (the run-on of a syntactical unit from one-line to the next, or from one hemistich to the next) in the way in which the rhythmic-melodic feet sometimes "overlap at expected cadential or caesural points, thus obscuring the sense of closure."[80]

Here we have a musical version of Kahn's theory of discontinuity (the oscillation between analog flows and punctuating breaks) or Seurat's dissolution of the painting into "all-over" textures and similar units of sensation. Some contemporaries decried this "microscopic" method in Debussy's music, insisting that it resulted in an "amorphous" quality "like a sort of musical protoplasm."[81] Yet as with Kahn's verse or Seurat's canvases, the key to the songs of Debussy's *Proses lyriques* rested in the proportions generated by the distribution of melodic-rhythmic cells in the musical tissue.

THE HIDDEN STRATA:
BETWEEN LABORATORY AND CAFÉ CONCERT

Around 1900 the original link between experimental phonetics and the new poetry was reinforced by alliances between several verslibristes and the newly formed Collège de France experimental phonetics laboratory of the Abbé Rousselot, which we examined in chapter 3. The poets Robert de Souza and Andre Spire, working together with the linguists George Lote and Eugene Landry, utilized Rousselot's apparatus to analyze modern pronunciation of the alexandrine and to experiment with new verse forms. With instruments like Rousselot's phonoscope, they set out to make scansion an experimental science, with the intention to "resolve rhythm as one does in phonetics, into its physical, physiological, and sociological parts."[82] For studies of the alexandrine, they brought in master enunciators, luminaries of the French stage such as Sarah Bernhardt and Benoît-Constant Coquelin, who read verse from the whole field of French literature. Studies such as Landry's *La Théorie du rythme et le rythme du français déclamé* (1911) and Lote's gargantuan three-volume *L'Alexandrin d'après la phonétique expérimentale* (1913–14) marshaled copious graphics traces and quantitative tables to show that the alexandrine is really not a twelve-syllable line, as the absolute law of French prosody maintained. Rather it constantly varies from nine to fourteen syllables, the strictness and scrupulousness of the poet notwithstanding. It was now manifestly clear how unfounded was the old theory that the alexan-

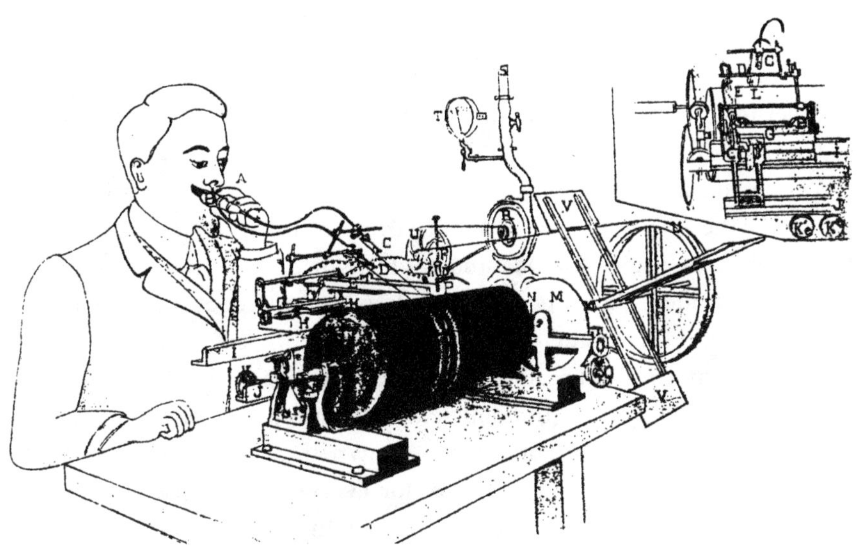

Rousselot phonoscope. From Georges Lote, *L'Alexandrin d'après la phonétique expéri-mentale*, 2nd ed. (Paris: Georges Crès, 1919).

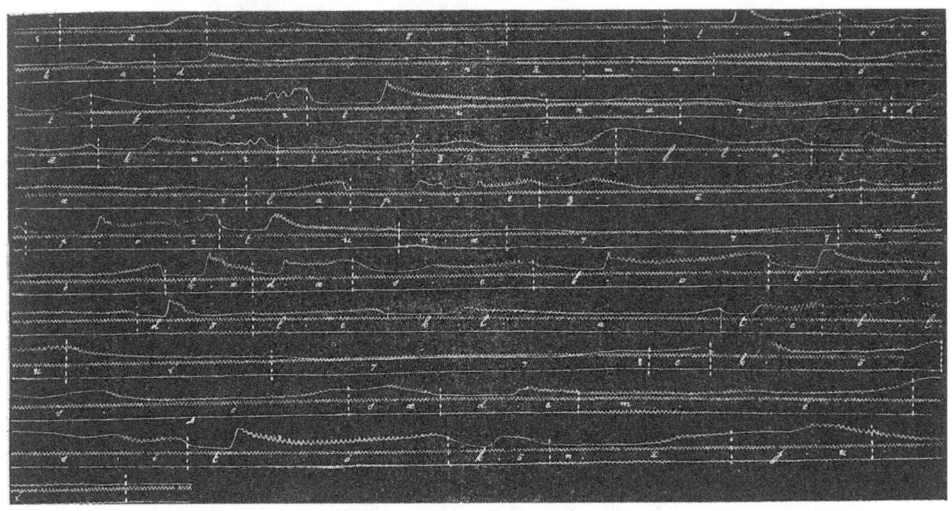

Graphical inscription of a quatrain from Corneille's *Cinna*. From Georges Lote, *L'Alexandrin d'après la phonétique expérimentale*, 2nd ed. (Paris: Georges Crès, 1919).

drine depended on the number twelve because that number held special magic for the French. Declaimed French, Landry and Lote argued, possessed a deeper tendency to follow an implicit generative rhythmic pulse—as Kahn had long insisted.

For de Souza and Spire, the laboratory provided an opportunity to examine by day the tumultuous declamatory rhythms that filled the café concerts and cabarets by night. Sounds and rhythms heard in the Chat noir were seen in the Collège de France laboratory, where the poet-linguists took up the task of what Mallarmé called "purifying the dialect of the tribe."[83] The sounds and rhythms of the so-called *caf'-conç* typically involved arabesques of gestures and brusquely immobilized postures, pantomimes and imitative contagions of rhythmical convulsions drawn from the popular images of hysterical bodies out of control.[84] Yet for every zig, zag, paf! given to the eye of beholder, there was an equally rich archive of phonetic gestures that had developed in and through the distinctive literary forms of the café concert. The enunciatory style of this mode of declamation valorized extreme suppleness, bending and shaping language to musical and rhythmic effects, with the French *e muet* as the most critical variable. De Souza and Spire graphically recorded all varieties of *e muet*. Lines like "Fluid' et douc' caress' d'cendr' bleue" revealed several *e*'s hidden beneath the silent written vowel, all pronounced with variable timbres, pitch, durations, and intensities.[85] For de Souza and Spire the laboratory was the touchstone of a campaign to make the *e muet* and related aspects of the *caf'-conç* style part of respectable declaimed French, bringing the transgressive rhythms of the nocturnal demimonde as a counter to stifling bourgeois institutions of poetry.[86] This was the original intention of the vers libre revolution, of course; but now it gained leverage in the metrological power of the laboratory. Just as the physiological measurement of human reaction times and "personal equations" held together countless technosocial systems, so the calibrated rhythms of speech would bring aesthetic and social life into a new modernist harmony.[87]

With these efforts toward the calibration of the personal and social rhythms, the parallel projects of verslibrisme and Rousselot's experimental phonetics fused. Ezra Pound, who was taken to Rousselot's laboratory by Spire and de Souza in 1913, described the odd collaboration between the priest and the radical poets as one focused on technique but carrying multiple levels of social meaning.

There was in those days still a Parisian research for technique. Spire wrangled as if vers libre were a political doctrine. De Souza had what the old Abbé called *une oreille très fine*, but he, the Abbé, wrapped up De Souza's poems and asked me to do likewise in returning them lest his *servante* should see what I was carrying.

The Abbé was M. Rousselot who had made a machine for measuring the duration of verbal components. A quill or tube held in the nostril, a less shaved quill or other tube in the mouth, and your consonants signed as you spoke them.

They return, One and by one, With fear, As half awakened, each letter with a double registration of quavering.[88]

Like other early twentieth-century artists, Pound spoke of rhythm and drew metaphors of it from a variety of contexts, but he frequently reiterated that Rousselot's work provided the critical resource for his own theory and practice of "absolute rhythm" as well as for the work of a broad and international selection of modern poets. From "The Return" cited above, to his magnum opus *Pisan Cantos*, he developed a prosody of "hidden"—inaudible and invisible—rhythms.[89]

Pound elsewhere described the collaboration of Rousselot and the poets as a hidden "strata" in the making of modernism, a place where investigations joined the rhythms of "spoken reality" with inaudible rhythms of invisible social orders converged.[90] For Pound, as for his French *confrères*, this stratum, revealed only through the intimacies of the artist's craft, would furnish the principles of new ways of acting together, new modes of civil governance, which we will examine further in chapter 7. But first we need to consider more ways that artists and physiologists sought to make the *senses* act together: before social symbiosis and synchronization there came synesthesia, the fusion of the senses.

6

SENSORY FUSION

Evolution and Synesthesia in Art and Aesthetics

The protoplasm develops to a point where it becomes a being. . . . Human beings wished to see, so developed eyes—to hear, so ears . . . to communicate, so vocal chords came.

Edvard Munch, Notebook (1906)

WE HAVE SEEN HOW FOR MANY SYMBOLIST PAINTERS AND POETS, what made the idea manifest in artwork was art's capacity to make the primordial rhythms of biological life perceptible to the beholder. In their quest for new forms of aesthetic experience, many artists delved ever more deeply into systems of evolutionary psychophysiology that treated biological life as essentially periodic or waveform.

There were several possible routes to these views, but for many the crucial mediator was once again the *esthétique scientifique* of Charles Henry. Protoplasm made brief but telling appearances in the work of Henry, who noted the parallels between protoplasmic heliotropisms studied by Paul Bert and the theory of aesthetic directions.[1] Reviewers like the physiologist Jules Héricourt in the *Revue scientifique* amplified the claim, noting that "among the waveform phenomena of life, nothing seems capable of escaping the rigors of the principles that [Henry] has established, from artistic productions to the beats of the heart. A veritable mechanics of the protoplasm is thus revealed."[2] Héricourt underscored that the human appreciation of art derived from an unconscious recognition of the rhythmic movements and automatisms stored in the cerebral unconscious, the legacy of the branching evolutionary waveform movements in the protoplasm.

The theory of organic plasticity anchored the doctrine of artistic plasticity. As we saw earlier (chapter 2), the protoplasm theory of life shored up physiological doctrines that treated life as pulsatile and vibratory. More specifically, it rooted the functional properties of automaticity, imitation, and plasticity in the very materiality of living substance and, by extension, the materiality of art. Thus, for the aestheticians, the protoplasm doctrine proved attractive because it provided a substrate for the very kinds of mobility, fluidity, and plasticity they aspired to in their arts. If protoplasm opened the biologists' imagination to what Jacques Loeb called "technologies of living substance," it similarly offered a role for artists as engineers of pulsatile life.[3] By understanding the mechanisms of the vibratory organism, the new art would aim at nothing less than the transformation of plastic human substance and function.

This chapter examines the efforts of the artists Edvard Munch and August Strindberg to build a new art out of the protoplasmic functions (or dysfunctions) of sensory fusion, imitation, automatism, and even what was known in the 1890s as ideoplasty.

Although Munch and Strindberg conducted some scientific experiments around these phenomena (together and separately), their primary involvements with the concepts were discursive, and their primary experiments were in artistic media. Their efforts to create an embodied, physiological art soon opened the path, paradoxically, to an art of disembodiment—an art of abstraction—based on the same principles of the vibratory organism.

THE MEANING OF MOLLUSKS

The most auspicious point of contact between evolutionary psychophysiology and aesthetics could be found in questions of sensory modalities, especially synesthesia, the sensory pathology à la mode around 1890. Synesthesia had been a feature of French vanguard poetry since Baudelaire's "Correspondences" and Rimbaud's "Vowels," both of which celebrated the arbitrary and subjective character of sensory fusion. But by the 1880s synesthesia had become a key topic of scientific physiology, leading a new generation of artists to set aside what Victor Segalen called the synesthetic "Old Testament" of Baudelaire and Rimbaud for the "New Testament" of sensory fusion based on scientific investigation.[4] The symbolist poet René Ghil, whose "evolutional-instrumentalist" doctrine of synesthesia was extremely influential, claimed to join Hermann Helmholtz's experimental investigation of tone-color with Wagner's ideal of the reunification of the different forms of art through crossovers of eye and ear.[5]

In December of 1891, the Paris dramaturge Paul Napoléon Roinard put Ghil's doctrine to work—staging an epic adaptation of the Song of Songs at Paul Fort's Théâtre des arts. Roinard's production put Ghil's ideas before *tout Paris*: a few critics were scathing, but most raved, and years later many would remember it as the work that consecrated the hallowed place of synesthesia within modernism. The performance inspired the physiological psychologist Alfred Binet to reflect upon the scientific causes and artistic possibilities of colored hearing before the readers of *Revue des deux mondes*:

> We already know that in colored hearing certain vowels are always accompanied by the same mental representations of color. The authors of the Song of Songs have given a material form to this association of ideas. We see a person who advances toward the footlights while holding forth in a manner that, by a happy choice of words, returns constantly to the same vowel, *i* for example. To indicate to the eyes of the spectators the idea of the color orange, which for a small number of persons, is associated with this vowel, the person in question presents himself in an orange set. There are others in which the narration has other dominant vowels and which move in [a] red, blue, or green set. Then, to augment the number of concordances and to make it more complete, the authors have linked each vowel and each color to a particular scent, with a musical note determined the same way. And, naturally, as it is necessary to translate all of this into a material form, while the recitative was on "I" and the set orange, a symphony was heard to play behind the curtains, and one pulverized the scent of white violet near the prompt box.[6]

Along with Ghil, who disavowed the production,[7] some critics found the play more redolent of Charles Henry's aesthetics: "Vaporizers fit to please Charles Henry, the father of the olfactometer, sprayed the house with incense and the scent of white violets, hyacinth, lilies, acacia, lily of the valley, seringa, orange blossoms and jasmine, while the music of Flamen de Labrely played on. And, under the coalition of these chromatic, auditory, and fragrant forces unleashed by M. Paul Roinard, the spectator surrendered to the Word of Solomon."[8]

The artists' fascination with sensory fusion encouraged scientists and doctors to reconsider various pathologies of synesthesia, especially so-called color hearing.[9] In this most frequent form of sensory confusion, sounds, or even the memory of sounds, awaken sensations of color or luminous images, which is always the same for the same letters, the same tone of voice or musical instrument. According to some, color hearing was a rare gift of exquisitely organized nervous systems; for others it was merely an accidental abnormal connection between the optic and acoustic brain-centers by means of nervous filaments. Because color hearing appeared to have a hereditary component, some scientists sought its source in evolutionary development, arguing that it was connected to an abnormal differentiation of sensory functions.

This explanation did not, however, cast any light on the larger animating question around synesthesia: was its presence a sign of regression or evolutionary advance? After all, it might represent a heightened access to the unseen physical vibrations, a human faculty akin to the most advanced recording device, cathode ray tube, or spectroscope. The biologist Felix Le Dantec pointed out that this would make artists akin to scientific instruments—or to protoplasmic beings: "The living protoplasms, very complex colloids, are highly susceptible to imitating . . . colors and sounds." This happened through a condition of "resonance" that established itself "between a colloid and its ambience."[10]

Raphaël Du Bois, a French comparative physiologist, provided what many considered a firm foundation for this view with a "general theory of sensation," based on studies of an ancestral mollusk, the common piddock (*Pholas dactylus*, Fr. *Pholade dactyle*).[11] Du Bois was able to investigate the primitive organism's modes of cognition of the ambient milieu. Unlike oysters and other bivalve mollusks, the piddock possessed a proboscis or siphon, through which it is sensible to all external impressions: light, noise, touch, smell, and so on. Thus, in contrast to "higher animals in which the protoplasm is differentiated" and "nerves, ganglia, brain, and sense apparatus are formed," this mollusk "sees, hears, smells, and feels with this one part of its body; its proboscis functions at once as a eye, ear, nose, finger, et cetera." For Du Bois

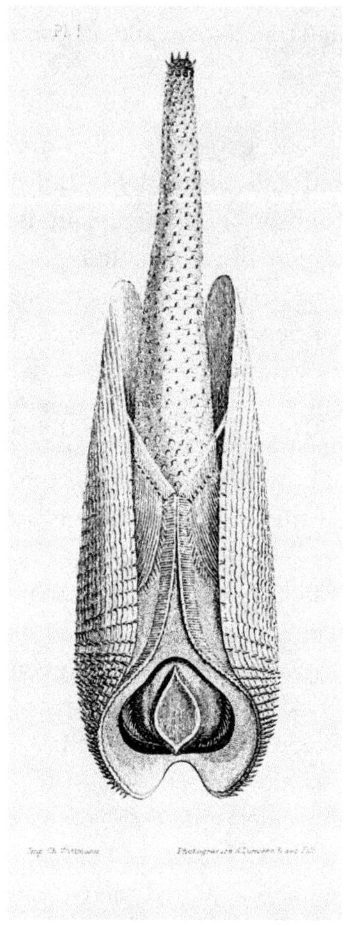

Morphology of *Pholas dactylu*s. From Raphaël Du Bois, *Anatomie et physiologie comparée de la pholade dactyle: Structure, locomotion, tact, olfaction, gestation, vision, dermoptique, photogénie, avec une théorie générale des sensations* (Paris: G. Masson, 1892).

this gave its study an important philosophical value in determining what is "fundamental in the play of organs and apparatus that perpetuate life and thought among humans."[12]

In Du Bois's experimental setup, the common piddock became the vibratory organism par excellence. Using a graphical recording system, Du Bois recorded the movements of the piddock's siphon. In the amplitude and the velocity of the contraction of peripheral contractile segments, he explained, the animal itself wrote its impressions of sensory stimuli. In effect, all senses were reduced to one, which Du Bois called "touch-vision" (*dermop-*

tique), but this did not mean that stimuli were undifferentiated. Different kinds of visual stimuli, odor, and pressure all resulted in different graphic curves. More remarkably, in response to different colors the piddock produced curves whose amplitudes corresponded to the order of the solar spectrum: yellow, blue, violet, red (white produced a curve in the middle). Sound produced a similar range of responses in accordance with the rapidity and intensity of vibrations. The piddock itself, in other words, closely resembled a graphical recording instrument, registering different sensations amodally as small variations in vibratory frequency and intensity. But it was its position within an evolutionary lineage that led to humans that won the lowly mollusk its status as a model organism.

If for some symbolist theorists Du Bois's work furnished needed justification for the synthesis of the senses, for certain critics it showed just the opposite.[13] Max Nordau, the Austrian neurologist turned cultural Jeremiah, used Du Bois's findings to build a pillar of his case against the symbolists in *Degeneration*, his condemnation of decadence in modern art and culture.[14] Nordau insisted that the valorization of synesthesia, the desire to exalt the perception of undifferentiated senses, presented a symptom of regression or atavism, in short, of a will to return to a condition of the "protoplasm in the living cell."[15] Nordau observed that from Du Bois one knew that primitive organisms like the piddock exist in a perfect condition of synesthesia, the very state idealized by the artistic avant-garde, who failed to see that this state was simply "evidence of diseased and debilitated brain-activity." Moreover, he mordantly concluded, "it is a retrogression to the very beginning of organic development. It is a descent from the height of human perfection to the low level of a mollusk. To raise the combination, transposition and confusion of the perceptions of sound and sight to the rank of a principle of art, to see futurity in this principle, is to designate the return from the consciousness of man to that of the oyster."[16] Nordau's form of argumentation—call it *reductio ad protoplasma*—charted a distinctive new mode of fin-de-siècle rhetoric.[17] The facts of evolution from protoplasm were not in dispute, however; only the prescriptions for the arts based in physiological aesthetics and prospects for a society that increasingly reveled in pathologies like synesthesia and the afflictions of imitation associated with hysteria, hypnotism, somnambulism, and the like.

MUNCH AND STRINDBERG IN BERLIN

When Edvard Munch and August Strindberg befriended each other in Berlin in 1892, protoplasmania and its elements—Ernst Haeckel's monist biology, French psychiatry and psychophysiology, and physiological aesthetic theories of art—formed a consecrating element of their friendship.[18] Yet, as Shelly Wood Cordulak has shown, the scientific interests of both men were deep and much more long-standing.[19] After an unsuccessful stint as a medical student at the University of Uppsala, Strindberg had made his dramaturgical reputation as a leading example of the "vivisectional" method pioneered by Émile Zola, itself based on the physiology of Claude Bernard.[20] Munch, the son and brother of doctors, had grown up surrounded by medicine and science and read widely in monism, medicine, and psychology all his life. Perhaps most importantly, he had been captivated by the physiological theories of art current among the French avant-garde during his Paris sojourn of 1889.

In Berlin, a critical personal influence for both Munch and Strindberg entered upon this well-prepared ground: Stanislaw Przybyszewski, a Polish architect turned medical student and physiologist, an *anarchisante* spirit who aspired to a literary career and lifestyle in the bohemian French mode of Baudelaire and his acolytes. Przybyszewski, known to his friends as the "gory physiologist" and "the ingenious Pole," had studied with Haeckel, Carl Vogt, and Jacob Moleschott and between 1890 and 1893 specialized in physiology and neurology, until his expulsion from the University of Berlin for "socialist activities."[21] One of Przybyszewski's crucial intellectual roles in the artists' circle revolved around his explanations of physiological doctrines of art and aesthetics, especially those emanating from France. Julius Meier-Graefe, the art critic and historian, later recalled strolling one night with Przybyszewski, who "as usual . . . expounded on physiology."[22] Meier-Graefe's ambivalence about Przybyszewski's physiological obsessions echoed the broader critical reception to his 1892 book, *Zur Psychologie des Individuums*, which ranged from those who derided it as a mere "sauce of medical terms" to others who lauded its "transmission of concepts and apparatus of exact scientific research to the field of intuitive psychology" and "energetic endeavor to formulate new concepts."[23]

Munch, Strindberg, and Przybyszewski famously gathered in Berlin at an Armenian tavern dubbed Zum Schwarzen Ferkel (the Black Pig) by Strindberg. The scene at the Ferkel involved a variety of other artists, intellectuals, and doctors and by all accounts featured a rather intense bohemianism, with lots of drinking, camaraderie, sexual intrigue, and heady conversation. Under Przybyszewski's guidance the circle read widely in the biological and psychiatric literature: Haeckel's writings on biology and monist philosophy, Helmholtz's *Sensations of Tone*, and Moleschott's *Der Kreislauf des Lebens*, Henry Maudsley's *Physiology of Mind and Pathology of Mind*, Théodule Ribot's *Les Maladies de la volonté* and *Les Maladies de la personnalité*, Hippolyte Bernheim's *De la suggestion*, works by Jean-Martin Charcot and his associates, and much more besides.[24]

They also read works by authors spurred by these kinds of biomedical works to literary, artistic, and social reflection, most notably Max Nordau and Friedrich Nietzsche. Both Nordau and Nietzsche embraced the 1880s wave of interest in evolutionary and physiological aesthetics, taking on board the assumption that works of art were both created and apprehended through the physiological conditions of senses and bodily functions, especially those pertaining to movement, emotion, attention, and perception. Evolutionary aesthetics, moreover, held that human physiology (sentience, motor function, emotion, and temperament) had evolved—and would continue to evolve—along Darwinian (or more often, Lamarckian) lines.[25] For these thinkers, and many others, part of the fascination with this mode of inquiry derived from the notion that the arts had been a critical component of evolution and would become even more decisive in the future of human development.

Nordau's 1885 work, *Paradoxes*, which unlike his later work presented a largely affirmative account of physiological aesthetics and a biomedical model of society, was particularly admired by Strindberg.[26] In the chapter "Psycho-Physiology of Genius and Talent," Nordau poised genius as a balance between Schopenhauerian will and Kantian judgment. The hinge between them was an effective division of protoplasmic labor. He argued that art, like complex tasks of respiration, circulation, and digestion, are more complex tasks than those performed "by a lump of protoplasm," and our apparatus is "organized with a view to the division of labor, as a cabinet minister, for instance, has neither time to cook his own dinner nor to mend his own clothes." Artists possessed a special psychophysiology that suited them for their work, centered on a highly developed sensory-motor apparatus: "This direct connection between the centres of light-sensations and those of motion, which is the organic foundation of the special artistic talent . . . the centre of light-sensations from some object . . . those few that are most essential, they retain, and imitate by muscular movements."[27]

Nordau refined his theory in his Zola-like experimental novel entitled *Die Krankheit des Jahrhunderts* (1887). Nordau was therefore viewed as an artistic and philosophical comrade by the Berlin Ferkel circle, whose members eagerly anticipated his next book, *Entartung* (*Degeneration*), which appeared in 1892.[28] But they were in for a surprise. In *Degeneration* Nordau reversed his progressive view of physiological aesthetics, arguing that it was both a symptom and cause of a deep sickness in fin-de-siècle civilization.[29]

Nietzsche's writings were similarly suffused with a fascination for biology and especially physiological aesthetics. This dimension of his thought was downplayed in late twentieth-century Nietzsche interpretation but has been recovered by recent criticism.[30] There are good reasons to assume that the Ferkel circle, and the especially the devoted Nietzsche enthusiast Przybyszewski, would have been particularly alert to this aspect of the philosopher's thinking. Nietzsche drew upon many of the same biological sources that the artists read, including Haeckel and the monists, and a variety of German, English, and French physiologists. While Michael Foster's protoplasm research gripped Nietzsche's late conception of the will to power, it was Charles Féré who gained a "massive presence" in Nietzsche's writings, shaping the philosopher's thought on the physiology of emotion, the role of suggestion, and the ideomotor theory of art, as well as critical materials for his key concepts of crime and decadence.[31]

In his critical writings on Munch's art, Przybyszewski positioned his friend at the vanguard of this new approach to art:

The last evolutionary stage of art—naturalism—has made us alien to psychic and mental phenomena, has made our views of deep and infinite thoughts so shallow, that it is now absolutely impossible to project ourselves into a new artistic idea that does not even make use of the technique of realism, which exists entirely in psychic areas, in the subtlest and finest emotions of the soul. . . . This is what makes Munch so great and so significant, that everything that is deep and dark, all that for which language has not yet found any words, and which expresses itself solely as a dark, foreboding instinct, that all this takes on color through him and enters our consciousness.[32]

Many of Munch's statements about his art from this period reflect his adherence to the doctrines of physiological aesthetics. "I don't paint from nature," Munch wrote in 1890. "I paint not what I see, but what I saw."[33] Over the course of his life, Munch often referred to this idea of painting from memories, whether conscious or unconscious, or more precisely from sensations or emotions stored within as the vibrational archive of different mental and physiological states. By "painting the colors and lines and shapes [he had] seen in a moment of emotional stress," Munch wrote of himself, he could "get the moment of stress to vibrate anew."[34] This is a clear expression of the French psychophysiological doctrine of symbol formation as a condensation of impressions in the protoplasm that then become externalized by the motor functions as idea or symbol in the work of art. Munch thought of this vibrating protoplasmic memory image in personal terms, as the bearer of emotion and sometimes mystical longings and perceptions. But it could also refer to transgenerational heredity and memory, as implied by Haeckel and developed in fin-de-siècle art history in Aby Warburg's notion of *Nachleben*, in which psychophysiological memory seamlessly encompassed human history and especially traumatic memory.[35]

Przybyszewski repeated this view with the addition of his interest in synesthesia, reporting his friend's aspiration to paint unconscious sensations that effaced the separation of the gates of sense, rechanneling the impressions of specific sense modalities through other ones. Munch, he wrote, sought to find the "knotting point" where "all impressions flow together, where the most heterogeneous things are sensed as equivalent" because individuality rendered them in the same emotional tone.[36] The result was synesthesia, Przybyszewski explained, with emphasis drawn from a line from Baudelaire's *Les Fleurs du mal*: "color becomes line, scent becomes sound: les parfums, les couleurs et les son se répondent."[37] Przybyszewski marked Munch's originality in his having renounced all painting from direct observation of nature, turning instead to congealed memories inscribed on his own sensorium, which he then rendered in form and line equivalents. The aim of painting was to recover that original protoplasmic unity in the higher form of the synesthetic *Gesamtkunstwerk*.[38]

The interest in synesthetic effects had been shared by Przybyszewski and Munch in a series of experimental events held in the Berlin home of the doctor and poet Carl Ludwig Schleich. The events, splendidly recounted by Sven Dierig, featured Przybyszewski playing works of Frédéric Chopin in a free-form, unconventional, and passionate manner on Schleich's Steinway piano.[39] "The tones," Max Dauthendey recalled, "wildly devoured order and laws and thoughts from the minds of all listeners, and tones, people, and times mixed to form chaos."[40] Przybyszewski described these performances as experiments in physiological aesthetics, where "Chopinesque sounds" might incite thought apparatus to vibrate creatively. Chopin was unique, he argued, because of his relentlessly synesthetic mode of composing. "It appears as if the law of specific energy of the sense organs has no validity for him [Chopin]," he wrote, "as if there were some point in this eternally fevering brain in which all sensations come together, some kind of interconnection of the sense organs so that a sensation of light or taste could proceed directly to the auditory nerves."[41] The Chopinesque manner of playing the piano would thus transform tones into writing, notes into letters, music into literature, until each of his auditors were "Chopinized," that is, when the listener "writhed in pain . . . , when a terrible scream was wrenched from his heart."[42]

Przybyszewski's words pointed directly to Munch's *The Scream*. The general monist character of the painting has been remarked by scholars. Reinhold Heller, for example, writes that "the curving lines of the sky, echoed in the curves of the figure's body, dominate. It is as if, in their essential form and color there was no distinction between the landscape, sky, and figure, and that all were fused in the symbolic flatness of Munch's pictorial representation of Monistic unity."[43] The monist unity of the painting might be said to concentrate around the melding of color and sound in the painting, borne perhaps through the swirling ether, whose waveforms flow from the perspectival back of the painting to converge on the humanoid figure with hands cupped around the face, which resembles typical period representations of cells with semipermeable membranes.

The relatively ambiguous boundaries between the figure and the swirling, enveloping atmosphere moreover suggest some clinical accounts of synesthesia. Synesthetics typically reported that they "heard colors" outside of themselves in an area just beyond the body, rather than internally, the way most sense perceptions are experienced. The suggestion that synesthesia marked a kind of projection in auratic space confirmed its association with the ambiguous boundaries of selfhood associated with protoplasm.

"I felt the great Scream through nature," read an inscription Munch wrote underneath the lithograph of the painting. The invocation of the "I" confers identification with the receiver figure, perhaps as a fellow receiver of the great Scream, much like the classic *repoussoir* figures used to orient the viewer in the painting's space. The presence of the central figure similarly draws the viewer into the painting's landscape, or rather, soundscape, inducing a synesthetic sense of hearing the scream represented in the painting. The painting thus constructs its own mode of apprehension, sets the conditions of its meaning, and requires the beholder for its completion. In this sense it might be said to function like an experiment in psychophysiological aesthetics.

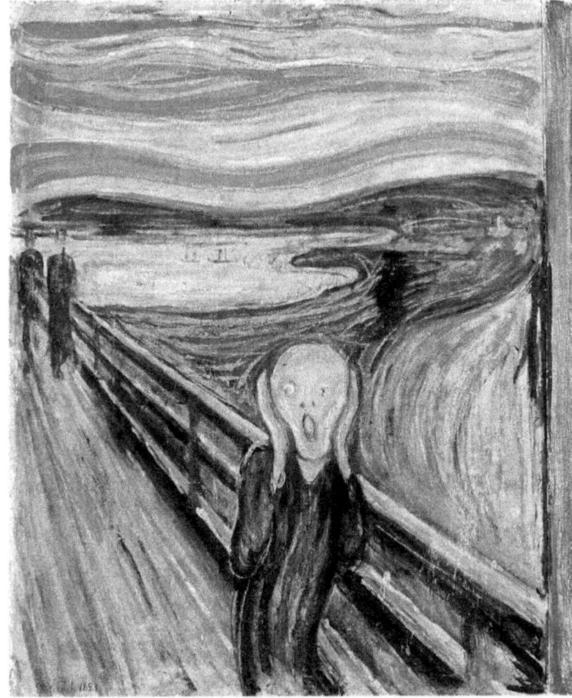

Edvard Munch, *The Scream*, 1893. Tempera and pastel on cardboard, 91 x 73.5 cm. Nasjonalgalleriet, Oslo. © The Munch Museum / The Munch-Ellingsen Group / SODRAC (2013).

Or more specifically, *The Scream* recalled several experiments conducted by Parisian psychiatrists and psychophysiologists on the effects of unexpected or extreme bursts of sound or light on experimental subjects, usually patients at the Salpetrière or Bicêtre psychiatric hospitals. In works widely known, and read by Munch and his circle, such as Désiré-Magloire Bourneville and Paul Régnard's, *Iconographie photographique de la Salpetrière* (1876–80), Régnard's, *Les Maladies épidémiques de l'esprit* (1887), Paul Richer's *Étude clinique sur la grande hystérie ou hystéro-épilepsie* (1881–85), and Charles Féré's *Sensation et mouvement* (1887), there were dramatic photographs and engravings depicting catalepsies, somnambulisms, and anesthesias induced by striking a gong, large tuning fork, or tam-tam, or igniting limelights, magnesium flames, or compounds with firework effects. The aim of these experiments, Georges Didi-Huberman has written, was for the sensory jolt to "produce an attitude, and the attitude to produce a tableau."[44] Exposed to a loud sound or fireworks, patients would typically freeze into an attitudinal position, often remaining there long after the sound or light had abated.

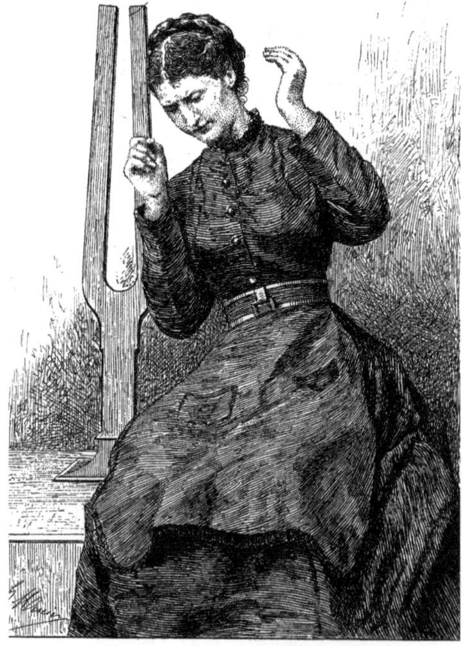

Experiments in the psychophysiology of sound with hysterics. From Paul Régnard, *Les Maladies épidémiques de l'esprit: Sorcellerie, magnétisme, morphinisme, délire des grandeurs* (Paris: Plon-Nourrit, 1887).

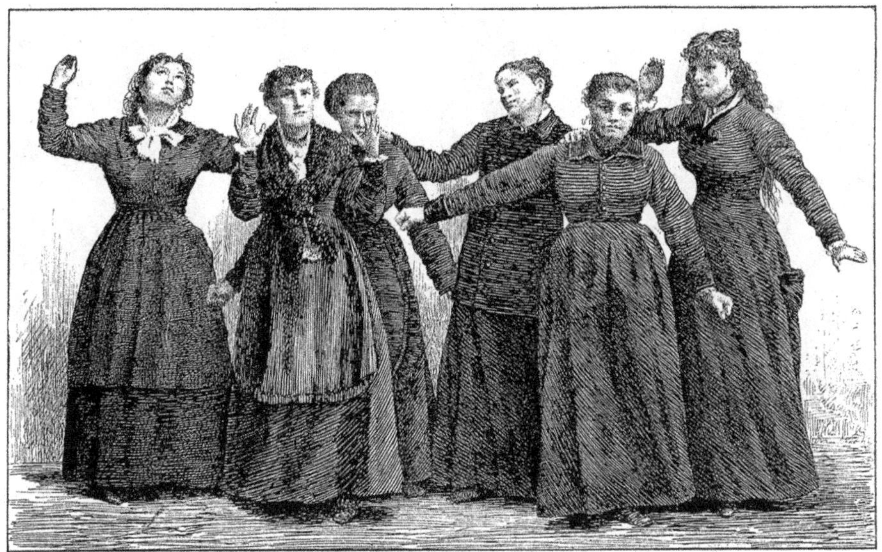

Aesthetic contagion: six hysterics suddenly hypnotized by an intense and unexpected noise. From Paul Régnard, *Les Maladies épidémiques de l'esprit: Sorcellerie, magnétisme, morphinisme, délire des grandeurs* (Paris: Plon-Nourrit, 1887).

Some studies, like Féré's well-known research, centered on instances of "involuntary imitation, of contagion of gestures through the visual sense."[45] In these experiments, undertaken "at the behest of M. Charles Henry" and reported in his *Sensation et mouvement*, Féré used graphical recording devices to gauge the transfer of movement from visual image to the mind, and then from mind to movements by the experimental subject. These experiments invested aesthetic phenomena with an eye to the broader social and epidemiological implications of the contagious effects of sensory-motor phenomena suggested in works like Régnard's. The latter explained his psychophysiological investigations with reference to universal vibrations that may come in the form of physical sensations or human gestures and create irresistible convulsive epidemics of mind: "The frequent sight of certain people pushes one, little by little, to reproduce their poses and gestures. Tics are contagious, external qualities and defects transmit themselves, and even

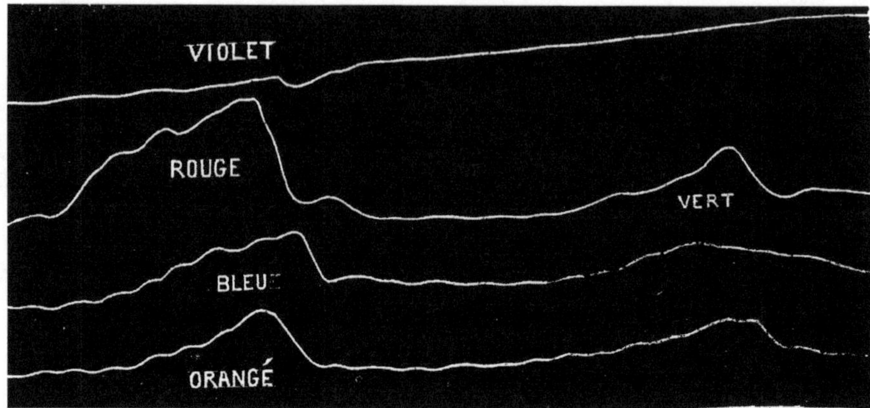

Psychophysiological experiments in color: plethysmograph studies. From Charles Féré, *Sensation et mouvement: Études expérimentales de psycho-mécanique* (Paris: F. Alcan, 1887).

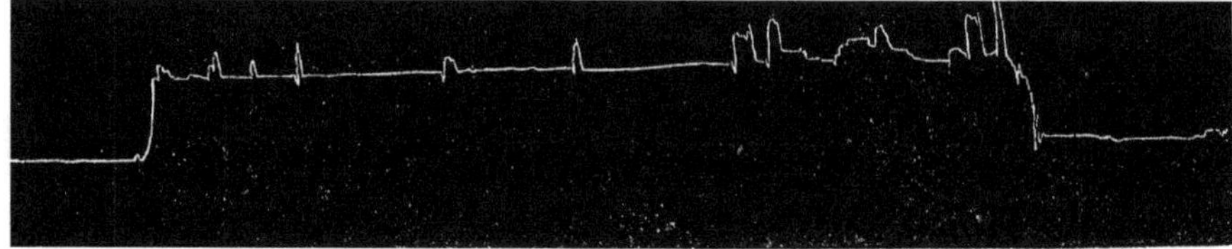

Psychophysiological experiments in sound: dynamograph recordings of subject reactions to the mute and continuous vibrations of a gong. From Charles Féré, *Sensation et mouvement: Études expérimentales de psycho-mécanique* (Paris: F. Alcan, 1887).

thoughts are modified by contact with certain individuals. How can these mysterious influences and reciprocity of action be explained? Authors have held that, in nature, the molecules of all bodies are animated by incessant vibrations, and that in subjects who are placed in identical conditions, the two nervous systems end up vibrating in unison."[46] These were the terms of an emerging physiological aesthetic model of spectatorship celebrated in both the new modernist arts and in popular entertainments, and of course decried in works like Nordau's *Degeneration*.[47]

Munch's *The Scream* might be read as an allegory, or pace Nordau, a manifesto for this conception of art.[48] The central figure in the painting assumes a pose or attitude similar to those depicted in the French experimental studies, while the fiery orange and red swirling sky could also suggest the pyrotechnic chemical flames, or more peevishly, a reference to Nordau's "sky [in which] the clouds are aflame in the weirdly beautiful glow which was observed for the space of years after the eruption of Krakatoa," the image of the ethereal contagion whereby the "whole of civilized human-ity" becomes "converted to the aesthetics of the Dusk of Nations."[49] *The Scream* might thereby depict a psychophysiological contagion or epidemic of the mind coursing through space, enveloping first the central figure of the painting and then the beholder of the canvas as well. The beholder is there-fore brought irresistibly into the event depicted, which leaves no possibility of perceiving the painting from a neutral or detached perspective. This is how art, or at least the new art conceptualized by the French avant-garde, might be seen to work its effects, as the painter's lines and color, the poet's vocal declamation, and the actor's gesture compel a vibratory imitative inner movement in the spectator. It might also serve as an account of the spread of the new art (and the worldview that underpinned it): radiating out from the vibrant bohemian precincts of European cities to engulf the bourgeois establishment, who react at first with similarly stricken attitudes.

Within the medical and scientific discussion of these "influences and reciprocity of action" lurked the question of the will, specifically the place of the demarcation between voluntary action and involuntary automatism, sometimes located directly in the activity of protoplasm, as an entry in Munch's notebooks indicated.[50] But it was easy to invoke the accumulating vibratory throb to explain the behaviors of protoplasmic or primitive organ-isms. In humans that would indicate the flight of the centralized control of reason. As the psychiatrists' studies suggested that the control function of reason was more fragile than people had generally supposed, the contagions of affect and emotions became a source of growing concern. "Social mimeti-cism . . . impels us [to imitate those around us]. . . . A form of madness by imitation exists," Régnard concluded.[51] By 1890 the psychiatric notion of social mimeticism had become the basis for a full-blown sociology in the writings of Collège de France professor Gabriel Tarde, for whom "society is imitation, and imitation is a type of somnambulism."[52]

Munch's painting *Angst* (*Anxiety*), which revisited the landscape of *The Scream* with an advancing crowd of spectral figures, amplified the human-

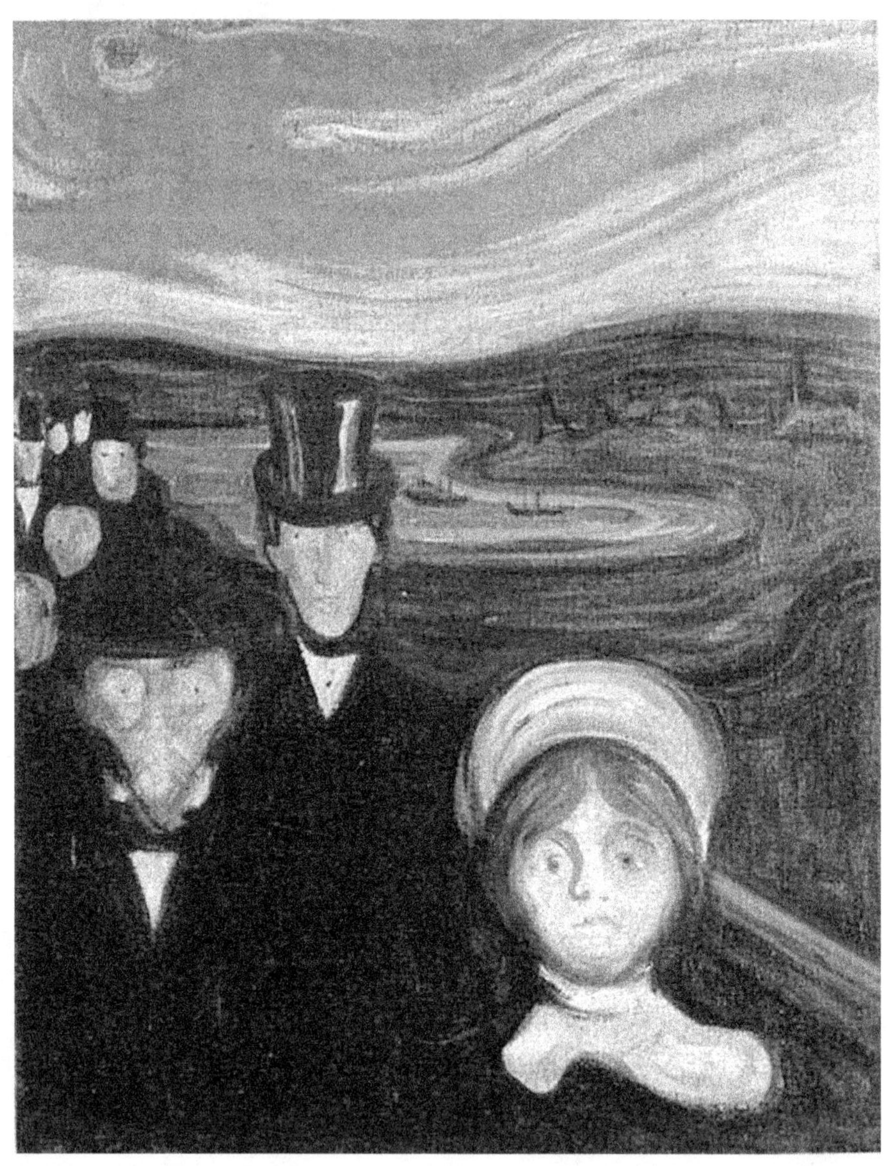

Edvard Munch, *Anxiety*, 1894. Oil on canvas, 94 x 73 cm. Munch Museum, Oslo, Norway. © The Munch Museum / The Munch-Ellingsen Group / SODRAC (2013).

to-human contagion of affect that he had previously depicted through sound and color.[53] If *The Scream* showed the contagion of the new art coursing through society, here were its minions in the public, zombies closing in on the Max Nordaus of the world.

Nordau's great worry, of course, concerned the fate of a society made in the image of an artistic culture that was itself made in the image of evolutionary neurophysiological pathology. It was not only the fact that artists had begun to adopt physiological theories as the basis for their art, but that their art had begun to create a new kind of spectator, a new public vibrating all too happily to representations of pathology. "It is certainly unnecessary to draw the reader's attention in a special manner to the complete coincidence of this clinical picture of hysteria with the description of the peculiarities of the fin-de-siècle public," Nordau observed.[54] The Parisian press (Nordau lived in Paris) was filled with accounts of performances and artworks that induced automatisms of the nervous system, leading onlookers to mime hysterics, somnambulists, and epileptics with abandon.[55] Nordau's screed was the most alarmist and most systematic produced by those worried about these arts, providing a medically informed critique and linking it with related contemporary fears of depopulation and crime.

Another of Munch's inscriptions on *The Scream*—"could have only been made by a madman"—teasingly suggested that Nordau might be right. It is quite possible that Munch intended this inscription as an affirmative rebuke to the Nordau discussion on everybody's lips in 1893. In any case, Munch was already an avid reader of the neuropsychiatric and physiological literature around which Nordau built his case, and a devotee of the approach to art recently developed among the Paris vanguard. Munch had already acquired the epithet of being this kind of refined, neurasthenic artist, "sickly sensitive," a decadent bohemian aristocrat of the spirit, with the talent to match the description.[56] And whether or not he had Nordau in mind, Munch would soon and repeatedly have to answer to Nordau-inspired critics, like the Norwegian medical student Johannes Schaffenberg in 1895, who, as Patricia Berman has shown, invoked the language of Nordau to accuse Munch of hereditary morbidity, dissolute living, and of unleashing a contagion of corruption among the youth of Norway.[57]

If Munch's madness was of the contagious variety, it remains unclear whether the painter would have been the source or recipient of the scourge, although there is no doubt he would have accelerated its spread. Either way, many of his contemporaries, like the English writer Edward Carpenter, believed there was a positive correlation between synesthesia and the shaman in so-called primitive societies, as well as between homosexuals and other "deviant" sexual orientations: all were examples of a fortunate failure of protoplasm to differentiate itself, a fate that conferred upon the individual not oysterhood but extraordinary powers to perceive the world in its original condition of undifferentiated unity.[58]

STRINDBERG IN PARIS AND BEYOND

Strindberg took up residence in Paris in 1894, plunging into several new intellectual currents there. Munch joined Strindberg in the French capital for several fateful months in 1896. This visit culminated in a break between the two friends, largely because of a complex swirl of events involving the arrest of Przybyszewski in Berlin on charges of murdering his first wife and two children, and a paranoid suspicion of Strindberg's that Munch conspired in a plot to murder him. Yet beyond the personal break there was a philosophical parting of the ways, as Strindberg delved more deeply into scientific experimentation, photography, and especially, occultism. Some commentators have described this as an evolution in Strindberg's thought from naturalism to supernaturalism. There is some truth in this characterization, of course, but Strindberg's changes equally took place within collective transformations among fin-de-siècle intellectuals of the "-isms" upon which he drew—symbolism, monism, transformism—as well as in the context of a turn among many leading European scientists to questions long associated with occultism, spiritualism, and psychical research. Within the general change of fashion, continuities in Strindberg's views remain discernable. Among these concerns, protoplasm doctrines provide a telltale marker.

While still in Berlin, Strindberg's scientific interests grew. One German member of the Ferkel group, Schleich, host of the "Chopinizing" musical salons and self-experimenting neuroscientist, reported on Strindberg's experimental trials that investigated the "electromolecular vibration of the protoplasm" using chemical preparations and spectral analysis.[59] Two years later, Strindberg described these laboratory experiments in an essay entitled "Wo sind die Nerven der Pflanzen?," in which he concluded that instead of nerves, energy in plants is "distributed—everywhere in the protoplasm," which meant that they use the protoplasm as a conductor.[60] Among the consequences Strindberg drew from his alleged discovery was the evolutionary basis of "sensory confusion," or synesthesia, which he championed as the basis of a new art.

Similar chemical studies began to appear in Strindberg's writing and correspondence from this time. In his *Antibarbarus* (1894), he described a number of chemical experiments that challenged the conventional division of the elements, following ideas taken from Haeckel's monism. As Strindberg explained in a letter to Torsten Hedlund, "I simply drew all the logical conclusions inherent in Transformism and Monism."[61] Strindberg wrote to Haeckel to explain his ideas but did not receive quite the response he had hoped for.[62] If he received no joy from the greatest monist, Strindberg found satisfaction among the transformists, especially when he found reviews in the *Journal des débats* of two new books describing experiments similar to his own: François Jollivet-Castelot's *La Vie et l'âme de la matière: Essai de physiologie chimique* and Claude Hemel's *Les Métamorphose de la matière*. Strindberg claimed that Jollivet-Castelot "repeats all the ideas of my *Antibarbarus* without even knowing it; he even dates his chapter on transmutation November 1893 as I did! Except that he was in Douai and I in Brünn." Even more delightful were the credentials of his newly discovered *compagnon du route*: "Chemist, member of the Astronomical Society of France and of the Independent Group of Esoteric Studies."[63]

Strindberg referred to himself as a "transformist," a term that in his usage joined the French doctrines of chemical neo-Lamarckism with a fascination for older esoteric alchemical doctrines. The notion of inner forces bearing signs or even hidden languages was an old one, of course, held by alchemists and Romantic *Naturphilosophen* alike and regenerated by the more occult versions of symbolism à la mode in 1890s France. These modes of thought joined forces with French transformists, many of whom affirmed their own roots in French romanticism, avidly extending their hypotheses beyond the organism to transmutations of the material world, the ether, and the heavens.[64] Strindberg imbibed deeply from these traditions. But his reformulation of these ideas grew from his experimental monism and gained a new plausibility through the doctrine of protoplasm as a medium of inscriptive memory. He remained particularly fascinated by the ways in which matter, especially crystals, could assume the appearance of plant or animal forms, looking like feathers or ears of corn. This suggested an "image-making drive" in nature itself: "Could water in the form of steam, having passed numerous times through the plants, have taken and retained the imprint of its form? Would this same water, leaving the primitive state of its crystalline form, have the possibility of developing and creating the free forms within the forms of crystal? Is it the water that gives its form to plants or the other way around?"[65] Matter thus showed evidence of a capacity to inscribe the "memory" of its previous states, so that it could represent them subsequently as images, forms, or symbols.

Strindberg now sought to extend the idea from physiology to ontology, showing how the principles of the organic world, of protoplasm, applied to the world of matter itself. "Silicon breathes and has the capacity for movement of protoplasm," wrote Strindberg in his 1896 essay "Das Seufzen der Steine."[66] This statement appeared in part as an answer to the wry question of why Paris is such a remarkable place. "After twenty years I have finally discovered Paris and found its secret," Strindberg began the essay. Despite the geographical superiority of other locales, the Romans already understood that silica and limestone made the best building materials and so made a little fishing spot on the Seine their key northern city and the eventual crossroads of Europe. Strindberg's assertion may have been tongue-in-cheek, but he was serious about the chain of chemical reasoning that allowed him to "dethrone" the notion of carbon as progenitor of organisms and replace it with a metal normally thought to be dead. After all, iron takes oxygen from the air and gives off carbon dioxide, water, and ammonia—it breathes, after a fashion. Similarly, "the protoplasma of a cell also contains, besides the albuminoids, granules of uric acid, silicon, and carbonate of lime."[67] Strindberg asserted that "stone is living and can bring forth life through fermentation. Coal is born of the mountain." Similar conditions obtained in the generation of primitive organisms, such as in the *Urschleim* of *Bathybius haeckeleii*, which Huxley pulled out of the depths of the oceans, "where lime and gelatinous silicon dioxide were in play."[68] Silicon thus bridged the inorganic stuff of the earth and the dynamic movement of life in its primordial protoplasmic form. These experiments also explained, Strindberg deadpanned, the vitality of Paris, the city built of limestone and silicon—and, of course, the city of transformist natural philosophy.

These speculations underwrote Strindberg's experiments with primitive photographic media during the 1890s.[69] Describing his trials as attempts to produce "natural art," Strindberg abjured available photographic equipment, noting his special distrust of lenses, which he believed obstructed certain chromatic rays of light and therefore distorted reality.[70] As in his paintings, Strindberg sought to achieve a tactile surface in his images consistent with his conviction that the images were themselves nature rather than images of nature.[71] Sometimes Strindberg built simple lensless pinhole cameras out of cigar boxes or other containers. But more interesting were his "celestographs," images produced by a direct method using neither lens nor camera obscura.

Working in Austria in the winter of 1894, Strindberg experimented with simply placing his photographic plates on the ground or a window sill, exposing them to the sky above. The images that gradually emerged from this process resembled the night sky. But as Douglas Feuk notes, it is just as easy to see them as gravel and dust, dark soil or asphalt.[72] Feuk suggests that it was exactly this interpenetration of earth and sky that Strindberg sought to produce, much like the interbraiding of organic and inorganic, spiritual and material. These image experiments exemplified Strindberg's emerging notion of "natural art, where the artist works in the same capricious way as nature, without a specific aim."[73]

Strindberg also described this as "automatic art," a way of seeing evanescent figures or symbols in ever-changing appearances of nature.[74] The capacity of nature to produce automatic art was also a feature of the best new modernist painting:

Does this not provide an analogy with the modernist paintings that philistines find so incomprehensible? At first, one sees only a chaos of colours; then it begins to assume a likeness, it resembles, but no: it resembles nothing. All at once a point defines itself, like the nucleus of a cell; it grows, the colours group themselves around it and accumulate; rays develop which sprout branches and twigs as ice crystals do on a window pane . . . and the image presents itself to the viewer, who has assisted at the birth of the picture. And, what is even better, the painting remains always new, it changes according to the light, never wears out, and is endowed with the gift of light.[75]

Strindberg very plausibly had Munch's *The Scream* in mind with this passage. In any case, he surely had Nordau in mind as the most notorious of the philistines. At the end of the essay he revealed that his theories of natural and automatic art served as a direct refutation of "that degenerate beast of a critic," who concludes from this "that he is mentally deranged and gives this sickness the scientific (!) name 'Echolalia.'" He continued:

> Every true poet since the creation of the world has been an echolaliac.
> With one exception, Max Nordau, who uses rhyme without being a
> poet. *Hinc Illae lacrimae!*
>
> The art of the future (which will pass away, like everything else)!
> Imitate nature closely; above all, imitate nature's way of creating![76]

Nordau used echolalia—the immediate and involuntary repetition of words or phrases just spoken by others, a symptom of autism and some types of derangement—to describe the disconnected rhyme patterns of free verse poets.[77] Echolalia, he insisted, represented yet another pathological contagion of involuntary movements or automatisms that characterized the neuropathic aesthetics of the avant-garde. With his notion of automatic art, Strindberg thus pushed the notion of imitative automatism back from the human or organic world (protoplasm) and into the realm of inorganic matter itself. Imitation was therefore not a pathology but a universal characteristic of all things, best manifested in the new modernist arts.

Strindberg was well along this path of thought when Munch joined him in Paris. During their months together Munch produced his famous lithograph, *Portrait of Strindberg*, which suggested some of Strindberg's ideas, or the condition of his soul at the time. Munch rather playfully represented Strindberg's wavy hair as waveforms, a motif repeated in the waveforms that adorn the border of the image. Both wave patterns conceal hidden images of naked women, one each emerging from Strindberg's wavy hair and waveform aura, suggesting a half-materialized Eros borne by the radiating medium.

Arne Eggum has noted that the waveform patterns that frame Strindberg suggest his obsession with Colonel Albert de Rochas de Aiglun's book, *Extériorisation de la sensibilité: Étude expérimentale et historique* (1895), a farrago of physiological aesthetics and spirit photography that argued that internal

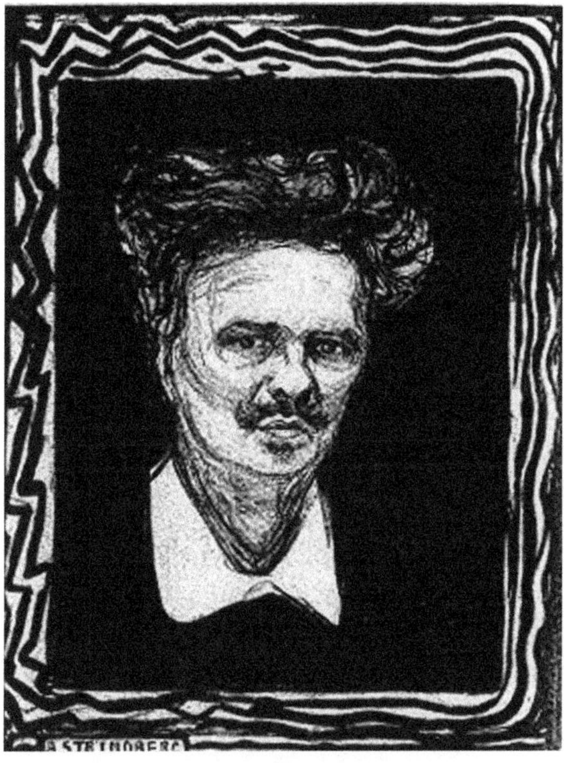

Edvard Munch, *Portrait of Strindberg*, 1896. Lithograph, composition: 19 7/8 x 14 7/8 in. (50.5 x 37.8 cm); sheet: 27 11/16 x 19 7/16 in. (70.3 x 49.4 cm). © The Munch Museum / The Munch-Ellingsen Group / SODRAC (2013).

energies—physiological and spiritual—can be "externalized" or projected beyond the human body by spirit mediums, artists, and other adepts.[78] Rochas was primarily concerned with auras and astral bodies that formed "sensible layers" (*couches sensibles*) that enveloped the body of a hypnotized subject or medium in trance states. As the notion of "exteriorized sensibility" indicates, the phenomena concerned the projection of inner sentiments or conditions toward exterior receptors, as pseudopods extruding the boundaries of the organism. The sensible layer thus appeared as a sort of extroflected inner double that enveloped the medium like a formfitted spectral garment.

Here the protoplasm discourse coalesced with a growing interest in a host of new discoveries and conjectures about infravisible physical or ethereal energies. This was a moment when even some leading scientists began to wonder openly whether new sensitive instruments like the spectrograph and new phenomena such as cathode rays, X-rays, and wireless telegraphy demonstrated that the ether represented a much wider spectrum of energies than had been hitherto imagined. A spate of books appeared in France that explored the new X-rays in conjunction with auratic photography and occult phenomena, such as E. N. Santini's *La Photographie à travers les corps opaques par rayons électriques, cathodiques et de Roentgen* (1896) and Hippolyte Baraduc's *L'Âme humaine, et méthode radiographique humaine, la force courbe cosmique: Photographies des vibrations de l'ether, lois des aura* (1897).[79] Strindberg read and discussed such work with friends, along with several others books dealing with images of auras, ods, ectoplasms, and other effluvia of the mediumistic body, such as Jean Finot's *La Photographie transcendentale*.[80] Reflecting on their conversations a few years later, Munch mused that "there must be something to Strindberg's idea of how waves that surround affect us. Perhaps we have a sort of receiver in our brain."[81]

These spontaneous images were of kindred variety to the protophotographic phenomena that fascinated Strindberg, in which matter's past survives to reproduce itself in images. Now the spirit medium herself became the medium of a special mode of "materialization," which seemed to mimic the process of photography or operate as a variant on a similar kind of image-making capacity. Withdrawing into a darkened room, the ectoplasm-producing medium, in Tom Gunning's words, "became a sort of camera, her spiritual negativity bodying forth a positive image, as the human body behaves like an uncanny photomat, dispensing images from its orifices."[82] Ectoplasmic and aural photography thus seemed to return to sort of essence of photography that Strindberg had been pursuing. The medium's body suggested an overall vision of matter as a vast system of radiating energy based on the model of protoplasm—or ether—as the conductor of light and sound waves.

Strindberg found these published investigations broadly in line with his own experimental trials in photography, and he eagerly joined the discussion. In his essay "Ueber die Lichtwirkung in der Fotografie: Betrachtungen aus Anlass der X-Strahlen" ("On the Action of Light in Photography: Reflections Occasioned by the X-Rays"), he noted he had often "not been surprised that light rays, which are said to be vibrations in the ether, cannot penetrate a door, while the notes of a piano, which are said to be merely air-waves, can penetrate a stone wall."[83] The discovery of X-rays confounded this notion, suggesting a type of light more akin to sound than normal light.

This suggested that the existing categories of physics and chemistry were inadequate, which he, Strindberg, had always assumed. Now people might be more able or willing to grasp what Strindberg had been up to in his own chemical photographic experiments: "Today, when people are amazed that X-rays require neither a camera nor a lens, it is a fitting moment for me to relate the real circumstances concerning my photographs of celestial bodies taken without a camera or lens in early spring 1894, which provoked considerable amusement at the time, and were near to ruining me, indeed perhaps did so." He reported several experiments of his own that had revealed similar kinds of luminous phenomena. The upshot of all of this, Strindberg suggested, was that the true nature of photography was not understood at all, nor was it really in question: "From having been a scientific experiment, photography has now become a game, and yet the whole process remains a mystery." Its value rested in its capacity to unmask invisibilities, give access to interiorities, or perceive an exteriorization of sensibility. For Strindberg these chemical transformations had both ontological and psychological significance. Or, in other words, photography offered the possibility of psychological experimentation through chemistry, a modern form of alchemy.

Strindberg's attempts fell within a broad fin-de-siècle movement to spiritualize the body as a means to materialize the spirit or mind. What began among as the symbolists as the impulse to "objectify the subjective" through the mechanisms of psychophysiological ideomotor principles increasingly became a quest to see material forms as vessels for spirit, ideas, and emotions. The passage of many fellow-traveling artists and scientists from the standard laboratory setups into the unconventional worlds of spiritualist séances, occultism, and psychical research followed directly from the convergence of physiological aesthetics, hysteria and hypnotism, and a new physics of unseen vibratory forces that passed through sensory thresholds that were often too subtle for human perception but could be registered by the sensitive instruments. Protoplasm, the storage medium of subtle vibrations, thus played a vital role in the experimental and conceptual systems that informed these attempts.

By 1910 the focus of these experiments intensified, with redoubled attempts by artists and scientists to discover the mechanisms of mind-to-mind—or soul-to-soul—communication in the form of empathic or even telepathic transfers of ideas and emotions in the pure formal media of lines, colors, and sounds. In the next chapter we will see how this impulse, usually described as the beginnings of modernism, extended the experimental system of physiological graphics to its ultimate expression in the new movements of abstraction in painting and poetry.

7

ART FOR LIFE'S SAKE

Kinesthesia, Empathy, and Abstraction in Early Modernism

> We may not be able to consciously comprehend an emotion that an artist
> tries to express but we can be made to feel it; artists set down those outward
> manifestations of their emotion that our body will mechanically imitate,
> however lightly, so as to place us in the indefinable psychological state that
> caused them.
>
> Henri Bergson, *Essai sur les données immédiates de la conscience* (1889)

INTO THE DEBATE OVER THE ORDER OF THE SENSES STEPPED THE BIOL-
ogist Félix Le Dantec, anarchist and friend of the artistic avant-garde, to
defend synesthesia. In several writings published just after the turn of the
century, Le Dantec maintained that in higher organisms there was a capacity—and a drive—to reunite the senses not in synesthesia per se, but in a
unification of the senses under the direction of single sense or principle. Le
Dantec's intervention ushered in a new debate among physiologists, aestheticians, and artists over the relative status of the senses—whether or
not sensory hierarchy was natural or desirable and whether or not a third
term, like *vision*, or something else, might unify fractious perceptions. That
something else soon appeared in the guise of a new "sixth" sense, called the
muscle sense, or kinesthesia: the sense of muscular tension, weight, rhythm,
motion, and orientation in space became the physiological key to the experience of making or beholding art. The "modernist" turn around 1910—the
turn toward abstraction—derived from the new fascination with kinesthesia
as the basis of both artistic creation and spectatorship.

The kinesthetic turn grew out of two decades of work in physiological aesthetics. But it also marked a change. Where Charles Henry, Gustave
Kahn, and the generation of 1886 had focused on developing the skills and

techniques of the laboratory and atelier to enhance effects of dynamogenic pleasure and inhibitory pain, the prewar avant-garde aestheticians and artists looked increasingly to the art of dance and burgeoning forms of physical culture and body techniques as a resource for cultivating artistic skills and practices. These body cultures also derived from the broader culture of experimental physiology, and they proceeded from the same utopian promise of personal and social transformation through the plasticity of living substance that had informed physiological aesthetics since its inception. The new somatic practices provided a set of valuable resources for artistic practice along the lines set in motion by physiological aesthetics, but they also anchored the new art within a wider cultural vanguard that valorized the quest for a newly disciplined and released body, with increased capacities for flexibility, efficiency, expression, and individuality. Across an increasingly varied ideological spectrum, the new art took a leading place among a variety of vehicles for elevating sensibilities and promoting mass activation.

VIVRE, C'EST VIBRER

There were different routes to the kinesthetic theory of art, but the most consequential French version passed through the vital properties of protoplasm. After a prodigious start to his career at the Institut Pasteur, investigating the nutritive physiology of protozoa, Le Dantec devoted much of his work to developing a general theory of life based on the processes of the physics and chemistry of the colloids in protoplasm.[1] Life, he contended, occurred at "roughly a half-distance" between the atomic or chemical scale of colloidal protoplasm and the scale of the mechanical individual organ.[2] Most of the critical functions of life took place out of interactions between these two scales, including the critical modes of habit taking that underwrote neo-Lamarckian doctrines of plasticity.[3] For Le Dantec the origins of aesthetics could be found in the fact that "living protoplasms, very complex colloids, are highly susceptible to imitate . . . colors and sounds." This imitation occurred, Le Dantec argued, through rhythmic movements, as well as the equilibrium maintained between "a colloid and its environment" through the "phenomenon of resonance."[4] Le Dantec's theory was intended to answer the synesthesia question posed by Max Nordau—the imitative function of the senses represented a cooperative drive to coordinate the senses to provide a complete picture of the external world. It was an anarchist vision of the senses operating through a system of mutual aid, reiterating inescapable questions of civil governance with respect to questions of aesthetics. But Le Dantec's formulation also put forward a fundamental biological doctrine of aesthetics that would shape the modernist moment as forcefully as his rival, Henri Bergson.[5]

Soon after articulating his theory of a cooperative drive in sensory physiology, Le Dantec backtracked somewhat, arguing that sensory unification in humans was fulfilled through the direction of vision, the sense with the unique capacity to largely supersede the other senses. If this was not self-evident, Le Dantec argued, the development of scientific instruments provided sufficient evidence of the inescapable primacy of vision: "The sense of vision encroaches very largely on the domains of all the other [senses] and, day by day, its efficacy grows by the invention of perfected apparatus; one can even wish that they will not arrive too late to give us a complete knowledge of the phenomena."[6] Le Dantec's prime examples were graphical recording instruments, which translated all sensory modalities into vibrations and rendered them to the eyes in graphical form. The Edison phonograph, for example, "translates in one sinuous line inscribed on its cylinder, the piece of music that one plays before it, and we know that the sinuous line suffices to integrally reproduce the piece of music."[7]

Similarly, pressure, heat, and even scent (as evidenced in a device constructed by M. Maneuvrier to determine the vintage of wine over the telephone line) could all be translated into the overarching sense modality of visuality though graphical inscription techniques, which Le Dantec liked to call "direct optics."[8] With the technical extensions of sense offered by recoding apparatus, all senses were subsumed into one, the visual. Humans could be said to have overcome the sensory compartmentalization bequeathed by evolution and effectively recovered the original protoplasmic unity of sense celebrated in the common piddock. "Science," wrote Le Dantec, "will perhaps lead us one day to know all phenomena of the world with just one of our senses; and that will truly be monism."[9] His argument effectively restated the original assumptions of Ernst Haeckel's perigenesis theory: the protoplasm served as a kind of graphical recording apparatus, a medium for the inscription of forces acting in the organic world.

Le Dantec's prophetic announcement of the hegemony of vision beautifully foretold the modernist obsession with pure opticality. Under the hege-

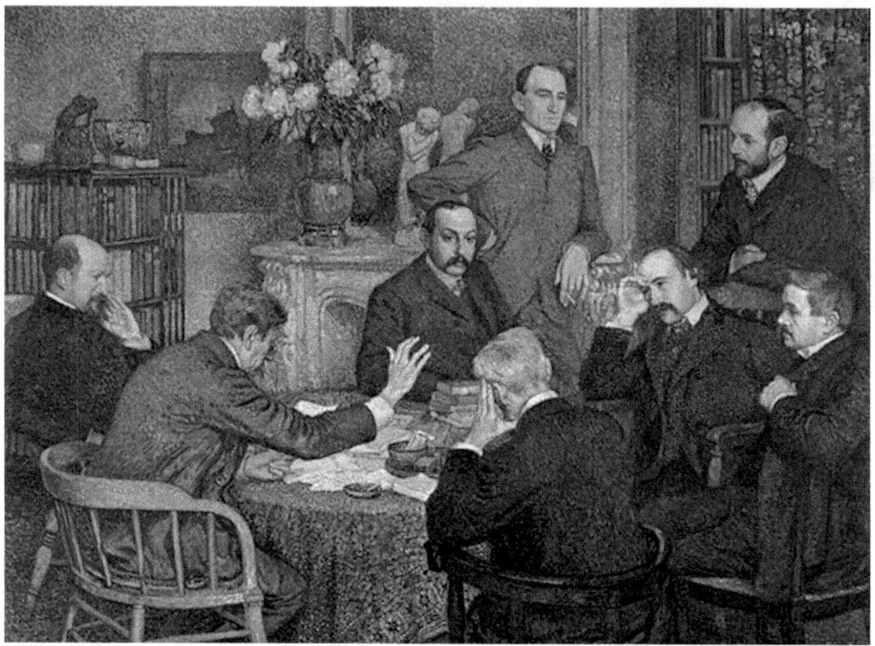

Théo Van Rysselberghe, *The Reading (La Lecture)*, 1903. Oil on canvas. Musée des Beaux-Arts, Gand.

mony of vision, the unification of the senses would enable the unification of the arts and of the sciences, respectively. In the case of science, the evolution of instrumental prosthesis was also on the verge of delivering a universal language, which would bring the end of "compartmentalized sciences."[10] Similarly, the opticalization of the arts would deflect any threat posed by the musicalization of painting or similar synesthetic projects. On the contrary, it would reinforce and facilitate the interchange of sense modalities.[11]

These ideas inspired a rich new wave of aesthetic theorizing. The most influential came from Albert Cozanet, alias Jean D'Udine, who adapted Le Dantec's notion of imitation in the colloidal protoplasm to a full-blown theory of art. Beginning with his *De la correlation des sons et des couleurs en art* (1897), D'Udine developed a theory of art as the reproduction of synesthetic waveforms on the model of the protoplasm. "Vivre, c'est vibrer," D'Udine asserted in the opening sentence of his 1910 work *L'Art et le Geste*, a work both dedicated to, and designed to unite the thought of, his teachers Le Dantec and the Swiss Émile Jaques-Dalcroze, the famous inventor of the pedagogy of modern dance. The task of D'Udine's book was to offer a "mechanical theory of artistic signs," joining Le Dantec's theory of "objective imitation" of external vibrations by colloidal compounds with Jaques-Dalcroze's ideas of "rhythmic gymnastics" (also, "eurhythmics"), in which the acoustic sensation of duration had its basis in kinesthetic memory. Life is movement, and underlying all feelings and states of mind are physiological rhythms, including those that are involuntary or hereditary. "What interests us," D'Udine wrote, "is the notion that the colloid particles that compose the human body are unified by complex relations . . ., our physiological modifications . . . by the presence of sonorous phenomena or colors . . ., rhythmic modifications at a very small scale."[12]

D'Udine argued that through the hereditary memory stored in protoplasm, a rich archive of rhythmic pulsation has been bequeathed to all organic beings. The task of the artist is to learn to access this archive through the bodily practices of each artistic medium, be it dance, painting, music, or poetry. Artistic creativity, then, involves tapping these resources and representing them in inventive combinations and sequences.

Each work of art is thus a series of signs of force, capable of stimulating a condition of recognition in the beholder or recipient of the work. Because arrangements of sounds and colors, lines and gestures, produce modifications of physiological states, they are all effectively synesthetic, although some are doubly or multiply so by virtue of the number of sense functions they engage. Yet D'Udine supported Le Dantec's claims for the hegemony of the visual sense, with its unique ability to govern and subsume the other senses. Since art is primarily a physiological phenomenon, the formal critical language of art or aesthetics should be similarly drawn from physiology, especially in its visually realized, graphical form.

D'Udine found the practical aesthetic complement to Le Dantec's doctrine in the methods of so-called eurhythmics, developed by Jaques-Dalcroze and his "College of Rhythm," based in the Dresden suburb of Hellerau and promoted by followers around Europe and North America.[13] Seeking to perfect the rhythmic sense, Dalcroze schools emphasized rhythmic gymnastics (eurhythmics) involving the entire body as the basis of all training, followed by solfège (ear training) and, finally, improvisation.[14] This progression allowed students to proceed from simple movements of the limbs to every time signature, to every note, to every beat, and ultimately, to every one of the innumerable rhythmic patterns produced in music. For D'Udine this training made accessible the primordial archive of rhythms stored within the colloidal protoplasm, thus implementing in art what Le Dantec had demonstrated in science. The Dalcroze method accomplished this, D'Udine argued, because it effectively made "gesture the basis of all synesthesia"—the unification of sense came through bodily gesture and the associated phenomena of the muscle sense.[15] If, as D'Udine insisted, every art was an imitative transcription of specific rhythms into one or another sensory modality, the Dalcroze method provided the most complete mode of general artistic training.

The most successful implementation of D'Udine's theories arrived in the work of French artist Francis Picabia, who met the aesthetician in 1909 and soon thereafter changed his style of painting.[16] While many of the so-called simultanist painters of Paris in this period breathed in the ubiquitous biological philosophy of Henri Bergson's *Creative Evolution*, Picabia drew upon the aesthetic theory of *L'Art et le geste*.[17] In a series of works initiated in 1913, just after returning from a voyage to New York, Picabia realized on canvas D'Udine's theories. During his stay in the American metropolis, Picabia remarked on the dizzying array of sensations generated by New World modernity: the crowds, the immense vertical architecture, the electrically illuminated night, the Babel-like language-scape of "all tongues of the world" merging in a great chorus.[18] In New York Picabia thus found the themes of his European artistic comrades magnified to unprecedented scale: the futurists' ecstasies of technological force and speed, the simultanists' fascination with the mind's grasp of an infinity of interrelated states of being.[19] In interviews Picabia stated repeatedly that in the face of these modern realities the painter's task was not to optically render the directly observed world, but to allow the sensations to condense into memories that would eventually provide material for artistic creation.

The "Udnie" paintings are entitled with an anagram of D'Udine, the pen name of Picabia's friend and theoretical inspiration, Albert Cozanet. The anagram, especially as used in the title of the painting *I See Again in My Memory My Dear Udnie*, underscored D'Udine's notion of artistic creation as an imaginative combinatorics of affective and aesthetic signs drawn from personal and organic memory. The personal memory was probably of a Polish dancer whom Picabia met on the ship to New York, although some have

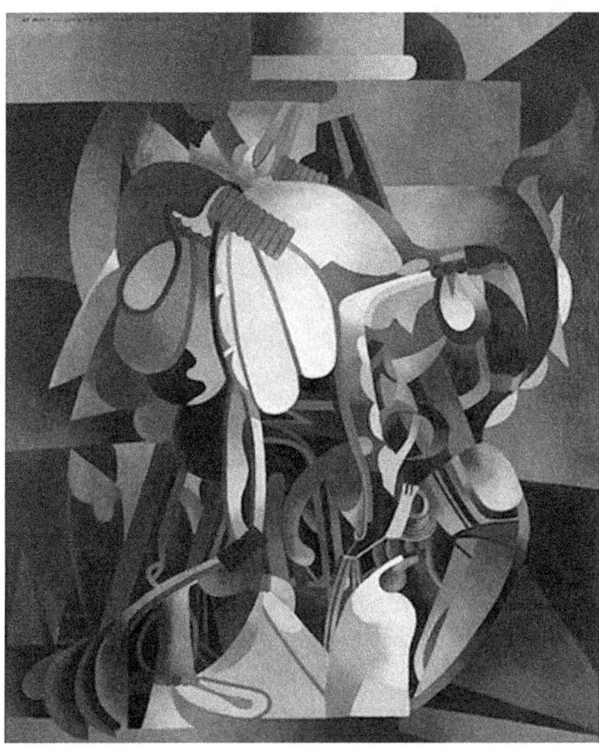

Francis Picabia, *I See Again in My Memory My Dear Udnie*, 1914, possibly begun 1913. Oil on canvas, 8 ft. 2 1/2 in. x 6 ft. 61/4 in. (250.2 x 198.8 cm). © Estate of Francis Picabia / SODRAC (2013).

suggested that it referred to Isadora Duncan, whose tragic death occurred around the time Picabia was in America. Rather than a literal reference to one or the other, Picabia probably brought several memories together to demonstrate the overdetermination of meanings that can be generated by the kind of combinatoric invention championed by D'Udine.

Some later remarks of the poet Gertrude Stein regarding the paintings of Picabia during this period tend to confirm the theoretical orientation of D'Udine: "Picabia had conceived and is struggling with the problem that a line should have the vibration of a musical sound and that this vibration should be the result of conceiving the human form . . . in so tenuous a fashion that it would induce vibration in the line forming it. It is his way of achieving the disembodied."[20] Stein explained that "the emotion of the object" creates a vibration that determines the character of the line.[21] In 1913 Picabia was reported to have said that he was attempting to represent "the emotion produced in our minds by things," remarks very close to those of Stein, who became a close friend many years later. Elsewhere Picabia spoke similarly of the analogy between painting and music, claiming that if a musician is inspired by a landscape, rather than describe it, "he expresses it in sound waves, he translates it into an expression of the impression, the mood. And as there are absolute sound waves, so there are absolute waves of color and form."[22]

These ideas were reinforced by the method of composition that Picabia developed for the New York paintings. He first improvised a linear structure based on an idea from memory, for example, of a dancer or, in another work, of African American singers in a Harlem church. The lines captured the remembered experience as form, energy, and emotion, rather than suggesting a particular grouping or scene (as he had previously done as an impressionist painter). Once the linear structure was in place, Picabia then began to improvise around it, building a composition out of form and color, which he believed could embody inner experience without recourse to the sphere of verbal consciousness. The improvisation proceeded by either affirming the areas bounded by the line, or breaking it down by continuing a color over a boundary, or fading one plane into the next. Picabia probably learned these techniques from his friends among the cubist painters, like Marcel Duchamp, but in his hands they served his distinctive idea of the self-generating evolution of a painting out of the phylogenetic and personal archive of organic memory. It was the painter's method of realizing what D'Udine called imagination: "the faculty of creating new rhythms through the combination of rhythms previously recorded."[23] These were an artist's rendering of the myriad interrelated rates of physiological time through which Étienne-Jules Marey sought to understand the organism.

Picabia's painting technique hewed closely to the Dalcroze method in dance, as well as D'Udine's generalization of it to a larger aesthetic principle. The emergence of dance as a key modernist art form around 1900 owed much to physiological aesthetics. For much of the nineteenth century, physiologists had been fascinated by phenomena variously known as inner sense, organic, and visceral sensibility, which referred to those unclassifiable sensations that could not be traced accurately to one of the five known sense organs. By late in the century, these phenomena became linked with the original undifferentiated sensations of protoplasm. Close to these sensations were the phenomena of muscle sense, or kinesthesia (eventually best known

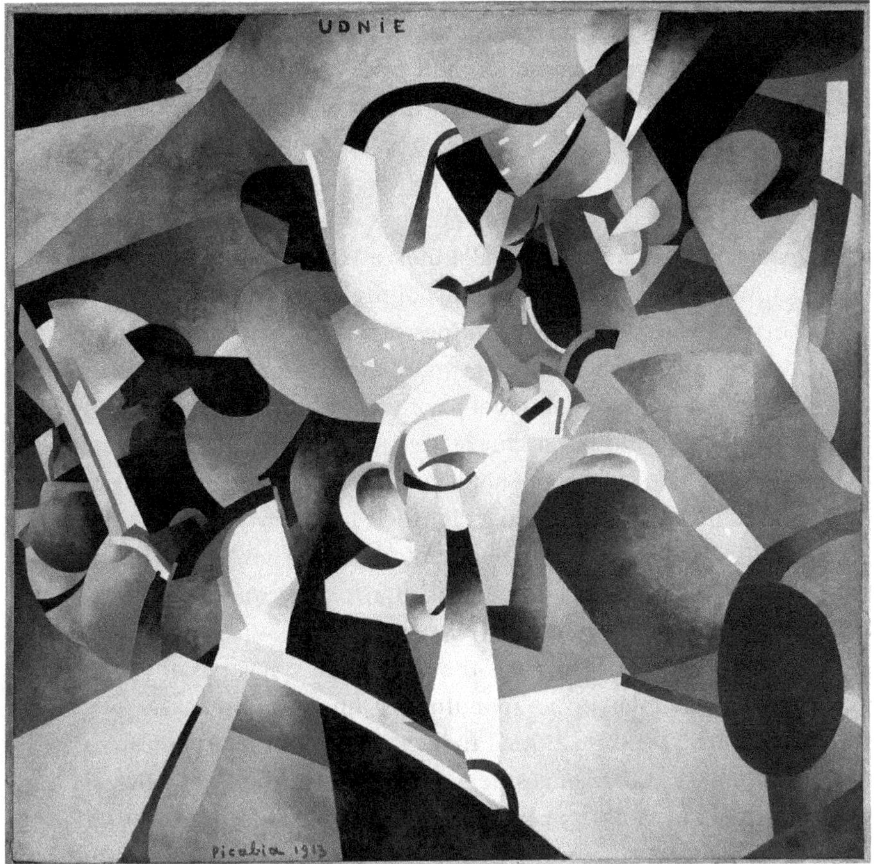

Francis Picabia, *Udnie (Young American Girl: Dance)*, 1913. 300 x 300 cm. Musée national d'art moderne, Paris. © Estate of Francis Picabia / SODRAC (2013).

as proprioception): the sense of movement, balance; the sense of weight and resistance to the force of gravity, which give the body its sense of orientation in space. Contemporary physiologists argued that kinesthetic sense emanated from the periphery of the body and communicated to a movement center in the brain located in the same area as the sense of touch.[24] Proponents of kinesthesia argued that its origins in peripheral sensation challenged the centralizing hypothesis of motor movement as resulting from a discharge of efferent energy from the brain, usually through an act of will.[25]

Kinesthesia acquired the status of the "sixth sense" because of the ability of muscles to receive sensation and carry out movements, a sentience comparable to the ear and eye. The primacy of dance grew from the idea that kinesthetic awareness functioned as a kind of primordial cognition, a touchstone for the unification of the differentiated senses and their corresponding special arts, like painting or music. Eurhythmic exercises became a touchstone for arts pedagogy of all kinds: a key to finding the thread of the *Gesamtkunstwerk* within the constraints of the specific arts.

In D'Udine's aesthetic theory, kinesthesia was represented by the primacy of the sense of touch as the primordial basis for the unification of the senses: "The sense of touch functions with us each time that life or a work of art interests one or another of our other senses, even when these appear to us impressed by the sensible phenomenon in isolation."[26] Touch was the educator of the other senses, the model for their function, much like the model developed in Raphaël Du Bois's notion of "touch-vision." D'Udine's term for the sense of touch in the automatisms of art was *gesture*. D'Udine situated this expanded sense of touch at the center of the synesthetic function in the arts, asserting that "gesture is the basis of all synesthesia."[27] It followed that dance should take a correspondingly prime position as the touchstone for all other arts. D'Udine argued that this order of the arts recapitulated a long evolutionary course of aesthetic education. In the beginning, the simple movements of walking gave rise to the acoustic sense of duration, to rhythms, cadences. Then music, which was "able to find in our muscular sensations the notions of duration that served as its primordial element,"

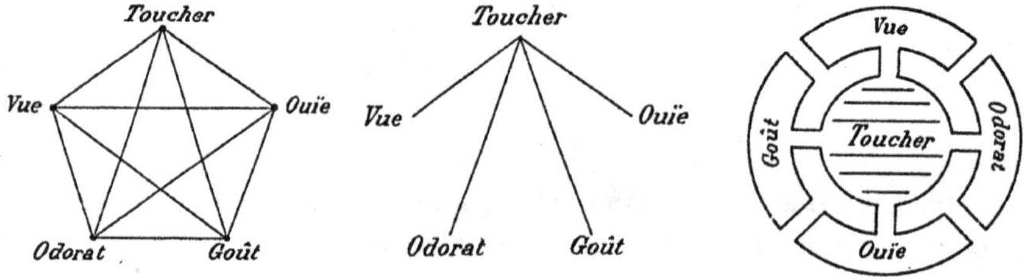

Diagram of the place of touch in the sensorium. From Jean D'Udine, *L'Art et le geste* (Paris: F. Alcan, 1910).

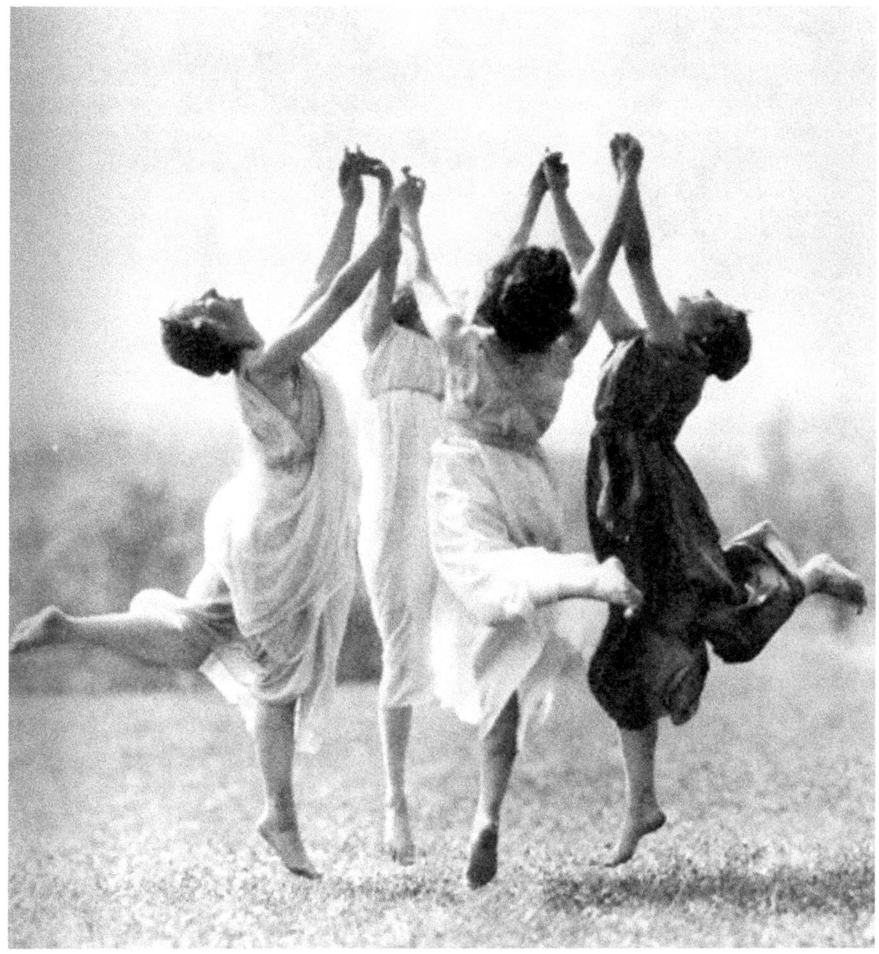

Dalcroze eurhythmic dance exercise. From M. E. Sadler, ed., *The Eurhythmics of Jacques-Dalcroze* (London: Constable & Co., 1912).

was born "of bodily movements accomplished by the first representatives of our species."[28]

Following this aesthetic theory, the challenge for the painter was to give tactile values to retinal impressions. Dance thus figured as the constant theme of Picabia's paintings in these years. Among the New York paintings, besides *Udnie (Young American Girl: Dance)*, dance appeared in *Edtaon-*

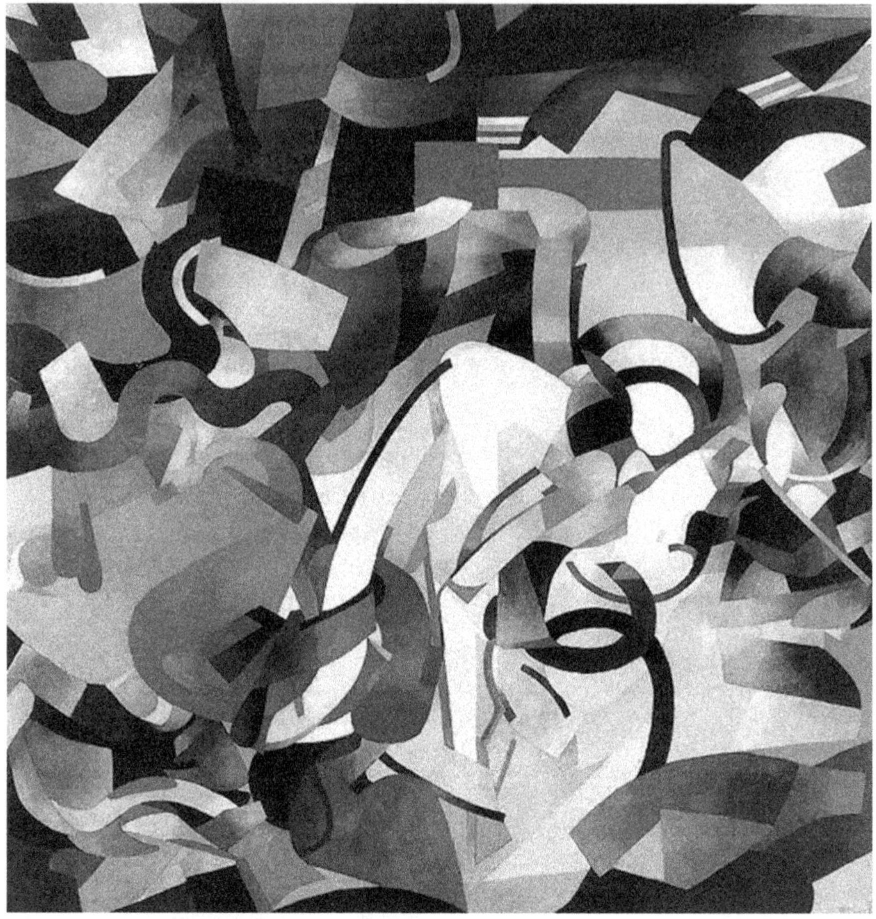

Francis Picabia, *Edtaonisl (Ecclésiastique)*, 1913. Oil on canvas. © Estate of Francis Picabia / SODRAC (2013).

isl (Ecclésiastique), whose title was an abbreviated anagram for *étoile danseuse* (star dancer) and subtitle conjured the painter's amused recollection of the dancer performing before a portly Dominican priest. Besides the obvious contrasts of secular eroticized entertainment and traditional religious asceticism, the amusement deepens when one remembers that, according to D'Udine's theory, the very purpose of art was to excite the memory of the affective rhythms in the observer through the microprocesses of inner imitation, or what German theorists called empathy (*Einfühlung*).[29] Picabia's canvas would thus suggest the awakening of the memory of the pulsating spirit within the cleric, a sense of life awakening within.

More generally, and even in secular observers, the dance paintings aimed to provoke kinesthetic self-awareness by calling attention to our orientation in space, using techniques such as posing movements that develop in different directions at different speeds, flouting the principle of gravity. In *Culture physique* (1913), for example, Picabia made ribbonlike forms coil over one another while refusing any focus or point of rest and effacing any distinction between form and space. These forms jolt the viewer out of passive viewing by provoking adjustments to his or her body in an attempt regain equilibrium. The "physical culture" of the title might therefore refer to the actions of the spectator, whose response to the painting increases vitality, beauty, health, and harmony. But the title might also call attention to what had become a fundamental convergence between this new mode of art and the new physical or body cultures, as exercises in regulating the body through rhythm or even achieving heightened function through training the muscles and nervous system. Modernist art *is* physical culture, the title might suggest, and vice versa, with a shared aim of achieving superior bodily control and, at its most utopian, of emancipating a new creative spirit of improvisation in all who participate in it.

RHYTHM AND ABSTRACTION IN VERSE: ONOMATOPOEIA AND THE FUTURIST MOMENT

A similar turn occurred in the arts of poetry and versification, as a sacralized Wagnerian poetics gave way to a dithyrambic modernism rooted in cabaret culture and based on imitative contagions of speech and gestural tics simulating hystero-epileptic bodies out of control. It was here that F. T. Marinetti, long before his fame as the proclaimer of futurism, made his literary debut, after his friend and patron Gustave Kahn secured him a literary prize in 1898 and arranged to have his award-winning poem recited by Sarah Bernhardt at the Théâtre de Odéon.[30] Although Marinetti found Bernhardt's rendering of his verse "a little monotonous due to her usual way of reciting alexandrines," the young poet took up the declamatory art with passion, touring regularly over the next decade in the cabaret circuits of both France and Italy, later proclaiming the variety theater and its "body madness" the birthplace and true home of futurism.[31]

In 1909, after a decade of working as a touring cabaret poet and anarchist troublemaker, Marinetti unleashed the battle cry of futurism, publishing the "Foundation and Manifesto of Futurism" in newspapers across Europe.[32] He also published the manifesto in a combined book edition with the *Enquête internationale sur le vers libre*, a survey of the state of free verse poetry that both canonized it as a critical avant-garde movement and signaled its supersession by futurism. The timing of the joint publication, in part due to delays resulting from Marinetti's automobile accident in 1908, has seldom been noted, but it provided a symbolic torch-passing gesture within the avant-garde.

One of the overriding lessons of the *Enquête* was that the French crisis in verse had become international and therefore universal in its implications for poetry. Although quarrels over vers libre remained, there was widespread agreement that rhythm remained essential to it, and to all future poetry. In later manifestos Marinetti promoted his futurist poetic doctrines as an evolutionary transformation of vers libre into a radicalization of the rhythmic imperative, paring vocal rhythm down to its atomistic essence and embedding it in a full-fledged performance sound art perfectly suited to the futurist variety theater.[33] While his futurist verse technique, *parole in libertà*, broke all ties with symbolist atmospherics—"moonlight" banished, epicene bodies pummeled with brass knuckles, "ritual pomp" killed off whenever it was found—it radicalized the phonetic and psychophysiological conceptions of vers libre, leaving only "art, this extension of the jungle of our veins that pours from our bodies into the infinity of space and time."[34]

In the "Technical Manifesto of Futurist Literature," Marinetti announced with his usual bombast, "In an airplane, sitting on the fuel tank, my belly warmed by the head of the pilot, I realized the utter folly of the antique syntax we have inherited from Homer. A furious need to liberate words, dragging them free of the prison of the Latin sentence!"[35] Marinetti's sky-born experience of dynamic balance and torsion revealed that words could be subjected to the same kinesthetic forces as the bodily gestures of dancers and painters.

The destruction of the supports of the Latin sentence had of course been more or less the project of the *verslibristes*. But now the radical poets of 1886 appeared still too imbued with the antique rules of prosody, despite having

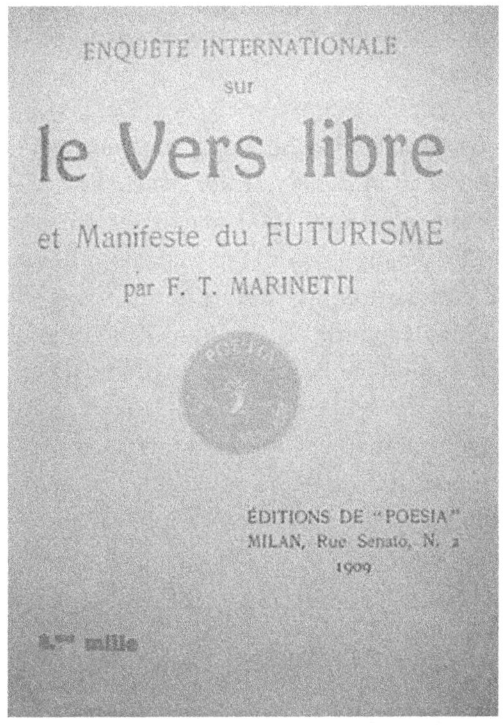

Cover of *Enquête internationale sur le vers libre et Manifeste du futurisme*, edited by F. T. Marinetti (Milan: Éditions de "Poesia," 1909).

delivered a mighty blow to meter and syllabism. "There have been a thousand reasons for the existence of free verse, but now its destiny is to be replaced by words-in-freedom," proclaimed Marinetti.[36] Where vers libre had destroyed the conventions of meter and elevated rhythm and the affective features of voice as the vehicles of meaning, parole in libertà sought to smash the last stifling supports of signification in grammar and syntax maintained by the verslibristes. "As poetry and sensibility have evolved," Marinetti charged, "two irremediable defects of free verse have become apparent":

1. Free Verse fatally urges the poet toward facile, sonorous effects, transparent tricks with mirrors, monotonous cadences, a ridiculous clanging of bells and the predictable ripostes of internal and external echoes.

2. Free Verse artificially channels the flow of lyrical emotion between the great walls of syntax and the locks of grammar. Free, intuitive inspiration, which is directed straight at the intuition of the ideal reader,

thus finds itself pent up and distributed, like drinking water, to slake the thirst of all obstinate, finicky intellects.[37]

Syntax had been the last refuge for some symbolists, most famously Mallarmé, who wrote, "What pivot, I understand, in these contrasts, for intelligibility? There must be a guarantee—Syntax."[38] Marinetti rejected this, proclaiming that poets must no longer arrange "words syntactically prior to hurling them forth."[39] Besides the elimination of syntax, the futurist poet should also jettison all other remaining supports of the traditional Latinate sentence: articles, pronouns, prepositions, conjunctions, auxiliary verbs, even punctuation.

But how to cultivate futurist inspiration and intuition? Marinetti imagined the futurist poet as an ordinary lyrical temperament, who would emerge spontaneously after finding himself in an "area of intensified life (revolution, war, shipwreck, earthquake, etc.)," and would instinctively compose in the futurist manner.

> He will begin by brutally destroying syntax as he talks. He won't waste time building sentences. He won't give a damn about punctuation and finding adjectives. He will ignore linguistic subtleties and nuances, and in his haste he will breathlessly fling his visual, auditory, and olfactory impressions at your nerve ends, precisely as they strike him. The vehemence of his emotional steam will burst the conduits of the sentence, the valves of punctuation, and the adjustable bolts of adjectivation. Handfuls of essential words in no conventional order. The sole purpose of the narrator is to convey all the vibrations of his being.[40]

In Marinetti's telling, the transition from vers libre to parole in libertà unfolded less from deliberation than from the necessities of communicating under the extreme conditions of modernity. While the technique of free verse might have sufficed in 1886, the newer material collisions of everyday life produced a different soundscape and a different sensorium, and therefore entailed a different poetics. Marinetti understood the innovations of vers libre as part of an incipient industrialization of language. Parole in libertà would further this process by eliminating frictions and introducing new efficiencies into prosody.

The key concept was onomatopoeia, which thoroughly collapsed sound and meaning and accelerated the velocity of verbal communication.

> Our growing love for matter, the will to penetrate it and to know its vibrations, the physical bonds that tie us to machines, urge us to THE USE OF ONOMATOPOEIA. Sound, which results from the rubbing together or the collision of solids, liquids, or gases at speed, requires that onomatopoeia, the reproduction of sound, be one of the most dynamic elements in poetry. And as such, onomatopoeia can take the place of the verb in the infinitive, particularly if it is set against one or more other onomatopoeias. (E.g., the onomatopoeic tatatata of machine guns opposing the urrraaaah of the Turks . . .) The brevity of the onomatopoeic words in this case allows us the use of the most versatile interweaving of rhythms.[41]

Onomatopoeia produced efficiencies by condensing phonic units to their smallest dimensions, allowing the emergence of a recombinant phonetics in which "our lyrical intensity must be free to dismantle and remake words, cutting them in half, extending and reinforcing their centers or their extremities, increasing or reducing the number of their vowels and consonants."[42] Such basic phonetic units would better realize the desideratum of an acoustic art organized around the subrhythms of the voice and organs of phonation.

Marinetti's doctrine of onomatopoeia fused a Bergsonian notion of musical suggestion or empathy with the modern soundscape. Since the symbolist moment of 1886, the two-way street of ideomotor theory and related doctrines of imitation and suggestion had entrenched themselves in the performance cultures of French and Italian cabaret, where machinelike tics of language and gesture became the vernacular representations of unconscious automatism. For the futurist narrator who sought "to communicate all of the vibrations of his being," the two-way street was now crowded with "an unending exchange of intuitions, rhythms, instincts, and metallic discipline," resulting in motorcars, airplanes, phonographs without, and a new technical sensorium within.[43] Hence Marinetti's boisterous claim in his "Technical Manifesto of Futurist Literature" that dictation taken from the propeller of his soaring biplane suggested that Homeric syntax be replaced with found sound.[44]

Onomatopoeia emerged as the unavoidable medium of dictation from the technological soundscape. Following the laws of onomatopoeia, the material body of the word mimicked the essence of the referent—this was the passage through the door opened by the phonetic investigations of the vers-slibristes. Phonic shards would gain meaning by blending with the "onomatopoeic orchestration or compendium of noises." Marinetti then passed to the next stage: hearing the sound drew the auditor into visceral union with the phoneme, with the object presented under the form of the word. Such a poetic soundscape would offer the possibility of reaching a "psychic onomatopoeic orchestration, the resonant yet abstract expression of an emotion or of pure thought."[45] With all extraneous elements stripped away, the power of an acoustic art was all that was left, kinships of assonance or alliteration coming together or apart, binding the sentient listener to the material field of language voiced aloud; in Marinetti's words, "the lyrical continuation and transfiguration of our animal magnetism," a vast undifferentiated aural expanse "spreading itself in universal vibration" and dissolving the self empathically within it.[46]

Marinetti found his muse in the Battle of Adrianople in the first Balkan War (1912–13), where the clamor of "onomatopoeic artillery" enabled him to transmute flying shrapnel into the hurling phonic shards of the poem *Zang tumb tumb*. He reported that he "finished that short synthesizing noise-making poem while witnessing the machine-gunning of three thousand horses ordered by the Turkish general"—the image of nineteenth-century horses annihilated by twentieth-century machines building an exact analogy to the effects of his own lyric. *Zang tumb tumb* took oral recitation far beyond the comparatively stuffy theatricality of the Parisian Samedis populaires, where Marinetti got his start some fifteen years earlier.[47] Wyndham Lewis attended a performance in London, listening in "astonishment at what Marinetti could do with his unaided voice."[48] Lewis recalled that "even at the front, when bullets whistled around him, he had never encountered such a terrifying volume of noise as Marinetti produced."[49] Marinetti's own description, from his "Dynamic, Multichanneled Recitation" (1916), gave some idea of what Lewis meant.

I recited several passages from my Zang Tumb Tumb: Adrianopoli in a dynamic and multichanneled fashion. On the table, arranged in front of me, I had a telephone, some boards, and the right sort of hammers so that I could act out the orders of the Turkish general and the sounds of rifle and machine-gun fire.

. . . My audience, continually turning so as to follow all of my movements, was utterly enthralled, their bodies alight with emotion at the violent effects of the battle described by my Words-in-Freedom.

. . .

The growing interest of the English audience turned into frenzied enthusiasm when I arrived at the peak of my dynamic performance, alternating the Bulgarian song "Sciumi Maritza" with my dazzling images and the rumble of the onomatopoeic artillery.[50]

The onomatopoeic clamor had varying effects on Marinetti's auditors who heard his performances across Europe. The war correspondent Harry Nevinson remarked that he had "heard many recitations and [had] tried to describe many battles. But listen to Marinetti's recitation of one of his battles scenes and . . . the noise, the confusion, the surprise of death, the terror and courage, the shouting, curses, blood, and agony—all were recalled by that amazing succession of words, performed or enacted by the poet with such passion and abandonment that no one could escape the spell of listening."[51]

Some of the most astute critics of Marinetti attacked the artistic validity of sympathetic experience through sound. After hearing Marinetti perform in London, the English critic Henry Newbolt bristled at vocal "mimicry" and the futurist's use of imitative sound and the physical sympathy ("nervous excitement") it induced in the auditor.

But whereas [Marinetti] mimics and declaims, the [proper] poet does something quite different. The poet changes the water of experience into the wine of emotion, not by the tones of his voice, but by the magic of ordered language. He does not give you the elements of matter and nervous excitement for you to make of them what you can; he gives you his own intuition already made, his own world already created, and so created as to exist externally, when the vibrations of the voice have long since passed into silence. The power of the Futurist . . . is gramophonic, and it has the limitations of the gramophone.[52]

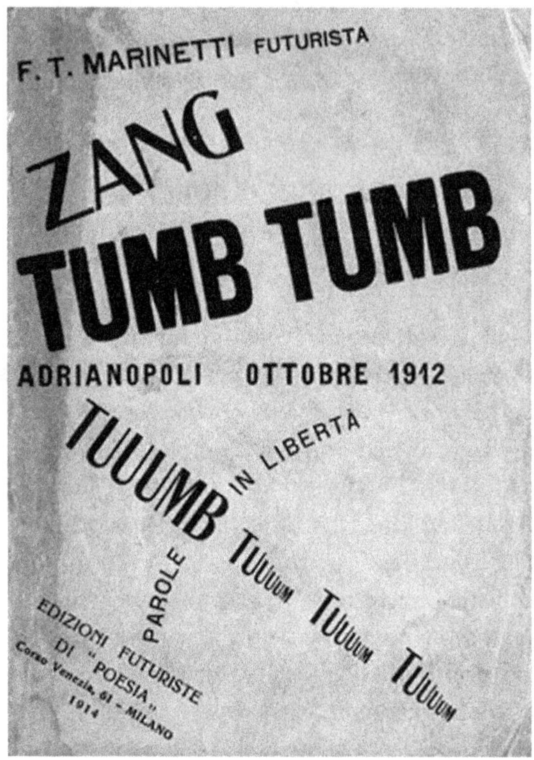

Cover of F. T. Marinetti, *Zang Tumb Tumb* (Milan, 1914).

Newbolt's charge of a "gramophonic" art shot through Marinetti's aesthetics and struck verslibrisme, an art invented in the image of the graphical recording of sound. The question came down to "intuition," or what happened between receiving the vibrations from the soundscape and the "imitative" repetition in the vocal performance. For Marinetti, the poet was the figure who underwent transformation in that moment, whose very "I" became reprogrammed by the propeller's whirl, so that there was no question of mere repetition or the "already made," but something new and evolved.

THE PERSONAL BOOMBOOM COLLECTIVE: ZURICH DADA

The sensory realignment of eye and ear was as political as it was epistemological. It resonated with the artists gathered in Zurich's Cabaret Voltaire, soon to be called Dadaists, who recognized the *anarchisante* political aesthetics of Marinetti's work yet utterly rejected its militarism and nationalism.[53] As Hugo Ball, the group's artistic leader, wrote, the very idea of Dada sound poetry began with Marinetti.

> With the sentence having given way to the word, the circle around Marinetti began resolutely with parole in libertà. They took the word out of the sentence frame (the world image) that had been thoughtlessly and automatically assigned to it, nourished the emaciated big-city vocables with light and air, and gave them back their warmth, emotion, and their original untroubled freedom. We others went a step further. We tried to give the isolated vocables the fullness of an oath, the glow of a star. And curiously enough, the magically inspired vocables conceived and gave birth to a new sentence that was not limited and confined by any conventional meaning.[54]

In the "Das erste dadaistische Manifest" (1916), Ball wrote that he wanted "no words that others have invented." This was a problem, of course, since "all words have been invented by others. I would like to add my own nonsense, my own rhythm and vowels and consonants that correspond to it. If these oscillations are seven yards long, then I want to rightly put forth words that are seven yards long. . . . Then one can really see how articulated language comes into being. . . . I want to have the Word where it ends and where it begins."[55] Rhythm here precedes language, measures its coming and going, and persists after it.

Ball regarded modern language as corrupted, but the redemption of European culture might be found in a deeper rhythm. "Our debates," he wrote, "are a burning search . . . for the specific rhythm and the buried face of this age . . . for the possibility of its being stirred, its awakening. Art is only an occasion for that, a method."[56] Ball and his Zurich Dada comrades looked to the cabaret as the experimental generator of regenerative rhythms, much like the Parisian poets Andre Spire and Robert de Souza.

Before coming to wartime Zurich, Ball had lived and studied in Munich, where he imbibed the particular blend of physiological aesthetics and avant-garde practice that flourished there.[57] From 1906 to 1910 he studied at the University of Munich, attending the lectures of Theodor Lipps on empathy and aesthetics, while writing a dissertation on Nietzsche. After 1910 Ball abandoned the university to study theater full-time, and he developed a fascination with the Dalcroze method of eurhythmic movements, which led him to visit the Dalcroze Institute in the garden city of Hellerau, outside of Dresden.[58] There he immersed himself in the kinesthetic movement arts, which valorized the special *Kennen* of the muscle sense over the conventional *Wissen* of cognition and language.

During his Munich years Ball also became friends with Wassily Kandinsky, with whom he had begun several collaborations before Germany declared war on Russia and Kandinsky was forced to return home.[59] Kandinsky published an essay on stage composition in *Der Blaue Reiter* in 1912, about the time he met Ball, in which he refined the ideas published the previous year in his text *Concerning the Spiritual in Art*.[60] In the earlier essay he argued that an artist must approach all types of artistic expression as different forms of bodily motion.[61] In the newer work on stage composition, he took the perspective of the spectator, in whom the artwork elicits "a vibration of the soul." The goal of any artistic medium is one of producing a "certain complex of vibrations." The dramatic work of art, he insisted, takes place neither on the stage nor in the script, but arises anew in every moment "out of the complex of inner experiences (soul vibrations) of the viewer."[62]

In Zurich, Ball and his associates at the Cabaret Voltaire collaborated with eurhythmatist and choreographer Rudolf Laban, who had also decamped from Munich after the outbreak of war.[63] Laban's choreography, known variously as *Freitanz*, *Ausdruckstanz*, or simply *Bewegungskunst*, broke down the dancer's bodily habits with spontaneous and counterintuitive movements. The larger aim was to increase sensitivity to new spatial rhythms and ultimately reconfigure the body's ambulatory systems of expression. Each new sensation of spatial rhythm generated a new sense of felt vibrations on the part of the performers and audience alike and opened new unanticipated physiological pathways of expression.

In the summer of 1916 Ball and company began to experiment with interactions between bodily movements and sound gestures in a semi-improvisational recitation of poetic script. Marinetti's onomatopoeic sound art showed the way to fashion the voice into an instrument that would reverberate through the tissues of performers and audience alike.

Abstract dancers: a gong beat is enough to stimulate the dancer's body to make the most fantastic movements. The dance has become an end in itself. The nervous system exhausts all the vibrations of sound, and perhaps all the hidden emotions of the gong beater too, and turns them into an image. Here, in this special case, a poetic sequence of sounds was enough to make each of the individual word particles produce the strangest visible effect on the hundred-jointed body of the dancer . . . a dance full of flashes and edges, full of dazzling light and penetrating intensity.[64]

Vibratory intensities would serve as the medium that would bind the performers and audience together. The Zurich Dadaists aimed to forge a social collective bound in felt vibrations of elemental rhythm, in shared experiences of gestures, noise and expressive movements that filled the performance space of the Cabaret Voltaire. More than simply a mode of social criticism, the energies of performance would forge a psychophysiological counterexample to the warmongers and their public supporters, honest and free of the illusions that supported the mechanical slaughter at the front. "To be demanding and cruel," wrote Tristan Tzara, "pure and honest towards the work one is preparing and which will be situating amongst men, new organisms, creations that live in the very bones of light in the imaginative focus that action will take—(REALITY)."[65]

In keeping with the experimental phoneticists' interest in vowels as bearers of communal synchronization, the Zurich Dadaists experimented obsessively with vowels and the coordination of different tonalities, extended utterance, and liaisons of vowel sounds into sound poems of varying sonorities. Early experiments in vowel combinations soon resulted in performances of phonetic poems Ball famously called *Verse ohne Worte* or *Lautgedichte*, notably the six-poem cycle "Gadji Beri Bimba." In this work Ball composed phonetic sequences in which the vowels were weighed and distributed solely according to the values of the beginning sequence.

gadji beri bimba glandridi lauli lonnii cadori
gadjama gramma berida bimbala glandri galassassa laulitalomini[66]

In these lines he conveyed the physical substance of sound, sound as guttural rumblings, sound as voice, generated by lungs, larynx, vocal chords, tongue, and lips, producing sudden trills and sibilations. Ball regarded these phonetic sequences as "abstract" (he was thinking of Kandinsky's recent work) and left it to the listener to grasp the cohesion offered through the rhythmicity and repetition of sounds. But unlike with the auditory blast of Marinetti's shows, the hearer of an oral performance of Ball's pieces is invariably prompted to repeat the sounds inwardly and to find through the inner rhythm of one's own subvocalizations, what Ball's comrade Tzara called one's "personal boomboom."[67]

Futurist and Dadaist vocal arts effectively finished the job launched by the symbolist *verslibristes* in 1886, eradicating all remaining conventions in verse, collapsing all meaning into the properties of sound, removing all fetters holding back the staging of the raw, naked, amplified human sensorium. But they also intervened in a European colloquy on political aesthetics that arose after 1910, having been shaped by the physiological turn in aesthetics and *verslibrisme* in particular. The 1886 French avant-garde's quest for social and political transformation, by means of a sentience transformed by new forms of art, had finally begun to be realized. But the question of what sort of civil governance was desirable, what ideas of political servitude and mastery were suggested by the new art, led to increasing divergences in preference for the physiology of ear or eye, respectively. In the French context one marker of the turn came from the pen of Remy de Gourmont, medievalizing symbolist and verslibriste protégé of Gustave Kahn and *La Vogue*, who by 1899 had begun to turn the arguments of vers libre into a case for aristocratic supremacy. Gourmont shared the assumption that "the true problem of style is a question of physiology," but which physiology, and to what end?[68]

Gourmont agreed that the voice and the ear, and indeed oral tradition, produced a rhapsodic bonding. But these were plebian senses, capable of empathic merging and unable to think, and therefore insufficient to lead or direct popular poetry. Gourmont wrote in his 1905 essay, "Le Vers populaire," that the voice and ear highlight the worst sense of musicality, in which the plebian mind, a veritable sensorium of acoustic impressions, shows its deformation in ways that illustrate the ear's intellectual inferiority to the eye. Popular poetry draws together in one sound vowels that are normally separate and introduces "deformities demanded by assonance." Only the eye can provide the necessary kind of distance and discrimination, among the senses and in politics.[69]

These ideas were echoed by numerous French thinkers, such as Julien Benda, who acknowledged that "the sensations of hearing . . . cause vibration in a nervous system connected with a vital organism which lies deeper than that affected by sensations of sight."[70] Yet this musicality only made hearing a birthright for the lower, "plebian" orders, which Benda contrasted with the visual or plastic sensibility of an antique aristocracy. European thinkers from Wilhelm Worringer and José Ortega y Gasset to Wyndham Lewis and Ezra Pound voiced similar ideas, with an insistent demand for political and social hierarchy rooted in a ranking of the senses. Against these calls the futurist and Dadaist performance arts appeared to have radicalized the 1886 imperatives of vers libre in order to preserve them, both as formal innovations and as the "social science" they were created to advance. To side with the oral and aural meant advocating *performance* against the operations of the eye. *Zang tumb tumb* and *gadji beri bimba* were the last anarchist battle cries against the burgeoning dictatorial ocular politics of modernism.

CONCLUSION

OVER THE COURSE OF THE EUROPEAN FIN DE SIÈCLE, EXPERIMENTAL physiology served as the key resource for innovation in the arts. Beginning in the late 1870s, physiologists and anthropologists put the role of sensory order and hierarchy in the public *sensus communis* on the table, and scientists, aestheticians, painters, and poets took up the issue with activist intentions, turning their crafts into experimental systems that might generate new modes of experience and new ways to synchronize sensibilities and shape social order. As we have seen, these attempts involved a variety of questions, from exaltations of the evolutionarily primitive senses of touch and olfaction, to synesthetic ecstasies, to explorations of the attunements of kinesthetic sense, to a rhythmic ordering of aesthetic experience. By the eve of the First World War, artwork became a mode of engineering sensory and pulsatile life, a means of intensifying the plasticity of the senses and the malleability of somatic functions.

But the project would not last. As it did with so many things, the First World War altered the course of modernism in the arts and sciences. The upheaval of the conflict dispersed people and things—networks disintegrated, and sensibilities changed. In *Belphégor* (1918), an influential expression of the changing sensibility, the French philosopher and critic Julien Benda took aim at what he described as the total domination of physiological aesthetics.[1] "Contemporary French society," he wrote, "demands that all works of art should arouse emotion and sensation: it insists that art shall cease to provide any form of intellectual pleasure."[2] Benda then systematically identified and challenged every element of the "worship of a curiously abstract idea of pure affectivity in the arts" associated with physiological aesthetics: the demand that art arouse sympathy (empathy) and emotion, even a mystic union between beholder and object, and that it achieve this through a plasticity and musicality of thought, typically achieved by intermixing the poised, form-giving senses of sight and touch with the diffuse, disintegrative sensations of smell, hearing, and taste. Everywhere, Benda complained, art was associated with the vital urge, essentially unconscious and devoid of understanding, which by dilation and expansion became aware of itself and capable of reflection on its object. Benda identified the most profound problem as "this desire that art shall be life itself, and not a picture which some intelligence paints of life."[3]

> The cult of our contemporaries for elementary life, their contempt for life that has evolved, appears not merely in their aesthetic. In their views on the living world, in their biological philosophy the only form of life that interests them is obviously elementary life, protoplasmic life; it is to this life alone—so exclusively that they do not even believe it necessary to warn us—that all their definitions of life apply (incessant change of direction, incommensurability with the idea, etc.); life that seeks to pass beyond this moment, to stabilize what is changeable, to solidify what is liquescent . . . ; this has no interest for them, in fact it is a defection from life, a return to inert matter.[4]

Benda regarded this conflation of art and life as a serious dereliction of the purpose of artists and intellectuals, a theme that he would take up again in his more famous *Treason of the Intellectuals* (1927).[5] For Benda the task—the civilizing mission—of artistic and intellectual work was to promote universality. The abandonment of that universalizing mission for the particularism of the body counted as a contributing condition for the catastrophic European conflict.

Benda's critique joined a pan-European colloquy of artists, critics, and philosophers who voiced suspicions about the social and political aspirations of physiological aesthetics. Thinkers like Wilhelm Worringer, T. H. Hulme, Remy de Gourmont, and José Ortega y Gasset, all of whom had begun as partisans of physiological aesthetics, turned against the quest to make empathy or psycho-physiological attunement the radical principle of demotic social transformation.[6] Each insisted that the project of grounding the social bond and principles of civil governance in the ear, muscles, and viscera had ended up contributing to the political cataclysm of the war. The solution was not to be found in the lower senses and peripheral body but in a governing rationality, often coordinated with the severe gaze of ocularity. Hulme's conversion from enthusiastic Bergsonian first to Worringer-inspired critic of boundary-less aesthetic empathy and then to champion of the austere precision of the analytical philosophy of G. E. Moore and Bertrand Russell is a well-known emblem for this turn.[7] Others featured more blatantly reactionary politics, such as Ortega y Gasset's demand to replace the mass sensibility of aesthetic empathy with a sensory hierarchy directed by the eye.

With time the critics of early modernist aesthetics hung the pejorative label *psychologism* on physiological aesthetics, a term that gathered up all of the defining elements of the methods and ambitions of the prewar arts and sciences: the emphasis on the body, on affect, and indeed all human psychology, evolution, and even history as the foundational source of art and aesthetic cognition.[8] In their place the high modernists vaunted logical universals and eternal principles that were uncontaminated by the body or any particularism.

Still, physiological aesthetics flowed on in many of the eddies and countercurrents within modernism, often finding employment in attempts to undermine pristine formalisms. Once the task of modernist (and especially formalist) art had been defined as the investigation of the fact of automatism itself, it fell to the surrealists, Marcel Duchamp, and others to resurrect fin-de-siècle notions of automatism as involuntary appearances of subconscious activity externalized in physiological activity.[9]

The course of European modernism contrasted with the United States, where physiological modernism continued to thrive. In an important new study, Robin Veder has shown how ideas and practices of physiological aesthetics, and especially kinesthesia, shaped the work of a broad spectrum of influential people in the American art world through the 1930s.[10] Modernists associated with the Armory Show, the Société Anonyme, the Stieglitz circle, and the Barnes Foundation combined research in physiological aesthetics with personal experimentation in a range of new body techniques, such as the Dalcroze method, the Alexander Technique, Rolf Structural Integration, and Mensendieck Functional Mechanics, as a means of harmonizing the body and refining new modes of abstraction in the arts. Not only did these forays into physiological aesthetics and body techniques shape the work of crucial artists like Arthur Davies, Alfred Stieglitz, and Georgia O'Keeffe, as well as important institutions like the Barnes Foundation, they formed the basis of the aesthetic writings of John Dewey, arguably the most influential American theorist of art in the interwar era.[11]

It is tempting to speculate about the reasons why physiological modernism continued to thrive in North America while it waned in interwar Europe. One obvious suggestion might be that having been spared from much of the carnage and devastation of the war, American artists and intellectuals were able to retain the utopian optimism that underpinned physiological modernism, while their European counterparts confronted a profound crisis of purpose and identity. There is certainly evidence on the European side that many artists and critics became sympathetic to the view that physiological aesthetics had been part of the problem, or at least to the idea that it could not be part of the solution to the hardened perceptions of the great crisis that remained largely unsolved after 1918. In some instances the conditions of the war helped worries about degeneration and effeminization renew the currency of Nordau-esque arguments about physiological aesthetics. But for others the problems with physiological aesthetics were epistemological or political, requiring entirely new foundations for modernist art.

In any event, high modernist principles eventually crossed the Atlantic, reaching their apotheosis in the United States of the 1950s. They were best exemplified in the criticism of Clement Greenberg, which, as Caroline Jones forcefully argues, derived its power from his mastery of the increasingly bureaucratic sensorium of high modernist New York. This was a world of segmented and divided senses, of mass-produced products and innumerable technologies that screened and filtered sense data according to bureaucratic logic. In such a world, Jones observes, "the body's place as undifferentiated corpus was nowhere," and the visual regulated and controlled all sense and bodily functions.[12] Twentieth-century industrial culture produced a sensorium different from that of the skill-based artisanal industrialism of the nineteenth century, altering the conditions of the possibility of aesthetics itself. Physiology was excised from art criticism and art history, even when it continued to play a regulative function in formalist analysis.

High modernism of this broadly Greenbergian type came to reshape our vision of the entire history of modernism. Not long after the theories and practices of physiological aesthetics were rejected, the history of how a broad spectrum of experimental physiology had contributed to early modernism was relegated to what Pound called modernism's "hidden strata," unknown or forgotten to all but a few old-timers and their confidants. This study has sought to recover this history, to put early aesthetic modernism and industrial modernity in their common context, mediated by the experimental systems of laboratory physiology.

NOTES

Introduction

1   *London Examiner*, quoted in Anonymous, review of *Physiological Aesthetics*, by Grant Allen, *Popular Science Monthly* 11, no. 41 (October 1877): 760.

2   William James, "What Is an Emotion?" *Mind* 9, no. 34 (1884): 188. See also the notes for a seminar on physiological aesthetics that James taught: William James, "Notes for Philosophy 20a: Psychological Seminary 1891–1892. Aesthetics," in *Manuscript Lectures: The Works of William James*, ed. F. Burkhardt (Cambridge, MA: Harvard University Press, 1988), 206–11. On James's aesthetics, see Francesca Bordogna, "The Psychology and Physiology of Temperament: Pragmatism in Context," *Journal of the History of the Behavioral Sciences* 37, no. 1 (2001): 3–25.

3   Claude Bernard, *Introduction to the Study of Experimental Medicine*, trans. Henry Copley Greene (1865; repr., New York: Dover, 1957), 40, 42–43. Bernard here alluded to a saying by Victor Hugo.

4   Much of the relevant literature appears throughout the notes in this book, but this is a good place to acknowledge several key early milestones in the scholarly literature: Judith Ryan, *The Vanishing Subject: Early Psychology and Literary Modernism* (Chicago: University of Chicago Press, 1991); Christoph Asendorf, *Ströme und Strahlen: Das langsame Verschwinden der Materie um 1900* (Berlin: Anabas, 1989); Tim Armstrong, *Modernism, Technology, and the Body* (Cambridge: Cambridge University Press, 1998); Caroline Jones and Peter Galison, eds., *Picturing Science, Producing Art* (London: Routledge,1998); Bruce Clarke and Linda Dalrymple Henderson, eds., *From Energy to Information: Representation in Science and Technology, Art and Literature* (Stanford, CA: Stanford University Press, 2002); and Mark Micale, ed., *The Mind of Modernism: Medicine, Psychology, and the Cultural Arts in Europe and America, 1880–1940* (Stanford, CA: Stanford University Press, 2004).

5   Terry Eagleton, *The Ideology of the Aesthetic* (Oxford: Basil Blackwell, 1990), 13–17.

6   The eighteenth-century aestheticians conceived the discipline in close adherence to the etymology and traditions of aesthetics. The term *aesthetics* derives from a quilt of Greek words that designate activities of sensory perception in a strictly physiological sense, as in *sensation*, as well as a mental sense, as in *apprehension*. *Aisthetikos* derives from *aistheta*, things perceptible by the senses, from *aesthesthai*, to perceive. For a complete etymology, see H. Liddell and R. Scott, *Greek-English Lexicon*, 9th ed. (Oxford: Oxford University Press, 1996). With the

resurgence of physiological aesthetics came an array of new terms built around *aesthesis*, some of which appear in this book, for example, *synesthesia* (overlapping sensory functions), *kinesthesia* (the "muscle sense"), *hyperesthesia* (excessive aesthetic sensibility), *archaestheticism* (pantheist monist doctrine of universal perceptibility), and so on.

7   See, for example, the English-language discussion in Edmund Burke, *A Philosophical Inquiry into the Origin of Our Ideas of the Sublime and the Beautiful* (Basel: J. J. Tourneisen, 1792); Daniel Webb, *Observations on the Correspondences between Poetry and Music* (London, 1769); and Uvedale Price, *Essays on the Picturesque, as Compared with the Sublime and the Beautiful*, 3 vols. (London: Mawman, 1811). The physiological doctrines of Burke's aesthetics are explicated in Aris Sarafianos, "The Contractility of Burke's Sublime and Heterodoxies in Medicine and Art," *Journal of the History of Ideas* 69, no. 1 (2008): 23–48; Sarafianos, "Pain, Labor, and the Sublime: Medical Gymnastics and Burke's Aesthetics," *Representations* 91 (2005): 58–83.

8   Eagleton, *Ideology of the Aesthetic*, 20.

9   See, for example, Johannes Müller, *Zur vergleichenden Physiologie des Gesichtsinnes des Menschen und der Thiere nebst einem Versuch über die Bewegungen der Augen und über den menschlichen Blick* (Leipzig: Knobloch, 1826); J. E. Purkyně, *Abhandlung über die physiologische Untersuchung des Sehorgans und des Hautsystems* (Breslau, 1823); K. T. Tourtual, *Die Sinne des Menschen in den wechselseitigen Beziehungen ihres psychischen und organischen Leben: Ein Beitrag zur physiologischen Aesthetik* (Münster, Germany: Friedrich Regensberg, 1827); Hermann Helmholtz, *Die Lehre von den Tonempfindungen als physiologische Grundlage für die Theorie der Musik* (Braunschweig, Germany: Vieweg, 1863); Ernst Brücke, *Die Physiologischen Grundlagen der neuhochdeutschen Verskunst* (Vienna: Carl Gerold's Sohn, 1887); and Ernst Brücke, *Principes scientifiques des beaux-arts* (Paris: G. Baillière et Cie, 1878). On the aesthetic concerns of these figures, see Timothy Lenoir, "The Politics of Vision: Optics, Painting, and Ideology in Germany, 1845–1895," in *Instituting Science: The Cultural Production of Disciplines*, ed. Lenoir (Stanford, CA: Stanford University Press, 1997), 131–38; Michael Hagner and Bettina Wahrig-Schmidt, *Johannes Mueller und die Philosophie* (Berlin: Akademie, 1992); and R. Steven Turner, *In the Mind's Eye: Vision and the Hering-Helmholtz Controversy* (Princeton, NJ: Princeton University Press, 1994).

10   Nicholas Jardine, "The Laboratory Revolution in Medicine as Rhetorical and Aesthetic Accomplishment," in *The Laboratory Revolution in Medicine*, ed. Andrew Cunningham and Perry Williams (Cambridge: Cambridge University Press, 1992), 304–23. Sven Dierig, *Wissenschaft in der Maschinenstadt: Emil Du Bois-Reymond und seine Laboratorien in Berlin* (Göttingen, Germany: Wallstein, 2006), develops this idea in the critical case of Emil Du Bois-Reymond.

11   I am referring primarily to the German archipelago of physiology laboratories,

which were emulated internationally to varying degrees. See Robert G. Frank Jr., "American Physiologists in German Laboratories, 1865–1914," in *Physiology in the American Context 1850–1940*, ed. Gerald L. Geison (Bethesda, MD: American Physiological Society, 1987), 11–47; and the essays in William Coleman and Frederick L. Holmes, eds., *The Investigative Enterprise: Experimental Physiology in Nineteenth-Century Medicine* (Berkeley: University of California Press, 1988).

12   G. Stanley Hall, "Is Aesthetics a Science?" *The Nation* 31 (1879): 380–81.

13   The notion of experimental system is taken from Hans-Jörg Rheinberger, *Toward a History of Epistemic Things: Synthesizing Proteins in the Test Tube* (Stanford, CA: Stanford University Press, 1997), and will be developed throughout this book.

14   For a sampling of this literature, see C. Di Dio and V. Gallese, "Neuroaesthetics: A Review," *Current Opinion in Neurobiology* 19 (2009): 682–87; D. J. Levitkin, *This Is Your Brain on Music* (New York: Dutton, 2006); A. P. Shimamura and S. E. Palmer, eds., *Aesthetic Science: Connecting Minds, Brains, and Experience* (New York: Oxford University Press, 2011); and M. Skov and O. Vartanian, eds., *Neuroaesthetics* (Amityville, NY: Baywood Publishing Co., 2010. For evolutionary approaches, see Eckart Voland and Karl Grammer, eds., *Evolutionary Aesthetics* (Berlin: Springer, 2003).

15   Mark Rollins, "What Monet Meant: Intention and Attention in Understanding Art," *Journal of Aesthetics and Art Criticism* 62 (2004): 175–88; and David Freedberg and Vittorio Gallese, "Motion, Emotion, and Empathy in Esthetic Experience," *Trends in Cognitive Science* 11 (2007): 197–203. For essays that bridge the earlier aesthetics and contemporary neuroscience, see Susan Lanzoni, Robert Brain, and Allan Young, eds., "Varieties of Empathy in Science, Art, and Culture," special issue, *Science in Context* 26 (2012).

16   For a contrasting approach, see the recent work by eminent neuroscientist Eric R. Kandel, *The Age of Insight: The Quest to Understand the Unconscious in Art, Mind, and Brain, from Vienna 1900 to the Present* (New York: Random House, 2012), which uses contemporary neuroscience to complete the dialogue between art and medicine begun in fin-de-siècle Vienna.

17   Compare bioartist Eduardo Kok, who writes in his introduction to a collection of essays entitled *Signs of Life: Bio Art and Beyond* (Cambridge, MA: MIT Press, 2007), 3:

>   Clearly, it is impossible—and unacceptable—to circumscribe the questions raised by biotechnology with the realm of scientific research or industrial production, precisely because they take place in society at large. They affect the health of the individual but they also impact social relations. . . . They create new life and unprecedented legal problems. They manufacture new products and redefine markets. Just as they influence notions of personal identity, they also change cultural patterns. . . . Artists openly defy pre-

mature obituaries of formal experimentation and innovation by literally
working with living media—biomedia—and inventing ideas and forms
impossible to reproduce until recently.
On contemporary bioart see Robert Mitchell, *Bioart and the Vitality of Media*
(Seattle: University of Washington Press, 2010); Ingeborg Reichle, *Art in the Age
of Technoscience: Genetic Engineering, Robotics, and Artificial Life in Contemporary Art*
(Vienna: Springer, 2009); and Peter Weibel and Ljiljana Fruk, *Molecular Aesthetics*
(Cambridge, MA: MIT Press, 2013).

18   See, especially, Bruno Latour and Steve Woolgar, *Laboratory Life: The Construction
of Scientific Facts*, 2nd ed. (Princeton, NJ: Princeton University Press, 1986); Latour,
"Give Me a Laboratory and I will Raise the World," in *Science Observed*, ed. K. D.
Knorr-Cetina and Michael Mulkay (London: Sage, 1983), 141–70; Latour, "Visual-
ization and Cognition: Thinking with Eyes and Hands," in *Knowledge and Society:
Studies in the Sociology of Culture Past and Present*, vol. 6, ed. H. Kuklick (Baltimore:
Johns Hopkins University Press, 1986), 1–40; and Latour, "Circulating Reference:
Sampling Soil in the Amazon Forest," in *Pandora's Hope: Essays on the Reality of Sci-
ence Studies* (Cambridge, MA: Harvard University Press, 1999), 24–79.

19   On Latour's abiding intellectual debt to Charles Péguy and Henri Bergson, see
Henning Schmidgen, "The Materiality of Things? Bruno Latour, Charles Péguy,
and the History of Science," *History of the Human Sciences* 26 (2013): 3–28; and
Schmidgen, *Bruno Latour: Zur Einführung* (Hamburg: Junius, 2011), which traces
these themes over Latour's entire career. See also Latour`s writings on Gabriel
Tarde as a precursor: Latour, "Gabriel Tarde and the End of the Social," in *The
Social in Question: New Bearings in the History and the Social Sciences*, ed. Patrick
Joyce (London: Routledge, 2002), 117–32; and Latour and Vincent Antoine Lépi-
nay, *The Science of Passionate Interests: An Introduction to Gabriel Tarde's Economic
Anthropology* (Chicago: Prickly Paradigm Press, 2009). Bruno Latour, *We Have
Never Been Modern*, trans. Catherine Porter (Hemel Hempstead, UK: Harvester
Wheatleaf, 1993), makes the case against the notion of modernity.

20   Richard Wagner, *"The Art-Work of the Future," and Other Works*, trans. and ed.
William Ashton Ellis (Lincoln: University of Nebraska Press, 1993).

21   Friedrich Nietzsche, *Nietzsche Contra Wagner* ("Where I Offer Objections"), in
Werke: Kritische Gesamtausgabe, ed. Giorgio Colli and Mazzino Montinari (Berlin:
De Gruyter, 1967–), 3:416.

22   Michael Marrinan, *Romantic Paris: Histories of a Cultural Landscape, 1800–1850*
(Stanford, CA: Stanford University Press, 2009), 173–77.

23   John Tresch, *The Romantic Machine: Utopian Science and Technology after Napoleon*
(Chicago: University of Chicago Press, 2012), 148, 128.

24   John Tresch, "The Prophet and the Pendulum: Sensational Science and Audiovisual Phantasmagoria around 1848," *Grey Room* 43 (2011): 16–41.

25   See the letters between Jules Laforgue and Gustave Kahn in Laforgue, *Lettres à*

un ami, 1880–1886, introduction and notes by G. Jean-Aubry (Paris: Mercure de France, 1941).

26 Paul Valéry, "On Literary Technique" (1889), in *The Art of Poetry*, ed. Jackson Mathews, trans. Denise Foliot (Princeton, NJ: Princeton University Press, 1989), 313.

27 Max Nordau, *Degeneration* (1892), translation of 2nd ed., with introduction by George L. Mosse (Lincoln: University of Nebraska, 1968).

28 Andreas Killen, "Psychiatry, Cinema, and Urban Youth in Early Twentieth-Century Germany," *Harvard Review of Psychiatry* 14 (2006): 38–43; and Scott Curtis, "Between Observation and Spectatorship: Medicine, Movies, and Mass Culture in Imperial Germany," in *Film 1900: Technology, Perception, Culture*, ed. Annemone Ligensa and Klaus Kreimeier (New Barnet, UK: John Libbey Publishing, 2009), 87–98.

29 Julien Benda, *Belphégor*, trans. S. J. I. Lawson, from the original *Belphégor: Essai sur l'esthétique de la présente société française* (1918) (New York: Payson and Clarke, 1929), 36.

30 Compare the fine study by Christopher Butler, *Early Modernism: Literature, Music, and Painting in Europe 1900–1916* (Oxford: Clarendon Press, 1994), which somewhat arbitrarily dates early modernism from 1900 while routinely reaching back to find key intellectual resources in the preceding decades.

31 Jonathan Crary, *Suspensions of Perception: Attention, Spectacle, and Modern Culture* (Cambridge, MA: MIT Press, 1990).

32 Lorraine Daston and Peter Galison, "The Image of Objectivity," *Representations* 40, no. 1 (1992): 83. See also Lorraine Daston and Peter Galison, *Objectivity* (New York: Zone Books, 2007).

33 In these domains the rhetoric of mechanical objectivity was not equally well received. On the one hand, George Biddell Airy's recourse to the precise impersonal measures of chronograph inscriptions appears to have conferred authority on the astronomical-time measurements of the Greenwich Observatory. British medical doctors, on the other hand, ran into resistance from well-heeled patients who disliked and distrusted the imposition of the machine in clinical diagnosis, preferring the educated judgment of a gentleman-physician. On Greenwich, see Simon Schaffer, "Astronomers Mark Time: Discipline and the Personal Equation," *Science in Context* 2 (1988): 115–45. On graphical recording instruments in medicine, see Christopher Lawrence, "Incommunicable Knowledge: Science, Technology and the Clinical Art in Britain 1850–1914," *Journal of Contemporary History* 20 (1985): 503–20.

34 Friedrich Schlegel, quoted in Tresch, *Romantic Machine*, 64.

35 Herbert Spencer, *The Principles of Psychology* (New York: D. Appleton & Co., 1877), 1:130.

36 Friedrich A. Kittler, *Discourse Networks 1800/1900*, trans. Michael Metteer, with

Chris Cullens (Stanford, CA: Stanford University Press, 1985); Kittler, *Gramophone, Film, Typewriter*, trans. Geoffrey Winthrop-Young and Michael Wutz (Stanford, CA: Stanford University Press, 1999); and Kittler, *Draculas Vermächtnis: Technische Schriften* (Leipzig: Reclam, 1993). See also Geoffrey Winthrop-Young, *Kittler and the Media* (Cambridge: Polity, 2011).

37   Kittler, *Gramophone, Film, Typewriter*, xxxix.

38   Friedrich A. Kittler, *Optical Media*, trans. Anthony Enns (Cambridge: Polity, 2010), 148.

39   John V. Pickstone, *Ways of Knowing: A New History of Science, Technology, and Medicine* (Chicago: University of Chicago Press, 2000). See also Pickstone's further development of the ideas in this book: Pickstone, "Working Knowledges Before and After circa 1900: Practices and Disciplines in the History of Science, Technology, and Medicine," *Isis* 98 (2007): 489–516; Pickstone, "The Analytical Revolutions and the Syntheses of Modernism," in *Histoire des sciences modernes*, ed. H. Otto Sibum and Kapil Raj, vol. 2 of *Les Sciences et la modernité* (Paris: Le Seuil, forthcoming).

40   Pickstone, "Analytical Revolutions and the Syntheses of Modernism."

41   Michael Baxandall, *Painting and Experience in Fifteenth-Century Italy*, 2nd ed.(Oxford: Oxford University Press, 1988), first published 1972; Samuel Edgerton, *The Renaissance Rediscovery of Linear Perspective* (New York: Harper and Row, 1975); Svetlana Alpers, *The Art of Describing: Dutch Art in the Seventeenth Century* (Chicago: University of Chicago Press, 1983); and Catherine Wilson, *The Invisible World: Early Modern Philosophy and the Invention of the Microscope* (Princeton, NJ: Princeton University Press, 1995).

42   Pickstone, *Ways of Knowing*, 14, 139, 158–60 (quotation 159), 163–65.

43   Ibid., 159.

44   On dynamite as a technology for transforming relations of time and space, see Thomas Brandstetter, "Entfesselte Kräfte: Der Sprengstoff als Kulturtechnik der Moderne," in *Zeichen der Kraft: Wissensformationen 1800–1900*, by Brandstetter and Christof Windätter (Berlin: Kadmos, 2008), 46–61. On dynamite in anarchist circles, see John Merriman, *The Dynamite Club: How a Bombing in Fin-de-Siècle Paris Ignited the Age of Modern Terror* (Boston: Houghton Mifflin Harcourt, 2009).

45   Pickstone, *Ways of Knowing*, 159.

46   I cannot resist noting the parallels between two synthetic objects invented in 1913: the paintings of Picabia (and others) based on notions of kinesthetic empathy (or the mass spectacles at Hellerau, Germany, designed to induce kinesthetic empathic reactions); and Anton Köllisch's chemical synthesis of the first empathogenic drug, MDMA, better known by its street name, Ecstasy. On the relations between drugs and human evolution, see Richard M. Doyle, *Darwin's Pharmacy: Sex, Plants, and the Evolution of the Noosphere* (Seattle: University of Washington Press, 2011).

47 Étienne-Jules Marey, *La Méthode graphique dans le sciences expérimentales et principalement en physiologie et en medicine* (Paris: G. Masson, 1878), xiii.

48 Laurent Loison, "The Notions of Plasticity and Heredity among French Neo-Lamarckians (1880–1940): From Complementarity to Incompatibility," in *Transformations of Lamarckism: From Subtle Fluids to Molecular Biology*, ed. Snait B. Gissis and Eva Jablonka (Cambridge, MA: MIT Press, 2011).

49 See H. G. Wells, "The Limits of Individual Plasticity" (1895), in *H. G. Wells: Early Writings in Science and Science Fiction*, ed. R. M. Philmus and D. Y. Hughes (Berkeley: University of California Press, 1975), 36–39. On scientists' interest in ectoplasm séances, see Robert Michael Brain, "Materialising the Medium: Ectoplasm and the Quest for Supra-normal Biology in Fin-de-Siècle Science and Art," in *Vibratory Modernism*, ed. Anthony Enns and Shelley Trower (London: Palgrave, 2013), 115–44.

50 Jacques Loeb, quoted in Philip J. Pauly, *Controlling Life: Jacques Loeb and the Engineering Ideal in Biology* (Berkeley: University of California Press, 1990), 5.

51 Philip J. Pauly, "Modernist Practice in American Biology," in *Modernist Impulses in the Human Sciences, 1870–1930*, ed. Dorothy Ross (Baltimore: Johns Hopkins University Press, 1994), 272–89.

52 Hugo Ball, *Diary*, March 5, 1917, cited in Hans Richter, *Dada: Art and Anti-Art* (London: Thames and Hudson, 1965), 41.

1. Representation on the Line

1   G. Stanley Hall], "The Graphic Method," *The Nation* 29, no. 745 (October 9, 1879): 238. Étienne-Jules Marey, *La Méthode graphique en sciences expérimentales et principalement en physiologie et en médicine* (Paris: G. Masson, 1878), iii.

2   Otto Wiener, *Die Erweiterung unserer Sinne: Akademische Antrittsvorlesung* (Leipzig: J. A. Barth, 1900), 23–24.

3   Marey, *La Méthode graphique*, iii, vi.

4   On the naming and nomenclature of scientific instruments, see Christian Licoppe, *La Formation de la pratique scientifique: Le Discours de l'expérience en France et en Angleterre (1630–1820)* (Paris: La Découverte, 1996), 270; and Lissa Roberts, "A Word and the World: The Significance of Naming the Calorimeter," *Isis* 79, no. 2 (1988): 199–232.

5   On the myriad mechanical drawing and tracing devices of the late eighteenth and early nineteenth centuries, see Martin Kemp, *The Science of Art: Optical Themes in Western Art from Brunelleschi to Seurat* (New Haven, CT: Yale University Press, 1990), 167–203.

6   Licoppe, *La Formation de la pratique scientifique*; and Simon Schaffer, "Self-Evidence," *Critical Inquiry* 18, no. 2 (Winter 1992): 327–62.

7   Schaffer, "Self-Evidence," 359–62.

8   Hans Blumenberg, *Die Lesbarkeit der Welt* (Frankfurt: Suhrkamp, 1981), especially 233–67.

9   John Bender and Michael Marrinan, *The Culture of Diagram* (Stanford, CA: Stanford University Press, 2010), 14.

10   Ibid., 34–35.

11   Samuel Y. Edgerton, *The Renaissance Rediscovery of Linear Perspective* (New York: Harper and Row, 1975); and Michael Lynch, "Laboratory Space and the Technological Complex: An Investigation of Topical Contextures," *Science in Context 4* (1991): 51–78.

12   Bender and Marrinan, *Culture of Diagram*, 106.

13   On Monge's gestural epistemology of graphical representation, see Lorraine Daston, "The Physicalist Tradition in Early Nineteenth-Century French Geometry," *Studies in the History and Philosophy of Science* 17, no. 3 (1986): 269–95.

14   William Playfair, *A Real Statement of the Finances and Resources of Great Britain* (London: Whittingham, 1796). On Lambert's graphical representations, see Sybille Nikolow, "Die Versinnlichung von Staatskräften: Statistische Karten um 1800," *Traverse* 6, no. 3 (1999): 63–82.

15   For a broad history of the forms of graphical representation, see H. G. Funkhouser, "Historical Development of the Graphical Representation of Statistical Data," *Osiris* 3 (1938): 269–404; and Thomas L. Hankins, "Blood, Dirt, and Nomograms: A Particular History of Graphs," *Isis 90*, no. 1 (1999): 50–80.

16   On the antiquity of copying techniques, see Georges Didi-Huberman, *L'Empreinte* (Paris: Centre Georges Pompidou, 1997).

17   Charles Babbage, *The Economy of Machinery and Manufactures* (London: Charles Knight, Pall Mall East, 1832), 51.

18   Georges Didi-Huberman, *La Ressemblance par contact: Archéologie, anachronisme et modernité de l'empreinte* (Paris: Minuit, 2008).

19   Katharine Park, "Impressed Images: Reproducing Wonders," in *Picturing Science, Producing Art*, ed. Caroline A. Jones and Peter Galison (London: Routledge, 1998), 256.

20   Hans Belting, *Bild und Kult: Eine Geschichte des Bildes vor dem Zeitalter der Kunst* (Munich: Beck, 1990); Ernst von Dobschuetz, *Christusbilder: Untersuchungen zur christlichen Legende* (Leipzig: Hinrichs, 1899); and Ewa Kuryluk, *Veronica and Her Cloth: History, Symbolism, and the Structure of a "True" Image* (Cambridge: Blackwell, 1991).

21   André Bazin, "The Ontology of the Photographic Image," in *What Is Cinema?*, trans. Hugh Gray (Berkeley: University of California Press, 1967), 1:14.

22   See "Special Issue: Cultural Techniques," *Theory, Culture, and Society* 30, no. 6 (2013), ed. Geoffrey Winthrop-Young, Jussi Parikka, and Ilinca Iurascu.

23   Thomas Macho, "Second-Order Animals: Cultural Techniques of Identity and Identification," *Theory, Culture, and Society* 30, no. 6 (2013): 30–47.

24   On the ubiquity of modern copying techniques, see Hillel Schwartz, *The Culture of the Copy: Striking Likenesses, Unreasonable Facsimiles* (New York: Zone Books,

1996); and Didi-Huberman, *L'Empreinte*. On the meanings of copying in modern art, see Richard Schiff, "Representation, Copying, and the Technique of Originality," *New Literary History* 14 (1983): 332–63.

25 Lorraine Daston and Peter Galison, "The Image of Objectivity," *Representations* 40, no. 1 (1992): 85. The notion of working objects receives a larger treatment in Daston and Galison, *Objectivity* (New York: Zone Books, 2009).

26 H. W. Dickinson, *A Short History of the Steam Engine* (Cambridge: Cambridge University Press, 1938), 85.

27 R. L. Hills and A. J. Pacey, "The Measurement of Power in Early Steam-Driven Textile Mills," *Technology and Culture* 13, no. 1 (1972): 25–43.

28 Quoted in ibid., 34.

29 Ken Alder, "Making Things the Same: Representation, Tolerance and the End of the Ancien Régime in France," *Social Studies of Science* 28, no. 4 (1998): 499–545; and H. Belofsky, "Engineering Drawing: A Universal Language in Two Dialects," *Technology and Culture* 32, no. 1 (1991): 23–46.

30 Charles Dupin, one of the most active proponents of new dynamic theories, summarized his teacher's views this way: "Although Monge did not direct his labors toward dynamics, he nevertheless very effectively served this science through his geometrical theories. Minds accustomed to clearly discerning in space coordinate frames, lines, and surfaces with simple and double curvature forming, cutting, touching, folding and developing according to various laws, have become minds eminently suited to conceive and to describe the general phenomena of the movement of bodies." Charles Dupin, *Essai historique sur les services et les travaux scientifiques de Gaspard Monge* (Paris: Bachelier, 1819), 144.

31 C. L. M. H. Navier, "Addition: Sur les principes du calcul et de l'établissement des machines, et sur les moteurs," in *Architecture Hydraulique*, by Bernard Forest de Bélidor (Paris: Firmin Didot, 1819), 376.

32 On the values of the concept of work in France in this period, see François Vatin, *Le Travail: Économie et physique* 1780–1830 (Paris: Presses Universitaires de France, 1993).

33 Jean-Victor Poncelet, quoted in Jean-Pierre Séris, *Machine et communication* (Paris: Vrin, 1987), 429.

34 Arthur Morin, "Descriptions des appareils chronométrique à style: Propres à la représentation graphique et la détermination des lois du mouvement dans divers genres d'expériences," in *Mémoires du Congrès scientifique de France: Cinquième session, tenue à Metz en septembre 1837* (Metz: S. Lamfort, 1838), 583–607.

35 Crosbie Smith, *The Science of Energy: A Cultural History of Energy Physics in Victorian Britain* (Chicago: University of Chicago Press, 1998); and Robert M. Brain and M. Norton Wise, "Muscles and Engines: Indicator Diagrams and Helmholtz's Graphical Methods," in *The Science Studies Reader*, ed. Mario Biagioli (London: Routledge, 1998), 51–66.

36   Arthur Morin, *Notice sur divers appareils dynamométriques: Propres à mesurer l'effort du travail développé par les moteurs animés ou inanimés, ou consommé par des machines de rotation, et sur un nouvel indicateur de la pression dans les cylindres des machines à vapeur* (Paris: Mathias, 1839), 1–2; and M. Norton Wise, "Mediations: Enlightenment Balancing Acts; or, The Technology of Rationalism," in *World Changes: Thomas Kuhn and the Nature of Science*, ed. P. Horwich (Cambridge, MA: MIT Press, 1993).

37   On the transition to the dynamic, steam-powered nineteenth-century world, see Ilya Prigogine and Isabelle Stengers, *Order Out of Chaos: Man's New Dialogue with Nature* (London: Flamingo, 1984); Anson Rabinbach, *The Human Motor: Energy, Fatigue, and the Origins of Modernity* (Berkeley: University of California Press, 1992); Simon Schaffer, "Nebular Hypothesis and the Science of Progress," in *History, Humanity, and Evolution: Essays for John C. Greene*, ed. James Moore (Cambridge: Cambridge University Press, 1989); Michel Serres, "Turner Translates Carnot," in *Hermes: Literature, Science, Philosophy*, trans. Josué Harari (Baltimore: Johns Hopkins University Press, 1982); John Tresch, *The Romantic Machine: Utopian Science after Napoleon* (Chicago: University of Chicago Press, 2012); and M. Norton Wise, "Work and Waste: Political Economy and Natural Philosophy in Nineteenth-Century Britain," *History of Science* 27 (1989): pt.1, 263–301; pt. 2, 391–449; pt. 3, vol. 28 (1990): 221–61.

38   Arthur Morin, *Leçons de mécanique pratique* (Paris: Hachette, 1846), 24.

39   Morin, *Notice sur divers appareils dynamométrique*, 29–30.

40   Karl Marx, *Capital*, trans. Ben Fowkes (New York: Random House, 1997), 1:129, 168.

41   On the introduction of Morin dynamometers to the United Kingdom, see Lewis Gordon, "On Dynamometrical Apparatus; or, The Measurement of Mechanical Effect of Moving Powers," *Proceedings of the Philosophical Society of Glasgow* (1841–42): 42–43. On the German reception, see Robert Michael Brain and M. Norton Wise, "Muscles and Engines: Indicator Diagrams and Helmholtz's Graphical Methods," in *The Science Studies Reader*, ed. Mario Biagioli, 51–66 (London: Routledge, 1998).

42   Brain and Wise, "Muscles and Engines"; Frederic L. Holmes and Kathryn M. Olesko, "The Images of Precision: Helmholtz and the Graphical Method in Physiology," in *The Values of Precision*, ed. M. Norton Wise (Princeton, NJ: Princeton University Press, 198–221; and Henning Schmidgen, *Die Helmholtz-Kurven: Auf der Spur der verlorenen Zeit* (Berlin: Merve, 2009).

43   Emil Du Bois-Reymond, letter to Hermann Helmholtz (1852), in Christa Kirsten, *Dokumente einer Freundschaft: Briefwechsel zwischen Hermann von Helmholtz und Emil Du Bois-Reymond 1846–1894* (Berlin: Akademie Verlag, 1986), 123. See also Brain and Wise, "Muscles and Engines"; and Sven Dierig, *Wissenschaft in der Machinenstadt: Emil Du Bois-Reymond und seine Laboratorien in Berlin* (Göttingen, Germany: Wallstein, 2006).

44 Emil Du Bois-Reymond, "Naturwissenschaft und bildende Kunst" (1890), in *Reden von Emil Du Bois-Reymond*, ed. Estelle Du Bois-Reymond (Leipzig: Veit & Co., 1912), 2:421–22.

45 Hans-Jörg Rheinberger, *Toward a History of Epistemic Things: Synthesizing Proteins in the Test Tube* (Stanford, CA: Stanford University Press, 1997). "Machines for making the future" comes from François Jacob, *The Statue Within: An Autobiography*, trans. Franklin Philip (New York: Basic Books, 1988), 234.

46 Ruth Benshop, "What Is a Tachistoscope? Historical Explorations of an Instrument," *Science in Context* 11, no. 1 (1998): 43.

47 Hebbel E. Hoff and Leslie A. Geddes, "The Technological Background of Physiological Discovery: Ballistics and the Graphic Method," *Journal of the History of Medicine and Allied Sciences* 15 (1960): 345–63.

48 Henning Schmidgen, "The Donders Machine: Matter, Signs, and Time in a Physiological Experiment, ca. 1865," *Configurations* 13 (2005): 217.

49 Franciscus Cornelis Donders, *Physiologie des Menschen*, vol. 1, *Die Ernährung*, 2nd ed. (Leipzig: Hirzel, 1859), 4, quoted in Schmidgen, "Donders Machine," 237.

50 James Clerk Maxwell, "General Considerations concerning Scientific Apparatus," In *Handbook to the Special Loan Collection of Scientific Apparatus, 1876, South Kensington* Museum (London: Chapman and Hill, 1876), 1–21. On Maxwell's discussion, see also Peter L. Galison, *How Experiments End* (Chicago: University of Chicago Press, 1987), 23–27.

51 Charles Sanders Peirce, *Collected Papers of Charles Sanders Peirce*, ed. Charles Hartshorne and Paul Weiss, vol. 6, *Scientific Metaphysics* (Cambridge, MA: Harvard University Press, 1935), 65.

52 Emil Du Bois-Reymond to Alexander von Humboldt, n.d., Alexander von Humboldt Nachlass, Archiv der Staatsbibliothek Preussischer Kulturbesitz, Berlin (West).

53 On the divergent traditions, compare Henning Schmidgen, "Physics, Ballistics, and Psychology: A History of the Chronoscope in/as Context, 1845–1890," *History of Psychology* 8 (2005): 46–78; and Soraya de Chadarevian, "Graphical Method and Discipline: Self-Recording Instruments in Nineteenth-Century Physiology," *Studies in History and Philosophy of Science* 24, no. 2 (1993): 267–91.

54 [Anonymous], "Distribution of Driving-Power in Laboratories," *Nature* 33 (January 14, 1886): 248–50.

55 Marey, *La Méthode graphique*, v, iii. On Marey, see Marta Braun, *Picturing Time: The Work of Étienne-Jules Marey (1830–1895)* (Chicago: University of Chicago Press, 1993); and François Dagognet, *Étienne-Jules Marey: La Passion de la trace* (Paris: Hazan, 1987).

56 Marey, *La Méthode graphique*, ii–v.

57 Jacques Derrida, *Of Grammatology*, trans. Gayatri Chakravorty Spivak (Baltimore: Johns Hopkins University Press, 1974), 155, 142.

58 Ibid., 157; Bruno Latour, "Circulating Reference," in *Pandora's Hope: Essays on the Reality of Science Studies* (Cambridge, MA: Harvard University Press, 1999). Latour's metaphor of inscription as "Ariadne's thread" first appeared in Latour and Steve Woolgar, *Laboratory Life: The Construction of Scientific Facts* in 1979 (2nd ed., Princeton, NJ: Princeton University Press, 1986), where Latour also cites Derrida's early work as a source of his notion of inscription.

59 Marey, *La Méthode graphique*, v.

60 Funkhouser, "Historical Development of Graphical Representation."

61 Giovanni Ferraro, "Analytical Symbols and Geometrical Figures in Eighteenth Century Calculus," *Studies in History and Philosophy of Science* 32, no. 3 (2001): 535–55.

62 Marey, *La Méthode graphique*, ii.

63 Ibid., xiii.

64 Charles Sanders Peirce, *The Essential Peirce: Selected Philosophical Writings*, ed. Nathan Houser and Christian Kloesel (Bloomington: Indiana University Press, 1992), 1:226. Indexicals were one element of Peirce's theory of signs, consisting of a tripartite division of icon, index, and symbol. Carlo Ginzburg, "Clues: Roots of an Evidential Paradigm," in *Clues, Myths, and the Historical Method*, trans. John and Anne C. Tedeschi (Baltimore: Johns Hopkins University Press, 1989), 96–125, famously argues that the late nineteenth-century was the age of an epistemological paradigm of indexicality, which Ginzburg contrasted with the "Galilean" model of vision and knowledge based on perspective and ocularity.

65 On tricks of scale as a key feature of Victorian science, see Heinz Otto Sibum, *Shifting Scales: Microstudies in Early Victorian Britain* (Berlin: Max-Planck Institute for History of Science Pre-print, 2001).

66 Bruno Latour, "Visualization and Cognition: Thinking with Eyes and Hands," *Knowledge and Society: Studies in the Sociology of Culture Past and Present*, vol. 6, ed. H. Kuklick (Baltimore: Johns Hopkins University Press, 1986), 1–40; and Latour, "Drawing Things Together," in *Representation in Scientific Practice*, ed. Michael Lynch and Steve Woolgar (Cambridge, MA: MIT Press, 1990), 19–68.

67 Jonathan Crary, *Techniques of the Observer: On Vision and Modernity in the Nineteenth Century* (Cambridge, MA: MIT Press, 1990), 113, describes this as the crucial learned subject position of the nineteenth century.

68 Étienne-Jules Marey, *Du mouvement dans les fonctions de la vie: Leçons faites au Collège de France* (Paris: Germer Baillière, 1868), 93. See also Ernst Mach, "Zur Theorie der Pulswellenzeichner," *Sitzungsberichte der mathematisch-naturwissenschaftliche Classe der Kaiserlichen Akademie der Wissenschaften* 46 (1862): 157–74.

69 W. F. Kümmel, *Musik und Medizin: Ihre Wechselbeziehungen in Theorie und Praxis von 800 bis 1800* (Freiburg: Karl Alber, 1977), especially chapter 1, "Puls und Musik," 23–32.

70 Eugen Adolf Hermann Petersen, "Rhythmus," In *Königliche Gesellschaft der Wis-

senschaften zu Göttingen: Philologisch-historische Klasse, N.F., vol. 16 (1917): 1–104.

71 Marey, *Du mouvement dans les fonctions de la vie*, 93.

72 Nadar (Gaspard-Félix Tournachon), *Quand j'étais photographe* (Paris: Flammarion, 1900), 257.

73 Ibid., 253–54.

74 Marey, *La Méthode graphique*, 108.

75 In the most glaring omission, Bergson never cited Marey, and Marey never cited Bergson, despite the fact that they were colleagues at the Collège de France and collaborators in various committees investigating hypnotism and spiritualism, with many more common friends and links besides. Perhaps it was tactful diplomacy, perhaps an unwillingness to cite the obvious. See, for example, their collaborative publication, Henri Bergson, M. [Étienne-Jules] Marey, et al., "Groupe d'études de phénomènes psychiques," 1901, in *Mélanges*, ed. André Robinet (Paris: Presses Universitaires de France, 1972), 509–15.

76 Henri Bergson, *Creative Evolution*, trans. Arthur Mitchell, edited by Keith Ansell Pearson, Michael Kolkman, and Michael Vaughn, with an introduction by Keith Ansell Pearson (London: Palgrave, 2007), xxxv.

77 Henri Bergson, *Time and Free Will: An Essay on the Immediate Data of Consciousness* (1889), authorized translation by F. L. Pogson, 3rd ed. (London: G. Allen, 1913). Georges Canguilhem wrote that Bergson was a "rare French philosopher" who "considered mechanical invention as a biological function," and he asserted that Bergson's *Creative Evolution* "is, in some sense, a treatise of general organology." Canguilhem, "Machine and Organism," trans. Mark Cohen and Randall Cherry, in *Incorporations*, ed. Jonathan Crary and Sanford Kwinter (New York: Zone Books, 1992), 69n50. I agree, and I would also say that this could be claimed to some degree of Bergson's earlier works.

78 Henri Bergson, "La Philosophie de Claude Bernard," 1913, in *Oeuvres*, ed. André Robinet, 5th ed. (Paris: Presses Universitaires de France, 1991), 1433–40.

79 Henri Bergson, "Discussion avec Einstein," in *Mélanges*, ed. André Robinet (Paris: Presses Universitaires de France, 1972), 1344. On the critique of measurement in Bergson's debates with Einstein over the theory of relativity, see Jimena Canales, *A Tenth of a Second: A History* (Chicago: University of Chicago Press, 2009), 179–203.

80 Bergson might well have appreciated the etymological explanation of the new apparatus given in a popular magazine just months after its invention: "*Cinematograph* is a compound Greek word signifying the registration of movements. The object of the apparatus is in fact to reproduce life and movement in all of their appearances." *Le Monde illustré*, January 25, 1896, quoted in Matt Matsuda, *The Memory of the Modern* (Oxford: Oxford University Press, 1996), 173.

81 Bergson, *Creative Evolution*, 195 (italics in original).

82 The technical origins of cinematography in experimental physiology were

echoed in the terminology used for early cinematographic apparatus—taken from Greek and Latin roots joining *life* or *movement* with *vision* or *writing*: vitascope, vitagraph, bioscope, biograph, kinetoscope, kinetograph, and cinematograph. See Georges Sadoul, *L'Invention du cinema* (Paris: Denoël, 1946), 298.

83 Bergson, *Creative Evolution*, 195.

2. The Vibratory Organism

1 Thanks to Richard Staley for calling the above-quoted *Encyclopedia Britannica* entry for "Life" to my attention.

2 "Given the elevated role that protoplasm performs in the theater of cell organization, it is easy to understand the unexpected interest . . . in the study of its constitution and to the unraveling of its three major problems, the anatomical one, the chemical one, and the evolutionary one, which are still waiting to be clarified. . . . Protoplasm will become the battlefield of the forthcoming science, and the discovery of the laws that this matter obeys in its distinct conditions of existence will be the greatest conquest of humanity." Santiago Ramon y Cajal, "El protoplasma," in *La clinica: Seminario de medicina, cirujía y farmacia* (1880), reprinted in Ramon y Cajal, *Discurso de doctorado y trabajos de juventud*, ed. A. Merchán-Perez (Madrid: Universidad-Europea—CEES Ediciones, 2001), 307. Of course, Ramon y Cajal later fought on the opposite flank in the protoplasm battlefield, becoming an arch opponent of the amoeboid theory of the nerve junction.

3 Hannah Landecker, *Culturing Life: How Cells Became Technologies* (Cambridge, MA: Harvard University Press, 2007), 10.

4 Philip J. Pauly, "Modernist Practice in American Biology," in *The Origins of American Social Science*, ed. Dorothy Ross (Cambridge: Cambridge University Press, 1991), 272–89.

5 Judy Johns Schloegel and Henning Schmidgen, "General Physiology, Experimental Psychology, and Evolutionism: Unicellular Organisms as Objects of Psychophysiological Research, 1877–1918," *Isis* 93, no. 4 (2002): 614–45. On Nietzsche and protoplasm, see Gregory Moore, *Nietzsche, Biology, and Metaphor* (Cambridge: Cambridge University Press, 2002).

6 I coin the term *protoplasmania* to describe the fin-de-siècle enthusiasm for protoplasm biology in Robert Brain, "Protoplasmania: The Vibratory Organism and Man's Glassy Essence in the Later 19th Century," in *Zeichen der Kraft: Wissensformationen 1800–1900*, ed. Thomas Brandstetter and Christof Windgätter (Berlin: Kadmos, 2008), 198–227. On the place of protoplasm theories within Haeckel's wider monist philosophy, see Ernst Haeckel, *The Riddle of the Universe at the Close of the Nineteenth Century* (New York: Harper, 1900).

7 My use of the term *vibratory organism* is intended to serve as the biological counterpart to the invisible physical vibrations, rays, waves, and forces that

Linda Dalrymple Henderson has shown to have animated the work of many fin-de-siècle artists who subscribed to different versions of the "psycho-physical" universe. See Henderson, "Vibratory Modernism: Boccioni, Kupka, and the Ether of Space," in *From Energy to Information: Representation in Science and Technology, Art, and Literature*, ed. Bruce Clarke and Linda Dalrymple Henderson (Stanford, CA: Stanford University Press, 2002), 126–49. It is worth noting that the term *vibratory organism* has a longer pedigree. Cultural historian Roger Shattuck used it to describe the method of Charles Baudelaire's prose poems in his *Inner Eye: On Modern Literature and the Arts* (New York: Farrar, Straus and Giroux, 1984), 135–48. Shattuck borrowed the phrase from the British philosopher Alfred North Whitehead, who described how individuals possess distinctive rhythms, acquired in part from "stray rhythms which pass over the face of nature using physical objects as transient vehicles for their expression." Alfred North Whitehead, *An Enquiry Concerning the Principles of Natural Knowledge* (1919) (London: Forgotten Books, 2013), 199.

8   Charles S. Peirce, "Man's Glassy Essence," in *Collected Papers of Charles Sanders Peirce*, ed. Charles Hartshorne and Paul Weiss, vol. 6, *Scientific Metaphysics* (Cambridge: Belknap Press of Harvard University Press, 1965), 264; originally published in *The Monist* 3 (1892).

9   Samuel Butler, *Luck, or Cunning, as the Main Means of Organic Modification* (London: A. C. Fifield, 1922), 64.

10   Ernst Haeckel, *Über die Wellenzeugung der Lebensteilchen oder die Perigenesis der Plastidule* (1875), in *Gemeinverständliche Vorträge und Abhandlungen aus dem Gebiete der Entwicklungslehre*, 2nd ed. (Berlin: Henschel; Leipzig: Kröner, 1924), 86–142. On the pangenesis theory, see Charles Darwin, *Variation of Animals and Plants Under Domestication*, reprint of 2nd ed. (1883), with new foreword by Harriet Ritvo (Baltimore: Johns Hopkins University Press, 1998).

11   For a late nineteenth-century view of the dispute, see the lengthy assessment in Yves Delage, *La Structure du protoplasma et les théories sur l'hérédité* (Paris: C. Reinwald, 1895). For neglected twentieth-century continuations, see Jan Sapp, *Beyond the Gene: Cytoplasmic Inheritance and the Struggle for Authority in Genetics* (Oxford: Oxford University Press, 1987).

12   Thomas S. Hall, *Ideas of Life and Matter: General Physiology 600 BC to 1900 AD*, vol. 2, *From the Enlightenment to the End of the Nineteenth Century* (Chicago: University of Chicago Press, 1969).

13   Thomas Henry Huxley, "On the Physical Basis of Life," *Fortnightly Review* 5, no. 26 (1869): 129–45. On Huxley's protoplasm theory, see Gerald L. Geison, "The Protoplasmic Theory of Life and the Vitalist-Mechanist Debate," *Isis* 60, no. 3 (1969): 272–92. For general accounts of the life and work of Huxley, see Adrian Desmond's two-volume biography, *Huxley: The Devil's Disciple* (London: Michael Joseph, 1994); *Huxley: Evolution's High Priest* (London: Michael Joseph, 1997); and

Paul White, *Thomas Huxley: Making the Man of Science* (Cambridge: Cambridge University Press, 2003).

14 Desmond, *Huxley: The Devil's Disciple*, 367.

15 Huxley, "Physical Basis of Life," 135.

16 Bruce J. Hunt, "Lines of Force, Swirl of Ether," *From Energy to Information: Representation in Science and Technology, Art, and Literature*, ed. Bruce Clarke and Linda Dalrymple Henderson (Stanford, CA: Stanford University Press, 2002), 100.

17 Huxley, "Physical Basis of Life," 136.

18 Ibid., 138.

19 Rev. Alexander Anderson, quoted in Anonymous, *Protoplasm, Powheads, and Porwiggles, and the Evolution of the Horse from the Rhinoceros, Illustrating Professor Huxley's Scientific Mode of Getting Up the Creation and Upsetting Moses* (London: Longmans and Co., 1875), 13.

20 Desmond, *Huxley: The Devil's Disciple*, 367.

21 Disraeli, quoted in Anonymous, *Protoplasm, Powheads, and Porwiggles, and the Evolution of the Horse from the Rhinoceros, Illustrating Professor Huxley's Scientific Mode of Getting Up the Creation and Upsetting Moses* (London: Longmans and Co., 1875). Two decades later the dignitary Pooh-Bah (Lord High Everything Else) of Gilbert and Sullivan's comic opera *Mikado* would claim a staggering list of titles on the basis of his ability to trace his lineage to "a primordial protoplasmal atomic globule." On the hilarity of Pooh-Bah's protoplasmic lineage, see the *Cambridge Review* 12 (February 5, 1891): 198; and W. S. Gilbert and Arthur Sullivan, *The Mikado; or, The Town of Titipu* (Woodford Green, Essex, UK: International Music Publications, 1996). On the context of the opera, see Christopher Hibbert, *Gilbert and Sullivan and Their Victorian World* (New York: American Heritage Publishing Co., 1976). I thank Ted Porter for pointing out this splendid allusion to me.

22 John Hutchinson Stirling, *As Regards Protoplasm: In Relation to Professor Huxley's Essay "On the Physical Basis of Life"* (New Haven, CT: Charles C. Chatfield, 1870), 58–59.

23 Not long after Haeckel speculated that an amorphous albumen was the primordial living matter, Huxley received an inchoate jelly creature retrieved from the depths of the English Channel from the diggers of the transatlantic undersea telegraph cable. Huxley christened it *Bathybius haeckeleii*, a gesture that greatly enthused Haeckel. Huxley then speculated further about a pulsating film of protoplasm carpeting the "whole sea bottom from the Persian Gulf round Cape of Good Hope & away by St. Helena to England," but was forced to admit several years later that the gelatinous substance was not an organism but an artifact, a precipitate of calcium sulfate from the seawater that had reacted with the alcohol used as a preservative liquid. Huxley, quoted in Desmond, *Huxley: The Devil's Disciple*, 365. See also Nicholas A. Rupke, "*Bathybius Haeckelii* and the Psychol-

ogy of Scientific Discovery," *Studies in the History and Philosophy of Science* 7, no. 1 (1976): 53–62.

24 The pioneering French work was Félix Dujardin, *Sur l'organisation des infusoires* (Paris: Renouard, 1838).

25 Max Schultze, "Die Gattung Cornuspira unter den Monothamien und Bemerkungen über die Organisation und Fortpflanzung der Polythamien," *Archiv für Naturgeschichte* 26 (1860): 287–310; and William Coleman, "Cell, Nucleus, and Inheritance: An Historical Study," *Proceedings of the American Philosophical Society* 109 (1965): 124–58.

26 For different views of Haeckel, see Robert J. Richards, *The Tragic Sense of Life: Ernst Haeckel and the Struggle over Evolutionary Thought* (Chicago: University of Chicago Press, 2008); Mario Di Gregorio, *From Here to Eternity: Ernst Haeckel and Scientific Faith* (Göttingen, Germany: Vandenhoeck and Ruprecht, 2005); and Olaf Breidbach, *Visions of Nature: The Art and Science of Ernst Haeckel* (Munich: Prestel, 2006). On the social context of Haeckel's cell theory in Germany, see Paul Weindling, "Ernst Haeckel, Darwinismus and the Secularization Nature," in *History, Humanity and Evolution: Essays for John C. Greene*, ed. James R. Moore (New York: Cambridge University Press, 1989), 311–28; Weindling, "Theories of the Cell State in Imperial Germany," in *Biology, Medicine and Society 1840–1940*, ed. Charles Webster (New York: Cambridge University Press, 1981), 99–155; and Sander Gliboff, *H. G. Bronn, Ernst Haeckel, and the Origins of German Darwinism: A Study in Translation and Transformation* (Cambridge, MA: MIT Press, 2008).

27 Ernst Haeckel, "Remarks on the Protoplasm Theory," *Quarterly Journal of Microscopical Science* 10 (1869): 229.

28 E. Ray Lankester, "A Theory of Heredity: A Review of Haeckel's Pamphlet Entitled 'Perigenesis der plastidule,'" in *The Advancement of Science: Occasional Essays and Addresses* (London: Macmillan and Co., 1890), 286; originally published in *Nature*, July 15, 1876.

29 Hans-Jörg Rheinberger, *Toward a History of Epistemic Things: Synthesizing Proteins in the Test Tube* (Stanford, CA: Stanford University Press, 1997).

30 Étienne-Jules Marey, "Le Transformisme et la physiologie expérimentale," *Revue scientifique* 11, no. 35 (1873): 818.

31 Laurent Loison, *Qu'est-ce que le néolamarckisme? Les Biologistes français et la question de l'evolution des espèces* (Paris: Vuibert, 2010), 40–46.

32 Marey, "Le Transformisme et la physiologie expérimentale," 818.

33 Ewald Hering, *Über das Gedächtnis als eine allgemeine Funktion der Organisierten Materie*, 2nd ed. (Vienna: Gerold, 1876).

34 Hering, *Über das Gedächtnis*; and R. Steven Turner, *In the Eye's Mind: Vision and the Helmholtz-Hering Controversy* (Princeton. NJ: Princeton University Press, 1994), 57–58.

35   Laura Otis, *Organic Memory: History and the Body in the Late Nineteenth and Early Twentieth Centuries* (Lincoln: University of Nebraska Press, 1994); E. S. Russell, "Samuel Butler and the Memory Theories of Heredity," in *Form and Function: A Contribution to the History of Animal Morphology* (1916; Chicago: University of Chicago Press, 1982), 335–34; Samuel Butler, *Unconscious Memory*, 3rd ed. (London: Cape, 1922); and Richard Semon, *Die Mneme als erhaltendes Prinzip im Wechsel des organischen Geschehens*, 5th ed. (Leipzig: Wilhelm Engelmann, 1920).

36   Haeckel, *Über die Wellenzeugung der Lebensteilchen*, 91.

37   Jane Bennett, *Vibrant Matter: A Political Ecology of Things* (Durham, NC: Duke University Press, 2010), 17.

38   Haeckel, *Über die Wellenzeugung der Lebensteilchen*, 109.

39   Ibid..

40   Ibid., 131.

41   Ibid., 122.

42   In the fifth edition of the *Origin of Species* (1869), Darwin proclaimed Haeckel's tree a bold and "great beginning" that showed "how classification will in the future be treated." Charles Darwin, *The "Origin of Species" by Charles Darwin: A Variorum Text*, ed. Morse Peckham (Philadelphia: University of Pennsylvania Press, 1959), 676. On Darwin's reception of Haeckel's tree diagrams, see Richards, *Tragic Sense of Life*, 136–42. I thank Bob Richards for tutoring me on the different forms of Haeckel's Descent Trees.

43   Haeckel, *Über die Wellenzeugung der Lebensteilchen*, 129 (italics added).

44   On the physiological division of labor see Haeckel, *Über die Wellenzeugung der Lebensteilchen*. See also Ernst Haeckel, *Über Arbeitstheilung in der Natur- und Menschenleben* (Berlin: Luederitz, 1869). On some of the roles of this principle in nineteenth-century, biology see Camille Limoges, "Darwin, Milne-Edwards, et le principe de divergence," in *XII Congrès international d'histoire des sciences* 8 (1968): 111–15; and Gerald L. Geison and Manfred D. Laublicher, "The Varied Lives of Organisms: Variation in the Historiography of the Biological Sciences," *Studies in History and Philosophy of Biological and Biomedical Sciences* 32, no. 1 (2001): 1–29.

45   Henri Milne-Edwards, *Rapport sur les progrès récents des sciences zoologiques en France* (Paris: Imprimerie Impériale, 1867), 435. Zoologists since antiquity had, to be sure, understood animal organs by analogy to tools or mechanisms suggested by the form or structure of the anatomical features at hand. Think of Aristotle comparing the bones of the forearm, flexed by the tendons, with the arms of the catapult drawn back by tightened cables; or Borelli explaining the swimming action of the fish by comparing the caudal fin with an oar used as a rudder. Milne-Edwards's analogy was *not* this kind of *de usu partium argument*, that is, not the embodiment of a function in structure. The analogy ran in the opposite direction: from function to part, the task taking precedence over the tool.

Instead of assembling analogous forms and inferring similar functions, Milne-Edwards brought together similar functions and discovered analogous forms.

46 Henri Milne-Edwards, *Introduction à la zoologie générale* (Paris: V. Masson, 1851), 35.

47 Ibid.

48 Ibid., 23

49 Historians of biology seem not to have noticed that Milne-Edwards' principal heir in physiology was É.-J. Marey, his former student and close family friend. On the close personal relations, see Marey's *éloge* to Milne-Edwards's son, the biologist Alphonse Milne-Edwards: "Discours à l'occasion du décès de M. Milne-Edwards," *Revue scientifique*, 4th ser., no. 13 (1900): 547.

50 Haeckel, *Über die Wellenzeugung der Lebensteilchen*, 129.

51 Ibid., 109.

52 Mary Bouquet, "Family Trees and Their Affinities: The Visual Imperative of the Genealogical Diagram," *Journal of the Royal Anthropological Institute* 2, no. 1 (1996): 43–66.

53 Robert J. Richards, *The Meaning of Evolution: The Morphological Construction and Ideological Construction of Darwin's Theory* (Chicago: University of Chicago Press, 1992), 108.

54 Santiago Ramon y Cajal, "Las maravillas de la histologia," *La Clinica* (1883), cited in Ramon y Cajal, *Recuerdos de mi vida* (Madrid: Imprenta y Libreria de N. Moya, 1917), 184. Similar views can also be found in Ramon y Cajal, "El protoplasma," in *La Clinica: Seminario de medicina, cirujía y farmacia* (1880), reprinted in *Discurso de doctorado y trabajos de juventud*, ed. A. Merchán-Perez (Madrid: Universidad-Europea—CEES Ediciones, 2001).

55 Balfour Stewart and Peter Guthrie Tait, *The Unseen Universe; or, Physical Speculation on a Future State* (New York: Macmillan and Co., 1875), 156. In 1886 the mathematician Charles Howard Hinton updated this notion by analogy to the recently invented phonograph, which serves as an interface between the third and fourth dimension. See Hinton, *A Picture of Our Universe: Scientific Romances*, 1st ser.(1886; repr., New York: Arno Press, 1976), 196–97.

56 For "Aether-Waves and the Organ of their Perception," see Grant Allen, *Physiological Aesthetics* (London: Henry S. King & Co., 1877), 137.

57 Ernst Haeckel, *Das Protistenreich* (Leipzig: Guenter, 1878). On the general importance of unicellular organisms in late nineteenth-century life sciences, see Andrew Reynolds, "Amoebae as Exemplary Cells: The Protean Nature of an Elementary Organism," *Journal of the History of Biology* 41 (2008): 307–37.

58 Michael Foster, *Textbook of Physiology* (London: Macmillan and Co., 1877), 1–8, 493 (quotation).

59 Foster, quoted in Gerald L. Geison, *Michael Foster and the Cambridge School of Physiology: The Scientific Enterprise in Late Victorian Society* (Princeton, NJ: Princeton University Press, 1978), 218.

60   Foster, quoted in ibid., 203. M. Norton Wise, "Machines without Kraft: On the Cultural Meaning of Automata," in *Zeichen der Kraft: Wissensformationen 1800–1900*, ed. Thomas Brandstetter and Christof Windgaetter (Berlin: Kulturverlag Kadmos, 2008), 97, places Foster's rhythmic conception of protoplasm in the context of nineteenth-century thinking about automata, especially the distinction between (masculine) force-expending engines and (feminine) mimetic automata.

61   Foster, quoted in Geison, *Michael Foster and the Cambridge School*, 193. Like Ramon y Cajal, Foster eventually recovered from his youthful bout with protoplasmania, as he explained in an 1895 review of Max Verworn's *General Physiology* (*Allgemeine Physiologie*): "It is not for me who in my rash youth had wild dreams of building up a new physiology by beginning with the study of the amoeba, and working upwards, to say one word against the experimental investigation of lower forms of life. But experience and reflection have shown me that, after all, the physiological world is wise in spending its strength on the study of higher animals." Michael Foster, review of *Allgemeine Physiologie: Ein Grundriss der Lehre vom Leben*, by Max Verworn, *Nature* 51, no. 1327 (1895): 529–30.

62   See, for example, the critical experiments leading to modern tissue culture: Ross Harrison, "The Outgrowth of Nerve Fiber as a Mode of Protoplasmic Movement," *Journal of Experimental Zoology* 9 (1910): 787–846; Alexis Carrel and Montrose Burrows, "Cultivation of Tissues in Vitro and Its Technique," *Journal of Experimental Medicine* 13 (1911): 387–96; and Alexis Carrel, ""Physiological Time," *Science* 74 (1931): 618–21. Also compare these studies with concurrent attempts to forge a "synthetic biology" based on the manipulation of protoplasm: Alfonso L. Herrera, *Una ciencia nueva, la plasmogenia* (Mexico City: F. Diaz de Léon, 1911); and Stéphane Leduc, *Biologie synthétique* (Paris: Poinat, 1912).

63   Ernst Haeckel, *Essais de psychologie cellulaire*, translated from the German by Jules Soury (Paris: Baillière, 1880), 17–18.

64   Ernst Haeckel, *Les Preuves du transformisme: Réponse à Virchow*, translated from the German by Jules Soury (Paris: Baillière, 1879), 63–64.

65   Haeckel, *Über die Wellenzeugung der Lebensteilchen*, 238.

66   Ernst Haeckel, "Zellseelen und Seelenzellen" (1878), in *Gemeinverständliche Vorträge und Abhandlungen aus dem Gebiete der Entwicklungslehre*, 2nd ed. (Berlin: Henschel; Leipzig: Kröner, 1924), 162–95; Haeckel, "Zellseele und Zellularpsychologie" (1878), pt. 4 of "Freie Wissenschaft und freie Lehre," in *Gemeinverständliche Vorträge und Abhandlungen aus dem Gebiete der Entwicklungslehre*, 236–46; and Haeckel, *Essais de psychologie cellulaire*. On the effects of this and other cell theories on late nineteenth-century thought, see Andrea Orsucci, *Dalla biologia cellular alle scienze dello spirito: Aspetti del dibattito sull'individualità nell'Ottocento tedesco* (Bologna: Società Editrice il Mulino, 1992).

67   Schloegel and Schmidgen, "General Physiology, Experimental Psychology, and Evolutionism."

68 Verworn (1887), quoted in ibid., 630.

69 Alfred Binet, *The Psychic Life of Microorganisms: A Study in Experimental Psychology*, trans. Thomas McCormack (Chicago: Open Court, 1897).

70 Ibid.

71 Théodule Ribot, "Les Mouvements et leur importance psychologiques," *Revue philosophique* 8 (1879): 383.

72 Frédéric Paulhan, *Les Phénomènes affectifs et les lois de leur apparition: Essai de psychologie générale* (Paris: Alcan, 1887); Charles Féré, *Sensation et mouvement: Études expérimentales de psycho-mécanique* (Paris: F. Alcan, 1887); and Charles Richet, *L'Homme et l'intelligence: Fragments de physiologie et de psychologie* (Paris: F. Alcan, 1884).

73 Jean Marie Guyau, "Mémoire et phonographe," *Revue philosophique* 4 (1880): 320.

74 Jules Soury, review of *Anatomie et physiologie comparée de la pholade dactyle*, by Raphaël Du Bois, *Revue philosophique* 40 (1895): 547.

75 Ibid., 543.

76 Peirce, "Man's Glassy Essence," 165.

77 Ibid., 171.

78 Henri Bergson, *Evolution créatrice* (Paris: Presses Universitaires de France, 1907). All citations of this work refer to the updated revised edition of Arthur Mitchell's authorized 1911 translation: Henri Bergson, *Creative Evolution*, trans. Arthur Mitchell, ed. Keith Ansell Pearson, Michael Kolkman, and Michael Vaughan with an introduction by Keith Ansell Pearson (London: Palgrave, 2007). On Bergson and biology, see Yvette Conry, *L'Évolution créatrice d'Henri Bergson: Investigations critiques* (Paris: L'Harmattan, 2000); and Keith Ansell Pearson, "Bergson's Encounter with Biology: Thinking Life," *Angelaki* 10 (2005): 59–72.

79 Spyridon Koutroufinis, "Ontogenetisches Werden im Lichte der Lebens-und Prozessphilosophie von Henri Bergson" (habilitation thesis, Technical University of Berlin, 2009).

80 Bergson, *Creative Evolution*, xxxviii.

81 On this point see the review by the biologist Félix Le Dantec, "La Biologie de M. Bergson," *Revue du mois* 4 (1907): 230–41, which endorsed Bergson's critique of Spencer and pointed out that it extended to "Darwin with his gemmules, Weismann with his determinants, and all the partisans of representative particles."

82 Bergson, *Creative Evolution*, 15.

83 Herbert Spencer Jennings, *Contributions to the Study of the Behavior of Lower Organisms* (Washington, DC: Carnegie Institution, 1904); Maupas, "Étude des infsoires ciliés," *Archive de zoologie expérimentale* 4 (1883): 4; P. Vignon, *Recherches de cytologie générale sur les épithéliums* (Paris, 1912).

84 Henri Bergson, *Matter and Memory*, trans. Nancy Margaret Paul and W. Scott Palmer (Mineola, NY: Dover, 2004), 22.

85 Bergson, *Creative Evolution*, 24.

86 Ibid., 28.

87 Ibid., 17 (italics in original).

88 Claude Bernard, *Leçons sur les phénomènes de la vie communs aux animaux et aux végétaux* (1978), ed. Georges Canguilhem (Paris: Vrin, 1966), 292–93.

89 Bergson, *Creative Evolution*, 23.

90 Ibid., 22. See also Otto Bütschli, *Über die Struktur des Protoplasmas: Untersuchungen über mikroskopische Schäume und das Protoplasma; Versuchen und Beobachtungen zur Lösung der Frage nach den physikalischen Bedingungen der Lebenserscheinungen* (Leipzig: Engelman, 1892).

91 This point would be contested by later biologists, like Constantin Monakow, who otherwise found great inspiration in Bergson's work. "In my view," Monakow wrote, "it is completely impossible to separate the psychic from the physical in living protoplasm." Monakow, letter to Bergson scholar Raoul Mourgue (1919), quoted in Anne Harrington, *Reenchanted Science: Holism in German Culture from Wilhelm II to Hitler* (Cambridge, MA: Harvard University Press, 1996), 92.

92 Bergson, *Creative Evolution*, 11.

93 Henri Bergson, *Matter and Memory*, 332.

94 Alexis Carrel, "Physiological Time," *Science* 74, no. 1929 (1931): 618–21; Carrel, *L'Homme, cet inconnu* (Paris: Plon, 1935); Constantin von Monakow and Raoul Mourgue, *Introduction biologique à l'étude de la neurologie et de la psychopathologie* (Paris: Alcan, 1928); Pierre Lecomte du Noüy, "Sur une constant d'activité physiologique ne dependant que de l'âge," *Sunti delle communcazioni scientiliche, XIV Congresso internazionale di fisiologia* (Rome, 1932); and Raoul Mourgue, "Une Découverte scientifique: La Durée bergsonienne," *Revue philosophique* 120 (1935): 350–66.

95 The experimental techniques are discussed in Jean Comandon, Constantin Levatidi, and Stefan Mutermilch, "Étude de la vie et de la croissance des cellules in vitro à l'aide de l'enregistrement cinématographique," *Comptes rendus des séances de la Société de la Biologie* 74 (1913): 464–67. On Carrel's cinematography and tissue culture, see Hannah Landecker's excellent studies, "Cellular Features: Microcinematography and Early Film Theory," *Critical Inquiry* 31 (2005): 903–37; and *Culturing Life: How Cells Became Technologies* (Cambridge, MA: Harvard University Press, 2007).

96 Carrel, "Physiological Time," 621.

97 Landecker, *Culturing Life*, 87.

98 Bergson, *Creative Evolution*, 114.

99 Ibid.

100 Ibid.

3. Visible Speech

1   Michel Bréal, "Les Lois phoniques: À propos de la création du laboratoire de phonétique expérimentale au Collège de France," *Mémoires de la Société de linguistique de Paris* 10 (1898): 11.

2   The description of the modern laboratory is from Bruno Latour and Steve Woolgar, *Laboratory Life: The Construction of Scientific Facts*, 2nd ed. (Princeton, NJ: Princeton University Press, 1986), first published 1979. See also Hans-Jörg Rheinberger, *Experiment, Differenz, Schrift* (Marburg, Germany: Basiliskenpresse, 1992). On the development of a modern science of signification see Hans Aarsleff, "Bréal, 'la sémantique,' and Saussure," in *From Locke to Saussure: Essays on the Study of Language and Intellectual History* (Minneapolis: University of Minnesota Press, 1982), 382–400.

3   A notable exception is Henning Schmidgen, "The Donders Machine: Matter, Signs, and Time in a Physiological Experiment, ca. 1865," *Configurations* 13, no. 2 (2005): 211–56.

4   The discontinuity is recounted in Aarsleff, *From Locke to Saussure*. One of the few works by a historian of linguistics to grant importance to the phonetics laboratory is Sylvain Auroux, "La Catégorie du *parler* et la linguistique," *Romantisme* 9, nos. 25–26 (1979): 170–73.

5   Auroux, "La Catégorie du *parler*," 169.

6   Michel Bréal, *Essai de sémantique*, 5th ed. (Paris: Hachette, 1911), 255–56. On the impact of the telegraph on the commodification of information in the nineteenth-century United States, see JoAnne Yates, *Control through Communication: The Rise of System in American Management* (Baltimore: Johns Hopkins University Press, 1989), 21–36.

7   Gabriel Tarde was elected to the Collège de France in 1900, as a result of his work in the 1890s.

8   For a study of the contributors and content of the principal organ of the Société de linguistique, see Piet Desmet, *"La Revue de linguistique et de philologie comparée* (1867–1916)—organe de la linguistique naturaliste en France," *Beiträge zur Geschichte der Sprachwissenschaft* 4, no. 1 (1994): 49–80.

9   Léon Vaïsse, "Discours du président," *Bulletin de la Société de linguistique* 1–5 (1869–85): cliii.

10   On nationalism in German philology, see Richard Bauman and Charles L. Briggs, *Voices of Modernity: Language Ideologies and the Politics of Inequality* (Cambridge: Cambridge University Press, 2003), especially chapters 5 and 6; and Olga Amsterdamska, *Schools of Thought: The Development of Linguistics from Bopp to Saussure* (Dordrecht: D. Reidel, 1987), especially chapter 3.

11   Bréal received much of his education in Germany. See his *Excursions pédagogique: Un Voyage scolaire en Allemagne* (Paris: A. Lahure, 1884). A brief biographical

sketch of Bréal is contained in the translator's preface to Michel Bréal, *The Beginnings of Semantics: Essays, Lectures and Reviews*, trans. and ed. George Wolf (London: Duckworth, 1991), 3–4.

12   Suzanne L. Marchand, *German Orientalism in the Age of Empire: Religion, Race, and Scholarship* (Cambridge: Cambridge University Press, 2009); Sabine Mangold, *Eine "weltbürgerliche Wissenschaft": Die deutsche Orientalistik im 19. Jahrhundert* (Stuttgart: Steiner, 2004); and Dietmar Rothermund, *The German Intellectual Quest for India* (New Delhi: Manihar, 1986).

13   François Bopp, *Grammaire comparée des langues indo-européenes comprenant le sanscrit, le zend, l'armenien, le grec, le latin, le lithuanien, l'ancien slave, le gothique et l'allemand*, trans. M. Michel Bréal, 2 vols. (Paris: Imprimerie Nationale, 1866). On Bopp, see also Michel Foucault, *The Order of Things* (New York: Random House, 1970).

14   Michel Bréal, introduction to *Grammaire comparée*, by François Bopp, xxiv.

15   Bréal reminded his readers that Parisians regularly took up linguistic affectations, such as the eighteenth-century vogue for pronouncing *r* like *s* and *s* like *r*: *Paris* became *Pazis*, *mari* became *mazi*, and conversely *un oiseau* became *un oireau*. Some affectations, such as this one, were duly discarded, but others could become incorporated into language. See Michel Bréal, "Le Langage et les nationalités," *Revue des deux mondes* 108 (1891): 622–23; and Bréal, "Les Lois phoniques," 3.

16   Vaïsse, "Discours du président," cliii.

17   Léon Vaïsse, "Notes pour servir à l'histoire des machines parlantes," *Mémoires de la Société de linguistique de Paris* 3 (1878): 257–68. On Kempelen's speaking automaton, see Brigitte Felderer and Ernst Stouhal, *Kempelen—Zwei Maschinen: Texte, Bilder und Modelle zur Sprechmaschinen und zum schachspielenden Androiden Wolfgang von Kempelens* (Vienna: Sonderzahl, 2003). On the history of talking machines, see Thomas L. Hankins and Robert J. Silverman, *Instruments and the Imagination* (Princeton, NJ: Princeton University Press, 1995); Briggite Felderer, "Stimm-Maschinen: Zur Konstruktion und Sichtbarmachung menschlicher Sprache im 18. Jahrhundert," in *Zwischen Rauschen und Offenbarung: Zur Kultur-und Mediengeschichte der Stimme*, ed. Friedrich Kittler, Thomas Macho, and Sigrid Weigel (Berlin: Akademie, 2002), 257–78; and Giulio Panconcelli-Calzia, *Geschichtszahlen der Phonetik: Quellenatlas der Phonetik*, ed. Konrad Koerner (Philadelphia: John Benjamins, 2003).

18   Alexander Melville Bell, *A New Elucidation of the Principles of Speech and Elocution* (1849), quoted in Robert V. Bruce, *Bell: Alexander Graham Bell and the Conquest of Solitude* (Boston: Little, Brown, 1973), 19.

19   Léon Vaïsse, "Notation des sons du langages," *Bulletin de la Société de linguistique de Paris* 1–5 (1869–85): clv.

20   Étienne-Jules Marey, *La Méthode graphique dans le sciences expérimentales et principalement en physiologie et en médicine* (Paris: G. Masson, 1878), v.

21 See Mara Mills, "The Dead Room: Deafness and Modern Communications Technologies" (PhD diss., Harvard University, 2006), especially chapter 3.

22 For contemporary French views of the Pratisakhya, see Adolphe Regnier, *Études sur la grammaire védique: Praticakya du Rig-Véda* (Paris: Imprimerie Impériale, 1859).

23 W. S. Allen remarked upon the mingling of prescription with description in the aphorisms of the *Pratisakhya*: "Their avowed purpose is to preserve the oral tradition of the sacred texts: to this end the direst penalties are threatened for mispronunciation, including descent to the hell of Kumbhipaka; the competent pupil, on the other hand, is encouraged by verses such as that which closes the Tattiriya-Pratisakhya—'He who knows the distinctions of tone and length may go and sit with the professors.'" See W. S. Allen, *Phonetics in Ancient India* (London: Geoffrey Cumberlege, 1953), 6.

24 For a twentieth-century discussion of the *yamas*, see Allen, *Phonetics in Ancient India*, 75–78.

25 This quarrel was part of the long engagement with premodern Sanskrit linguistics through which modern linguistics was forged. As Sheldon Pollock observes in his magisterial *Language of the Gods and the World of Men: Sanskrit, Culture, and Power in Premodern India* (Berkeley: University of California Press, 2006): "In one of the subtler ironies of Western intellectual history, Franz Bopp, William Dwight Whitney, Ferdinand de Saussure, Emile Benveniste, Leonard Bloomfield, and Noam Chomsky learning both substantively and theoretically from Indian premodernity (being all them Sanskritists or students of Sanskrit-knowing scholars), developed successively historical, structural, and transformational linguistics and, by these new forms of thought . . . some basic conceptual components of Western modernity itself" (164).

26 Charles Rosapelly, "Inscription de mouvements phonétiques," *Physiologie expérimentale: Travaux du laboratoire de M. Marey* (Paris: G. Masson) 2 (1875): 113, 110.

27 Étienne-Jules Marey, "Inscription des phénomènes phonétiques d'après les travaux de divers auteurs," *Journal des savants* 20 (October 1897): 564.

28 Rosapelly, "Inscription de mouvements phonétiques."

29 Ibid., 113.

30 On Rudolph Koenig, see David Pantalony, *Altered Sensations: Rudolph Koenig's Acoustical Workshop in 19th Century Paris* (New York: Springer, 2009).

31 The term *phoneme* was initially used in conjunction with these experiments. First used in a paper delivered to the Société de linguistique by the philologist A. Dufriche-Desgenettes as an alternative to the inelegant *son du langage*, it was taken up by Louis Havet, who is credited by historians of phonetics with authoring the term and disseminating it through the auspices of the International Phonetic Association, which he helped inaugurate in 1886. See Jiri Kramsky, *The Phoneme: Introduction to the History and Theories of a Concept* (Munich: Wilhelm

Fink, 1974), 21; and David Jones, *The History and Meaning of the Term "Phoneme"* (London: International Phonetic Association, 1957).

32 Wilbur A. Benware, *The Study of Indo-European Vocalism in the 19th Century* (Amsterdam: John Benjamins, 1974), 13–14. See also the Leipzig dissertation of Ferdinand de Saussure, *Mémoire sur le système primitif des voyelles dans les langues indoeuropéenes* (Leipzig: Vieweg, 1878).

33 Robert Willis, "On Vowel Sounds, and on Reed Pipes," *Transactions of the Cambridge Philosophical Society* 3 (1830): 231–68.

34 On this question, see Hans Günter Tillman, "Early Modern Instrumental Phonetics," in *Concise History of the Language Sciences: From Sumerians to the Cognivitists*, ed. E. F. K. Koerner and R. E. Asher (Oxford: Pergamon, 1995), 401–15.

35 Julia Kursell, "A Gray Box: The Phonograph in Laboratory Experiments and Field Work, 1900–1920," in *The Oxford Handbook of Sound Studies*, ed. Karin Bijsterveld and Trevor Pinch (New York: Oxford University Press, 2011), 176–97.

36 Léon Scott de Martinville, *La Fixation graphique de la voix* (Paris: Société d'Encouragement, 1857), 1. On Scott, see also Hankins and Silverman, *Instruments and the Imagination*, 133–37. On the growth of stenographic instruments in the United States, see Yates, *Control through Communication*, 36–45.

37 Léon Scott de Martinville, *Histoire de la sténographie depuis les temps anciens jusqu'à nos jours; ou précis historique et critique des divers moyens qui ont été proposés ou employés pour rendre l'écriture aussi rapide que la parole* (Paris: Charles Tondeur, 1849).

38 Jonathan Sterne, *The Audible Past: Cultural Origins of Sound Reproduction* (Durham, NC: Duke University Press, 2003), 34–39.

39 Ibid., 34.

40 Ernst Brücke, *Grundzüge der Physiologie und Systematik der Sprechlaute für Linguisten und Taubstummlehrer* (Vienna: Gerold, 1856), 29–30.

41 Franciscus Cornelis Donders, "Ueber die Natur der Vocale (Erste briefliche Mittheilung an Herrn Prof. Bruecke von F. C. Donders)," *Archiv für die holländischen Beiträge zur Natur-und Heilkunde* 1 (1858): 157–62.

42 Franciscus Cornelius Donders, "Zur Klangfarbe der Vocale," *Annalen der Physik* 199 (1864): 527–28. See also Schmidgen, "Donders Machine."

43 Kursell, "Gray Box," 183–85.

44 Rudolph Koenig, *Quelques expériences de l'acoustique* (Paris: Lahure, 1882). Koenig won gold medals for his apparatus at both the International Exhibition of 1862 in London and at the Philadelphia Centennial Exposition of 1876. For further description, see Koenig, *Catalogue des appareils d'acoustique* (Paris, 1882); and Jules Gavarret, *Phénomènes physique de la phonation* (Paris: G. Masson, 1877). On Koenig's vowel studies, see David Pantalony, "Seeing a Voice: Rudolph Koenig's Instruments for Studying Vowel Sounds," *American Journal of Psychology* 117, no. 3 (2004): 271–86. For Koenig more broadly, see Pantalony, *Altered Sensations*.

45 Kursell, "Gray Box," 179–81.

46 W. H. Barlow, *Popular Science Review* 13 (1874): 278–88; and Barlow, *Proceedings of the Royal Society* 22 (1873–74): 277–89.

47 Alexander Graham Bell, "Researches in Electric Telephony," *Journal of the Society of Telegraph Engineers* 6 (1877): 385–416, quoted in Charles Snyder, "Clarence John Blake and Alexander Graham Bell: Otology and the Telephone," *Annals of Otology, Rhinology and Laryngology* 83, no. 2, S13 (1974): 3–31.

48 Clarence J. Blake, "The Use of the Membrana Tympani as a Phonautograph and Logograph," *Archives of Ophthalmalogy and Otology* 5 (1876): 108–13. See also Comte Th. A. L. Du Moncel, *The Telephone, the Microphone, and the Phonograph* (New York: Harpers, 1879); and G. B. Prescott, *The Speaking Telephone, Talking Phonograph, and other Novelties* (New York: Appleton, 1878).

49 Although he lost the competition over the original voice transmission patent to Alexander Graham Bell—often described as the single most valuable patent in the world (before the MS-DOS computer operating system)—Edison continued to churn out scads of patents concerned with telephonic improvements and microphones. See Oliver Read and Walter L. Welch, *From Tin Foil to Stereo: Evolution of the Phonograph* (Indianapolis, IN: H. W. Sams, 1959), 11.

50 Marey, "Inscription des phénomènes phonétiques," 583.

51 See L. Hermann, "Phonophotographische Untersuchungen," *Archive für die gesammte Physiologie* 45 (1889): 582; Hermann, "Über das Verhalten der Vokale am neuen Edison'schen Phonographen," *Archive für die gesammte Physiologie* 47 (1890): 44; Ph. Wagner, "Über die Verwendung der Grützner-Marey'schen Apparats u.d. Phonographen zur phonetischen Untersuchungen," *Phonetische Studien* 4 (1890): 68; and J. McKendrick, G. Murray, and D. Wingate, "Committee Report on the Physiological Application of the Phonograph and on the Form of the Voice Curves by the Instrument," *Reports of the British Association for the Advancement of Science* (1896): 669.

52 H. Marichelle, *La Parole d'après le tracé du phonographe* (Paris: Delagrave, 1897); and Marichelle and Hémardinger, "Études des sons de la parole par le phonographe," *Comptes rendues de l'Académie des sciences de Paris* 135 (1897): 884.

53 Georges-René-Marie Marage, "Formation des voyelles," *L'Année psychologique* 6 (1899): 485–92. See also Hankins and Silverman, *Instruments and the Imagination,* 210–11.

54 Georges Demeny, "Analyse des mouvements de la parole par la chronophotographie," *Comptes rendues de l'Académie des sciences* 113 (1891): 216–17. See also Demeny, "Les Photographies parlantes," *La Nature* 20 (April 16, 1892): 311–15; and Demeny, "La Photographie de la parole," *Paris-Photographe* 1, no. 7 (1891): 306–8.

55 Marta Braun, *Picturing Time: The Work of Étienne-Jules Marey (1830–1904)* (Chicago: University of Chicago Press, 1992), 180–82.

56 Marey, "Inscription des phénomènes phonétiques," 582.

57   Yates, *Control through Communication*, 45.

58   Louis Couturat, *Les Nouvelles Langues internationales* (Paris: Hachette, 1907); Otto Jespersen, *Phonetische Grundfragen* (Leipzig: B. G Teubner, 1904); and John G. McKendrick, "Experimental Phonetics," *Nature* 65, no. 1678 (1901): 182–89.

59   Eduard Koschwitz, "La Phonétique expérimentale et la philologie Franco-Provençal," *Revue des patois gallo-romanes* 4 (1891): 215.

60   See the review of a course at the École des hautes études entitled "Phonétique des patois" in Abbé Rousselot, "Introduction a l'étude des patois," *Revue des patois gallo-roman*s 1 (1887): 1–23.

61   Lucien Adam, *Les Patois lorrains* (Paris: Maisonneuve, 1881); and Adam, *Les Classifications, l'objet, la méthode, les conclusions de la linguistique* (Paris: Maisonneuve, 1882). The rapid disappearance of the patois can be attributed in part to the previous attempts to eradicate them, as well as to the zealous program of public education in the Third Republic. Already in 1887, in "Introduction a l'étude des patois," the Abbé Rousselot wrote, "The patois are disappearing and it is already late to recover them" (3). By the early twentieth century, the attempt to recover disappearing languages had become an urgent international project, carried out by ethnologists and several state-sponsored phonographic archives.

62   Koschwitz, "La Phonétique expérimentale et la philologie Franco-Provençal," 215.

63   Hubert Pernot, "L'Abbé Rousselot (1846–1924)," *Revue de l'alliance française* 22 (1925): 135.

64   Abbé Rousselot, *Les Modifications phonétiques du langage étudiée dans le patois d'une famille de Cellefrouin* (Paris: H. Welter, 1891); and Rousselot, *La Méthode graphique appliquée à la phonétique* (Paris: Macon, 1890).

65   Compare the methods of visualizing speech and geographical mapping in the Humboldtian tradition described in Matti Bunzl, "Franz Boas and the Humboldtian Tradition: From Volksgeist and Nationalcharakter to an Anthropological Concept of Culture," in *Volksgeist as Method and Ethic: Essays on Boasian Ethnography and the German Anthropological Tradition*, ed. George Stocking (Madison: University of Wisconsin Press, 1996), 17–78; and Michael Dettelbach, "The Face of Nature: Precise Measurement, Mapping, and Sensibility in the Work of Alexander von Humboldt," *Studies in the History and Philosophy of Biological and Biomedical Sciences* 30 (1999): 473–504.

66   Rousselot, *Les Modifications phonétiques*, 2.

67   Ibid., 23.

68   On Gregoire's policy of *écraser les patois,* see David Bell, "Lingua Populi, Lingua Dei: Language, Religion, and the Origins of French Revolutionary Nationalism," *American Historical Review* 100, no. 5 (1995): 1403–37; Michel de Certeau, Dominique Julia, and Jacques Revel, *Une Politique de la langue: La Revolution française et le patois* (Paris: Gallimard, 1975); and R. D. Grillo, *Dominant Languages: Language*

and Hierarchy in Britain and France (Cambridge: Cambridge University Press, 1989), 24.

69 In his treatise on Hebrew grammar, Spinoza expressed it thus: "Vowels are not letters, but their 'soul,' and letters without vowels, or consonants, are the 'bodies without soul.'" See de Certeau, Julia, and Revel, *Une Politique de la langue*, 97.

70 De Certeau, Julia, and Revel, *Une Politique de la langue*, 114.

71 Rousselot, *Les Modifications phonétiques*, 10.

72 Ibid.

73 Rousselot, *Les Modifications phonétiques*, 7–8. In the wake of Rousselot's enormous international success among linguists and ethnographers, Verdin sold many examples of the kit, especially in Germany, for 1,724 francs. See Charles Verdin, *Catalogue des instruments de précision pour la physiologie et la medicine* (Paris: Verdin, 1890); and Eduard Koschwitz, "Der Registrierapparat," *Archiv für das Studium der neueren Sprachen* 88 (1892): 244–53.

74 Rousselot, *Les Modifications phonétiques*, 8–19.

75 Two celebrated examples of such works from the period are Rudolfo Livi, *Antropometria militare, risultati ottenuti dallo spoglio dei fogli sanitarii dei militari delle classi 1859–63*, 2 vols. (Roma: Presso il Giornale Medico del Regio Esercito, 1896); and John Beddoe, *The Races of Britain, a Contribution to the Anthropology of Western Europe* (Bristol: Arrowsmith, 1885).

76 Rousselot, *Les Modifications phonétiques*, 147.

77 Ibid., 97.

78 The Abbé Gorse gave a similar account, in an anecdote recounted by Eugen Weber: "'Parlez français,' says the master to the pupil. 'Monsieur, je parle comme je save et comme je poude.' The villager forgets a little of his mother tongue at school, and learns only a parody of French." See Weber, *Peasants into Frenchmen: The Modernization of Rural France, 1870–1914* (London: Chatto and Windus, 1979), 67.

79 Rousselot, *Les Modifications phonétiques*, 98.

80 Hermann Breymann, *Die phonetische Literatur von 1876–1895* (Leipzig: Deichert, 1897), 129–35. A list of reviews of Rousselot's work appears on page 55.

81 Anonymous, review of *Les Modifications phonétique du langage étudiée dans le patois d'une famille de Cellefrouin and Paul Passy, étude sur les changements phonétiques et leurs caractères généraux*, by Abbé Rousselot, *Literaturblatt für germanische und romanische Philologie* 9 (1892): 314.

82 L. Azoulay, "L'Ère nouvelle des sons et des bruits—musées et archives phonographiques," *Bulletins et Mémoires de la Société d'anthropologie de Paris* 1 (1900): 172–78. This article was also published in *Revue scientifique* 13 (1900): 712–15.

83 Quoted in McKendrick, "Experimental Phonetics," 1678.

84 Azoulay, "L'Ère nouvelle des sons et des bruits," 178.

85 McKendrick, "Experimental Phonetics," 1678.

86   Rousselot, *Les Modifications phonétiques.*

87   Hubert Pernot, "L'Abbé Rousselot (1846–1924)," *Revue de phonétiques* 5 (1928): 17–21.

88   Gabriel Tarde, *Les Lois sociales: Esquisse d'une sociologie* (Paris: F. Alcan, 1898), 65–66. Bruno Latour describes Tarde as a precursor to the actor-network approach to the sociology of innovation. See Latour, "Gabriel Tarde and the End of the Social," in *The Social in Question: New Bearings in History and the Social Sciences*, ed. Patrick Joyce, (London: Routledge, 2002), 117–32.

89   St. Thomas Aquinas, *Summa contra gentiles* 1.2.c.77.

90   Gabriel Tarde, "Les Vers impairs," *Le Semeur* 19 (1890): 601. See also the continuation in *Le Semeur* 20 (1890): 639–43, which includes two of Tarde's own poems.

4. Algorithms of Pleasure

1   Quoted in Anonymous, review of *Physiological Aesthetics*, by Grant Allen, *Popular Science Monthly* 11, no. 41 (October 1877): 760.

2   Grant Allen, *Physiological Aesthetics* (London: Henry S. King & Co., 1877); and Herbert Spencer developed his "Aestho-Physiology," in *The Principles of Psychology* (1877), reprinted in *The Works of Herbert Spencer*, 3rd ed. (Osnabrueck, Germany: Otto Zeller, 1966), vol. 2, pt. 9, chapter 9. Spencer's "Origin and Function of Music" (1857), reprinted in *Essays: Moral, Political, and Aesthetic* (New York: D. Appleton, 1889), contained his account of speech and musical expression, which also found broad influence in the literature of physiological aesthetics. See Jean-Marie Guyau, *Problèmes de l'esthétique contemporaine* (Paris: F. Alcan, 1884); Gabriel Séailles, *Essai sur le génie dans l'art* (Paris: Baillière, 1883); and Émile Hennequin, *La Critique scientifique* (Paris: Perrin, 1888).

3   On Charles Henry, see especially, Michael Zimmerman, *Les Mondes de Seurat: Son oeuvre et le débat artistique de son temp*, trans. J. Ferry, S. Schnall, K. F. Willems (Paris: Fonds Mercator/Albin Michel, 1991); and Robert L. Herbert, "'Parade de cirque' de Seurat et l'esthétique scientifique de Charles Henry." *Revue de l'art* 50 (1980): 9–23. José A. Argüelles, *Charles Henry and the Formation of a Psycho-Physical Aesthetic* (Chicago: University of Chicago Press, 1972), is less reliable. For good summaries of Henry's work by contemporaries, see Jules Héricourt, "Une Théorie mathématique de l'expression: Le Contraste, le rythme et la mesure d'après les travaux de M. Charles Henry," *Revue scientifique* 44 (1889): 586–93; and Anonymous, "Psychophysics," *The Nation* 1319 (October 9,1890): 290–92. For posthumous appreciation and reminiscences, see the special issue "Hommage à Charles Henry," *Cahiers de l'étoile* 13 (January–February 1930).

4   Harry M. Collins, "Expert Systems and the Science of Knowledge," in *The Social Construction of Technological Systems*, ed. Wiebe J. Bijker, Thomas P. Hughes, and Trevor J. Pinch (Cambridge, MA: MIT Press, 1987), 329–48.

5   Paul Signac, *D'Eugène Delacroix au néo-impressionnisme* (1899; Paris: Hermann, 1964), 158.

6   Charles Henry, "Introduction à une esthétique scientifique," *La Revue contemporaine* 2 (1885): 466.

7   Ibid., 444–45.

8   Ibid., 28.

9   Judith Wechsler, *A Human Comedy: Physiognomy and Caricature in Nineteenth-Century Paris* (Chicago: University of Chicago Press, 1982), 16.

10   Jennifer Montagu, *The Expression of the Passions: The Origin and Influence of Charles Le Brun's "Conférence sur l'expression générale et particulière"* (London: Yale University Press, 1994). On physiognomy in French art education, see Anthea Callen, *The Spectacular Body: Science, Method, and Meaning in the Work of Degas* (London: Yale University Press, 1995), 1–35.

11   Charles Blanc, *Grammaire des arts du dessin: Architecture, sculpture, peinture* (Paris: Henri Lauren, 1867).

12   David Pierre Giottino Humbert de Superville, *Essai sur les signes inconditionnels dans l'art* (Leiden: Hoek, 1827–32). On Humbert, see Barbara Maria Stafford, *Symbol and Myth: Humbert de Superville's Essay on Absolute Signs in Art* (London: Associated University Presses, 1979).

13   Blanc, *Grammaire*, 35.

14   Ibid., 30.

15   Ibid., 27–30, 560–65.

16   For Henry's relations to Mosso's experiments, see Charles Henry, *Cercle chromatique, presentant tous les compléments et toutes les harmonies de couleurs* (Paris: Charles Verdin, 1888), 7. See also the many studies of color and sound in Charles Féré, *Sensation et mouvement: Études expérimentales de psycho-mécanique* (Paris: F. Alcan, 1887), 36–48.

17   For this work Brown-Séquard won the prestigious Lallemand Prize of the Academy of Sciences in 1885. For accounts of his work, see the summary of his course at the Collège de France in Charles-Édouard Brown-Séquard, "Collège de France: Cours de médecine par. M. Brown-Séquard," *Gazette hebdomadaire de médecine et de chirurgue* 16 (1879): 771. See also Brown-Séquard, *Recherches expérimentales et cliniques sur l'inhibition et la dynamogénie—Application des connaissances fournies par ces recherches aux phénomènes principaux de l'hypnotisme et du transfert* (Paris: G. Masson, 1882); Brown-Séquard, "Champ d'action de l'inhibition en physiologie, en pathogénie et en thérapeutique," *Archives de physiologie normales et pathologique* (Paris: G. Masson) 5, no. 1 (1889): 1–23; and Charles François-Franck, *Leçons sur les fonctions motrices du cerveau et sur l'épilepsie cérébrale* (Paris: Octave Doin, 1887). On Brown-Séquard's life and work, see Michael J. Aminoff, *Brown-Séquard: A Visionary of Science* (New York: Raven Press, 1993); and J. M. D. Olmsted, *Charles-Édouard Brown-Séquard: A Nineteenth Century Neurologist and Endocrinologist* (Baltimore: Johns Hopkins Press, 1946).

18   Charles Henry, "Sur la dynamogénie et l'inhibition: Note de M. Charles Henry

présentée par M. Brown-Séquard," *Comptes rendues de l'Académie des sciences* 108 (January 7, 1889): 70.

19 For a general history of the concept of inhibition, see Roger Smith, *Inhibition: History and Meaning in the Sciences of Mind and Brain* (Berkeley: University of California Press, 1992).

20 Charles-Édouard Brown-Séquard, "Expérience démontrant la puissance dynamogénique chez l'homme d'un liquide extrait de testicules d'animaux," *Archives de physiologie normale et pathologique* (Paris: G. Masson), 5th ser., vol. 1 (1889): 651–58. On the sensational reception of Brown-Séquard's experiments in the United States, see Merriley Borell, "Brown-Séquard's Organotherapy and Its Appearance in America at the End of the Nineteenth Century," *Bulletin of the History of Medicine* 50 (1976): 309–20.

21 Michael Zimmerman points out that Henry's formulation of the dynamogeny/inhibition principle deviates in important ways from Brown-Séquard. The most crucial difference lies in the requirement that every act of perception requires a supplementary quantity of work by the organism. See Zimmerman, *Les Mondes de Seurat*, 256–57.

22 Herbert Spencer, *Les Bases de la moral évolutionniste* (Paris: Ballière, 1880), 74. Charles Féré also refers to Spencer on this point.

23 Charles Richet, *Recherches expérimentales et clinique sur la sensibilité* (Paris: G. Masson, 1877); and Richet, "La Douleur: Étude de psychologie physiologique," *Revue philosophique* 4 (1877): 457–81. On Richet, see Stewart Wolf, *Brain, Mind, and Medicine: Charles Richet and the Origin of Physiological Psychology* (New Brunswick, NJ: Transaction Publishing, 1993).

24 Richet, "La Douleur," 480.

25 To augment the general biological significance of his findings, Richet took on board Mantegazza's clinical findings that certain organic functions diminished after dolorous stimuli. Richet conducted experiments to test this claim, finding that the pain made the pulse subside and respiration accelerate in rabbits and dogs. But Richet, sticking to his contention that pain is a cerebral act, would not link pain with inhibition, which was a more general physiological state, except when the stimuli were extremely strong. Only then, he allowed, could there be not a stimulus of the marrow, but a suspension of its action: "This is one of the phenomena of arrest, of inhibition, which M. Brown-Séquard and others have for some time subjected to patient research." See Charles Richet, *L'Homme et l'intelligence: Fragments de physiologie et de psychologie* (Paris: F. Alcan, 1884), 462; and Paolo Mantegazza, *La fisiologia del dolore* (Florence: Poggi, 1880).

26 Henry, "Sur la dynamogénie et l'inhibition," 70–71.

27 Féré, *Sensation et mouvement*, 84.

28 Deborah Silverman, *Art Nouveau in Fin-de-Siècle France: Politics, Psychology, and Style* (Berkeley: University of California Press, 1989), 75–106.

29 Féré, *Sensation et mouvement*, 14.

30 Ibid., 33–34.

31 Ibid., 36.

32 Ibid., 46.

33 Charles Henry, *Rapporteur esthétique: Notice sur ses applications à l'art industriel, à l'histoire de l'art, à l'interprétation de la méthode graphique* (Paris: G. Séguin, 1888), 15.

34 Ibid.

35 One critic who seems to have comprehended most of Henry's mathematics was Jules Héricourt; see his "Théorie mathématique de l'expression." Féré rejected the mathematical interpretation of the ideomotor function. In remarks presumably directed at Henry, he insisted that "it is necessary to resist the temptation to make a psychomechanical law in mathematical form" on the grounds that the "dynamic state of an experimental subject varies incessantly under the influence of ingesta and of circumfusa," influences "impossible to rigorously determine." See Féré, *Sensation et mouvement*, 49.

36 Henry, *Cercle chromatique*, 105–11.

37 On Helmholtz's theory and its sources, see the excellent chapter by Timothy Lenoir, "The Eye as Mathematician: Clinical Practice, Instrumentation, and Helmholtz's Construction of an Empiricist Theory of Vision," in *Hermann von Helmholtz and the Foundations of Nineteenth-Century Science*, ed. David Cahan (Berkeley: University of California Press, 1993), 109–53. See also H. J. Simonsz and I. Den Tonkelaar, "19th Century Models of Eye Movements, Donder's Law, Listing's Law and Helmholtz's Directional Circles," *Documenta Opthamologica* 74 (1990): 95–112.

38 Henry, "Introduction à une esthétique scientifique," 6.

39 Charles Henry, "Société de psychologie physiologique: Sur une loi générale de réactions psychomotrices," *Revue philosophique* 2 (1890): 108.

40 Argüelles, *Charles Henry and the Formation of a Psycho-Physical Aesthetic*.

41 Henry, *Cercle chromatique*, 105–9. Again, for a clearer account, see Lenoir, "Eye as Mathematician," 142–48. For Helmholtz's discussion, see his "Ueber die normalen Bewegungen des menschlichen Auges," in *Wissenschaftliche Abhandlungen* (Leipzig: J. A. Barth, 1882–1895), 2:360–419.

42 Henry, *Cercle chromatique*, 11–12.

43 Henry, "Société de psychologie physiologique."

44 Ibid., 107–8

45 Henry, "Introduction à une esthétique scientifique," 9.

46 Ibid., 10.

47 Ibid., 11.

48 Henry, *Cercle chromatique*, 14.

49 Ibid.

50 Charles Henry, "Le Contraste, le rythme, la mesure," *Revue philosophique* 28 (October 1889): 357.

51 Henry, *Rapporteur esthétique*, 9.

52 Henry, "Introduction à une esthétique scientifique," 12–13.

53 See Josef Hoëné de Wronski, *Introduction à la philosophie des mathématiques et technie de l'algorithmie* (Paris: Courcier, 1811).

54 In an interview Henry also announced that he had constructed and would soon publish an instrument for working poets: an apparatus for analyzing the modifications of emitted noises and sounds in terms of the expression of feelings. But this instrument never appeared. See "M. Charles Henry," in *Enquête sur l'evolution littéraire*, ed. Jules Huret (Paris: Charpentier, 1891), 399.

55 Harry M. Collins and Robert Evans, *Rethinking Expertise* (Chicago: University of Chicago Press, 2007).

56 Ibid., 35.

57 Monika Cwiartka, "Materiality and the Discourse of Science" (PhD diss., University of British Columbia, 2012), 142–43.

58 See Joan Ungersma Halperin, *Félix Fénéon: Aesthete and Anarchist in Fin-de-Siècle Paris* (New Haven, CT: Yale University Press, 1988).

59 Frederick W. Taylor, *The Principles of Scientific Management* (1911; New York: 1967), 111.

60 Henry, *Rapporteur esthétique*, 5.

61 Reviewers of Henry's instruments were divided in their opinions. George Lechalas was largely critical; see his review of *Cercle chromatique*, vol. 1, by Charles Henry, *Revue philosophique* 28 (1889): 635–45. Emile Meyerson, on the other hand, provided a mostly appreciative account in "Les Travaux de M. Charles Henry sur une théorie mathématique de l'expression," *Bulletin scientifique* (December 20, 1889): 98–100.

62 On the interactions between art and medicine, see Barbara Maria Stafford, "Presuming Images and Consuming Goods: The Visualization of Knowledge from the Enlightenment to Post-modernism," in *Consumption and the World of Goods*, ed. John Brewer and Roy Porter (London: Routledge, 1992), 462–77.

63 Robert G. Frank Jr., "The Telltale Heart: Physiological Instruments, Graphic Methods, and Clinical Hopes, 1854–1914," in *The Investigative Enterprise: Experimental Physiology in Nineteenth Century Medicine*, ed. William Coleman and Frederic L. Holmes (Berkeley: University of California Press, 1988), 211–90; Christopher Lawrence, "Incommunicable Knowledge: Science, Technology and the Clinical Art in Britain, 1850–1914," *Journal of Contemporary History* 20, no. 4 (1985): 503–520; J. Rosser Matthews, *Quantification and the Quest for Medical Certainty* (Princeton, NJ: Princeton University Press, 1995); and Stanley Joel Reiser, *Medicine and the Reign of Technology* (Cambridge: Cambridge University Press, 1978).

64 Paul Lorain, *Études de médicine clinique faites avec l'aide de la méthode graphique et des appareils enregistreurs*, 2 vols. (Paris: P. Brouardel, 1877). The case history Henry considered is in vol. 2, pp. 349–51.

65 Henry, *Rapporteur esthétique*, 14.

66 Lorain, cited in ibid., 14.

67 Henry, *Rapporteur esthétique*, 14.

68 Ibid., 15.

69 Henry, *Cercle chromatique*. See also Charles Henry, *Harmonies de formes et de couleurs: Demonstrations pratiques* (Paris: A. Hermann, 1891). An extended treatment of Henry's color theory is beyond the compass of this book.

70 Floyd Ratliff, *Paul Signac and Color in Neo-Impressionism* (New York: Rockefeller University Press, 1992).

71 Eugène Delacroix, quoted in Signac, *D'Eugène Delacroix au néo-impressionnisme*, 54.

72 Robert L. Herbert, *Neo-Impressionism* (New York: Solomon Guggenheim Foundation, 1968).

73 Joris-Karl Huysmans, *Against Nature (À Rebours)*, trans. Robert Baldick (London: Penguin Classics, 1956), 104–15.

74 Charles Henry, "Odors and the Sense of Smell," *Popular Science Monthly* 41 (September 1892): 689–90. This article is a translation from the *Revue scientifique*.

75 Charles Henry, "Sur un olfactomètre de M. Charles Henry," *Revue philosophique* 184 (1891): 448.

76 There are many possible modes of transmission, of course. One obvious one would come from Proust's father, the prominent physician Adrian Proust, who collaborated with Marey (among others) on a report on the 1884 cholera epidemic in Paris.

77 Proust's remark appeared in his published notes to two lectures by John Ruskin that he translated: John Ruskin, *Sésame et les lys: Traduction et notes de Marcel Proust; Précéde de "Sur la lecture" de Marcel Proust* (1906) (Brussels: Editions Complexe, 1987), 146.

78 Henry, *Rapporteur esthétique*, 15.

79 The physiologist Jules Héricourt hailed Henry's technique as a "great moral project," since, "if the rhythmic movements are the expression of the normal functioning of the organism, the view and execution of movements of the same order will by a sort of suggestion give the intimate phenomena the same qualities as those which are its spontaneous expression." Héricourt, "Une Théorie mathématique de l'expression," 593.

80 Henry, *Rapporteur esthétique*, 15.

81 Charles Albert, "La 21ème exposition des artistes indépendents," *Les Temps nouveaux* 10 (1905): 7.

82 Jules Christophe, quoted in Sven Lövgren, *The Genesis of Modernism* (Stockholm: Almqvist & Wiksell, 1959), 81.

83 On the rise of independent art markets, see Robert Jensen, *Marketing Modernism in Fin-de-Siècle Europe* (Princeton, NJ: Princeton University Press, 1994).

84 Ibid., 8–9.

85 Among political economists the key figures were Richard Jennings, William Stanley Jevons, and Francis Ysidro Edgeworth, while in the art world the writings of Ruskin, William Morris, Walter Pater, and Grant Allen figured prominently. On these interactions, see Regenia Gagnier, *The Insatiability of Human Wants: Economics and Aesthetics in Market Society* (Chicago: University of Chicago Press, 2000); and Catherine Gallagher, *The Body Economic: Life, Death, and Sensation in Political Economy and the Victorian Novel* (Princeton, NJ: Princeton University Press, 2006).

86 On Signac's reluctance to make true decorative art, see Phillippe Thiebaut, "Art nouveau et néo-impressionnisme: Les Atéliers de Signac," *Revue de l'art* 92 (1991): 72–78. Katherine Brion shows that Signac in the 1890s developed a new decorative approach to painting around a didactic logic of anarchist propaganda and "purely aesthetic emotion" based on Henry's methods. See Katherine Brion, "Paul Signac's Decorative Propaganda of the 1890s," *RIHA Journal* 44 (2012): 1–20.

87 Miriam R. Levin, *Republican Art and Ideology in Late Nineteenth-Century France* (Ann Arbor, MI: UMI Research Press, 1986).

88 John G. Hutton shows how in the early Third Republic the anarchists and republicans "swam in the same stream" with respect to many political issues, including the ideology of art. See Hutton, *Neo-Impressionism and the Search for Solid Ground: Art, Science and Anarchism in Fin-de-Siècle France* (Baton Rouge: Louisiana State University Press, 1994). On networks of anarchist artists, see Robyn Roslak, *Neo-Impressionism and Anarchism in Fin-de-Siècle France: Painting, Politics, and Landscape* (Burlington, VT: Ashgate, 2007); and Eugenia W. Herbert, *The Artist and Social Reform: France and Belgium, 1885–1898* (New Haven, CT: Yale University Press, 1961). On anarchism in the Third Republic more generally, see also Jean Maitron, *Histoire du mouvement anarchiste en France (1880–1914)*, 2nd ed. (Paris, 1955); Marie Fleming, *The Anarchist Way to Socialism: Élisée Réclus and Nineteenth Century European Anarchism* (London: Rowman & Littlefield, 1979); Caroline Cahm, *Kropotkin and the Rise of Revolutionary Anarchism 1872–1886* (Cambridge: Cambridge University Press, 1989); Vivian Bouhey, *Les Anarchistes contre la République 1880 à 1914* (Rennes: Presses Universitaires de Rennes, 2008); and George Woodcock, *Anarchism* (Peterborough, ON: Broadview, 2004).

89 Leora Auslander, *Taste and Power: Furnishing Modern France* (Berkeley: University of California Press, 1996), 398.

90 Paul Signac, "Excerpts from the Unpublished Diary of Paul Signac, pt. 1," ed. and trans. J. Rewald, *Gazette des beaux-arts* 91 (July–December 1941): 169.

91 Scarry develops the relation between beauty, justice, and John Rawl's notion of fairness in her "Fairness as a Symmetry of Everyone's Relation to One Another,"

On Beauty and Being Just (Princeton, NJ: Princeton University Press, 1999), 63–75.

92 For accounts of the plight of the French decorative-arts industries, see Edmond Plauchut, "La Rivalité des industries d'art en Europe," *Revue des deux mondes* 105 (1891): 630–43; Marius Vachon, *Les Musées et les écoles d'art industriel en Europe* (Paris: Imprimerie Nationale, 1890); Henry Havard and Marius Vachon, *Les Manufactures nationales: Les Gobelins, la Savonnerie, Sèvres, Beauvais* (Paris: G. Decaux, 1889); Vachon, *Pour la défense de nos industries d'art* (Paris: Lahure, 1899); and Vachon, "Rapport de M. George Berger," *Revue des arts décoratifs* 12 (1891–92): 360–61.

93 Pierre Du Maroussem, *Les Ébenistes du Faubourg Saint-Antoine: Grands magasins, "sweating system"* (Paris: Rousseau, 1892), 142.

94 Jacques Rancière, *The Politics of Aesthetics: The Distribution of the* Sensible, trans. Gabriel Rockhill (London: Continuum, 2006).On French republican scientists and sensory order, see Nelia Dias, *La Mesure du sens: Les Anthropologues et le corps humain au XIXe siècle* (Paris: Aubier, 2004).

95 Henry, *Harmonies de formes et de couleurs*, 64.

96 Paul Signac to Vincent van Gogh, letter 584a, in *The Complete Letters of Vincent Van Gogh*, 2nd ed. (Boston: New York Graphic Society, 1978), 3:153. In a similar journal entry, Signac remarked on the sight of some ugly houses: "This again gives me the wish to publish a small device—a chromatic circle with a screen—giving the two, three, or four tones and tints which go well together and harmonize with one another. It would render the greatest service to dressmakers, fashion designers, house painters, upholsterers, and would prevent them from falling into those serious errors which too frequently spoil their best creations. It would lead them toward harmony, without groping. A small 10-line note would tell them: 'If you have a red and want to make it agree with two other tints . . . turn the disk and you will find the three tints which harmonize best.'" Signac, "Excerpts from the Unpublished Diary of Paul Signac, pt. 1," 167–68.

97 Recent anarchist writings had elevated the problems of head and hand, and the role of education for ameliorating them, to the top of the agenda. See Peter Kropotkin, "Travail intellectuel et travail manuel," *La Révolte* (March 1890): 22–26. See also Kropotkin, "La division du travail," *La Révolte* (April 21, 1889): 20.

98 On the fashion for historicist pastiche in fin-de-siècle France, see Auslander, *Taste and Power*; and Silverman, *Art Nouveau in Fin-de-Siècle France*.

99 Fénéon found this comparative method especially valuable. "The confrontation of the two images," he wrote, "is edifying for every normal eye that knows how to abstract from utilitarian or logical convenience, and from this point of view the plates constitute unique and probing experiments. Nonrhythmics are not only the examples to avoid in industrial the art, they are the examples to follow each time it is necessary to obtain a form with more visual acuity, or, to speak vaguely, more utility. The disagreeable hyperesthesia, the agreeable anesthesia. Ugliness is

'practical': there are in these experiments the characteristics and the justification of the most generous efforts of this scientific age." Félix Fénéon, "Paul Signac," in *Au-déla de l'impressionnisme*, ed. Françoise Cachin (Paris: Hermann, 1966), 119.

100 Henry and Signac found an institutional home for their work in the Bibliothèque Forney, a lending library and apprenticeship school for artisans established in the workers' district of the Faubourg Saint-Antoine with the aim of overcoming "the egocentricity of capital and dominating spirit of the clergy" by making "available to the poor man and to the worker the means that are necessary for him to be given a more scientific and elevated character to his knowledge." Henry, *Harmonies de formes et de couleurs*, 2. On the Forney library, see Auslander, *Taste and Power*, 362.

101 Charles Henry, *Application de nouveaux instruments de précision (cercle chromatique, rapporteur et triple décimetre esthétique) a l'archéologie* (Paris: E. Leroux, 1890). Also published in the *Revue archéologique* (1890): 187–213.

102 Albert Dumont, "Inscriptions céramiques de Grèce," *Archives des missions scientifiques et littéraires*, 2nd ser., vol. 6 (1871): 13–15. The amphoras also appeared in Albert Dumont, *Les Céramiques de la Grèce propre*, 2 vols. (Paris: Firmin Didot, 1888–90).

103 Henry, "Application de nouveaux instruments de précision," 193–94.

104 See, for example, Franz Wickhoff, "On the Historical Unity in the Universal Evolution of Art," in *German Essays on Art and History*, trans. Peter Wortsman, ed. Gert Schiff (New York: Continuum, 1988), 165–72; and Riegl, "Late Roman or Oriental?," in *German Essays on Art History*, 173–91. On Alois Riegl, see the discussion in Michael Ann Holly, *Panofsky and the Foundations of Art History* (Ithaca, NY: Cornell University Press, 1984), 69–96.

105 Henry, "Application de nouveaux instruments de précision," 190–91.

106 Signac, *D'Eugène Delacroix au néo-impressionnisme*, 67.

107 Seurat, quoted in David W. Galenson, *Painting between the Lines: Patterns of Creativity in Modern Art* (Cambridge, MA: Harvard University Press, 2001), 42.

108 Seurat, letter to Signac, August 26, 1888, cited in Henri Dorra and John Rewald, *Seurat: L'Œuvre peinte: Biographie et catalogue critique* (Paris: Les Beaux-Arts, 1959), lvx.

109 John Rewald, *Georges Seurat* (Paris: Albin Michel, 1948); and William Innes Homer, *Seurat and the Science of Painting* (Cambridge, MA: MIT Press, 1964). For revisionist challenges, see especially John Gage, "The Technique of Seurat: A Reappraisal," *Art Bulletin* 69, no. 3 (1987): 448–54; and Paul Smith, *Seurat and the Avant-Garde* (New Haven, CT: Yale University Press, 1997).

110 The exact dates of their meeting are unknown. Laforgue had known Seurat for years, having been a classmate at the École des Beaux-Arts (Seurat attended Laforgue's funeral in 1886). Kahn and Fénéon were more recent acquaintances of the painter, but Kahn soon became one of his closer friends.

111 Félix Fénéon "L'Impressionnisme aux Tuileries," *L'Art moderne* 6 (September 19, 1886): 300–302, reprinted in Fénéon, *Œuvres: Plus que complètes*, vol. 1, *Chroniques d'art*, ed. Joan Ungersma Halperin (Paris: Droz, 1970), 54. Several reviews published by other members of the circle also made this claim. See especially Gustave Kahn, "Peinture: Exposition des indépendants," *Revue indépendante* 7, no. 18 (April 1888): 160–63.

112 Félix Fénéon, "Le Néo-impressionnisme à la IVᵉ exposition des artistes indépendants," *L'Art moderne* 8 (April 15, 1888): 14.

113 Ibid.

114 Félix Fénéon, "Dix Marines d'Antibes, de M. Claude Monet," *La Revue indépendante* (August 1888), in *Œuvres*, 1:113. Camille Pissarro, in a letter to his son Lucien, attributed "the old Impressionists" remark to Seurat; quoted in Richard Thomson, *Seurat* (Oxford: Phaidon Press, 1985), 129.

115 Félix Fénéon, "L'Exposition des artistes independentes à Paris," *L'Art moderne* 9 (October 27, 1889): 339.

116 R. Herbert, "'Parade de cirque' de Seurat."

117 See, for example, Svetlana Alpers's analysis of the interiors by Pieter Saenredam in *The Art of Describing: Dutch Art in the Seventeenth Century* (Chicago: University of Chicago Press, 1983), 172–83.

118 Anonymous, "Le Salon de 1888, III," *Gazette des Beaux-Arts* 38, no. 2 (1888): 138–39.

119 R. Herbert, "'Parade de cirque' de Seurat,'" 14.

120 Henry van de Velde, "Notes sur l'art: Chahut," *La Wallonie* 5 (May 1890): 123. Van de Velde would go on to write an important essay on line in art, which would become a principle document of the theory and pedagogy of German Jugendstil. See Henry van de Velde, "Die Linie," *Die Zukunft* 40, no. 49 (1902): 385–88.

121 [Paul Signac], "Variétés: Impressionnistes et révolutionnaires," *La Révolte* 4 (June 13–19, 1891): 4.

122 Richard Schiff, "Realism of Low Resolution: Digitisation and Modern Painting," in *Impossible Presence: Surface and Screen in the Photogenic Era*, ed. Terry Smith (Chicago: University of Chicago Press, 2001), 124–56.

123 Blanc, *Grammaire*, 21.

124 Ibid.

125 Fénéon, "L'Impressionnisme aux Tuileries," 58.

126 Ibid., 74.

127 On photography and author's rights, see Bernard Edelman, *Le Droit saisi par la photographie* (1973), 3rd ed. (Paris: Flammarion, 2001); and Jane M. Gaines, *Contested Culture: The Image, the Voice and the Law* (Chapel Hill: University of North Carolina Press, 1991).

128 For a very sensitive account of the rift between Seurat and his friends, including full quotations of all of the central documents, see Halperin, *Félix Fénéon*, 136–43.

129 The painter Charles Angrand, one of the few to visit Seurat in his studio in

the months before his death, reportedly found Seurat in an ebullient mood, explaining his measurements and notions of the universal sign language of painting.

130 Paul Valéry, "On Literary Technique" (1889), in *The Art of Poetry*, ed. Jackson Mathews, trans. Denise Foliot (Princeton, NJ: Princeton University Press, 1989), 313. For Valéry's views on Charles Henry, see Paul Valéry et al., eds., "Hommage à Charles Henry," special issue, *Cahiers de l'étoile* 13 (January–February 1930).

131 Paul Valéry, "Introduction à la méthode de Léonardo de Vinci" (1894), in *Paul Valéry: Œuvres*, ed. Jean Hytier (Paris: Gallimard, 1957), 1:1185.

132 Ibid., 1:1205.

133 Paul Valéry, *Degas, Manet, Morisot* (Princeton, NJ: Princeton University Press, 1960), 19–20.

134 Valéry, "Note et digression" (1919), in *Paul Valéry: Œuvres*, 1:1205.

135 "The automatic machinery of a big factory is much more despotic than the small capitalists who employ workers have ever been," Engels wrote in his attack on the anarchists. "If man," he continued, "by dint of his knowledge and inventive genius, has subdued the forces of nature, the latter avenge themselves by subjecting him, in so far as he employs them, to a veritable despotism." See Friedrich Engels, "On Authority," (1874) in Karl Marx and Friedrich Engels, *The Marx-Engels Reader*, 2nd ed., ed. Robert C. Tucker (New York: W. W. Norton and Co., 1978), 730–33. On Engels's essay as a wellspring of thinking about essential differences between authoritarian and democratic technologies, especially in the work of Lewis Mumford, see Langdon Winner, "Do Artifacts Have Politics?," *Daedelus* 109 (1980): 121–36.

136 See, for example Peter Kropotkin, "Le Machinisme et la révolution," *Le Révolté* (April 13, 1884).

137 T. J. Clark, *Farewell to an Idea: Episodes in the History of Modernism* (New Haven, CT: Yale University Press, 1999), 102.

138 Thomson, *Seurat*, 206.

139 Thadée Natanson, "Expositions," *La Revue blanche* 6, no. 28 (February 1894): 187. Part of this vignette serves as the epigraph to Robert L. Herbert, Gary Tinterow, and Anne Distel, *Georges Seurat 1859–1891* (New York: Metropolitan Museum of Art, 1991), 3.

140 Henry Fox Talbot, *The Pencil of Nature* (1844–46; New York: Da Capo, 1969), n.p.

141 Félix Fénéon, "L'Impressionnisme" (1887), in *Œuvres: Plus que complètes*, vol. 1, *Chroniques d'art*, ed. Joan U. Halperin (Paris: Droz, 1970), 67.

142 Schiff, "Realism of Low Resolution," 142.

143 Thomson, *Seurat*, 156.

144 Joan Wallach Scott, "'L'Ouvrière! Mot impie, sordide . . .' Women Workers in the Disourse of French Political Economy, 1840–1860," in *Gender and the Politics of History* (New York: Columbia University Press, 1988), 139–63.

145 Ibid., 148.

146 Anonymous, "Un Cri de femme révoltée," *Le Révolté* (September 18–24, 1886).

147 J. Scott, "L'Ouvrière," 149.

148 The question of the dancer's wage was not unlike the one pondered by Seurat when asked by Octave Maus how much one of his paintings might cost: "As for my *Poseuses*, I am very much at a loss to fix a price for it. I compute my expenses on the basis of one year at seven francs a day: thus you can see where that leads me." Seurat, letter to Octave Maus, quoted in Norma Broude, ed., *Seurat in Perspective* (Englewood Cliffs, NJ: Prentice-Hall, 1978), 15.

149 Clark, *Farewell to an Idea*, 109–12.

150 [Signac], "Variétés."

151 W. J. T. Mitchell, *Iconology: Image, Text, Ideology* (Chicago: University of Chicago Press, 1986). In *Picture Theory: Essays on Verbal and Visual Representation* (Chicago: University of Chicago Press, 1994), Mitchell describes metapictures as "not merely epistemological models, but ethical, political, and aesthetic 'assemblages' that allow us to observe observers" (49). They "don't merely serve as illustrations to theory; they picture theory," he adds.

152 Schiff, "Realism of Low Resolution," 154.

153 Gustave Kahn, *Les Dessins de Georges Seurat (1859–1891)* (Paris: Bernheim-Jeune, 1928), n.p.

154 Gustave Kahn, "Le Vers libre: Conférence de M. Gustave Kahn, aux XX," *L'Art moderne* 11, no. 7 (February 15, 1891): 53.

155 Richard Schiff, "Grave Seurat," in *Seurat Re-viewed*, ed. Paul Smith (University Park: Pennsylvania State University Press, 2009), 171.

5. Liberating Verse

1 Mallarmé regarded Gustave Kahn as a protégé and in 1891 named him, along with Jules Laforgue and Francis Vielé-Griffin, as one of "three of the principal poets who have contributed to the Symbolist movement." Quoted in Jules Huret, *Enquête sur l'évolution littéraire* (Paris: Charpentier, 1891), 492. Around the same time, Mallarmé pledged to the anarchist Jean Grave that he, too, would "contribute a few humble words to his oeuvre." Quoted in Richard Shryock, "Becoming Political: Symbolist Literature in the Third Republic," *Nineteenth-Century French Studies* 33, nos. 3–4 (2005): 394.

2 Clive Scott, *Vers Libre: The Emergence of Free Verse in France, 1886–1914* (New York: Oxford University Press, 1990), 74–88, 146–49.

3 Benjamin Hrushovski, "On Free Rhythms in Modern Poetry," in *Style in Language*, ed. Thomas A. Sebeok (Cambridge, MA: MIT Press, 1960), 173–90.

4 In private letters, Laforgue uncharacteristically reproached Kahn for having accused their mutual friend Henry of stealing his (Kahn's) ideas. See Laforgue,

Lettres à un ami, 1880–1886, introduction and notes by G. Jean-Aubry (Paris: Mercure de France, 1941).

5   Gustave Kahn, "Réponse des symbolistes," *L'Évenement,* September 28, 1886.

6   G. Kahn, "Réponse des symbolistes."

7   Gustave Kahn, "Ce qui se détache nettement comme résultat tangible de l'année 1886, ce fut l'instauration du vers libre," in *Symbolistes et décadents* (Paris: L. Vanier, 1902; Geneva: Slatkine Reprints, 1977), 52. Page citations refer to the Slatkine edition.

8   On the symbolist movement more generally, see Richard Cándida-Smith, *Mallarmé's Children: Symbolism and the Renewal of Experience* (Berkeley: University of California Press, 1999); Julia Kristeva, *La Révolution du langage poétique: L'Avant-garde à la fin du XIXe siècle; Lautrémont et Mallarmé* (Paris: Éditions du Seuil, 1974).

9   Jean Moréas published "Le Symbolisme" in *Le Figaro,* in which he both coined the term *symbolism* and called for the "assouplissement" of certain classical rules of verse: caesura, hiatus, alternation of rhythms, and so on. Since the article appeared ten days before G. Kahn's "Réponses des symbolists," in *L'Événement* (September 28, 1886), Moréas was publicly recognized as the inventor of symbolist and vers libre. Kahn and many others argued at the time, and scholars have agreed, that Moréas's poetry was not vers libre in the strict sense they advocated. See Bonner Mitchell, *Les Manifestes littéraires de la Belle Époque 1886–1914: Anthologie critique* (Paris: Seghers, 1966).

10   Paul Valéry, *Variété* (Paris: Nouvelle Revue Française, 1924–44), 1:97–98.

11   As Clive Scott describes it, *vers libéré* refers to a "liberated" form of regular verse, which came into its own in the latter half of the nineteenth century, especially through the efforts of Hugo, Verlaine, Rimbaud, and others. It "makes free with the rules of rhyme, and uses a variety of devices to destabilize the rhythmic structure of the line." But, for all its liberties, *vers libéré* "maintains the conventions of isosyllabism and the indispensability of rhyme." See C. Scott, *Vers Libre,* 74–88, 310.

12   Gustave Kahn and Félix Fénéon, "Le Courrier social," *La Vogue* 1 (April 4, 1886): 27.

13   Some period definitions of *vers libre,* besides those discussed here, can be found in Remy de Gourmont, "Le Vers libre," in *Esthétique de la langue française,* 222–60 (Paris: Mercure de France, 1905); Édouard Dujardin, *Les Premiers poètes du vers libre* (Paris: Mercure de France, 1922); and the many responses in F. T. Marinetti, *Enquête internationale sur le vers libre* (Milan: Éditions de "Poesia," 1909). See also the skeptical view of T. S. Eliot in his "Reflections on Vers Libre," *New Statesman* 8 (1917): 518–19.

14   Ezra Pound put forth his definition of free verse as a maxim in the famous imagist manifesto, published in the March 1913 issue of *Poetry*: "As regarding rhythm: to compose in the sequence of the musical phrase, not in sequence of a

metronome." Ezra Pound, "A few Don'ts for an Imagiste," *Poetry* 1 (March 1913): 200–206.

15 Daniel Grojnowski, "Laforgue fumiste: L'Esprit de cabaret," *Romantisme* 64 (1989): 5–16.

16 Regarding Henry's interest in poetry, it is worth noting that Laforgue continually urged him to give up science and devote himself to poetry. A prose poem by Henry, entitled, "Vision," appeared in the first issue of *La Vogue* (April 4, 1886). One wonders what Laforgue was thinking . . .

17 Gustave Kahn developed his main theoretical ideas in "Réponse des symbolistes"; the interview in Huret, *Enquête sur l'évolution littéraire*; "Préface sur les vers libres," in *Premiers Poèmes* (Paris: Mercure de France, 1897); *Symbolistes et décadents* (Paris: L. Vanier, 1902); and his response in Marinetti, *Enquête internationale sur le vers libre*, 21–31. On Kahn's early work, see J. C. Ireson, *L'Œuvre poétique de Gustave Kahn (1859–1936)* (Paris: A. G. Nizet, 1962).

18 Charles O. Hartman, *Free Verse: An Essay on Prosody* (Princeton, NJ: Princeton University Press, 1980), 13–14.

19 On prosodic effects as "shapes of energy," see W. K. Wimsatt Jr. and Monroe Beardsley, "The Concept of Meter: An Exercise in Abstraction," *PMLA* 74, no. 5 (1959): 597.

20 Charles Henry, "Introduction à une esthétique scientifique," *La Revue contemporaine* 2 (1885): 466. On Henry's relations to experimental phonetics and symbolist poetry, see George Lote, "La Poétique du symbolisme," *Revue des cours et conferences* 35, no. 2 (1934): 120; and André Spire, *Plaisir poétique et plaisir musculaire: Essai sur l'évolution des techniques poétiques* (Paris: José Corti, 1949), 13–14.

21 Howard Nemerov, *Figures of Thought* (Boston: David Godine, 1978), 129.

22 Henry, "Introduction à une esthétique scientifique," 29.

23 Ernst Brücke, *Die Physiologischen Grundlagen der neuhochdeutschen Verskunst* (Vienna: Carl Gerold's Sohn, 1871).

24 Hermann Helmholtz, *Die Lehre von den Tonempfindungen als physiologische Grundlage für die Theorie der Musik* (Braunschweig, Germany: Vieweg, 1863); and Helmholtz, *On the Sensations of Tone as a Physiological Basis for the Theory of Music*, 2nd ed., trans. Alexander J. Ellis (London: Longmans, Green, and Co., 1885; repr., New York: Dover, 1954). Page citations refer to the Dover edition.

25 On Helmholtz's theory of music as an outgrowth of the inherent experimentalism of Western music, see Myles W. Jackson, *Harmonious Triads: Physicists, Musicians, and Instrument Makers in Nineteenth-Century Germany* (Cambridge, MA: MIT Press, 2006).

26 Brücke, *Die Physiologischen Grundlagen der neuhochdeutschen Verskunst*, iv.

27 Ibid.

28 Gaston Paris, "Études historiques et philologiques sur la rime française," *Romania* 6 (1877): 625.

29 G. Kahn, in *Enquête internationale sur le vers libre*, 26.

30 G. Kahn, "Préface sur le vers libre," 24–27.

31 Ibid., 25.

32 Ibid.

33 Ibid., 27.

34 Ibid., 6. See also C. Scott, *Vers Libre*, 122.

35 G. Kahn, "Préface sur le vers libre," 27.

36 Emile Hennequin, "L'Esthétique de Wagner et les doctrines spenceriennes," *La Revue wagnérienne* 1, no 10. (1885–86): 282–86.

37 G. Kahn, "Préface sur le vers libre," 27.

38 Gustave Kahn, "Response of the Symbolists" (1886), in *Art in Theory, 1815–1900: An Anthology of Changing Ideas*, ed. Charles Harrison, Paul Wood, and Jason Gaiger (Oxford: Blackwell, 1998), 1016–17.

39 On Henry's critical role in the early verslibristes' turn to phonetics, see Lote, "La Poétique du symbolisme," 120; and Andre Spire, *Plaisir poétique et plaisir musculaire*, 13–14.

40 G. Kahn, "Préface sur le vers libre," 29.

41 Ibid., 33.

42 Camille Mauclair, in Marinetti, *Enquête internationale sur le vers libre*, 64.

43 Ibid., 66.

44 Jimena Canales, *A Tenth of a Second: A History* (Chicago: University of Chicago Press, 2009).

45 G. Kahn, "Préface sur le vers libre," 16.

46 Mauclair, in *Enquête internationale sur le vers libre*, 65.

47 Ibid.

48 Paul Valéry, "Existence du symbolisme" (1936), in *Paul Valéry: Œuvres*, vol. 1, ed. Jean Hytier (Paris: Gallimard, 1957), 703.

49 G. Kahn, "Préface sur le vers libre," 17.

50 Charles Henry, "M. Charles Henry," in *Enquête sur l'évolution littéraire*, ed. Jules Huret (Paris: Charpentier, 1891), 399. Henry also mentioned that he had constructed an apparatus for analyzing the modifications of emitted noises and sounds in terms of the expression of feelings, but the instrument was never published.

51 Charles Henry, "Loi d'évolution de la sensation musicale," *Revue philosophique* 22 (1886): 81–87. Saint-Saëns's musical ideas were probably taken from his *Harmonie et mélodie* (Paris: Calmann Lévy, 1885).

52 Henry, "Loi d'évolution de la sensation musicale," 86–87.

53 Ibid., 87.

54 For an overview of French Wagnerism, see Gerald D. Thurow, "Art and Politics: Wagnerism in France," in *Wagnerism in European Culture and Politics*, ed. David C. Large and William Weber (Ithaca, NY: Cornell University Press, 1984), 134–66.

On Wagnerism and the French avant-garde, see Martha Calhoun, "The *Revue Wagnérienne* and the Literature of Music: The Translation of an Aesthetic" (PhD diss., State University of New York, Stony Brook, 1987); Édouard Dujardin, *"La Revue wagnérienne,"* in *Mallarmé par un des siens* (Paris: Albert Messein, 1936); Isabelle Wyzewska, *"La Revue wagnérienne": Essai sur l'interpretation esthétique de Wagner en France* (Paris: Perrin, 1934); Wolfgang Storch and Josef Mackert, eds., *Die Symbolisten und Richard Wagner* (Berlin: Edition Hentrich, 1991); Martine Kahane, *Wagner et la France* (Paris: Bibliothèque Nationale, 1983); Léon Guichard, *La Musique et les lettres en France au temps du wagnérisme* (Paris: Presses Universitaires de France, 1963); Richard Sieburth, "The Music of the Future" (1885), in *A New Literary History of French Literature*, ed. Denis Hollier (Cambridge, MA: Harvard University Press, 1994), 789–98; and Raymond Furness, *Wagner and Literature* (New York: St. Martin's, 1982).

55 Richard Wagner, *"The Art-Work of the Future," and Other Works*, trans. and ed. William Ashton Ellis (Lincoln: University of Nebraska Press, 1993).

56 Hennequin, "L'Esthétique de Wagner," 282–86. Hennequin, author of a work on physiological aesthetics (*La Critique scientifique* [Paris: Perrin, 1888]), was a critic for the *Revue indépendante* and a member of the circle of Fénéon and Henry. In his dramatic conclusion, Hennequin declared that "Wagner's *Ring* and Spencer's First Principles are the wave upon which humanity mounts to the universal."

57 Richard Wagner, "The Arts of Poetry and Tone in the Drama of the Future," in *Opera and Drama*, trans. William Ashton Ellis, 2nd ed. (London: Kegan Paul, Trench, Trubner & Co., 1900), 123–88.

58 Herbert Spencer, "The Origin and Function of Music," *Fraser's Magazine* 56, no. 334 (October 1857): 397–98.

59 Jules de Gaultier, "Essai de physiologie poétique," *La Revue blanche* 7, nos. 31–33 (1894): 393–408, 527–35. The British poet T. H. Hulme, who along with Ezra Pound imported verslibrisme into English poetry, described Gaultier's work as "a sign of the times." T. H. Hulme, "Searchers after Reality: Jules de Gaultier," *New Age* 6, no. 5 (December 2, 1909): 107.

60 Gaultier, "Essai de physiologie poétique," 394.

61 Ibid., 398.

62 Ibid., 399.

63 Ibid., 403.

64 Ibid.

65 Ibid., 404.

66 Ibid., 407.

67 See Robert de Souza, *Rhythme poétique* (Paris: Perrin, 1892), 4; Louis Becq de Fouquières, *Traité général de versification française* (Paris: Charpentier, 1879); and Paul Pierson, *Métrique naturelle du langage* (Paris: F. Vieweg, 1884). Pierson's book was published posthumously, after he died in 1880 at the age of twenty-nine.

68 Becq de Fouquières, *Traité général de versification française*, 182.

69 Nietzsche called Wagner "our greatest musical miniaturist" for his inventions
at the level of the smallest detail." Friedrich Nietzsche, *Der Fall Wagner* (1888), in
Werke: Kritische Gesamtausgabe, ed. Giorgio Colli and Mazzino Montinari (Berlin:
De Gruyter, 1969), 3:22. On Wagner's technique, see also Edward Lippman, *A
History of Western Musical Aesthetics* (Lincoln: University of Nebraska Press, 1993),
238–69.

70 Robert de Souza, *Rhythme poétique* (Paris: Perrin, 1892), 211.

71 Robert de Souza, *La Poésie populaire et le lyrisme sentimental* (Paris: Mercure de
France, 1899).

72 According to David Arkell, Debussy's character Monsieur Croche, which first
appeared in *La Revue blanche*, was based on Charles Henry, both directly and by
pillaging Paul Valéry's figure of Monsieur Teste, much to the irritation of Valéry.
See David Arkell, *Looking for Laforgue: A Biography of Jules Laforgue* (Manchester,
UK: Carcanet, 1979).

73 Stefan Jarocinski uses a palette of synonyms to describe Debussy's methods:
decomposed, dematerialized, divided, extinguished, separated, isolated, to name but
a few. See Jarocinski, *Debussy: Impressionism and Symbolism*, trans. Rollo Myers
(London: Eulenberg, 1976).

74 Roy Howat, *Debussy in Proportion: A Musical Analysis* (Cambridge: Cambridge University Press, 1983).

75 Margaret Cobb, *The Poetic Debussy: A Collection of His Song Texts and Selected Letters*
(Boston: Northeastern University Press, 1982), reports that the first two songs,
"De rêve" and "De grève," were published in the journal *Entretiens politiques et
littéraires* in December 1892, while the last, "De Soir," was complete in July 1893
(p. 133).

76 Theo Hirsbunner, "Musik und Dichtung im französischen Fin de Siècle am
Beispiel der Proses Lyriques von Debussy," in *Dichtung und Musik: Kaleidoskop
ihrer Beziehungen*, ed. Guntar Schnitzler (Stuttgart: Klett-Cotta, 1979), 152–74.

77 Sharon S. Prado, "The Decadent Aesthetic in France, 1880–1914: Musical Manifestations in the Works of Debussy and his Contemporaries" (PhD diss., University of Cincinnati, 1992).

78 Ibid., 253–55.

79 Ibid., 259–63, and especially appendix 2.

80 Ibid., 264.

81 Raphael Cor, "M. Claude Debussy et le snobisme contemporaine," in *Le Cas
Debussy*, ed. C.-Francis Caillard and José de Berys (Paris: Bibliothèque du Temps
Présent, 1909), 21.

82 Eugene Landry, *La Théorie du rythme et le rythme du français déclamé* (Paris: H.
Champion, 1911), 7.

83 The original phrase, from Mallarmé's dedication on the tomb of Edgar Allan

Poe, read "Donner un sens plus pur aux mots de la tribu." T. S. Eliot later famously incorporated it in *Four Quartets*: "Since our concern was speech, and speech impelled us / To purify the dialect of the tribe / And urge the mind to aftersight and foresight." T. S. Eliot, "Little Gidding," *Four Quartets* (London: Faber & Faber, 1944).

84 Rae Beth Gordon, *Why the French Love Jerry Lewis: From Cabaret to Early Cinema* (Stanford, VA: Stanford University Press, 2001); and Gordon, *Dances with Darwin 1875–1910: Vernacular Modernity in France* (Burlington, VT: Ashgate, 2009).

85 This work was described disparagingly by fellow Rousselot student Marcel Jousse, who, in lectures at the École d'anthropologie, alleged that Rousselot was alarmed by the agenda of de Souza and Spire. Jousse, quoted in Rémy Guérinel, "De la phonétique vivante et expérimentale du Professeur Jean-Pierre Rousselot (1846–1924) à l'anthropologie du geste et du rhythme du Professeur Marcel Jousse (1886–1961)" (unpublished manuscript, 2009), 8–9.

86 This project invites comparison with Erik Satie's efforts to bring the musical forms of the cabaret to the concert hall. Around 1912 Satie even jocularly described himself as a "phonometrician" and wrote a humorous piece on "the first time I used a phonoscope" for the "filthy business" of "cleaning sounds." See Satie, "What I Am," *The Writings of Erik Satie*, trans. and ed. Nigel Wilkins (London: Eulenburg, 1980), 58. On Satie and the cabaret, see Nancy Perloff, *Art and the Everyday: Popular Entertainment and the Circle of Erik Satie* (Oxford: Clarendon Press, 1991); and Steven Moore Whiting, *Satie the Bohemian: From Cabaret to Concert Hall* (Oxford: Oxford University Press, 1999).

87 Canales, *Tenth of a Second*. On discussions of rhythm in industrial life, see Robert Michael Brain, "The Ontology of the Questionnaire: Max Weber on Measurement and Mass Investigation," *Studies in the History and Philosophy of Science* 32, no. 4 (2001): 647–84.

88 Ezra Pound, *Polite Essays* (London: Faber & Faber, 1937).

89 Michael Golston, *Rhythm and Race in Modernist Poetry and Science* (New York: Columbia University Press, 2008).

90 "There was a strata in Paris which mere criticism of books fails to get hold of, a strata that goes either into literature itself, I means as its subject, or remains unrecorded. It is the tone of the time." Pound, *Polite Essays*, 130–31.

6. Sensory Fusion

1 Charles Henry, "Introduction à une esthétique scientifique," *La Revue contemporaine* 2 (1885): 468–69.

2 Jules Héricourt, "Une Théorie mathématique de l'expression: Le Contraste, le rythme et la mesure d'après les travaux de M. Charles Henry," *Revue scientifique* 44 (1889): 593.

3 Jacques Loeb, quoted in Philip J. Pauly, *Controlling Life: Jacques Loeb and the Engi-*

neering Ideal in Biology (Berkeley: University of California Press, 1990), 4.

4   Victor Segalen, "Les Synesthésies et l'École symboliste," *Mercure de France* 42, no. 148 (April 1902): 64. See also Pascal Rousseau, "Confusion des sens: Le Débat évolutionniste sur la synesthésie dans les débuts de l'abstraction en France," *Le Cahiers du Musée nationale de l'art moderne* 74 (2001): 5–33.

5   René Ghil, *Traité du verbe* (Paris: Giraud, 1886). On Ghil, see Louis W. Marvick, "René Ghil and the Contradictions of Synesthesia," *Comparative Literature* 51, no. 4 (1999): 297. Gustave Kahn, too, explored the synesthetic relations between directions, colors, and sounds in an early article for *La Vogue*: "De l'esthétique du verre polychrome," *La Vogue* 1 (April 18, 1886): 54–65.

6   Alfred Binet, "Le Problème de l'audition colorée," *Revue des deux mondes* 113 (1892): 611.

7   Ghil objected that *instrumentation verbale* was a theory and method of poetry alone, not a theatrical total work of art: if executed properly, all colors, music, scents, and emotions would be elicited within the austere medium of verse itself. But he also complained that correspondences used in the play were incorrect. See René Ghil, *Traité du verbe: États successifs (1885–1886–1887–1888–1891–1904)*, ed. Tizana Goruppi (Paris: A. G. Nizet, 1978).

8   Quoted in Joan Ungersma Halperin, *Félix Fénéon: Aesthete and Anarchist in Fin-de-Siècle Paris* (New Haven, CT: Yale University Press, 1988), 199.

9   Kevin T. Dann reports that while before 1870 scientific papers on synesthesia in France appeared only sporadically, between 1870 and 1883 there were about three papers per year, and after 1884 around sixteen papers annually. When the first Congrès international de psychologie physiologique met in Paris in 1889 to hear papers on hypnotism, attention, volition, suggestion, somnambulism, double consciousness, and the role of electricity in psychic phenomena, it was *audition colorée* (colored hearing) that caused the greatest stir. See Dann, *Bright Colors Falsely Seen: Synaesthesia and the Search for Transcendental Truth* (New Haven, CT: Yale University Press, 1998), 31.

10 Le Dantec, quoted in Jean D'Udine, *L'Art et le geste* (Paris: F. Alcan, 1910), 116.

11 Raphaël Du Bois, *Anatomie et physiologie comparée de la pholade dactyle: Structure, locomotion, tact, olfaction, gestation, vision, dermatoptique, photogénie, avec une théorie générale des sensations* (Paris: G. Masson, 1892).

12 Ibid.; and Jules Soury, "Review of *Anatomie et physiologie comparée de la pholade dactyle*, by Raphaël Du Bois, *Revue philosophique* 40 (1895): 541–51.

13 Albéric Magnard, "La Synthèse des arts," *La Revue de Paris* 5 (1894): 424–42.

14 Max Nordau, *Degeneration* (1892), translation of 2nd ed., with introduction by George L. Mosse (Lincoln: University of Nebraska Press, 1968).

15 Ibid., 142.

16 Ibid.

17 On Nordau and the rhetoric of degeneration, see Daniel Pick, *Faces of Degenera-*

tion: A European Disorder, c. 1848–c. 1918 (Cambridge: Cambridge University Press, 1989); and Sander L. Gilman and Edward I. Chamberlain, eds., *Degeneration: The Dark Side of Progress* (New York: Columbia University Press, 1985).

18　On the Scandinavian circle of artists in turn-of-the-century Berlin, see the contributions by Robert Fuchs, Asbjörn Aarseth, and Göran Söderstöm in Bernd Henningsen, Janine Klein, Helmut Müssener, and Solfrid Söderlind, eds., *Wahlverwandtschaft: Skandinavien und Deutschland, 1800 bis 1914* (Berlin: Jovis, 1997).

19　Shelly Wood Cordulak, *Edvard Munch and the Physiology of Symbolism* (London: Associated University Presses, 2002).

20　Amy Strahler Holzapfel, "Strindberg as Vivisector: Physiology, Pathology, and Anti-Mimesis in *The Father and Miss Julie*," *Modern Drama* 51, no. 3 (2008): 329–52.

21　On Przybyszewski, see Gabriela Matuszek, *"Der Geniale Pole?"—Stanislaw Przybyszewski in Deutschland, 1892–1992* (Paderborn, Germany: Igel, 1996); and Gabriela Matuszek, ed., *Über Stanislaw Przybyszewski: Rezensionen-Errinerungen—Porträts—Studien (1892–1995); Rezeptionsdokumente aus 100 Jahren* (Paderborn, Germany: Igel, 1995).

22　Meier-Graefe, quoted in Mary Kay Norseng, *Dagny: Dagny Juel Przybyszewska, the Woman and the Myth* (Seattle: University of Washington Press, 1991), 158.

23　Stanislaw Przybyszewski, *Zur Psychologie des Individuums* (Berlin: Fontane, 1892). The critical reactions are from Julius Bab, "Zur Psychologie des Individuums" (1892), in Matuszek, *Über Stanislaw Przybyszewski*, 10–13.

24　These are some of the works mentioned in Carla Lathe, "Munch's Dramatic Images 1892–1909," *Journal of the Warburg and Courtauld Institutes* 46 (1983): 191–206. For a more complete discussion, see Carla Lathe, "The Group Zum Schwarzen Ferkel: A Study in Early Modernism" (PhD diss., University of East Anglia, 1972).

25　On evolutionary aesthetics, see Kurt Bayertz, "Biology and Beauty: Science and Aesthetics in Fin-de-Siècle Germany," in *Fin de Siècle and its Legacy*, ed. Mikulas Teich and Roy Porter, 278–296 (Cambridge: Cambridge University Press, 1990). On the uses of Monism in German art, see Marsha Morton, "From Monera to Man: Ernst Haeckel, *Darwinismus*, and Nineteenth-Century German Art," in *The Art of Evolution: Darwin, Darwinisms, and Visual Culture*, ed. Barbara Larson and Fae Brauer, 59–91 (Hanover, NH: Dartmouth College Press, 2009).

26　John L. Greenway, "Strindberg and Suggestion in 'Miss Julie,'" *South Atlantic Review* 51, no. 2 (1986): 30.

27　Max Simon Nordau, *Paradoxes: From the German of Max Nordau* (1885) (Chicago: L. Schick, 1886), 128, 165.

28　Max Nordau, *Entartung* (Berlin: Duncker & Humblot, 1892).

29　On Nordau's transitions from liberal naturalist to cultural pessimist to Zionist, see P. M. Baldwin, "Liberalism, Nationalism, and Degeneration: The Case of Max Nordau," *Central European History* 13, no. 2 (1980): 99–120.

30   After a profound effacement in the mid-twentieth century, Nietzsche's physi-
     ological interests have come back into the view of scholars. See especially
     Bettina Wahrig-Schmidt, "'Irgendwie-jedenfalls physiologisch': Friedrich
     Nietzsche, Alexandre Herzen (fils) und Charles Féré 1888," *Nietzsche-Studien* 17
     (1988): 434–74; Helmut Pfotenhauer, *Die Kunst als Physiologie: Nietzsche's ästhetische
     Theorie und literarische Produktion* (Stuttgart: Metzler, 1985); and Gregory Moore,
     Nietzsche, Biology, and Metaphor. On Nietzsche's relation to science more broadly,
     see Gregory Moore and Thomas Brobjer, eds., *Nietzsche and Science* (Hampshire,
     UK: Ashgate, 2004), especially the essays by Brobjer, "Nietzsche's Reading and
     Knowledge of Natural Science: An Overview," 21–50, and Richard S. G. Brown,
     "Nietzsche: 'That Profound Physiologist,'" 51–70, which provides a useful discus-
     sion of the way leading interpreters of Nietzsche have treated his physiology.

31   Hans Erich Lampl, "Ex Oblivione: Das Féré-Palimpsest; Noten zur Beziehung
     Friedrich Nietzsche—Charles Féré," *Nietzsche-Studien* 15 (1986): 225–64.

32   Stanislaw Przybyszewski, *Das Werk des Edvard Munch: Vier Beiträge* (Berlin:
     Fischer, 1894), 4–5.

33   Quoted in Cordulak, *Edvard Munch and the Physiology of Symbolism,* 43.

34   Edvard Munch, quoted in Johan Langaard, *Edvard Munch: The University Murals*
     (Oslo: Norsk Kunstreproduksjon, 1960).

35   See especially Aby Warburg, *Grundlegende Bruchstücke zu einer monistischen
     Kunstpsychologie* (1888–1905), III: 43.1–2, Warburg Institute Archive, London. On
     Warburg's notion of *Nachleben,* see Georges Didi-Huberman, *L'Image survivante:
     Histoire de l'art et temps des fantômes sélon Aby Warburg* (Paris: Minuit, 2002).

36   Przybyszewski, *Das Werk des Edvard Munch: Vier Beiträge,* 13.

37   The French lines are of course a direct quotation from Charles Baudelaire's
     poem "Correspondances" (line 8), from *Les Fleurs du mal* (1857; Paris: Poutlet-
     Malassis, 1861).

38   On Przybyszewski's views of art, see Jörg Marx, *Lebenspathos und "Seelenkunst"
     bei Stanislaw Przybyszewski* (Frankfurt: Lang, 1990); and George Klim, *Stanislaw
     Przybyszewski—Leben, Werk und Weltanschauung im Rahmen der deutschen Literatur
     der Jahrhundertwende* (Paderborn, Germany: Igel, 1992).

39   Sven Dierig, "Con Sordino for Piano and Brain: Bohemian Neuroscience in a
     1900 Cultural Metropolis," *Configurations* 9 (2001): 413–40. Dierig shows how these
     events were used by Schleich as self-experiments that resulted in a theory of an
     active, neuroglia-based switching apparatus in the brain based on the variable
     fluid states of the protoplasmic glial cells.

40   Max Dauthendey, quoted in Matuszek, *Der geniale Pole,* 104. Julius Bab, biogra-
     pher of these Berlin bohemians, wrote that "people who heard Przybyszewski
     play Chopin considered this experience among the strongest artistic impressions
     in their lives." Ibid, 103.

41   Przybyszewski, *Zur Psychologie des Individuums,* 108.

42 Stanislaw Przybyszewski, *Ferne komm ich her . . . Errinerungen an Berlin und Krakau* (Leipzig: Kiepenheuer, 1985), 175.

43 Reinhold Heller, *Munch: His Life and Work* (Chicago: University of Chicago Press, 1984), 116.

44 Georges Didi-Huberman, *The Invention of Hysteria: Charcot and the Photographic Iconography of the Salpetrière*, trans. Alisa Hartz (Cambridge, MA: MIT Press, 2003), 210. On Charcot and hysteria discourse in the artistic culture of France, see Deborah Silverman, *Art Nouveau in Fin-de-Siècle France: Politics, Psychology, and Style* (Berkeley: University of California Press, 1989); and Barbara Larson, *The Dark Side of Nature: Science, Society, and the Fantastic in the Work of Odilon Redon* (University Park: Pennsylvania State University Press, 2005).

45 Charles Féré, "Exemple d'induction psychomotrice chez un chat," *Journal de psychologie normale et pathologique* 3 (1906): 26.

46 Paul Régnard, *Les Maladies épidémiques de l'esprit: Sorcellerie, magnétisme, morphinisme, délire des grandeurs* (Paris: Plon-Nourrit, 1887), 20.

47 On physiological models of spectatorship, see the essays in Mark Micale, ed., *The Mind of Modernism: Medicine, Psychology, and the Cultural Arts in Europe and America, 1880–1940* (Stanford, CA: Stanford University Press, 2004).

48 Strindberg, as we will see below, would soon mount his own response to Nordau in the context of putting forth a similar "automatic theory of art." See August Strindberg, "The New Arts! Or the Role of Chance in Artistic Creation," in *Selected Essays by August Strindberg*, trans. and ed. Michael Robinson (Cambridge: Cambridge University Press, 1996), 107.

49 Nordau, *Degeneration*, 6.

50 Munch, undated notebook, cited in Cordulak, *Edvard Munch and the Physiology of Symbolism*, 58.

51 Régnard, *Les Maladies épidémiques de l'esprit*, x.

52 Gabriel Tarde, *Les Lois de l'imitation: Étude sociologique* (Paris: Alcan, 1890), 97.

53 Reinhold Heller argues that in this painting Munch composed directly from the line and color directions of Charles Henry and Charles Féré. Heller observes that this explains why Munch, in making a woodcut of the painting, did not reverse the composition of the painting in the transfer to the print, as standard practice would have demanded: "Had Munch reversed the composition, the directional movement of the lines would have become a 'happy' one, thus destroying the intensity of the sunset's drastic mood." Heller, *Edvard Munch: The Scream* (London: Penguin, 1973), 117n38.

54 Nordau, *Degeneration*, 26.

55 Rae Beth Gordon, *Why the French Love Jerry Lewis: From Cabaret to Early Cinema* (Stanford, CA: Stanford University Press, 2001); and Gordon, *Dances with Darwin, 1875–1910: Vernacular Modernity in France* (Burlington, VT: Ashgate, 2009).

56 The Norwegian critic Andreas Aubert's 1890 description of Munch invoked

the standard imagery of Bohemian decadence: "nervously sensitive, seeking stimulation to the very point of sickness; in his veins is the blood of an extraordinarily noble race. . . . Among our artists, Munch is one whose entire temperament is formed by the neurasthenic. . . . He belongs to the generation of fine, sickly sensitive nerves that we encounter more and more frequently in the newest art. And not seldomly do they find a personal satisfaction in calling themselves 'Decadents,' the children of a refined, overly civilized age." A. Aubert, "Høstudstillingen: Aarsarbeidet IV; Edward Munch," *Dagbladet* (November 5, 1890): 2–3, trans. and cited in Heller, *Edvard Munch*, 81.

57 Patricia G. Berman, "Edvard Munch's Self-Portrait with Cigarette: Smoking and the Bohemian Persona," *Art Bulletin* 75 (1993): 627–46.

58 Edward Carpenter, *The Art of Creation: Essays on the Self and Its Powers* (London: George Allen, 1900), 2–7. See also Carpenter, *Intermediate Types among Primitive Folk: A Study in Social Evolution* (New York: Mitchell Kennerley, 1914); and Carpenter, *Love's Coming of Age* (London: Methuen, 1896). On the role of protoplasm in Carpenter's notion intermediate types, see Judy Smith, "Genealogies of Desire: 'Uranianism,' Mysticism, and Science in Britain, 1889–1940" (master's thesis, University of British Columbia, 2008).

59 Carl Ludwig Schleich, "Strindberg-Errinnerungen," in *Besonnte Vergangenheit: Lebenserinnerungen, 1859–1919* (Berlin: Rowohlt, 1924), 254–55.

60 August Strindberg, "Wo sind die Nerven der Pflanzen?," in *Verwirrte Sinneseindrücke: Schriften zu Malerei, Fotografie und Naturwissenschaften* (Dresden: Verlag der Kunst, 1998), 191.

61 August Strindberg to Torsten Hedlund, July 23, 1894, letter 318, in *Strindberg's Letters*, trans. and ed. Michael Robinson, vol. 2, *1892–1912* (Chicago: University of Chicago Press, 1992), 489. The text in question was Strindberg's *Antibarbarus I oder die Welt für sich und die Welt für mich* (Berlin: Verlag des Bibliographischen Bureaus, 1894).

62 As he explained in the same letter to Hedlund cited above, "I thought I had expressed the secret thoughts of my contemporaries and didn't expect to be received as a charlatan or lunatic; thus I was feeling somewhat depressed when Haeckel, in Jena, wrote to say that these ideas about the transformation of matter were not unfamiliar to him, for he had heard them from a recently deceased chemist whose work he respected, etc." Strindberg to Hedlund, *Strindberg's Letters*, 2:489.

63 Ibid.

64 J. L. de Lanessan, *Le Transformisme: Évolution de la matière et des êtres vivants* (Paris: Doin, 1883), is the key text. Lanessan's views are already present in his doctoral thesis "Du protoplasma végétal" (1876), but they developed into a monist transformism in the 1880s. This neo-Lamarckism updated the original outlook of Lamarck's theories of organic evolution, which were focused on transmutations

in cellular tissues and fluids and depended on his original chemical theory, itself largely opposed to the established Lavoisierien approach of his time. On French romanticism more generally, see John Tresch, *The Romantic Machine: Utopian Science and Technology after Napoleon* (Chicago: University of Chicago Press, 2012).

65 Strindberg, quoted in Per Hemmingsen, *Strindberg som fotograph* (Malmö: Kalejdoskop Förlag, 1989), 163.

66 August Strindberg, "Das Seufzen der Steine," in *Verwirrte Sinneseindrücke*, 141. This essay forms part of a series of essays with the overarching title "Jardins des Plantes." It was originally published in Paris as "Sylva Sylvarum" in January 1896, then in an expanded Swedish edition as "Jardin des Plantes" in Gothenburg in May 1896. Strindberg's mentions of Haeckel in this essay are not referenced but may have referred to Ernst Haeckel, *Die Kalkschwaemme. eine monographie*, 2 vols. (Berlin: Reimer, 1872).

67 Strindberg, "Das Seufzen der Steine," 164.

68 Ibid., 164–65.

69 On Strindberg as visual artist, see the essays in the exhibition catalog, Torsten Gunnarsson, Per Hedström, and Göran Söderström, eds., *Strindberg: Painter and Photographer* (New Haven, CT: Yale University Press, 2001).

70 Clément Chéroux, *L'Expérience photographique d'August Strindberg* (Paris: Actes Sud, 1994), 36.

71 On Strindberg and visual art, see Göran Söderstrom, *Strindberg och bildkonsten* (Uddevalla, Sweden: Forum, 1972). For Strindberg's relations with Nordic art, see Michelle Facos, "Strindberg and Scandinavian Painting: 1880–1900," in *Strindberg and Genre*, ed. Michael Robinson (Norwich, UK: Norvik, 1991), 276–86.

72 Douglas Feuk, *August Strindberg: Inferno Painting and Pictures of Paradise* (Copenhagen: Edition Bløndal, 1991).

73 Strindberg, "New Arts!," 103.

74 Ibid., 105.

75 Ibid., 105–6.

76 Ibid., 107.

77 Nordau, *Degeneration*, 65.

78 Arne Eggum, *Munch and Photography*, trans. Birgit Holm (New Haven, CT: Yale University Press, 1989), 61.

79 Clement Chéroux, "Photographs of Fluids: An Alphabet of Invisible Rays," in *The Perfect Medium: Photography and the Occult*, ed. C. Chéroux, A. Fischer, P. Apraxine, D. Canguilhem, and S. Schmit (New Haven, CT: Yale University Press, 2005), 114–25.

80 Strindberg carried Finot's *La Photographie transcendentale* in his "green sack," a bag of indispensable books and papers he kept with him at all times, which remains in the Strindberg archive at the Royal Library in Stockholm. Chéroux, *L'Expérience photographique*, 59.

81 Edvard Munch, quoted in Rolf Stenersen, *Edvard Munch: Close-Up of a Genius*, trans. and ed. Reidar Dittmann (Oslo: Gyldendal, 1969), 21.

82 Tom Gunning, "Phantom Images and Modern Manifestations," in *Fugitive Images: From Photography to Video*, ed. Patrice Petro (Bloomington: Indiana University Press, 1995), 58.

83 August Strindberg, "Ueber die Lichtwirkung in der Fotographie: Betrachtungen aus Anlass der X-Strahlen," in Strindberg, *Verwirrte Sinneseindruecke*, 122 (for all quotations in this paragraph).

7. Art for Life's Sake

1   On Le Dantec's career, see Laurent Loison, *Qu'est-ce que le néolamarckisme? Les biologistes français et la question de l'évolution des espèces* (Paris: Vuibert, 2010); and Stuart M. Persell, *Neo-Lamarckism and the Evolution Controversy in France, 1870–1920* (Lewiston, NY: Edwin Mellen Press, 1999), 101–40.

2   Félix Le Dantec, *Évolution individuelle et hérédité*, 2nd ed. (Paris: Alcan, 1913): ix.

3   Loison, *Qu'est-ce que le néolamarckisme?*, 68–70.

4   Félix Le Dantec, quoted in Jean D'Udine, *L'Art et le geste* (Paris: F. Alcan, 1910), 116.

5   Le Dantec agreed with many of Bergson's ideas, especially what he called the critique of the "false evolutionism" expressed in Darwin's doctrine of gemmules and Weismann's theory of the germ plasm. But Le Dantec also accused Bergson of stealing many of his ideas, including the notions of the "logic of solids," "the cinematographical mechanism of thought," and even the "élan vital." See Félix Le Dantec, "La Biologie de M. Bergson," *Revue de mois* 2 (1907): 230–41; and Bergson's letter to the editor of the same publication in the August 20, 1907, issue.

6   Félix Le Dantec, "L'Intuition," *Les Arts de la vie* 1 (1904): 31.

7   Ibid., 32.

8   Ibid., 30–32.

9   Ibid., 32.

10 Ibid., 33.

11 Pascal Rousseau, "Confusion des sens: Le Débat sur la synesthésie dans les débuts de l'abstraction en France," *Le Cahiers du Musée nationale de l'art moderne* 74 (2000–2001): 14–15.

12 D'Udine, *L'Art et le geste*, 115.

13 On the life and work of Dalcroze, see Percy B. Ingham, "The Method: Growth and Practice," in *The Eurhythmics of Jaques-Dalcroze*, ed. M. E. Sadler (London: Constable & Co., 1912), 31–47; and Adolphe Appia, "Über Ursprung und Anfang der rhythmischen Gymnastik," in *Der Rhythmus: Ein Jahrbuch* (Jena, Germany: Eugen Diederichs, 1911), 1:20–31.

14 Émile Jaques-Dalcroze, *Rhythmische Gymnastik* (Leipzig: Verlag von Sandoz, 1907).

15 D'Udine, *L'Art et le geste*, xvi.

16 Maria Lluïsa Borràs, *Picabia* (London: Thames and Hudson, 1985).

17 Arnaud Pierre, *Francis Picabia: La Peinture sans aura* (Paris: Gallimard, 2002), 102–5.

18 Francis Picabia, "How New York Looks to Me," *New York American* (March 30, 1913), 11.

19 On the Paris and New York contexts of Picabia's turn to nonfigurative painting, see the fine study by Virginia Spae, *Orphism: The Evolution of Non-figurative Painting in Paris, 1910–1914* (Oxford: Clarendon Press, 1979).
RMB: Please change the author's name to Virginia Spate; also in the bibliography.

20 Gertrude Stein, *The Autobiography of Alice B. Toklas* (New York: Random House, 1961), 210.

21 Ibid.

22 Francis Picabia in *New York Tribune* (1913), quoted in Spate, *Orphism*, 320.

23 D'Udine, *L'Art et le geste*, 6.

24 H. C. Bastian, *The Brain as an Organ of Mind* (New York: Appleton, 1880), 543.

25 W. B. Pillsbury, "The Place of Movement in Consciousness," *Psychological Review* 18 (1911): 83–89.

26 D'Udine, *L'Art et le geste*, 118.

27 Ibid., 234.

28 Ibid., 245.

29 The works of empathy theorists had been discussed in various French periodicals between 1900 and 1910. See, for example, Vernon Lee, "La Sympathie esthétique d'après Th. Lipps," *Revue philosophique* 64 (1905): 620–22. Charles Lalo, "Les Sens esthétiques," *Revue philosophique* 65 (1908): 449–70, joined the empathy theorists "aesthetic mechanics" with received theories of line, sound, and color promoted by Henry and his colleagues.

30 Scholars often note the important patronage relationship of Kahn and Marinetti, without noting their profound intellectual and artistic relations. Yet Marinetti's contemporaries appear to have known otherwise: an influential essay by the British poet and critic F. S. Flint, "Contemporary French Poetry," *Poetry Review* 1:8 (1912): 355–414, portrayed Marinetti's futurist poetics as the culmination of French vers libre. Peter Demetz, *Worte in Freiheit: Der italienische Futurismus und die deutsche literarische Avantgarde (1912–1934)* (Munich: Piper, 1990), 42–62, shows that Germans similarly understood Marinetti's words-in-freedom as a radicalization of Kahn's poetics.

31 F. T. Marinetti, "The Variety Theater," in *Critical Writings*, ed. Günter Berghaus, trans. Doug Thompson (New York: Farrar, Straus and Giroux, 2006), 185–92. See also Günter Berghaus, *The Genesis of Futurism: Marinetti's Early Career and Writings, 1899–1909* (Leeds, UK: Society for Italian Studies, 1995).

32 On the 1909 manifesto, see Jean-Pierre A. de Villers, ed., *Le Premier Manifeste du*

futurisme: Édition critique avec, en facsimile, le manuscrit original de F. T. Marinetti (Ottawa: Éditions de l'Université d'Ottawa, 1986).

33 Marinetti, "Variety Theater," 185–92.

34 F. T. Marinetti, "Technical Manifesto of Futurist Literature," in *Critical Writings*, 113.

35 Ibid., 107.

36 Ibid., 124.

37 F. T. Marinetti, "Destruction of Syntax—Untrammeled Imagination—Words-in-Freedom," in *Critical Writings*, 124.

38 Quoted in Richard Cándida-Smith, *Mallarmé's Children: Symbolism and the Renewal of Experience* (Berkeley: University of California Press, 1999), 26.

39 Marinetti, "Destruction of Syntax," 131.

40 Ibid., 123.

41 F. T. Marinetti, "Geometrical and Mechanical Splendor and Sensitivity toward Numbers," in *Critical Writings*, 140.

42 Marinetti, "Destruction of Syntax," 131.

43 F. T. Marinetti, "Extended Man and the Kingdom of the Machine," in *Critical Writings*, 86.

44 See Jeffrey T. Schnapp, "Propeller Talk," *Modernism/modernity* 1, no. 3 (1994): 153–78.

45 Marinetti, "Destruction of Syntax," 131.

46 Marinetti, "Geometrical and Mechanical Splendor," 139.

47 Günter Berghaus, *Italian Futurist Theatre, 1909–1944* (Oxford: Clarendon Press, 1998).

48 Wyndham Lewis, *Blasting and Bombardiering: An Autobiography (1914–1926)* (London: Calder and Boyars, 1967), 37. First published 1937 by Eyre & Spottiswoode; page numbers refer to the 1967 edition.

49 Lewis, quoted in F. T. Marinetti, *Let's Murder the Moonshine: Selected Writings of F. T. Marinetti*, ed. R. W. Flint, trans. R. W. Flint and Arthur A Coppotelli (Los Angeles: Sun and Moon Classics, 1991), 26.

50 F. T. Marinetti, "Dynamic, Multichanneled Recitation," in *Critical Writings*, 199.

51 Henry Nevinson, quoted in Douglas Kahn, *Noise, Water, Meat: A History of Sound in the Arts* (Cambridge, MA: MIT Press, 1999), 60.

52 Henry Newbolt, "Futurism and Form in Poetry," *Fortnightly Review* 95, no. 569 (1914): 812.

53 D. Kahn, *Noise Water Meat*; and Harold B. Segal, *Turn of the Century Cabaret: Paris, Barcelona, Berlin, Munich, Vienna, Cracow, Moscow, St. Petersburg, Zurich* (New York: Columbia University Press, 1987).

54 Hugo Ball, "Die Reise nach Dresden," *Der Künstler und die Zeitkrankheit: Ausgewählte Schriften*, ed. Hans-Burkhard Schlichtling (Frankfurt: Suhrkamp, 1984), 315.

55 Hugo Ball, "Das erste dadaistische Manifest" (Zürich, July 14, 1916), in *Der Künstler und die Zeitkrankheit*, ed. Schlichtling , 40.

56 Hugo Ball, entry for April 5, 1916, in *Flight Out of Time: A Dada Diary*, ed. John Elderfield, trans. Ann Raimes (New York: Viking Press, 1974), 59.

57 On Ball's Munich years, see Erdmute Wenzel White, *The Magic Bishop: Hugo Ball, Dada Poet* (Columbia, SC: Camden House, 1998), 61–83.

58 Dalcroze discusses applications of his methods in the theater, including the work of Ball's teacher Max Reinhardt, in Émile Jaques-Dalcroze, *Rhythm, Music, and Education* (New York: G. P. Putnam's Sons, 1921), 202.

59 White, *Magic Bishop*, 73–83.

60 Wassily Kandinsky, "On Stage Composition," in *The Blaue Reiter Almanac*, trans. Henning Falkenstein, ed. Klaus Lankheit (Boston: MFA Publications, 1965) 190–206.

61 Wassily Kandinsky, *Concerning the Spiritual in Art* (1911), trans. M. T. H. Sadler (New York: Dover, 1977), 51.

62 Kandinsky, "On Stage Composition," 205.

63 Hans Bolliger, Guido Magnaguagno, and Raimund Meyer, eds., *Dada in Zürich* (Zürich: Kunsthaus Zürich, 1985).

64 Ball, entry for March 30, 1917, in *Flight Out of Time*, 102.

65 Tristan Tzara, "Note on Poetry," *Dada* 4–5 (May 1919), reprinted and translated in Barbara Wright, ed., *Seven Dada Manifestoes and Lampisteries* (London: John Calder, 1977), 76.

66 Hugo Ball, "Gadji Beri Bimba," in *Gesammelte Gedichte*, ed. Annemarie Schütt-Hennings (Zurich: Die Arche, 1963), 27.

67 For performances of Ball's phonetic poems, visit UbuWeb, www.ubu.com/sound/ball.html (accessed May 10, 2010). On the "personal boomboom," see Tristan Tzara, "Dada Manifesto 1918," trans. Ralph Mannheim, in *The Dada Painters and Poets: An Anthology*, ed. Robert Motherwell (Cambridge, MA: Belknap Press of Harvard University Press, 1981), 79.

68 Remy de Gourmont, *Le Problème du style* (Paris: Mercure de France, 1902), 9.

69 Remy de Gourmont, *Esthétique de la langue française* (Paris: Mercure de France, 1905), 315–16.

70 Julien Benda, *Belphégor*, trans. S. J. I. Lawson, from the original *Belphégor: Essai sur l'esthétique de la présente société française* (1918) (New York: Payson and Clarke, 1929), 144.

Conclusion

1 Julien Benda, *Belphégor: Essai sur l'esthétique de la présente société française* (1918). All quotations are from the English translation: Julien Benda, *Belphégor*, trans. S. J. I. Lawson (New York: Payson and Clarke, 1929).

2 Benda, *Belphégor*, 3.

3   Ibid., 52.

4   Ibid,. 82.

5   Julien Benda, *La Trahison des clercs* (Paris: B. Grasset, 1927). There are several translations, most recently, *The Treason of the Intellectuals* (Piscataway, NJ: Transaction Publications, 2006).

6   Vincent Sherry, *Ezra Pound, Wyndham Lewis, and Radical Modernism* (Oxford: Oxford University Press, 1993).

7   Michael Levenson, *A Genealogy of Modernism: A Study of English Literary Doctrine, 1908–1922* (Cambridge: Cambridge University Press, 1984), 37–47; Karen Csengari, "The Chronology of T. H. Hulme's *Speculations*," *Papers in the Bibliographical Society of America* 80 (1986): 105–9; and Jesse Matz, "Hulme, Bergson, and Psychologism," in *The Mind of Modernism: Medicine, Psychology, and the Cultural Arts in Europe and America, 1880–1940*, ed. Mark Micale (Stanford, CA: Stanford University Press, 2004), 339–51.

8   Martin Jay, "Modernism and the Specter of Psychologism," *Modernism/modernity* 3, no. 2 (1996): 93–111; and John Fizer, *Psychologism and Psychoaesthetics* (Amsterdam: J. Benjamins, 1981). On the philosophical debate around psychologism in Germany, see Martin Kusch, *Psychologism: A Case Study in the Sociology of Philosophical Knowledge* (London: Routledge, 1995).

9   David Lomas, "Modest Recording Instruments: Science, Surrealism, and Visuality," *Art History* 27 (2004): 627–50; and Rosalind E. Krauss, *The Optical Unconscious* (Cambridge, MA: MIT Press, 1993).

10 Robin Maremant Veder, *The Living Line: Modern Art and the Economy of Energy* (University Press of New England, forthcoming). See also Robin Veder, "The Expressive Efficiencies of American Delsarte and Mensendieck Body Cultures," *Modernism/modernity* 17, no. 4 (2010): 819–38.

11 Veder, *Living Line*, chapter 7, reads Dewey's key texts, such as "Affective Thought in Logic and Painting," from *Art as Experience* (1934), against a rich archive of correspondence with Alfred C. Barnes and Leo Stein about art, physiological aesthetics, and their experiences with the Alexander Technique.

12 Caroline Jones, *Eyesight Alone: Clement Greenberg's Modernism and the Bureaucratization of the Senses* (Chicago: University of Chicago Press, 2006), 391.

BIBLIOGRAPHY

Archives

Archiv der Staatsbibliothek Preussischer Kulturbesitz, Berlin (West)

College de France, Paris

Conservatoire des Arts et Métiers, Paris

Étienne-Jules Marey Collection, Cinématheque Française, Paris

Hotel de Ville, Beaune, France

Hotel de Ville, Paris

Musée Marey, Beaune, France

Warburg Institute Archive, London

Printed Sources

Aarsleff, Hans. *From Locke to Saussure: Essays on the Study of Language and Intellectual History.* Minneapolis: University of Minnesota Press, 1982.

Adam, Lucien. *Les Classifications, l'objet, la methode, les conclusions de la linguistique.* Paris: Maisonneuve, 1882.

———. *Les Patois lorrains.* Paris: Maisonneuve, 1881.

Albert, Charles. "La 21ème exposition des artistes indépendents." *Les Temps nouveaux* 10 (April 8–14, 1905): 6–7.

Alder, Ken. "Making Things the Same: Representation, Tolerance and the End of the Ancien Régime in France." *Social Studies of Science* 28, no. 4 (1998): 499–545.

Allen, Grant. *Physiological Aesthetics.* London: Henry S. King & Co., 1877.

Allen, W. S. *Phonetics in Ancient India.* London: Geoffrey Cumberlege, 1953.

Alpers, Svetlana. *The Art of Describing: Dutch Art in the Seventeenth Century.* Chicago: University of Chicago Press, 1983.

Aminoff, Michael J. *Brown-Séquard: A Visionary of Science.* New York: Raven Press, 1993.

Amsterdamska, Olga. *Schools of Thought: The Development of Linguistics from Bopp to Saussure.* Dordrecht: D. Reidel, 1987.

Andry-Bourgeois, C. *L'Œuvre de Charles Henry et le probleme de la survie.* Paris: Jean Meyer, 1931.

Anonymous. "Un Cri de femme revoltée." *Le Révolté* (September 18–24, 1886).

———. "Distribution of Driving-Power in Laboratories." *Nature* 33 (January 14, 1886): 248–50.

———. "La Machine à synthèse des voyelles du docteur Marage." *La Nature* 2, no. 7 (1908): 160.

———. *Protoplasm, Powheads, and Porwiggles, and the Evolution of the Horse from the Rhinoceros, Illustrating Professor Huxley's Scientific Mode of Getting Up the Creation and Upsetting Moses.* London: Longmans and Co., 1875.

———. "Psychophysics." *The Nation* 1319 (October 9, 1890): 290–92.

———. Review of *Les Modifications phonétique du langage étudiée dans le patois d'une famille de Cellefrouin and Paul Passy, étude sur les changements phonétiques et leurs caractères généraux,* by Abbé Rousselot. *Literaturblatt für germanische und romanische Philologie* 9 (1892): 314.

———. Review of *Physiological Aesthetics,* by Grant Allen. *Popular Science Monthly* 11, no. 41 (October 1877): 760.

———. "Le Salon de 1888, III." *Gazette des Beaux-Arts* 38, no. 2 (1888): 138–39.

Appia, Adolphe. "Über Ursprung und Anfang der rhythmischen Gymnastik." In *Der Rhythmus: Ein Jahrbuch,* vol. 1, 20–31. Jena, Germany: Eugen Diederichs, 1911.

Aquinas, St. Thomas. *Summa contra Gentiles.* Translated by Anton C. Pegis et al. 5 vols. 1955. Reprint, Notre Dame, IN: University of Notre Dame Press, 1975.

Argüelles, José A. *Charles Henry and the Formation of a Psycho-Physical Aesthetic.* Chicago: University of Chicago Press, 1972.

Arkell, David. *Looking for Laforgue: A Biography of Jules Laforgue.* Manchester, UK: Carcanet, 1979.

Armstrong, Tim. *Modernism, Technology, and the Body.* Cambridge: Cambridge University Press, 1998.

Asendorf, Christoph. *Batteries of Life: On the History of Things and Their Perception in Modernity.* Translated by Don Renau. Berkeley: University of California Press, 1993.

———. *Ströme und Strahlen: Das langsame Verschwinden der Materie um 1900.* Berlin: Anabas, 1989.

Auerbach, Felix. *Die graphische Darstellung: Eine allgemeinverständliche, durch zahlreiche Beispiele aus allen Gebieten der Wissenschaft und Praxis erläuterte Einführung in den Sinn und den Gebrauch der Methode.* Leipzig: B. G. Teubner, 1914.

Auroux, Sylvain. "La Catégorie du *parler* et la linguistique." *Romantisme* 9, nos. 25–26 (1979): 157–78.

Auslander, Leora. *Taste and Power: Furnishing Modern France.* Berkeley: University of California Press, 1996.

Azoulay, L. "L'Ère nouvelle des sons et des bruits—musées et archives phonographiques." *Revue scientifique* 13 (1900): 712–15.

Babbage, Charles. *The Economy of Machinery and Manufactures.* London: Charles Knight, Pall Mall East, 1832.

Baldwin, P. M. "Liberalism, Nationalism, and Degeneration: The Case of Max Nordau." *Central European History* 13, no. 2 (1980): 99–120.

Ball, Hugo. *Flight Out of Time: A Dada Diary.* Edited by John Elderfield. Translated by Ann Raimes. New York: Viking Press, 1974.

———. *Gesammelte Gedichte*. Edited by Annemarie Schütt-Hennings. Zurich: Die Arche, 1963.

———. *Der Künstler und die Zeitkrankheit: Ausgewählte Schriften*. Edited by Hans-Burkhard Schlichtling. Frankfurt: Suhrkamp, 1984.

Barlow, W. H. *Popular Science Review* 13 (1874): 278–88.

———. *Proceedings of the Royal Society* 22 (1873–74): 277–89.

Bastian, H. C. *The Brain as an Organ of Mind*. New York: Appleton, 1880.

Baudelaire, Charles. *Les Fleurs du mal*. 1857. Paris: Poutlet-Malassis, 1861.

Bauman, Richard, and Charles L. Briggs. *Voices of Modernity: Language Ideologies and the Politics of Inequality*. Cambridge: Cambridge University Press, 2003.

Baxandall, Michael. *Painting and Experience in Fifteenth-Century Italy: A Primer on the Social History of Pictorial Style*. 2nd ed. Oxford: Oxford University Press, 1988. First published 1972.

Bayertz, Kurt. "Biology and Beauty: Science and Aesthetics in Fin-de-Siècle Germany." In *Fin de Siècle and Its Legacy*, edited by Mikulas Teich and Roy Porter, 278–96. Cambridge: Cambridge University Press, 1990.

Bazin, André. "The Ontology of the Photographic Image." In *What Is Cinema?*, translated by Hugh Gray, vol. 1, 9–16. Berkeley: University of California Press, 1967.

Beatty, John, and Piers Hale. "Water Babies: An Evolutionary Parable." *Endeavour* 32 (2008): 141–46.

Becq de Fouquières, Louis. *Traité général de versification française*. Paris: Charpentier, 1879.

Beddoe, John. *The Races of Britain, a Contribution to the Anthropology of Western Europe*. Bristol, UK: Arrowsmith, 1885.

Bell, Alexander Graham. "Researches in Electric Telephony." *Journal of the Society of Telegraph Engineers* 6 (1877): 385–416.

Bell, David. "Lingua Populi, Lingua Dei: Language, Religion, and the Origins of French Revolutionary Nationalism." *American Historical Review* 100, no. 5 (1995): 1403–37.

Belofsky, H. "Engineering Drawing: A Universal Language in Two Dialects." *Technology and Culture* 32, no.1 (1991): 23–46.

Belting, Hans. *Bild und Kult: Eine Geschichte des Bildes vor dem Zeitalter der Kunst*. Munich: Beck, 1990.

Benda, Julien. *Belphégor*. Translated by S. J. I. Lawson, from the original *Belphégor: Essai sur l'esthétique de la présente société française*. 1918. New York: Payson and Clarke, 1929.

Bender, John, and Michael Marrinan. *The Culture of Diagram*. Stanford, CA: Stanford University Press, 2010.

Bennett, Jane. *Vibrant Matter: A Political Ecology of Things*. Durham, NC: Duke University Press, 2010.

Benshop, Ruth. "What Is a Tachistoscope? Historical Explorations of an Instrument." *Science in Context* 11, no. 1 (1998): 23–50.

Benware, Wilbur A. *The Study of Indo-European Vocalism in the 19th Century*. Amsterdam: John Benjamins, 1974.

Berghaus, Günter. *The Genesis of Futurism: Marinetti's Early Career and Writings, 1899–1909*. Leeds, UK: Society for Italian Studies, 1995.

———. *Italian Futurist Theatre, 1909–1944*. Oxford: Clarendon Press, 1998.

Bergson, Henri. *Creative Evolution*. Translated by Arthur Mitchell. Edited by Keith Ansell Pearson, Michael Kolkman, and Michael Vaughn, with an introduction by Keith Ansell Pearson. London: Palgrave, 2007.

———. "Discussion avec Einstein." In *Mélanges*, edited by André Robinet, 1340–47. Paris: Presses Universitaires de France, 1972.

———. *Evolution créatrice*. Paris: Presses Universitaires de France, 1907.

———. *Matter and Memory*. Translated by Nancy Margaret Paul and W. Scott Palmer. Mineola, NY: Dover, 2004.

———. "La Philosophie de Claude Bernard." 1913. In *Oeuvres*, 5th ed., edited by André Robinet, 1433–40. Paris: Presses Universitaires de France, 1991.

———. *Time and Free Will: An Essay on the Immediate Data of Consciousness*. 1889. Authorized translation by F. L. Pogson. 3rd ed. London: G. Allen, 1913.

Bergson, Henri, M. [Étienne-Jules] Marey, et al. "Groupe d'études de phénomènes psychiques." 1901. In *Mélanges*, edited by André Robinet, 509–15. Paris: Presses Universitaires de France, 1972.

Berman, Patricia G. "Edvard Munch's Self-Portrait with Cigarette: Smoking and the Bohemian Persona." *Art Bulletin* 75 (1993): 627–46.

Bernard, Claude. *Introduction to the Study of Experimental Medicine*. Translated by Henry Copley Greene. 1865. Reprint, New York: Dover, 1957.

———. *Leçons sur les phénomènes de la vie communs aux animaux et aux végétaux*. 1878. Edited by Georges Canguilhem. Paris: Vrin, 1966.

Binet, Alfred. "Le Problème de l'audition colorée." *Revue des deux mondes* 113 (1892): 586–614.

———. *The Psychic Life of Microorganisms: A Study in Experimental Psychology*. Translated by Thomas McCormack. Chicago: Open Court, 1897.

———. *La Suggestibilité*. 1900. Reprint. Philadelphia: D. N. Goodchild, 2006.

Blake, Clarence J. "The Use of the Membrana Tympani as a Phonautograph and Logograph." *Archives of Ophthalmalogy and Otology* 5 (1876): 108–13.

Blanc, Charles. *Grammaire des arts du dessin: Architecture, sculpture, peinture*. Paris: Henri Lauren, 1867.

Blumenberg, Hans. *Die Lesbarkeit der Welt*. Frankfurt: Suhrkamp, 1981.

Bolliger, Hans, Guido Magnaguagno, and Raimund Meyer, eds. *Dada in Zürich*. Zürich: Kunsthaus Zürich, 1985.

Bolton, Thaddeus. "Rhythm." *American Journal of Psychology* 6, no. 2 (1894): 145–238.

Bonah, Christian. *Les Sciences physiologiques en Europe: Analyse comparées du XIXe siècle*. Paris: Vrin, 1995.

Bopp, François. *Grammaire comparée des langues indo-européenes comprenant le sanscrit, le zend, l'armenien, le grec, le latin, le lithuanien, l'ancien slave, le gothique et l'allemand.* Translated by M. Michel Bréal. 2 vols. Paris: Imprimerie Nationale, 1966.

Borck, Cornelius. *Hirnströme: Eine Kulturgeschichte der Elektroenzephalogie.* Göttingen, Germany: Wallstein, 2005.

Bordogna, Francesca. "The Psychology and Physiology of Temperament: Pragmatism in Context." *Journal of the History of the Behavioral Sciences* 37, no. 1 (2001): 3–25.

Borell, Merriley. "Brown-Séquard's Organotherapy and Its Appearance in America at the End of the Nineteenth Century." *Bulletin of the History of Medicine* 50 (1976): 309–20.

———. "Extending the Senses: The Graphic Method." *Medical Heritage* 2, no. 2 (1986): 114–21.

———. "Instruments and an Independent Physiology: The Harvard Physiological Laboratory, 1876–1906." In *Physiology in the American Context, 1850–1940*, edited by Gerald L. Geison, 293–321. Bethesda, MD: American Physiological Society, 1987.

———. "Training the Senses, Training the Mind." In *Medicine and the Five Senses*, edited by William F. Bynum and Roy Porter, 244–61. Cambridge: Cambridge University Press, 1993.

Borràs, Maria Lluïsa. *Picabia*. London: Thames and Hudson, 1985.

Bouhey, Vivian. *Les Anarchistes contre la République 1880 à 1914.* Rennes: Presses Universitaires de Rennes, 2008.

Bouquet, Mary. "Family Trees and Their Affinities: The Visual Imperative of the Genealogical Diagram." *Journal of the Royal Anthropological Institute* 2, no. 1 (1996): 43–66.

Brain, Robert Michael. "Genealogy of *Zang Tumb Tumb*: Experimental Phonetics, Vers Libre, and Modernist Sound Art." *Grey Room: Architecture, Art, Media, Politics*, no. 43 (2011): 88–117.

———. "How Edvard Munch and August Strindberg Contracted Protoplasmania: Memory, Synesthesia and the Vibratory Organism in Fin-de-Siècle Aesthetics." *Interdisciplinary Science Reviews* 35, no. 1 (2010): 7–38.

———. "Materialising the Medium: Ectoplasm and the Quest for Supra-normal Biology in Fin-de-Siècle Science and Art." In *Vibratory Modernism*, edited by Anthony Enns and Shelley Trower. London: Palgrave, 2013.

———. "The Ontology of the Questionnaire: Max Weber on Measurement and Mass Investigation." *Studies in the History and Philosophy of Science* 32, no. 4 (2001): 647–84.

———. "Protoplasmania: Huxley, Haeckel, and the Vibratory Organism in Late Nineteenth-Century Science and Art." In *The Art of Evolution: Darwin, Darwinisms, and Visual Cultures*, edited by Fae Brauer and Barbara Larson, 92–123. Lebanon, NH: University Presses of New England, 2009.

———. "The Pulse of Modernism: Experimental Physiology and Aesthetic Avant-Gardes circa 1900." *Studies in History and Philosophy of Science* 39 (2008): 393–417.

———. "Representation on the Line: The Graphic Method and the Instruments of Scientific Modernism." In *From Energy to Information: Representation in Science, Art, and Literature*, edited by Bruce Clark and Linda D. Henderson, 155–78. Stanford, CA: Stanford University Press, 2002.

———. "The Romantic Experiment as Fragment." In *Hans-Christian Ørsted and the Romantic Legacy in Science: Ideas, Disciplines, Practices*, edited by Robert M. Brain. R. S. Cohen, and Ole Knudsen, 217–34. Dordrecht: Springer, 2007.

———. "Self-Projection: Empathy and Oscillation in Hugo Münsterbergs Film Theory." *Science in Context* 25 (2012): 329–53.

———. "Standards and Semiotics." In *Inscribing Science*, edited by Timothy Lenoir, 249–85. Stanford, CA: Stanford University Press, 1998.

Brain, Robert Michael, and M. Norton Wise. "Muscles and Engines: Indicator Diagrams and Helmholtz's Graphical Methods." In *The Science Studies Reader*, edited by Mario Biagioli, 51–66. London: Routledge, 1998.

Brandstetter, Thomas. "Entfesselte Kräfte: Der Sprengstoff als Kulturtechnik der Moderne." In *Zeichen der Kraft: Wissensformationen 1800–1900*, by Thomas Brandstetter and Christof Windätter, 46–61. Berlin: Kadmos, 2008.

Brauer, Fae, and Barbara Larson, eds. *The Art of Evolution: Darwin, Darwinisms, and Visual Cultures*. Lebanon, NH. University Presses of New England. 2009.

Braun, Marta. *Picturing Time: The Work of Étienne-Jules Marey (1830–1904)*. Chicago: University of Chicago Press, 1992.

Bréal, Michel. *The Beginnings of Semantics: Essays, Lectures and Reviews*. Translated and edited by George Wolf. London: Duckworth, 1991.

———. *Essai de sémantique*. 5th ed. Paris: Hachette, 1911.

———. *Excursions pédagogique: Un Voyage scolaire en Allemagne*. Paris: A. Lahure, 1884.

———. "Le Langage et les nationalités." *Revue des deux mondes* 108 (1891): 615–39.

———. "Les Lois phoniques: À propos de la création du laboratoire de phonétique expérimentale au College de France." *Mémoires de la Société de linguistique de Paris* 10 (1898): 1–18.

Breidbach, Olaf. *Visions of Nature: The Art and Science of Ernst Haeckel*. Munich: Prestel, 2006.

Breymann, Hermann. *Die phonetische Literatur von 1876–1895*. Leipzig: Deichert, 1897.

Brion, Katherine. "Paul Signac's Decorative Propaganda of the 1890s." *RIHA Journal* 44 (2012): 1–20.

Brion-Guerry, Liliane, ed. *L'Année 1913: Les Formes esthétiques de l'oeuvre de l'art à la veille de la première guerre mondiale*. 3 vols. Paris: Klincksieck, 1971.

Broude, Norma, ed. *Seurat in Perspective*. Englewood Cliffs, NJ: Prentice-Hall, 1978.

Brown, Richard S. G. "Nietzsche: 'That Profound Physiologist.'" In *Nietzsche and Science*, edited by Gregory Moore and Thomas Brobjer, 51–70. Hampshire, UK: Ashgate, 2004.

Brown-Séquard, Charles Édouard. "Champ d'action de l'inhibition en physiologie, en pathogénie et en thérapeutique." *Archives de physiologie normales et pathologique* (Paris: G. Masson) 5, no. 1 (1889): 1–23.

———. "Collège de France: Cours de médecine par. M. Brown-Séquard." *Gazette hebdomadaire de médecine et de chirurgue* 16 (1879): 771.

———. "Expérience démontrant las puissance dynamogénique chez l'homme d'un liquide extrait de testicules d'animaux." *Archives de physiologie normale et pathologique* (Paris: G. Masson), 5th series, vol. 1 (1889): 651–58.

———. "Faits montrant combien est grande et variée l'influence du systeme nerveux sur la nutrition et les secretions." *Archives de physiologique normale et pathologique* (Paris: G. Masson), 5th series, vol. 5 (1891): 747–61.

———. *Recherches expérimentales et cliniques sur l'inhibition et la dynamogénie—Application des connaissances fournies par ces recherches aux phénomènes principaux de l'hypnotisme et du transfert.* Paris: G. Masson, 1882.

Bruce, Robert V. *Bell: Alexander Graham Bell and the Conquest of Solitude.* Boston: Little, Brown, 1973.

Brücke, Ernst. *Grundzüge der Physiologie und Systematik der Sprechlaute für Linguisten und Taubstummlehrer.* Vienna: Gerold, 1856.

———. *Die Physiologischen Grundlagen der neuhochdeutschen Verskunst.* Vienna: Carl Gerold's Sohn, 1871.

———. *Principes scientifiques des beaux-arts.* Paris: G. Baillière et Cie, 1878.

Bunzl, Matti. "'Franz Boas and the Humboldtian Tradition: From Volksgeist and Nationalcharakter to an Anthropological Concept of Culture." In Volksgeist as Method and Ethic: Essays on Boasian Ethnography and the German Anthropological Tradition, edited by George Stocking, 17–78. Madison: University of Wisconsin Press, 1996.

Bürger, Peter. *Theory of the Avant-Garde.* Translated by Michael Shaw. Minneapolis: University of Minnesota Press, 1984.

Burke, Edmund. *A Philosophical Inquiry into the Origin of Our Ideas of the Sublime and the Beautiful.* Basel: J. J. Tourneisen, 1792.

Butler, Christopher. *Early Modernism: Literature, Music and Painting in Europe, 1900–1916.* Oxford: Clarendon Press, 1994.

Butler, Samuel. *Luck, or Cunning, as the Main Means of Organic Modification.* London: A. C. Fifield, 1922.

———. *Unconscious Memory.* 1880. 3rd ed. London: Cape, 1922.

Bütschli, Otto. *Über die Struktur des Protoplasmas: Untersuchungen über mikroskopische Schäume und das Protoplasma; Versuchen und Beobachtungen zur Lösung der Frage nach den physikalischen Bedingungen der Lebenserscheinungen.* Leipzig: Engelman, 1892.

Cahm, Caroline. *Kropotkin and the Rise of Revolutionary Anarchism, 1872–1886.* Cambridge: Cambridge University Press, 1989.

Calhoun, Martha. "The *Revue Wagnérienne* and the Literature of Music: The Translation of an Aesthetic." PhD dissertation, State University of New York, Stony Brook, 1987.

Callen, Anthea. *The Spectacular Body: Science, Method, and Meaning in the Work of Degas.* New Haven: Yale University Press, 1995.

Calvo-Merino, B., D. E. Glaser, J. Grèzes, R. E. Passingham, and P. Haggard. "Action Observation and Acquired Motor Skills: An fMRI Study with Expert Dancers." *Cerebral Cortex* 15, no. 8 (2005): 1243–49.

Canales, Jimena. *A Tenth of a Second: A History.* Chicago: University of Chicago Press, 2009.

Cándida-Smith, Richard. *Mallarmé's Children: Symbolism and the Renewal of Experience.* Berkeley: University of California Press, 1999.

Canguilhem, George. "Machine and Organism." Translated by Mark Cohen and Randall Cherry. In *Incorporations,* edited by Jonathan Crary and Sanford Kwinter, 45–65. New York: Zone Books, 1992.

Carpenter, Edward. *The Art of Creation: Essays on the Self and Its Powers.* London: George Allen, 1900.

———. *Intermediate Types among Primitive Folk: A Study in Social Evolution.* New York: Mitchell Kennerley, 1914.

———. *Love's Coming of Age.* London: Methuen, 1896.

Carrel, Alexis. *L'Homme, cet inconnu.* Paris: Plon, 1935.

———."Physiological Time." *Science* 74, no. 1929 (1931): 618–21.

Carrel, Alexis, and Montrose Burrows. "Cultivation of Tissues in Vitro and Its Technique." *Journal of Experimental Medicine* 13 (1911): 387–96.

Cartwright, Lisa. "'Experiments of Destruction': Cinematic Inscriptions of Physiology." *Representations* 40 (1992): 129–52.

Chéroux, Clément. *Des couleurs et de leurs applications aux arts industriels, à l'aide des cercles chromatiques.* Paris: J. B. Baillière, 1864.

———. *L'Expérience photographique d'August Strindberg.* Paris: Actes Sud, 1994.

———. "Photographs of Fluids: An Alphabet of Invisible Rays." In *The Perfect Medium: Photography and the Occult,* edited by C. Chéroux, A. Fischer, P. Apraxine, D. Canguilhem, and S. Schmit, 114–25. New Haven, CT: Yale University Press, 2005.

Chevreul, Michel Eugène. *De la loi du contraste simultané des couleurs et de l'assortment des objets colorés. 1839.* Paris: Gauthier, 1886.

———. *The Principles of Harmony and Contrast of Colors.* Reprint of the 1854 English translation, with an introduction by Faber Birren. New York: Van Nostrand, 1972.

Cheysson, Ernest. "Les Méthodes de statistique graphique à l'Exposition universelle de 1878." *Journal de la Société de statistique de Paris* 12 (1878): 323–33.

Clark, T. J. *Farewell to an Idea: Episodes in the History of Modernism.* New Haven, CT: Yale University Press, 1999.

Clarke, Bruce, and Linda Dalrymple Henderson. *From Energy to Information: Representation in Science and Technology, Art and Literature*. Stanford, CA: Stanford University Press, 2002.

Cobb, Margaret. *The Poetic Debussy: A Collection of His Song Texts and Selected Letters*. Boston: Northeastern University Press, 1982.

Coen, Deborah R. *Vienna in the Age of Uncertainty: Science, Liberalism, and Private Life*. Chicago: University of Chicago Press, 2007.

Coleman, William. "Cell, Nucleus, and Inheritance: An Historical Study." *Proceedings of the American Philosophical Society* 109, no. 3 (1965): 124–58.

Coleman, William, and Frederick L. Holmes, eds. *The Investigative Enterprise: Experimental Physiology in Nineteenth-Century Medicine*. Berkeley: University of California Press, 1988.

Collins, Harry M. "Expert Systems and the Science of Knowledge." In *The Social Construction of Technological Systems: New Directions in the Sociology and History of Technology*, edited by Wiebe J. Bijker, Thomas P. Hughes, and Trevor J. Pinch, 329–48. Cambridge, MA: MIT Press, 1987.

Collins, Harry M., and Robert Evans. *Rethinking Expertise*. Chicago: University of Chicago Press, 2007.

Comandon, Jean, Constantin Levatidi, and Stefan Mutermilch. "Étude de la vie et de la croissance des cellules in vitro à l'aide de l'enregistrement cinématographique." *Comptes rendus des séances de la Société de la biologie* 74 (1913): 464–67.

Conry, Yvette. *L'Évolution créatrice d'Henri Bergson: Investigations critique*. Paris: L'Harmattan, 2000.

———. *L'Introduction du Darwinisme en France au XIXe siècle*. Paris: J. Vrin, 1974.

Cor, Raphael. "M. Claude Debussy et le snobisme contemporaine." In *Le Cas Debussy*, edited by C.-Francis Caillard and José de Berys. Paris: Bibliothèque du Temps Présent, 1909.

Cordulak, Shelly Wood. *Edvard Munch and the Physiology of Symbolism*. London: Associated University Presses, 2002.

Couturat, Louis. *Les Nouvelles Langues internationales*. Paris: Hachette, 1907.

Cowles, Virginia. *1913: An End and a Beginning*. New York: Harper and Row, 1968.

Crary, Jonathan. *Suspensions of Perception: Attention, Spectacle and Modern Culture*. Cambridge, MA: MIT Press, 2000.

———. *Techniques of the Observer: On Vision and Modernity in the Nineteenth Century*. Cambridge, MA: MIT Press, 1990.

Crookes, William. "Some Possibilities of Electricity." *Fortnightly Review* 51, no. 302 (1892): 173–81.

Cunningham, Andrew, and Perry Williams, eds. *The Laboratory Revolution in Medicine*. Cambridge: Cambridge University Press, 1992.

Curtis, Scott. "Between Observation and Spectatorship: Medicine, Movies, and

Mass Culture in Imperial Germany." In *Film 1900: Technology, Perception, Culture*, edited by Annemone Ligensa and Klaus Kreimeier, 87–98. New Barnet, UK: John Libbey Publishing, 2009.

Cwiartka, Monika. "Materiality and the Discourse of Science." PhD dissertation, University of British Columbia, 2012.

Cyon, Elie. *Atlas zur Methodik der physiologischen Experimente und Vivisektion*. Giessen: Ricker, 1876.

Dagognet, François. *Étienne-Jules Marey: La Passion de la trace*. Paris: Hazan, 1987.

Dann, Kevin T. *Bright Colors Falsely Seen: Synaesthesia and the Search for Transcendental Truth*. New Haven, CT: Yale University Press, 1998.

D'Arsonval, A. "Observations sur les effets des injections de liquide testiculaire." *Archives de physiologique normale et pathologique* (Paris: G. Masson), 5th series, vol. 5 (1891): 816–17.

Darwin, Charles. *The "Origin of Species" by Charles Darwin: A Variorum Text*. Edited by Morse Peckham. Philadelphia: University of Pennsylvania Press, 1959.

———. *Variation of Animals and Plants Under Domestication*. Reprint of 2nd ed. (1883), with new foreword by Harriet Ritvo. Baltimore: Johns Hopkins University Press, 1998.

Daston, Lorraine. "The Physicalist Tradition in Early Nineteenth-Century French Geometry." *Studies in the History and Philosophy of Science* 17, no. 3 (1986): 269–95.

Daston, Lorraine, and Peter Galison. "The Image of Objectivity." *Representations* 40, no. 1 (1992): 81–128.

———. *Objectivity*. New York: Zone Books, 2007.

Daston, Lorraine, and Elizabeth Lunbeck. *Histories of Scientific Observation*. Chicago: University of Chicago Press, 2011.

de Certeau, Michel, Dominique Julia, and Jacques Revel. *Une Politique de la langue: La Revolution française et le patois*. Paris: Gallimard, 1975.

de Chadarevian, Soraya. "Graphical Method and Discipline: Self-Recording Instruments in Nineteenth-Century Physiology." *Studies in the History and Philosophy of Science* 24, no. 2 (1993): 267–91.

Delage, Yves. *La Structure du protoplasma et les théories sur l'hérédité et les grand problems de la biologie générale*. Paris: C. Reinwald, 1895.

de Lanessan, J. L. *Du protoplasma végétal*. Paris: Doin, 1876.

———. *Le Transformisme: Évolution de la matière et des êtres vivants*. Paris: Doin, 1883.

Deleuze, Gilles, and Felix Guattari. *A Thousand Plateaus: Capitalism and Schizophrenia*. Translated by Brian Massumi. Minneapolis: University of Minnesota Press, 1987.

Scott de Martinville, Léon. *La Fixation graphique de la voix*. Paris: Société d'Encouragement, 1857.

———. *Histoire de la sténographie depuis les temps anciens jusqu'à nos jours; ou précis historique et critique des divers moyens qui ont été proposés ou employés pour rendre l'écriture aussi rapide que la parole*. Paris: Charles Tondeur, 1849.

Demeny, Georges. "Analyse des mouvements de la parole par la chronophotogra-phie." *Comptes rendues de l'Académie des sciences* 113 (1891): 216–17.

———. "La Photographie de la parole." *Paris-Photographe* 1, no. 7 (1891): 306–8.

———. "Les Photographies parlantes." *La Nature* 20 (April 16, 1892): 311–15.

Demetz, Peter. *Worte in Freiheit: Der italienische Futurismus und die deutsche literarische Avantgarde (1912–1934)*. Munich: Piper, 1990.

Derrida, Jacques. *Of Grammatology*. Translated by Gayatri Chakravorty Spivak. Balti-more: Johns Hopkins University Press, 1974.

Desmet, Piet. "*La Revue de linguistique et de philologie comparée (1867–1916)*—organe de la linguistique naturaliste en France." *Beiträge zur Geschichte der Sprachwissenschaft* 4, no. 1 (1994): 49–80.

Desmond, Adrian. *Huxley: The Devil's Disciple*. London: Michael Joseph, 1994.

de Souza, Robert. *La Poésie populaire et le lyrisme sentimental*. Paris: Mercure de France, 1899.

———. *Rhythme poétique*. Paris: Perrin, 1892.

Dettelbach, Michael. "The Face of Nature: Precise Measurement, Mapping, and Sensibility in the Work of Alexander von Humboldt." *Studies in the History and Philosophy of Biological and Biomedical Sciences* 30 (1999): 473–504.

de Villers, Jean-Pierre A., ed. *Le Premier Manifeste du futurisme: Édition critique avec, en facsimile, le manuscript original de F. T. Marinetti*. Ottawa: Éditions de l'Université d'Ottawa, 1986.

Dias, Nelia. *La Mesure du sens: Les Anthropologues et le corps humain au XIXe siècle*. Paris: Aubier, 2004

Dickinson, H. W. *A Short History of the Steam Engine*. Cambridge: Cambridge Univer-sity Press, 1938.

Didi-Huberman, Georges. *L'Empreinte*. Paris: Centre Georges Pompidou, 1997.

———. *L'Image survivante: Histoire de l'art et temps des fantômes sélon Aby Warburg*. Paris: Minuit, 2002.

———. *The Invention of Hysteria: Charcot and the Photographic Iconography of the Sal-petrière*. Translated by Alisa Hartz. Cambridge, MA: MIT Press, 2003.

———. *La Ressemblance par contact: Archéologie, anachronisme et modernité de l'empreinte*. Paris: Minuit, 2008.

Di Dio, C., and V. Gallese. "Neuroaesthetics: A Review." *Current Opinion in Neurobiol-ogy* 19 (2009): 682–87.

Dierig, Sven. "Con Sordino for Piano and Brain: Bohemian Neuroscience in a 1900 Cultural Metropolis." *Configurations* 9 (2001): 413–40.

———. *Wissenschaft in der Maschinenstadt: Emil Du Bois-Reymond und seine Laboratorien in Berlin*. Göttingen, Germany: Wallstein, 2006.

Di Gregorio, Mario. *From Here to Eternity: Ernst Haeckel and Scientific Faith*. Göttingen, Germany: Vandenhoeck and Ruprecht, 2005.

Donders, Franciscus Cornelis. "Ueber die Natur der Vocale (Erste briefliche Mittheilung an Herrn Prof. Bruecke von F. C. Donders)." *Archiv für die holländischen Beiträge zur Natur-und Heilkunde* 1 (1858): 157–62.

———. "Zur Klangfarbe der Vocale." *Annalen der Physik* 199 (1864): 527–28.

Dorra, Henri, and John Rewald. *Seurat: L'Œuvre peint; Biographie et catalogue critique.* Paris: Les Beaux-Arts, 1959.

Doyle, Richard M. *Darwin's Pharmacy: Sex, Plants, and the Evolution of the Noosphere.* Seattle: University of Washington Press, 2011.

Du Bois, Raphaël. *Anatomie et physiologie compares de la pholade dactyle: Structure, locomotion, tact, olfaction, gestation, vision, dermatoptique, photogénie, avec une théorie générale des sensations.* Paris: G. Masson, 1892.

Du Bois-Reymond, Emil. "Naturwissenschaft und bildende Kunst." 1890. In *Reden von Du Bois-Reymond,* edited by Estelle Du Bois-Reymond, vol. 2, 421–22. Leipzig: Veit & Co., 1912.

———. "Der physiologische Unterricht sonst und jetzt." In *Reden von Emil Du Bois-Reymond,* edited by Estelle Du Bois-Reymond, vol. 1, 359–83. Leipzig: Veit & Co., 1912.

Duchenne de Boulogne, Guillaume-Benjamin-Amand. *The Mechanism of Human Facial Expression.* Edited and translated by Andrew Cuthbertson. Cambridge: Cambridge University Press, 1990.

D'Udine, Jean [Albert Cozanet]. *L'Art et le geste.* Paris: F. Alcan, 1910.

Dujardin, Édouard. *Les Premiers Poètes du vers libre.* Paris: Mercure de France, 1922.

———. "*La Revue wagnérienne.*" In *Mallarmé par un des siens,* 194–234. Paris: Albert Messein, 1936.

Dujardin, Félix. *Sur l'organisation des infusoires.* Paris: Renouard, 1838.

Du Maroussem, Pierre. *Les Ébenistes du Faubourg Saint-Antoine: Grands magasins, "sweating system."* Paris: Rousseau, 1892.

Du Moncel, Comte Th. A. L. *The Telephone, the Microphone, and the Phonograph.* New York: Harpers, 1879.

Dumont, Albert. *Les Céramiques de la Grèce propre.* 2 vols. Paris: Firmin Didot, 1888–90.

———. "Inscriptions céramiques de Grèce." *Archives des missions scientifiques et littéraires,* 2nd series, vol. 6 (1871): 13–15.

Dupin, Charles. *Essai historique sur les services et les travaux scientifiques de Gaspard Monge.* Paris: Bachelier, 1819.

Dutton, Denis. *The Art Instinct: Beauty, Pleasure, and Human Evolution.* New York: Bloomsbury, 2009.

Eagleton, Terry. *The Ideology of the Aesthetic.* Oxford: Basil Blackwell, 1990.

Edelman, Bernard. *Le Droit saisi par la photographie.* 1973. 3rd ed. Paris: Flammarion, 2001.

Edgerton, Samuel Y. *The Renaissance Rediscovery of Linear Perspective.* New York: Harper and Row, 1975.

Edison, Thomas A. *The Phonograph and Its Future; and the Auriphone and Its Future.*

With "On the Hypothesis That Animals Are Automata, and Its History," by T. H. Huxley. Toronto: Rose-Belford Publishing Company, 1878.

Eggum, Arne. *Munch and Photography*. Translated by Birgit Holm. New Haven, CT: Yale University Press, 1989.

Eliot, T. S. "Little Gidding." In *Four Quartets*, 35–44. London: Faber & Faber, 1944.

———. "Reflections on Vers Libre." *New Statesman* 8 (1917): 518–19.

Encyclopedia Britannica. 11th ed. 33 vols. Cambridge: Cambridge University Press, 1910–11.

Engels, Friedrich. "On Authority." 1874. In Karl Marx and Friedrich Engels, *The Marx-Engels Reader*, 2nd ed., edited by Robert C. Tucker, 730–33. New York: W. W. Norton and Co., 1978.

Facos, Michelle. "Strindberg and Scandinavian Painting: 1880–1900." In *Strindberg and Genre*, edited by Michael Robinson, 276–86. Norwich, UK: Norvik, 1991.

Fechner, Gustav Theodor. *Vorschule der Aesthetik*. Leipzig: Breitkopf, 1876.

Felderer, Briggite. "Stimm-Maschinen: Zur Konstruktion und Sichtbarmachung menschlicher Sprache im 18. Jahrhundert." In *Zwischen Rauschen und Offenbarung: Zur Kultur-und Mediengeschichte der Stimme*, edited by Friedrich Kittler, Thomas Macho, and Sigrid Weigel, 271–79. Berlin: Akademie, 2002.

Felderer, Brigitte, and Ernst Stouhal. *Kempelen—Zwei Maschinen: Texte, Bilder und Modelle zur Sprechmaschinen und zum schachspielenden Androiden Wolfgang von Kempelens*. Vienna: Sonderzahl, 2003.

Fénéon, Félix. *Au-déla de l'impressionnisme*. Edited by Françoise Cachin. Paris: Hermann, 1966.

———. "Dix Marines d'Antibes, de M. Claude Monet." *La Revue indépendante* (August 1888). In *Œuvres: Plus que complètes*, vol. 1, *Chroniques d'art*, edited by Joan U. Halperin, 113. Paris: Droz, 1970.

———. "L'Exposition des artistes independentes à Paris" *L'Art moderne* 9 (October 27, 1889): 339–41.

———. "L'Impressionnisme." 1887. In *Œuvres: Plus que complètes*, vol. 1, *Chroniques d'art*, edited by Joan Ungersma Halperin, 64–68. Paris: Droz, 1970.

———. "L'Impressionnisme aux Tuileries." *L'Art moderne* 6 (September 19, 1886): 300–302. Reprinted in *Œuvres: Plus que complètes*, vol. 1, *Chroniques d'art*, edited by Joan Ungersma Halperin, 53–55. Paris: Droz, 1970.

———. *Les Impressionnistes en 1886*. Paris: Publications de la Vogue, 1886.

———. "Le Néo-impressionnisme à la IVe exposition des artistes indépendants." *L'Art moderne* 8, no. 16 (April 15, 1888): 121–23.

———. "Paul Signac." In Fénéon, *Au-dela de l'impressionnisme*, edited by Françoise Cachin. Paris: Hermann, 1966.

———. *Petit Bottin des Lettres et des Arts*. Paris: E. Giraud, 1886.

Féré, Charles. "Exemple d'induction psychomotrice chez un chat." *Journal de psychologie normale et pathologique* 3 (1906): 26–30.

———. *La Pathologie des emotions.* Paris: F. Alcan, 1892.

———. *Sensation et mouvement: Études expérimentales de psycho-mécanique.* Paris: F. Alcan, 1887.

Ferraro, Giovanni. "Analytical Symbols and Geometrical Figures in Eighteenth Century Calculus." *Studies in History and Philosophy of Science* 32, no. 3 (2001): 535–55.

Feuk, Douglas. *August Strindberg: Inferno Painting and Pictures of Paradise.* Copenhagen: Edition Bløndal, 1991.

Fizer, John. *Psychologism and Psychoaesthetics.* Amsterdam: J. Benjamins, 1981.

Fleming, Marie. *The Anarchist Way to Socialism: Élisée Réclus and Nineteenth Century European Anarchism.* London: Rowman & Littlefield, 1979.

Flint, F. S. "Contemporary French Poetry." *Poetry Review* 1:8 (1912): 355–414.

Fontanon, Claudine. "Un Ingénieur militaire au service de l'industrialisation: Arthur Jules Morin (1795–1880)." *Les Cahiers d'histoire et de philosophie des sciences* 29 (1990): 89–118.

Foster, Michael. Review of *Allgemeine Physiologie: Ein Grundriss der Lehre vom Leben,* by Max Verworn. *Nature* 51, no. 1327 (1895): 529–30.

———. *Textbook of Physiology.* London: Macmillan and Co., 1877.

Foucault, Michel. *The Order of Things.* New York: Random House, 1970.

Fox Talbot, Henry. *The Pencil of Nature.* 1844–46. New York: Da Capo, 1969.

François-Franck, Charles. *Leçons sur les fonctions motrices du cerveau et sur l'épilepsie cérébrale.* Paris: Octave Doin, 1887.

Frank, Robert G., Jr. "American Physiologists in German Laboratories, 1865–1914." In *Physiology in the American Context, 1850–1940,* edited by Gerald L. Geison, 11–47. Bethesda, MD: American Physiological Society, 1987.

———. "The Telltale Heart: Physiological Instruments, Graphic Methods, and Clinical Hopes, 1854–1914." In *The Investigative Enterprise: Experimental Physiology in Nineteenth-Century Medicine,* edited by William Coleman and Frederick L. Holmes, 211–90. Berkeley: University of California Press, 1988.

Freedberg, David, and Vittorio Gallese. "Motion, Emotion, and Empathy in Esthetic Experience." *Trends in Cognitive Science* 11, no. 5 (2007): 197–203.

Frizot, Michel. *Avant la cinématographie, la chronophotographie: Temps, photographie et mouvement autour de É.-J. Marey.* Beaune, France: Association des Amis de Marey, 1984.

———. *Étienne-Jules Marey.* Paris: Centre National de la Photographie, 1984.

———, ed. *A New History of Photography.* Cologne: Koenemann, 1998.

Funkhouser, H. G. "Historical Development of the Graphical Representation of Statistical Data." *Osiris* 3 (1937): 269–404.

Furness, Raymond. *Wagner and Literature.* New York: St. Martin's, 1982.

Fye, W. Bruce. *The Development of American Physiology: Scientific Medicine in the Nineteenth-Century.* Baltimore: Johns Hopkins University Press, 1987.

Gage, John. "The Technique of Seurat: A Reappraisal." *Art Bulletin* 69, no. 3 (1987): 448–54.

Gagnier, Regenia. *The Insatiability of Human Wants: Economics and Aesthetics in Market Society.* Chicago: University of Chicago Press, 2000.

Gaines, Jane M. *Contested Culture: The Image, the Voice and the Law.* Chapel Hill: University of North Carolina Press, 1991.

Galenson, David W. *Painting between the Lines: Patterns of Creativity in Modern Art.* Cambridge, MA: Harvard University Press, 2001.

Galison, Peter L. "Aufbau/Bauhaus: Logical Positivism and Architectural Modernism." *Critical Inquiry* 16 (1990): 709–52.

———. *How Experiments End.* Chicago: University of Chicago Press, 1987.

Gallagher, Catherine. *The Body Economic: Life, Death, and Sensation in Political Economy and the Victorian Novel.* Princeton, NJ: Princeton University Press, 2006.

Galvez, Paul. "Register and Copy: John Herschel Photographic Observations." Senior honor's thesis, Harvard University, 1997.

Gaultier, Jules de. "Essai de physiologie poétique." *La Revue blanche* 7, nos. 31–33 (1894): 393–408, 527–35.

Gavarret, Jules. *Phénomènes physique de la phonation.* Paris: G. Masson, 1877.

Geimer, Peter. "L'Autorité de la photographie: Révélations d'un suaire." *Études photographiques* 6 (May 1999): 67–99.

Geison, Gerald L. *Michael Foster and the Cambridge School of Physiology: The Scientific Enterprise in Late Victorian Society.* Princeton, NJ: Princeton University Press, 1978.

———. "The Protoplasmic Theory of Life and the Vitalist-Mechanist Debate." *Isis* 60, no. 3 (1969): 272–92.

Geison, Gerald L., and Manfred D. Laublicher. "The Varied Lives of Organisms: Variation in the Historiography of the Biological Sciences." *Studies in History and Philosophy of Biological and Biomedical Sciences* 32, no. 1 (2001): 1–29.

Genet-Delacroix, Marie-Claude. "Vies d'artistes, art academique, art officiel et art libre en France à la fin du dix-neuvième siècle." *Revue d'histoire moderne et contemporaine* 33, no. 1 (1986): 40–73.

Ghil, René. *Traité du verbe.* Paris: Giraud, 1886.

———. *Traité du verbe: États successifs (1885–1886–1887–1888–1891–1904).* Edited by Tizana Goruppi. Paris: A. G. Nizet, 1978.

Gilbert, W. S., and Arthur Sullivan. *The Mikado; or, The Town of Titipu.* Woodford Green, Essex, UK: International Music Publications, 1996.

Gilman, Sander L., and Edward I. Chamberlain, eds. *Degeneration: The Dark Side of Progress.* New York: Columbia University Press, 1985.

Ginzburg, Carlo. "Clues: Roots of an Evidential Paradigm." In *Clues, Myths, and the Historical Method.* Translated by John and Anne C. Tedeschi, 96–125. Baltimore: Johns Hopkins University Press, 1989.

———. "Morelli, Freud, and Sherlock Holmes: Clues and Scientific Method." *History Workshop* 9 (Spring 1980): 5–29.

Gliboff, Sander. *H. G. Bronn, Ernst Haeckel, and the Origins of German Darwinism: A Study in Translation and Transformation.* Cambridge, MA: MIT Press, 2008.

Golinski, Jan. "Precision Instruments and the Demonstrative Order." *Osiris* 9 (1994): 30–47.

Golston, Michael. *Rhythm and Race in Modernist Poetry and Science.* New York: Columbia University Press, 2008.

Gordon, Lewis. "On Dynamometrical Apparatus; or, The Measurement of Mechanical Effect of Moving Powers." *Proceedings of the Philosophical Society of Glasgow* (1841–42): 42–43.

Gordon, Rae Beth. *Dances with Darwin, 1875–1910: Vernacular Modernity in France.* Burlington, VT: Ashgate, 2009.

———. *Why the French Love Jerry Lewis: From Cabaret to Early Cinema.* Stanford, CA: Stanford University Press, 2001.

Gourmont, Remy de. *Le Problème du style.* Paris: Mercure de France, 1902.

———. "Le Vers libre." In *Esthétique de la langue française,* 222–60. Paris: Mercure de France, 1905.

Gratiolet, Louis Pierre. *De la physiognomie et des mouvements d'expression.* Paris: Hetzel, 1869.

Green, Nicholas. "All of the Flowers in the Field: The State, Liberalism, and Art under the Early Third Republic." *Oxford Art Journal* 10, no. 1 (1987): 77–84.

———. "Circuits of Production, Circuits of Consumption: The Case of Mid-Nineteenth-Century French Art Dealing." *Art Journal* 48, no. 1 (1989): 29–34.

———. "Dealing in Temperaments: Economic Transformation of the Artistic Field During the Second Half of the Nineteenth-Century." *Art History* 10, no. 1 (1987): 59–87.

Greenberg, Clement. *Clement Greenberg: The Collected Essays and Criticism.* 4 vols. Edited by John O'Brian. Chicago: University of Chicago Press, 1986.

———. "Modernist Painting." In *The New Art: A Critical Anthology,* edited by Gregory Battcock, 66–77. New York: Dutton, 1973.

Greenway, John L. "Strindberg and Suggestion in 'Miss Julie.'" *South Atlantic Review* 51, no. 2 (1986): 21–34.

Grillo, R. D. *Dominant Languages: Language and Hierarchy in Britain and France.* Cambridge: Cambridge University Press, 1989.

Grojnowski, Daniel. "Laforgue fumiste: L'Esprit de cabaret." *Romantisme* 64 (1989): 5–16.

Guérinel, Rémy. "De la phonétique vivante et expérimentale du Professeur Jean-Pierre Rousselot (1846–1924) à l'anthropologie du geste et du rhythme du Professeur Marcel Jousse (1886–1961)." Unpublished manuscript, 2009.

Guichard, Léon. *La Musique et les lettres en France au temps du wagnérisme.* Paris: Presses Universitaires de France, 1963.

Gumbrecht, Hans-Ulrich. *In 1926: Living at the Edge of Time.* Cambridge, MA: Harvard University Press, 1997.

Gunnarsson, Torsten, Per Hedström, and Göran Söderström, eds. *Strindberg: Painter and Photographer.* New Haven, CT: Yale University Press, 2001.

Gunning, Tom. "Phantom Images and Modern Manifestations." In *Fugitive Images: From Photography to Video*, edited by Patrice Petro. Bloomington: Indiana University Press, 1995).

Günther, Siegmund. "Die Anfänge und Entwicklungsstadien des Coordinaten-Princi-pes." *Abhandlungen der naturhistorischen Gesellschaft zu Nürnberg* 6 (1877): 3–50.

Guyau, Jean-Marie. "Mémoire et phonographe." *Revue philosophique* 4 (1880): 319–22.

———. *Problèmes de l'esthétique contemporaine*. Paris: F. Alcan, 1884.

Haeckel, Ernst. *Anthropogenie*. Leipzig: W. Engelman, 1874.

———. *Essais de psychologie cellulaire*. Translated from the German by Jules Soury. Paris: Baillière, 1880.

———. *Gemeinverständliche Vorträge und Abhandlungen aus dem Gebiete der Entwicklungslehre*. 2nd ed. Berlin: Henschel; Leipzig: Kröner, 1924.

———. *Generelle Morphologie*. Berlin: Reimer, 1866.

———. *Die Kalkschwaemme: Eine Monographie*. 2 vols. Berlin: Reimer, 1872.

———. *Les Preuves du transformisme: Réponse à Virchow*. Translated from the German by Jules Soury. Paris: Baillière, 1879.

———. *Das Protistenreich*. Leipzig: Guenter, 1878.

———. "Remarks on the Protoplasm Theory." *Quarterly Journal of Microscopical Science* 10 (1869): 223–29.

———. *The Riddle of the Universe at the Close of the Nineteenth Century*. New York: Harper, 1900.

———. *Über die Wellenzeugung der Lebensteilchen oder die Perigenesis der Plastidule*. 1875. In *Gemeinverständliche Vorträge und Abhandlungen aus dem Gebiete der Entwicklungslehre*, 2nd ed., 86–142. Berlin: Henschel; Leipzig: Kröner, 1924.

———. *Ueber Arbeitstheilung in der Natur- und Menschenleben*. Berlin: Luederitz, 1869.

———. "Zellseelen und Seelenzellen." 1878. In *Gemeinverständliche Vorträge und Abhandlungen aus dem Gebiete der Entwicklungslehre*, 2nd ed., 162–95. Berlin: Henschel; Leipzig: Kröner, 1924.

———. "Zellseele und Zellularpsychologie." 1878. In *Gemeinverständliche Vorträge und Abhandlungen aus dem Gebiete der Entwicklungslehre*, 2nd ed., 236–46. Berlin: Henschel; Leipzig: Kröner, 1924.

Hagner, Michael, and Bettina Wahrig-Schmidt. *Johannes Mueller und die Philosophie*. Berlin: Akademie, 1992.

Hall, G. Stanley. "The Graphic Method." *The Nation* 29, no. 745 (October 9, 1879): 238–39.

———. "Is Aesthetics a Science?" *The Nation* 31 (1879): 380–81.

Hall, Thomas S. *Ideas of Life and Matter: General Physiology 600 BC to 1900 AD*. Vol. 2, *From the Enlightenment to the End of the Nineteenth Century*. Chicago: University of Chicago Press, 1969.

Halperin, Joan Ungersma. *Félix Fénéon: Aesthete and Anarchist in Fin-de-Siècle Paris*. New Haven, CT: Yale University Press, 1988.

Hankins, Thomas L. "Blood, Dirt, and Nomograms: A Particular History of Graphs." *Isis* 90, no. 1 (1999): 50–80.

Hankins, Thomas L., and Robert J. Silverman. *Instruments and the Imagination.* Princeton, NJ: Princeton University Press, 1995.

Hansen, Mark B. N. "Media Theory." *Theory, Culture, Society* 23, nos. 2–3 (2006): 206–306.

———. *New Philosophy for New Media.* Cambridge, MA: MIT Press, 2004.

Harrington, Anne. *Reenchanted Science: Holism in German Culture from Wilhelm II to Hitler.* Cambridge, MA: Harvard University Press, 1996.

Harrison, Ross. "The Outgrowth of Nerve Fiber as a Mode of Protoplasmic Movement." *Journal of Experimental Zoology* 9 (1910): 787–846.

Hartman, Charles O. *Free Verse: An Essay on Prosody.* Princeton, NJ: Princeton University Press, 1980.

Havard, Henry, and Marius Vachon. *Les Manufactures nationales: Les Gobelins, la Savonnerie, Sèvres, Beauvais.* Paris: G. Decaux, 1889.

Heller, Reinhold. *Edvard Munch: The Scream.* London: Penguin, 1973.

———. *Munch: His Life and Work.* Chicago: University of Chicago Press, 1984.

Helmholtz, Hermann. "The Application of the Law of the Conservation of Force to Organic Nature." 1861. In *Selected Writings of Hermann von Helmholtz*, edited by Russell Kahl, 109–21. Middleton, CT: Wesleyan University Press, 1971.

———. *Die Lehre von den Tonempfindungen als physiologische Grundlage für die Theorie der Musik.* Braunschweig, Germany: Vieweg, 1863.

———. *On the Sensations of Tone as a Physiological Basis for the Theory of Music.* 2nd ed. Translated by Alexander J. Ellis. London: Longmans, Green, and Co., 1885. Reprint, New York: Dover, 1954.

———. "Über die Methoden, kleiste Zeittheile zu messen, und ihre Anwendungen für physiologische Zwecke." In *Wissenschaftliche Abhandlungen*, vol. 2, 862–80. Leipzig: J. A. Barth, 1883.

———. "Ueber die normalen Bewegungen des menschlichen Auges." In *Wissenschaftliche Abhandlungen*, vol. 2, 360–419. Leipzig: J. A. Barth, 1883.

Hemmingsen, Per. *Strindberg som fotograph.* Malmö: Kalejdoskop Förlag, 1989.

Henderson, Linda Dalrymple. *Duchamp in Context: Science and Technology in the Large Glass and Related Works.* Princeton, NJ: Princeton University Press, 1998.

———. *The Fourth Dimension and Non-Euclidean Geometry in Modern Art.* Princeton, NJ; Princeton University Press, 1983. New ed., Cambridge, MA: MIT Press, 2012.

———. "Vibratory Modernism: Boccioni, Kupka, and the Ether of Space." In *From Energy to Information: Representation in Science and Technology, Art, and Literature*, edited by Bruce Clarke and Linda Dalrymple Henderson, 126–49. Stanford, CA: Stanford University Press, 2002.

Hennequin, Émile. *La Critique scientifique.* Paris: Perrin, 1888.

———. "L'Esthétique de Wagner et les doctrines spenceriennes." *La Revue wagnérienne* 1, no. 10 (1885–86): 282–86.

Henningsen, Bernd, Janine Klein, Helmut Müssener, and Solfrid Söderlind, eds.,

Wahlverwandtschaft: Skandinavien und Deutschland, 1800 bis 1914. Berlin: Jovis, 1997.

Henry, Charles. *Application de nouveaux instruments de précision (cercle chromatique, rapporteur et triple décimetre esthétique) à l'archéologie*. Paris: E. Leroux, 1890.

———. *Cercle chromatique, presentant tous les compléments et toutes les harmonies de couleurs*. Paris: Charles Verdin, 1888.

———. "Cercle chromatique et sensation de couleur." *La Revue indépendante* 7, no. 19 (May 1888): 238–89.

———. "Le Contraste, le rythme, et le mesure." *Revue philosophique* 28 (October 1889): 356–81.

———. "L'Esthétique des formes." *La Revue blanche* 7 (August 1894): 118–29; (October 1894): 308–32; (December, 1894): 511–25; 8 (1895): 117–20.

———. "Formes, couleurs, mouvements." *Gazette des beaux-arts* 7, no. 1 (1882): 165–69.

———. "Harmonie de couleurs." *La Revue indépendante* 7, no. 20 (June 1888): 458–78.

———. *Harmonies de formes et de couleurs: Demonstrations pratique*. Paris: A. Hermann, 1891.

———. "Influence de l'odeur sur les mouvementes respiratoires et sur l'effort musculaire." *Comptes rendus hebdomadaires des séances et mémoires de la Société de biologie* 43 (June 6, 1891): 443–53.

———. "Introduction à une esthétique scientifique." *La Revue contemporaine* 2 (1885): 441–69.

———. "Loi d'évolution de la sensation musicale." *Revue philosophique* 22 (1886): 81–87.

———. "M. Charles Henry." In *Enquète sur l'évolution littéraire*, edited by Jules Huret, 395–99. Paris: Charpentier, 1891.

———. *Mesure des capacités intellectuelle et energetique*. Brussels: Institut Solvay, Travaux de l'Institut de Sociologie, 1906.

———. *Notice sur les travaux scientifiques de M. Charles Henry*. Rome: Imprimerie des Sciences Mathématiques et Physiques, 1891.

———. "Odors and the Sense of Smell." *Popular Science Monthly* 41 (September 1892): 689–90.

———, ed. *Œuvres de Fermat: Publiées par les soins de MM. Paul Tannery et Charles Henry sous les auspices du Ministre de l'Instruction publique*. 4 vols. Paris: Gauthier-Villars, 1891–1912.

———. "Olfactomètre fondé sur les diffusion à travers les membranes flexibles." *Comptes rendues de l'Académie des sciences* 112 (February 9, 1891): 344–47.

———. "Rapporteur esthétique et sensation de forme." *La Revue indépendante* 7, no. 18 (April 1888): 73–90.

———. *Rapporteur esthétique: Notice sur ses applications à l'art industriel, à l'histoire de l'art, à l'interpretation de méthode graphique*. Paris: G. Séguin, 1888.

———. "Recherches nouvelles d'olfactométrie." *Comptes rendues de l'Académie des sciences* 112 (April 20, 1891): 885–87.

———. *Recherches sur les manuscrits de Pierre de Fermat, suivies de fragments inédits de Bachet et de Malebranche.* 2 vols. Rome: Imprimerie des Sciences Mathématiques et Physiques, 1880.

———. "Société de psychologie physiologique: Sur une loi generale de réactions psychomotrices." *Revue philosophique* 2 (1890): 108.

———. "Sur la dynamogénie et l'inhibition: Note de M. Charles Henry présentée par M. Brown-Séquard." *Comptes rendues de l'Académie des sciences* 108 (January 7, 1889): 70–71.

———. "Sur un cercle chromatique, un rapporteur et un triple décimetre esthétique." *Comptes rendus de l'Académie des sciences* 108 (January 28, 1889): 169–71.

———. "Sur un olfactomètre de M. Charles Henry." *Revue philosophique* 31 (1891): 447–48.

———. "Vision." *La Vogue* 1 (April 4, 1886).

Herbert, Eugenia W. *The Artist and Social Reform: France and Belgium, 1885–1898.* New Haven, CT: Yale University Press, 1961.

Herbert, Robert L. "Les Artistes et l'anarchisme d'après les lettres inédites de Pissaro, Signac et autres." *Le Mouvement social* 36 (July–September 1961): 2–19.

———. *Impressionism: Art, Leisure, and Parisian Society.* New Haven, CT: Yale University Press, 1988.

———. *Neo-Impressionism.* New York: Solomon Guggenheim Foundation, 1968.

———. "'Parade de cirque' de Seurat et l'esthétique scientifique de Charles Henry." *Revue de l'art* 50 (1980): 9–23.

Herbert, Robert L., and Eugenia W. Herbert. "Artists and Anarchism: Unpublished Letters of Pissarro, Signac, and Others." *Burlington Magazine* 102 (1960): 473–82.

Herbert, Robert L., Gary Tinterow, and Anne Distel. *Georges Seurat, 1859–1891.* New York: Metropolitan Museum of Art, 1991.

Héricourt, Jules. "Une Théorie mathématique de l'expression: Le contraste, le rythme et la mesure d'après les travaux de M. Charles Henry." *Revue scientifique* 44 (1889): 586–93.

Hering, Ewald. *Über das Gedächtnis als eine allgemeine Funktion der Organisierten Materi.* 2nd ed. Vienna: Gerold, 1876.

Hermann, L. "Phonophotographische Untersuchungen." *Archive für die gesammte Physiologie* 45 (1889): 579–90.

———. "Über das Verhalten der Vokale am neuen Edison'schen Phonographen." *Archive für die gesammte Physiologie* 47 (1890): 41–45.

Herrera, Alfonso L. *Una ciencia nueva, la plasmogenia.* Mexico City: F. Diaz de Léon, 1911.

Herschel, John. "On the Action of the Rays of the Solar Spectrum on the Daguerreotype Plate." *Philosophical Magazine* 22 (1843): 120–32.

Hessenbruch, Arne. "Science as Public Sphere: X-Rays between Spiritualism and Physics." In *Wissenschaft und Öffentlichkeit in Berlin, 1870–1930*, edited by Constantin Goschlar, 89–126. Stuttgart: F. Steiner, 2000.

Hibbert, Christopher. *Gilbert and Sullivan and Their Victorian World*. New York: American Heritage Publishing Co., 1976.

Hills, R. L., and A. J. Pacey. "The Measurement of Power in Early Steam-Driven Textile Mills." *Technology and Culture* 13, no. 1 (1972): 25–43.

Hinton, Charles Howard. *A Picture of Our Universe: Scientific Romances*. 1886. Reprint, New York: Arno Press, 1976.

Hirsbunner, Theo. "Musik und Dichtung im französischen Fin de Siècle am Beispiel der Proses Lyriques von Debussy." In *Dichtung und Musik: Kaleidoskop ihrer Beziehungen*, edited by Guntar Schnitzler, 152–74. Stuttgart: Klett-Cotta, 1979.

Hirth, Georg. *Aufgaben der Kunstphysiologie*. 2nd ed. Munich: Hirth, 1897.

Hoff, Hebbel E., and Leslie. A. Geddes. "The Beginning of Graphic Recording." *Isis* 53, no. 3 (1962): 287–324.

———. "Graphic Recording before Carl Ludwig: An Historical Summary." *Archives internationales d'histoire des sciences* 12 (1959): 1–25.

———. "A Historical Perspective on Physiological Monitoring: Chaveau's Projecting Kymograph and the Projecting Physiograph." *Cardiovascular Research Center Bulletin* 14 (1975): 3–35.

———. "A Historical Perspective on Physiological Monitoring: Sherrington's Mammalian Laboratory and its Antecedents." *Cardiovascular Research Center Bulletin* 13 (1974): 19–39.

———. "The Technological Background of Physiological Discovery: Ballistics and the Graphic Method." *Journal of the History of Medicine and Allied Sciences* 15 (1960): 345–63.

Hoff, Hebbel E., Leslie. A. Geddes, and Roger Guillemin. "The Anemograph of Onsen-Bray: An Early Self-Registering Predecessor of the Kymograph." *Journal of the History of Medicine and Allied Sciences* 12 (1957): 424–48.

Holmes, Frederic L., and Kathryn M. Olesko. "The Images of Precision: Helmholtz and Graphical Methods in Physiology." In *The Values of Precision*, edited by M. Norton Wise, 198–221. Princeton, NJ: Princeton University Press, 1994.

Holzapfel, Amy Strahler. "Strindberg as Vivisector: Physiology, Pathology, and Anti-Mimesis in *The Father and Miss Julie*." *Modern Drama* 51, no. 3 (2008): 329–52.

Homer, William Innes. *Seurat and the Science of Painting*. Cambridge, MA: MIT Press, 1964.

Hopkinson, John. *The Working of the Steam Engine Explained by the Use of the Indicator*. London: Simpkin, Marshall, & Co., 1851.

Howat, Roy. *Debussy in Proportion: A Musical Analysis*. Cambridge: Cambridge University Press, 1983.

Hrushovski, Benjamin. "On Free Rhythms in Modern Poetry." *Style in Language*, edited by Thomas A. Sebeok, 173–90. Cambridge, MA: MIT Press, 1960.

Hulme, T. H. "Searchers after Reality: Jules de Gaultier." *New Age* 6, no. 5 (December 2, 1909): 107–8.

Humbert de Superville, David Pierre Giotinno. *Essai sur les signes inconditionnels dans l'art*. Leiden: Hoek, 1827–32.

Hunt, Bruce J. "Lines of Force, Swirl of Ether." In *From Energy to Information: Representation in Science and Technology, Art, and Literature*, edited by Bruce Clarke and Linda Dalrymple Henderson, 99–113. Stanford, CA: Stanford University Press, 2002.

Huret, Jules. *Enquête sur l'évolution littéraire*. Paris: Charpentier, 1891.

Hutton, John. *Neo-Impressionism and the Search for Solid Ground: Art, Science, and Anarchism in Fin-de-Siècle France*. Baton Rouge: Louisiana State University Press, 1994.

Huxley, Thomas Henry. "On the Physical Basis of Life." *Fortnightly Review* 5, no. 26 (1869): 129–45.

Huysmans, Joris-Karl. *Against Nature (À Rebours)*. Translated by Robert Baldick. London: Penguin Classics, 1956.

Ingham, Percy B. "The Method: Growth and Practice." In *The Eurhythmics of Jaques-Dalcroze*, edited by M. E. Sadler, 31–47. London: Constable & Co., 1912.

Ireson, J. C. *L'Œuvre poétique de Gustave Kahn (1859–1936)*. Paris: A. G. Nizet, 1962.

Jackson, Myles W. *Harmonious Triads: Physicists, Musicians, and Instrument Makers in Nineteenth-Century Germany*. Cambridge, MA: MIT Press, 2006.

Jacob, François. *The Statue Within: An Autobiography*. Translated by Franklin Philip. New York: Basic Books, 1988.

James, William. *Essays, Comments, and Reviews: The Works of William James*. Edited by Frederick Burkhardt. Cambridge, MA: Harvard University Press, 1987.

———. "Notes for Philosophy 20a: Psychological Seminary, 1891–1892. Aesthetics." In *Manuscript Lectures: The Works of William James*, edited by F. Burkhardt, 206–11. Cambridge, MA: Harvard University Press, 1988.

———. "What Is an Emotion?" *Mind* 9, no. 34 (1884): 188–205.

Janet, Pierre. *L'Automatisme psychologique: Essai de psychologie expérimentale sur les formes inférieures de l'activité humaine*. Paris: F. Alcan, 1889.

Jaques-Dalcroze, Émile. *Rhythm, Music, and Education*. New York: G. P. Putnam's Sons, 1921.

———. *Rhythmische Gymnastik*. Leipzig: Verlag von Sandoz, 1907.

Jardine, Nicholas. "The Laboratory Revolution in Medicine as a Rhetorical and Aesthetic Accomplishment." In *The Laboratory Revolution in Medicine*, edited by Andrew Cunningham and Perry Williams, 304–23. Cambridge: Cambridge University Press, 1992.

Jarocinski, Stefan. *Debussy: Impressionism and Symbolism*. Translated by Rollo Myers. London: Eulenberg, 1976.

Jarry, Alfred. *Exploits and Opinions of Dr. Faustroll, Pataphysician: A Neo-Scientific Novel*. 1911. Translated by Simon Watson Taylor. Boston: Exact Change Press, 1996.

Jarzombek, Mark. *The Psychologizing of Modernity: Art, Architecture, and History*. Cambridge: Cambridge University Press, 2000.

Jay, Martin. "Modernism and the Specter of Psychologism." *Modernism/modernity* 3, no. 2 (1996): 93–111.

Jennings, Herbert Spencer. *Contributions to the Study of the Behavior of Lower Organisms*. Washington, DC: Carnegie Institution, 1904.

Jensen, Robert. *Marketing Modernism in Fin-de-Siècle Europe*. Princeton, NJ: Princeton University Press, 1944.

Jespersen, Otto. *Phonetische Grundfragen*. Leipzig: B. G. Teubner, 1904.

Jones, Caroline. *Eyesight Alone: Clement Greenberg's Modernism and the Bureaucratization of the Senses*. Chicago: University of Chicago Press, 2006.

Jones, Caroline, and Peter Galison. *Picturing Science, Producing Art*. London: Routledge, 1998.

Jones, David. *The History and Meaning of the Term "Phoneme."* London: International Phonetic Association, 1957.

Jun, H. H. "Account of a Steam-Engine Indicator." *Quarterly Journal of Science, Literature, and the Arts* 13, no. 25 (1822): 91–95.

Kahane, Martine. *Wagner et la France*. Paris: Bibliotheque1 Nationale, 1983.

Kahn, Douglas. *Noise, Water, Meat: A History of Sound in the Arts*. Cambridge, MA: MIT Press, 1999.

Kahn, Gustave. "Au temps du pointillisme." *Mercure de France* 171 (April 1, 1924): 5–22.

———. "De l'esthétique du verre polychrome." *La Vogue* 1 (April 18, 1886): 54–65.

———. *Les Dessins de Georges Seurat (1859–1891)*. Paris: Bernheim-Jeune, 1928.

———. In *Enquête internationale sur le vers libre*, by F. T. Marinetti, 21–31. Milan: Éditions de "Poesia," 1909.

———. "Peinture: Exposition des indépendants." *Revue indépendante* 7, no. 18 (April 1888): 160–64.

———. *Premiers poèmes*. Paris: Mercure de France, 1897.

———. "Réponse des symbolistes." *L'Événement* (September 28, 1886).

———. "Response of the Symbolists." 1886. In *Art in Theory, 1815–1900: An Anthology of Changing Ideas*, edited by Charles Harrison, Paul Wood, and Jason Gaiger, 1016–17. Oxford: Blackwell, 1998.

———. *Symbolistes et décadents*. Paris: L. Vanier, 1902; Geneva: Slatkine Reprints, 1977.

———. "Le Vers libre: Conference de M. Gustave Kahn aux XX." *L'Art moderne* 11, no. 7 (February 15, 1891): 51–55.

Kahn, Gustave, and Felix Fénéon. "Le Courrier social." *La Vogue* 1 (April 4, 1886): 27–28.

Kandel, Eric R. *The Age of Insight: The Quest to Understand the Unconscious in Art, Mind, and Brain, from Vienna 1900 to the Present*. New York: Random House, 2012.

Kandinsky, Wassily. *Concerning the Spiritual in Art*. 1911. Translated by M. T. H. Sadler. New York: Dover, 1977.

———. "On Stage Composition." In *The Blaue Reiter Almanac*, translated by Henning Falkenstein, edited by Klaus Lankheit, 190–206. Boston: MFA Publications, 1965.

Kaplan, Louis. *The Strange Case of William Mumler, Spirit Photographer*. Minneapolis: University of Minnesota Press, 2008.

Kemp, Martin. *The Science of Art: Optical Themes in Western Art from Brunelleschi to Seurat*. New Haven, CT: Yale University Press, 1990.

Killen, Andreas. "Psychiatry, Cinema, and Urban Youth in Early Twentieth-Century Germany." *Harvard Review of Psychiatry* 14 (2006): 38–43.

Kim, Mi Gyung. *Affinity, That Elusive Dream: A Genealogy of the Chemical Revolution* Cambridge, MA: MIT Press, 2003.

Kirsten, Christa. *Dokumente einer Freundschaft: Briefwechsel zwischen Hermann von Helmholtz und Emil Du Bois-Reymond 1846–1894*. Berlin: Akademie Verlag, 1986.

Kittler, Friedrich A. *Discourse Networks 1800/1900*. Translated by Michael Metteer, with Chris Cullens. Stanford, CA: Stanford University Press, 1985.

———. *Draculas Vermächtnis: Technische Schriften*. Leipzig: Reclam, 1993.

———. *Gramophone, Film, Typewriter*. Translated by Geoffrey Winthrop-Young and Michael Wutz. Stanford, CA: Stanford University Press, 1999.

———. *Optical Media*. Translated by Anthony Enns. Cambridge: Polity, 2010.

Klim, George. *Stanislaw Przybyszewski—Leben, Werk und Weltanschauung im Rahmen der deutschen Literatur der Jahrhundertwende*. Paderborn, Germany: Igel, 1992.

Koenig, Rudolph. *Catalogue des appareils d'acoustique*. Paris, 1882.

———. *Quelques expériences de l'acoustique*. Paris: Lahure, 1882.

Kojevnikov, Alexei, Cathryn Carson and Helmuth Trischler, eds. *Weimar Culture and Quantum Mechanics: Selected Papers by Paul Forman and Contemporary Perspectives on the Forman Thesis*. London: World Scientific Press, 2011.

Kok, Eduardo. *Signs of Life: Bio Art and Beyond*. Cambridge, MA: MIT Press, 2007.

Koschwitz, Eduard. "La Phonétique expérimentale et la philologie Franco-Provençal." *Revue des patois gallo-romans* 4 (1891): 211–20.

———. "Der Registrierapparat." *Archiv für das Studium der neueren Sprachen* 88 (1892): 244–53.

Koutroufinis, Spyridon. "Ontogenetisches Werden im Lichte der Lebens-und Prozessphilosophie von Henri Bergson." Habilitation thesis, Technical University of Berlin, 2009.

Kramsky, Jiri. *The Phoneme: Introduction to the History and Theories of a Concept*. Munich: Wilhelm Fink, 1974.

Kremer, Richard L. "Building Institutes for Physiology in Prussia: Contexts, Interests, and Rhetoric." In *The Laboratory Revolution in Medicine*, edited by Andrew Cunningham and Perry Williams, 72–109. Cambridge: Cambridge University Press, 1992.

———. *The Thermodynamics of Life and Experimental Physiology, 1770–1880*. London: Taylor and Francis, 1990.

Kristeva, Julia. *La Révolution du langage poétique: L'Avant-garde à la fin du XIXe siècle; Lautrémont et Mallarmé*. Paris: Éditions du Seuil, 1974.

Kropotkin, Peter. "La Division du travail." *La Révolte* (April 21 1889): 20.

———. "Le Machinisme et la révolution." *Le Révolté* (April 13, 1884).

———. "Modern Science and Anarchism." In *Kropotkin's Revolutionary Pamphlets*, edited by Roger N. Baldwin, 145–94. New York: Vanguard Press, 1927.

———. "Travail intellectuel et travail manuel." *La Révolte* (March 1890): 22–26.

Kümmel, W. F. *Musik und Medizin: Ihre Wechselbeziehungen in Theorie und Praxis von 800 bis 1800.* Freiburg: Karl Alber, 1977.

Kursell, Julia. "A Gray Box: The Phonograph in Laboratory Experiments and Field Work, 1900–1920." In *The Oxford Handbook of Sound Studie*s, edited by Karin Bijsterveld and Trevor Pinch, 176–97. New York: Oxford University Press, 2011.

Kuryluk, Ewa. *Veronica and Her Cloth: History, Symbolism, and the Structure of a "True" Image.* Cambridge: Blackwell, 1991.

Kusch, Martin. *Psychologism: A Case Study in the Sociology of Philosophical Knowledge.* London: Routledge, 1995.

Laforgue, Jules. *Lettres à un ami, 1880–1886.* Introduction and notes by G. Jean-Aubry. Paris: Mercure de France, 1941.

Laguerre, M. E. *Oeuvres de Laguerre.* With a preface by Henri Poincaré. 2 vols. Paris: Gauthier-Villars, 1898.

Lalo, Charles. "Les Sens esthétiques." *Revue philosophique* 65 (1908): 449–70.

Lampl, Hans Erich. "Ex Oblivione: Das Féré-Palimpsest; Noten zur Beziehung Friedrich Nietzsche—Charles Féré." *Nietzsche-Studien* 15 (1986): 225–64.

Landecker, Hannah. "Cellular Features: Microcinematography and Early Film Theory." *Critical Inquiry* 31 (2005): 903–37.

———. *Culturing Life: How Cells Became Technologies.* Cambridge, MA: Harvard University Press, 2007.

Landry, Eugene. *La Théorie du rythme et le rythme du français déclamé.* Paris: H. Champion, 1911.

Langaard, Johan. *Edvard Munch: The University Murals.* Oslo: Norsk Kunstreproduksjon, 1960.

Langendorff, Oskar. *Physiologische Graphik: Ein Leitfaden in der Physiologie gebräuchlichen Registrirmethoden.* Leipzig: Deuticke, 1891.

Lankester, E. Ray. "A Theory of Heredity: A Review of Haeckel's Pamphlet Entitled 'Perigenesis der plastidule.'" In *The Advancement of Science: Occasional Essays and Addresses,* 271–86. London: Macmillan and Co., 1890.

Lanzoni, Susan. "Practicing Psychology in an Art Gallery: Vernon Lee's Aesthetics of Empathy." *Journal of the History of the Behavioral Sciences* 45 (2009): 330–54.

Lanzoni, Susan, Robert Brain, and Allan Young, eds. "Varieties of Empathy in Science, Art, and Culture." Special issue, *Science in Context* 26 (2012).

Larson, Barbara. *The Dark Side of Nature: Science, Society, and the Fantastic in the Work of Odilon Redon.* University Park: Pennsylvania State University Press, 2005.

Lathe, Carla. "The Group Zum Schwarzen Ferkel: A Study in Early Modernism." PhD dissertation, University of East Anglia, 1972.

———. "Munch's Dramatic Images, 1892–1909." *Journal of the Warburg and Courtauld Institutes* 46 (1983): 191–206.

Latour, Bruno. "Drawing Things Together." In *Representation in Scientific Practice*, edited by Michael Lynch and Steve Woolgar, 19–68. Cambridge, MA: MIT Press, 1990.

———. "Gabriel Tarde and the End of the Social." In *The Social in Question: New Bearings in History and the Social Sciences*, edited by Patrick Joyce, 117–32. London: Routledge, 2002.

———. "Give Me a Laboratory and I Will Raise the World." In *Science Observed*, edited by K. D. Knorr-Cetina and M. Mulkay, 141–70. London: Sage, 1983.

———. *Pandora's Hope: Essays on the Reality of Science Studies.* Cambridge, MA: Harvard University Press, 1999.

———. "Visualization and Cognition: Thinking with Eyes and Hands." *Knowledge and Society: Studies in the Sociology of Culture Past and Present*, vol. 6, edited by H. Kuklick, 1–40. Baltimore: Johns Hopkins University Press, 1986.

———. *We Have Never Been Modern.* Translated by Catherine Porter. Hemel Hempstead, UK: Harvester Wheatleaf, 1993.

Latour, Bruno, and Vincent Antoine Lépinay. *The Science of Passionate Interests: An Introduction to Gabriel Tarde's Economic Anthropology.* Chicago: Prickly Paradigm Press, 2009.

Latour, Bruno, and Steve Woolgar. *Laboratory Life: The Construction of Scientific Facts.* 2nd ed. Princeton, NJ: Princeton University Press, 1986. First published 1979.

Lawrence, Christopher. "Incommunicable Knowledge: Science, Technology, and the Clinical Art in Britain, 1850–1914." *Journal of Contemporary History* 20, no. 4 (1985): 503–20.

Le Brun, Charles. *Conférence sur l'expression générale et particulière.* Paris, 1698.

———. *Conférence sur l'impression des differents caractères des passions.* Paris, 1667.

Lechalas, George. Review of *Cercle chromatique*, vol. 1, by Charles Henry. *Revue philosophique* 28 (1889): 635–45.

Le Dantec, Félix. "La Biologie de M. Bergson." *Revue du mois* 4 (1907): 230–41.

———. *Évolution individuelle et héredité.* 2nd ed. Paris: Alcan, 1913.

———. "L'Intuition." *Les Arts de la vie* 1 (1904): 30–32.

Leduc, Stéphane. *Biologie synthétique.* Paris: Poinat, 1912.

Lee, Alan. "Seurat and Science." *Art History* 10, no. 2 (1987): 203–26.

Lee, Vernon. "La Sympathie esthétique d'après Th. Lipps." *Revue philosophique* 64 (1905): 620–22.

Legroux. "De la methode graphique appliquée à la clinique; des progrès qu'elle peut realiser; à propos de l'oeuvre derniere de Lorain." *Archives générale de médecine* 141 (1878): 335–52.

Lenoir, Timothy. "The Eye as Mathematician: Clinical Practice, Instrumentation, and Helmholtz's Construction of an Empiricist Theory of Vision." In *Hermann von Helmholtz and the Foundations of Nineteenth-Century Science*, edited by David Cahan, 109–53. Berkeley: University of California Press, 1993.

———. "Laboratories, Medicine, and Public Life in Germany, 1830–1849: Ideological Roots of the Institutional Revolution." In *The Laboratory Revolution in Medicine*, edited by Andrew Cunningham and Perry Williams, 14–71. Cambridge: Cambridge University Press, 1992.

———. "Models and Instruments in the Development of Electrophysiology, 1845–1912." *Historical Studies in the Physical and Biological Sciences* 17, no. 1 (1986): 1–54.

———. "The Politics of Vision: Optics, Painting, and Ideology in Germany, 1845–1895." In *Instituting Science: The Cultural Production of Scientific Disciplines*, edited by Timothy Lenoir, 131–38. Stanford, CA: Stanford University Press, 1997.

———. "Science for the Clinic: Science Policy and the Formation of Carl Ludwig's Institute in Leipzig." In *The Investigative Enterprise: Experimental Physiology in Nineteenth-Century Medicine*, edited by William Coleman and Frederick L. Holmes, 139–78. Berkeley: University of California Press, 1988.

———. "Social Interests and the Organic Physics of 1847." In *Science in Reflection*, edited by Edna Ullmann-Margalit, 169–81. Dordrecht: D. Reidel, 1988. Reprinted in Lenoir, *Instituting Science: The Cultural Production of Scientific Disciplines*, 75–95. Stanford, CA: Stanford University Press, 1997.

Levenson, Michael. *A Genealogy of Modernism: A Study of English Literary Doctrine, 1908–1922.* Cambridge: Cambridge University Press, 1984.

Levin, Miriam. *Republican Art and Ideology in the Late Nineteenth Century France.* Ann Arbor, MI: UMI Research Press, 1986.

Levitkin, D. J. *This Is Your Brain on Music.* New York: Dutton, 2006.

Lewis, Wyndham. *Blasting and Bombardiering: An Autobiography (1914–1926).* London: Calder and Boyars, 1967. First published 1937 by Eyre & Spottiswoode.

Licoppe, Christian. *La Formation de la pratique scientifique: Le Discours de l'expérience en France et en Angleterre (1630–1820).* Paris: La Découverte, 1996.

Liddell, H., and R. Scott. *Greek-English Lexicon.* 9th ed. Oxford: Oxford University Press, 1996.

Limoges, Camille. "Darwin, Milne-Edwards, et le principe de divergence." *XII Congrès international d'histoire des sciences* 8 (1968): 111–15.

Lippman, Edward. *A History of Western Musical Aesthetics.* Lincoln: University of Nebraska Press, 1993.

Livi, Rudolfo. *Antropometria militare, risultati ottenuti dallo spoglio de fogli sanitari dei militari delle classi 1859–63.* 2 vols. Roma: Presso il Giornale Medico del Regio Esercito, 1896.

Loison, Laurent. "The Notions of Plasticity and Heredity among French Neo-Lamarckians (1880–1940): From Complementarity to Incompatibility." In *Transformations of Lamarckism: From Subtle Fluids to Molecular Biology*, edited by Snait B. Gissis and Eva Jablonka, 67–76. Cambridge, MA: MIT Press, 2011.

———. *Qu'est-ce que le néolamarckisme? Les Biologistes français et la question de l'evolution des espèces*. Paris: Vuibert, 2010.

Lomas, David. "Modest Recording Instruments: Science, Surrealism, and Visuality." *Art History* 27 (2004): 627–50.

Lorain, Paul. *Études de medicine clinique faites avec l'aide de la méthode graphique et des appareils enregistreurs*. 2 vols. Paris: P. Brouardel, 1877.

———. "La Médicine scientifique; la methode graphique appliquée à l'étude clinique des maladies." *Revue des cours scientifiques de la France et de l'étranger* 7 (1870): 282–88.

Lote, Georges. *L'Alexandrin d'après la phonétique expérimentale*. 2nd ed. Paris: Georges Crès, 1919.

———. "La Poétique du symbolisme." *Revue des cours et conferences* 35, no 2 (1934).

Lövgren, Sven. *The Genesis of Modernism: Seurat, Gauguin, Van Gogh and French Symbolism in the 1880's*. Stockholm: Almqvist & Wiksell, 1959.

Ludwig, Carl. "Beiträge zur Kenntnis des Einflusses der Respirationsbewegungen auf den Blutlauf im Aortensysteme." *Müller's Archiv für Anatomie, Physiologie, und wissenschaftliche Medizin* 3 (1847): 242–302.

———. *Lehrbuch der Physiologie des Menschens*. 2 vols. Heidelberg: Winter, 1852–56.

Lynch, Michael. "Laboratory Space and the Technological Complex: An Investigation of Topical Contextures." *Science in Context* 4, no. 1 (1991): 51–78.

Mach, Ernst. "Zur Theorie der Pulswellenzeichner." *Sitzungsberichte der mathematisch-naturwissenschaftliche Classe der Kaiserlichen Akademie der Wissenschaften* 46 (1862): 157–74.

Macho, Thomas. "Second Order Animals: Cultural Techniques of Identity and Identification." *Theory, Culture, and Society* 30, no. 6 (2013): 30–47.

Magnard, Albéric. "La Synthèse des arts." *La Revue de Paris* 5 (1894): 424–42.

Main, Thomas J., and Thomas Brown. *The Indicator and the Dynamometer, with Their Practical Applications*. London: Hebert, 1847.

Maitron, Jean. *Histoire du mouvement anarchiste en France (1880–1914)*. 2nd ed. Paris: Société Universitaire d'Éditions et de Librairie, 1955.

Mallarmé, Stéphane. "La Musique et les lettres." 1894 In *Oeuvres complètes de Stéphane Mallarmé*, vol. 1, edited by Henri Mondor and G. Jean-Aubry, 635–57. Paris: Gallimard, 1945.

Manganaro, Marc. *Culture, 1922*. Princeton, NJ: Princeton University Press, 2002.

Mangold, Sabine. *Eine "weltbürgerliche Wissenschaft": Die deutsche Orientalistik im 19. Jahrhundert*. Stuttgart: Steiner, 2004.

Mantegazza, Paolo. *La fisiologia del dolore*. Florence: Poggi, 1879.

Marage, Georges-René-Marie. "Formation des voyelles." *L'Année psychologique* 6 (1899): 485–92.

Marchand, Suzanne L. *German Orientalism in the Age of Empire: Religion, Race, and Scholarship*. Cambridge: Cambridge University Press, 2009.

Maréchal, Gaston. "Photographie de la parole." *L'Illustration* 2543 (November 21, 1891): 406–7.

Marey, Étienne-Jules. *Animal Mechanism: A Treatise on Terrestrial and Aërial Locomotion.* New York: D. Appleton, 1874.

———. *Appareils et instruments de physiologie.* Paris: Lahure, 1879.

———. "Discours à l'occasion du décès de M. Milne-Edwards." *Revue scientifique,* 4th series, no. 13 (1900): 547.

———. *Du mouvement dans les fonctions de la vie: Leçons faites au Collège de France.* Paris: Germer Baillière, 1868.

———. "Du moyen d'économiser le travail moteur de l'homme et des animaux." *Travaux du laboratoire de M. Marey* (Paris: G. Masson) 1 (1875): 1–18.

———. "The History of Chronophotography." *Annual Report of the Board of Regents of the Smithsonian Institution for 1901* (1902): 314–40.

———. "L'Inscription des phénomènes phonétiques." Part 1, "Méthodes directes." Part 2, "Méthodes indirectes: Critique des résultats." *Revue générale des sciences* 9 (1898): 445–56, 482–90.

———. "Inscription des phénomènes phonétiques d'après les travaux de divers auteurs." *Journal des savants* 20 (October 1897): 561–85.

———. *La Machine animale: Locomotion terrestre et aérienne.* Paris: Baillière, 1873.

———. "Mesures à prendre pour l'uniformisation des méthodes et le contrôle des instruments employés en physiologie." *Comptes rendus de l'Académie des sciences* 127 (1898): 375–81.

———. *La Méthode graphique dans le sciences expérimentales et principalement en physiologie et en médicine.* Paris: G. Masson, 1878.

———. *Le Mouvement.* Paris: G. Masson, 1894.

———. "Nécessité de créer une commission internationale pour l'unification et le côntrole des instruments inscripteurs physiologiques." *Journal of Physiology* 23 (1898–99): 6–7.

———. "La Photographie du mouvement." *La Nature* (July 22, 1882): 115–16.

———. *Physiologie médicale de la circulation du sang basée sur l'étude graphique des mouvements du coeur et du pouls artériel, avec application aux maladies de l'appareil circulatoire.* Paris: Delahaye, 1863.

———. "Recherches hydrauliques sur la circulation du sang." *Annales des sciences naturelles (zoologie)* 9 (1858): 53–58.

———. "Recherches sur le pouls au moyen d'un nouvel appareil enregistreur: Le sphygmographe." *Comptes rendus des séances et mémoires de la Société de biologie* 11 (1859): 281–309.

———. "La Station physiologique de Paris." *La Nature* (September 8, 1883): 226–30; and (September 29, 1883): 275–79.

———. "Sur un nouveaux polygraphe, appareil inscripteur applicable aux recherches physiologiques et cliniques." *Comptes rendus de l'Académie des sciences* 89 (1879): 8–11.

———. "Le Transformisme et la physiologie expérimentale." *Revue Scientifique* 11, no. 35 (1873): 813–22.

———. "The Work of the Physiological Station at Paris." *Annual Report of the Board of Regents of the Smithsonian Institution for 1894* (1895): 391–412.

Marichelle, H. *La Parole d'après le tracé du phonographe.* Paris: Delagrave, 1897.

———. *Phonétique expérimentale: La parole d'après le tracé du phonographe.* Paris: Delagrave, 1897.

Marichelle, H., and Hémardinger. "Études des sons de la parole par le phonographe." *Comptes rendues de l'Académie des sciences de Paris* 135 (1897): 884–86.

Marinetti, F. T. *Critical Writings.* Edited by Günter Berghaus. Translated by Doug Thompson. New York: Farrar, Straus and Giroux, 2006.

———. *Enquête internationale sur le vers libre.* Milan: Éditions de "Poesia," 1909.

———. *Let's Murder the Moonshine: Selected Writings of F. T. Marinetti.* Edited by R. W. Flint. Translated by R. W. Flint and Arthur A. Coppotelli. Los Angeles: Sun and Moon Classics, 1991.

Marrinan, Michael. *Romantic Paris: Histories of a Cultural Landscape, 1800–1850.* Stanford, CA: Stanford University Press, 2009.

Marvick, Louis W. "René Ghil and the Contradictions of Synesthesia." *Comparative Literature* 51, no. 4 (1999): 289–308.

Marx, Jörg. *Lebenspathos und "Seelenkunst" bei Stanislaw Przybyszewski.* Frankfurt: Lang, 1990.

Marx, Karl. *Capital.* Vol. 1. Translated by Ben Fowkes. New York: Random House, 1997.

Matsuda, Matt. *The Memory of the Modern.* Oxford: Oxford University Press, 1996.

Matthews, J. Rosser. *Quantification and the Quest for Medical Certainty.* Princeton, NJ: Princeton University Press, 1995.

Matuszek, Gabriela. *"Der Geniale Pole?"—Stanislaw Przybyszewski in Deutschland, 1892–1992.* Paderborn, Germany: Igel, 1996.

———, ed. *Über Stanislaw Przybyszewski: Rezensionen-Errinerungen—Porträts—Studien (1892–1995); Rezeptionsdokumente aus 100 Jahren.* Paderborn, Germany: Igel, 1995.

Mauclair, Camille. In *Enquête internationale sur le vers libre,* by F. T. Marinetti, 65–68. Milan: Éditions de "Poesia," 1909.

Maupas. "Étude des infusoires ciliés." *Archive de zoologie expérimentale* 4 (1883): 4–9.

Maxwell, James Clerk. "General Considerations concerning Scientific Apparatus." In *Handbook to the Special Loan Collection of Scientific Apparatus, 1876, South Kensington Museum,* 1–21. London: Chapman and Hill, 1876.

Mayer, Andreas. *Mikroskopie der Psyche: Die Anfänge der Psychoanalyse im Hypnose-Labor.* Göttingen, Germany: Wallstein, 2002.

McKendrick, John G. "Experimental Phonetics." *Nature* 65, no. 1678 (1901): 182–89.

McKendrick, J., G. Murray, and D. Wingate. "Committee Report on the Physiological Application of the Phonograph and on the Form of the Voice Curves by the Instrument." *Reports of the British Association for the Advancement of Science* (1896): 666–73.

McLuhan, Marshall. *Understanding Media: The Extensions of Man*. New York: McGraw-Hill, 1964.

Mendelsohn, Everett. "The Social Locus of Scientific Instruments." In *Invisible Connections: Instruments, Institutions, and Science*, edited by Robert Bud and Susan E. Cozzens, 5–22. Bellingham, WA: SPIE Optical Engineering Press, 1992.

Merriman, John. *The Dynamite Club: How a Bombing in Fin-de-Siècle Paris Ignited the Age of Modern Terror*. Boston: Houghton Mifflin Harcourt, 2009.

Meyerson, Emile. "Les Travaux de M. Charles Henry sur une théorie mathématique de l'expression." *Bulletin scientifique* (December 20, 1889): 98–100.

Micale, Mark, ed. *The Mind of Modernism: Medicine, Psychology, and the Cultural Arts in Europe and America, 1880–1940*. Stanford, CA: Stanford University Press, 2004.

Mills, Mara. "The Dead Room: Deafness and Modern Communications Technologies." PhD dissertation, Harvard University, 2006.

Milne-Edwards, Henri. *Introduction à la zoologie générale*. Paris: V. Masson, 1851.

———. *Rapport sur les progrès récents des sciences zoologiques en France*. Paris: Imprimerie Impériale, 1867.

Mitchell, Bonner. *Les Manifestes littéraires de la Belle Époque 1886–1914: Anthologie critique*. Paris: Seghers, 1966.

Mitchell, Robert. *Bioart and the Vitality of Media*. Seattle: University of Washington Press, 2010.

Mitchell, W. J. T. *Iconology: Image, Text, Ideology*. Chicago: University of Chicago Press, 1986.

———. *Picture Theory: Essays on Verbal and Visual Representation*. Chicago: University of Chicago Press, 1994.

Monakow, Constantin von, and Raoul Mourgue. *Introduction biologique à l'étude de la neurologie et de la psychopathologie*. Paris: Alcan, 1928.

Montagu, Jennifer. *The Expression of the Passions: The Origin and Influence of Charles Le Brun's "Conférence sur l'expression générale et particulière."* London: Yale University Press, 1994.

Moore, Gregory. *Nietzsche, Biology, and Metaphor*. Cambridge: Cambridge University Press, 2002.

———. "Nietzsche's Reading and Knowledge of Natural Science: An Overview." In *Nietzsche and Science*, edited by Gregory Moore and Thomas Brobjer, 21–50. Hampshire, UK: Ashgate, 2004.

Moore, Gregory, and Thomas Brobjer, eds. *Nietzsche and Science*. Hampshire, UK: Ashgate, 2004.

Morin, Arthur. "Descriptions des appareils chronométrique à style: Propres à la représentation graphique et la détermination des lois du mouvement dans divers genres d'expériences." In *Mémores du Congrès scientifique de France: Cinquième session, tenue à Metz en septembre, 1837*, 583–607. Metz: S. Lamfort, 1838.

———. *Leçons de mécanique pratique*. Paris: Hachette, 1846.

———. *Notice sur divers appareils dynamométriques: Propres à mesurer l'effort du travail développé par les moteurs animés ou inanimés, ou consommé par des machines de rotation, et sur un nouvel indicateur de la pression dans les cylindres des machines a vapeur.* Paris: Mathias, 1839.

Morton, Frederick. *Thunder at Twilight: Vienna, 1913–14.* Cambridge, MA: Da Capo Press, 2001.

Morton, Marsha. "From Monera to Man: Ernst Haeckel, *Darwinismus*, and Nineteenth-Century German Art." In *The Art of Evolution: Darwin, Darwinisms, and Visual Culture*, edited by Barbara Larson and Fae Brauer, 59–91. Hanover, NH: Dartmouth College Press, 2009.

Mourgue, Raoul. "Une Découverte scientifique: La Durée bergsonienne." *Revue philosophique* 120 (1935): 350–66.

Müller, Johannes. *Zur vergleichenden Physiologie des Gesichtssinnes des Menschen und der Thiere nebst einem Versuch über die Bewegungen der Augen und über den menschlichen Blick.* Leipzig: Knobloch, 1826.

Muybridge, Eadweard. *Animals in Motion . . . An Electro-Photographic Investigation of Consecutive Phases of Muscular Motions . . . Commenced 1872, Completed 1885.* London: Chapman Hall, 1925.

Nadar [Gaspard-Félix Tournachon]. *Quand j'étais photographe.* Paris: Flammarion, 1900.

Natanson, Thadée. "Expositions." *La Revue blanche* 6, no. 28 (February 1894): 185.

Navier, C. L. M. H. "Addition: Sur les Principes du calcul et de l'établissement des machines, et sur les moteurs," in *Architecture Hydraulique*, by Bernard Forest de Bélidor. Paris: Firmin Didot, 1819.

Nemerov, Howard. *Figures of Thought.* Boston: David Godine, 1978.

Neswald, Elisabeth. *Thermodynamik als kultureller Kampfplatz: Eine Faszinationsgeschichte der Entropie 1850–1915.* Freiburg: Rombach, 2006.

Newbolt, Henry. "Futurism and Form in Poetry." *Fortnightly Review* 95, no. 569 (1914): 804–18.

Nietzsche, Friedrich. *Nietzsche Contra Wagner.* In *Werke: Kritische Gesamtausgabe*, vol. 3, edited by Giorgio Colli and Mazzino Montinari. Berlin: De Gruyter, 1969.

Nikolow, Sybille. "Die versinnlichung von staatskräften: Statistische Karten um 1800." *Traverse* 6, no. 3 (1999): 63–82.

Noakes, Richard. "The 'World of the Infinitely Little': Connecting Physical and Psychical Realities Circa 1900." *Studies in History and Philosophy of Science* 39 (2008): 323–34.

Noble, David. *The Religion of Technology: The Divinity of Man and the Spirit of Invention.* New York: Alfred A. Knopf, 1997.

Nordau, Max Simon. *Degeneration.* 1892. Translation of 2nd ed., with introduction by George L. Mosse. Lincoln: University of Nebraska Press, 1968.

———. *Entartung.* Berlin: Duncker & Humblot, 1892.

———. *Paradoxes: From the German of Max Nordau.* 1885. Chicago: L. Schick, 1886.

Norseng, Mary Kay. *Dagny: Dagny Juel Przybyszewska, the Woman and the Myth.* Seattle: University of Washington Press, 1991.

Noüy, Pierre Lecomte du. "Sur une constante d'activité physiologique ne dependant que de l'âge." *Sunti delle communcazioni scientiliche, XIV Congresso internazionale di fisiologia.* Rome, 1932.

Nyhart, Lynn K. *Biology Takes Form: Animal Morphology and the German Universities, 1800–1900.* Chicago: University of Chicago Press, 1995.

Olmsted, J. M. D. *Charles-Édouard Brown-Séquard: A Nineteenth Century Neurologist and Endocrinologist.* Baltimore: Johns Hopkins University Press, 1946.

Orsucci, Andrea. *Dalla biologia cellular alle scienze dello spirito: Aspetti del dibattito sull'individualità nell'Ottocento tedesco.* Bologna: Società Editrice il Mulino, 1992.

Osietzki, Maria. "Körpermaschinen und Dampfmaschinen: Vom Wandel der Physiologie und des Körpers unter dem Einfluss von Industrialisierung und Thermodynamik." In *Physiologie und industrielle Gesellschaft: Studien zur Verwissenschaftlichung des Körpers im 19. und 20. Jahrhundert,* edited by Philipp Sarasin and Jakob Tanner, 313–46. Frankfurt: Suhrkamp, 1998.

Otis, Laura. *Organic Memory: History and the Body in the Late Nineteenth and Early Twentieth Centuries.* Lincoln: University of Nebraska Press, 1994.

Panconcelli-Calzia, Giulio. *Geschichtszahlen der Phonetik: Quellenatlas der Phonetik.* Edited by Konrad Koerner. Philadelphia: John Benjamins, 2003.

Pantalony, David. *Altered Sensations: Rudolph Koenig's Acoustical Workshop in 19th Century Paris.* New York: Springer, 2009.

———. "Seeing a Voice: Rudolph Koenig's Instruments for Studying Vowel Sounds." *American Journal of Psychology* 117, no. 3 (2004): 271–86.

Paris, Gaston. "Études historiques et philologiques sur la rime française." *Romania* 6 (1877): 622–25.

Park, Katharine. "Impressed Images: Reproducing Wonders." In *Picturing Science, Producing Art,* edited by Caroline A. Jones and Peter Galison, 254–71. London: Routledge, 1998.

Paulhan, Frédéric. *Les Phénomènes affectifs et les lois de leur apparition: Essai de psychologie générale.* Paris: Alcan, 1887.

Pauly, Philip J. *Controlling Life: Jacques Loeb and the Engineering Ideal in Biology.* Berkeley: University of California Press, 1990.

———. "Modernist Practice in American Biology." In *Modernist Impulses in the Human Sciences, 1870–1930,* edited by Dorothy Ross, 272–89. Baltimore: Johns Hopkins University Press, 1994.

Pearson, Keith Ansell. "Bergson's Encounter with Biology: Thinking Life." *Angelaki* 10 (2005): 59–72.

Peirce, Charles S. *Collected Papers of Charles Sanders Peirce,* edited by Charles Hartshorne and Paul Weiss, vol. 6, *Scientific Metaphysics.* Cambridge, MA: Harvard University Press, 1935.

———. *The Essential Peirce: Selected Philosophical Writings.* Vol. 1. Edited by Nathan Houser and Christian Kloesel. Bloomington: Indiana University Press, 1992.

———. "Man's Glassy Essence." 1892. In *Collected Papers of Charles Sanders Pierce,* edited by Charles Hartshorne and Paul Weiss, vol. 6, *Scientific Metaphysics,* 155–77. Cambridge, MA: Belknap Press of Harvard University Press, 1935.

Perloff, Nancy. *Art and the Everyday: Popular Entertainment and the Circle of Erik Satie.* Oxford: Clarendon Press, 1991.

Pernot, Hubert. "L'Abbé Rousselot (1846–1924)." *Revue de l'alliance française* 22 (1925): 135.

———. "L'Abbé Rousselot (1846–1924)." *Revue de phonétiques* 5 (1928): 17–21.

Persell, Stuart M. *Neo-Lamarckism and the Evolution Controversy in France, 1870–1920.* Lewiston, NY: Edwin Mellen Press, 1999.

Petersen, Eugen Adolf Hermann. "Rhythmus." *Königliche Gesellschaft der Wissenschaften zu Göttingen: Philologisch-historische Klasse,* n.F., vol. 16 (1917): 1–104.

Pfotenhauer, Helmut. *Die Kunst als Physiologie: Nietzsche's ästhetische Theorie und literarische Produktion.* Stuttgart: Metzler, 1985.

Pick, Daniel. *Faces of Degeneration: A European Disorder, c. 1848–c. 1918.* Cambridge: Cambridge University Press, 1989.

Pickstone, John V. "The Analytical Revolutions and the Syntheses of Modernism." In *Histoire des sciences modernes,* edited by H. Otto Sibum and Kapil Raj, vol. 2 of *Les Sciences et la modernité.* Paris: Le Seuil, forthcoming.

———. *Ways of Knowing: A New History of Science, Technology, and Medicine.* Chicago: University of Chicago Press, 2000.

———. "Working Knowledges Before and After circa 1900: Practices and Disciplines in the History of Science, Technology, and Medicine." *Isis* 98 (2007): 489–516.

Pierre, Arnaud. *Francis Picabia: La Peinture sans aura.* Paris: Gallimard, 2002.

Pierson, Paul. *Métrique naturelle du langage.* Paris: F. Vieweg, 1884.

Pillsbury, W. B. "The Place of Movement in Consciousness." *Psychological Review* 18 (1911): 83–89.

Plauchut, Edmond. "La Rivalité des industries d'art en Europe." *Revue des deux mondes* 105 (1891): 630–43.

Playfair, William. *A Real Statement of the Finances and Resources of Great Britain.* London: Whittingham, 1796.

Pollock, Sheldon. *The Language of the Gods and the World of Men: Sanskrit, Culture, and Power in Premodern India.* Berkeley: University of California Press, 2006.

Porter, Theodore M. *The Rise of Statistical Thinking, 1820–1900.* Princeton: Princeton University Press, 1986.

———. *Trust in Numbers: The Pursuit of Objectivity in Science and Public Life.* Princeton, NJ: Princeton University Press, 1995.

Pound, Ezra. "A Few Don'ts for an Imagiste." *Poetry* 1 (March 1913): 200–206.

———. *Polite Essays.* London: Faber & Faber, 1937.

Prado, Sharon S. "The Decadent Aesthetic in France, 1880–1914: Musical Manifestations in the Works of Debussy and His Contemporaries." PhD dissertation, University of Cincinnati, 1992.

Prescott, G. B. *The Speaking Telephone, Talking Phonograph, and Other Novelties*. New York: Appleton, 1878.

Preyer, W. T. *Zur Psychologie des Schreibens*. Hamburg: Voss, 1896.

Price, Uvedale. *Essays on the Picturesque, as Compared with the Sublime and the Beautiful*. 3 vols. London: Mawman, 1811.

Prigogine, Ilya, and Isabelle Stengers. *Order Out of Chaos: Man's New Dialogue with Nature*. London: Flamingo, 1984.

Prodger, Phillip. *Time Stands Still: Muybridge and the Instantaneous Photography Movement*. New York: Oxford University Press, 2003.

Przybyszewski, Stanislaw. *Ferne komm ich her . . . Errinerungen an Berlin und Krakau*. Leipzig: Kiepenheuer, 1985.

———. *Das Werk des Edvard Munch: Vier Beiträge*. Berlin: Fischer, 1894.

———. *Zur Psychologie des Individuums*. Berlin: Fontane, 1892.

Purkyně, Jan. *Abhandlung über die physiologische Untersuchung des Sehorgans und des Hautsystems*. Breslau, 1823.

Rabaté, Jean-Michel. *1913: The Cradle of Modernism*. Oxford: Blackwell, 2007.

Rabinbach, Anson. *The Human Motor: Energy, Fatigue, and the Origins of Modernity*. Berkeley: University of California Press, 1992.

Ramon y Cajal, Santiago. "Las maravillas de la histologia." 1883. In *Recuerdos de mi vida*. Madrid: Imprenta y Libreria de N. Moya, 1917.

———. "El protoplasma." In *La Clinica: Seminario de medicina, cirujía y farmacia*. 1880. Reprinted in *Discurso de doctorado y trabajos de juventud*, edited by A. Merchán-Perez. Madrid: Universidad-Europea—CEES Ediciones, 2001.

Rancière, Jacques. *The Politics of Aesthetics: The Distribution of the* Sensible. Translated by Gabriel Rockhill. London: Continuum, 2006.

Rapp, Dietmar. "Quantitative Untersuchungen über die Zunahme der physiologischen Forschungsgeräte von 1784 bis 1911." Inaug. Diss. Med Münster, 1970.

Ratliff, Floyd. *Paul Signac and Color in Neo-Impressionism*. New York: Rockefeller University Press, 1992.

Read, Oliver, and Walter L. Welch. *From Tin Foil to Stereo: The Evolution of the Phonograph*. Indianapolis, IN: H. W. Sams, 1959.

Régnard, Paul. *Les Maladies épidémiques de l'esprit: Sorcellerie, magnétisme, morphinisme, délire des grandeurs*. Paris: Plon-Nourrit, 1887.

Regnier, Adolphe. *Études sur la grammaire védique: Pratiçakya du Rig-Véda*. Paris: Imprimerie Impériale, 1859.

Reiser, Stanley Joel. *Medicine and the Reign of Technology*. Cambridge: Cambridge University Press, 1978.

Rewald, John, ed. *Camille Pissarro: Lettres à son fils Lucien*. By Camille Pissarro. Paris: Albin Michel, 1947.

———. *Georges Seurat*. Paris: Albin Michel, 1948.

Reynolds, Andrew. "Amoebae as Exemplary Cells: The Protean Nature of an Elementary Organism." *Journal of the History of Biology* 41 (2008): 307–37.

Rheinberger, Hans-Jörg. *Experiment, Differenz, Schrift.* Marburg, Germany: Basiliskenpresse, 1992.

———. *Toward a History of Epistemic Things: Synthesizing Proteins in the Test Tube.* Stanford, CA: Stanford University Press, 1997.

Rheinberger, Hans-Jörg, and Michael Hagner, eds. *Die Experimentalisierung des Lebens: Experimentalsysteme in den biologischen Wissenschaften, 1850–1950.* Berlin: Akademie Verlag, 1993.

Ribot, Théodule. "L'Abstraction des émotions." *L'Année psychologique* 3 (1896–97): 1–9.

———. "Les Mouvements et leur importance psychologiques." *Revue philosophique* 8 (1879): 371–86.

Richards, Robert J. *The Meaning of Evolution: The Morphological Construction and Ideological Reconstruction of Darwin's Theory.* Chicago: University of Chicago Press, 1992.

———. *The Tragic Sense of Life: Ernst Haeckel and the Struggle over Evolutionary Thought.* Chicago: University of Chicago Press, 2008.

Richardson, Alan. "Philosophy as Science: The Modernist Agenda of Philosophy of Science, 1900–1950." In *In the Scope of Logic, Methodology, and Philosophy of Science,* vol. 2, edited by P. Gardenfors, J. Wolenski, and K. Kijania-Placek, 621–39. Dordrecht: Kluwer, 2002.

Richet, Charles. "La Douleur: Étude de psychologie physiologique." *Revue philosophique* 4 (1877): 457–81.

———. *L'Homme et l'intelligence: Fragments de physiologie et de psychologie.* Paris: F. Alcan, 1884.

———. *Recherches expérimentales et clinique sur la sensibilité.* Paris: G. Masson, 1877.

Richter, Hans. *Dada: Art and Anti-Art.* London: Thames and Hudson, 1965.

Riegl, Alois. "Late Roman or Oriental?" In *German Essays on Art History,* translated by Peter Wortsman, edited by Gert Schiff, 173–91. New York: Continuum, 1988.

Reichle, Ingeborg. *Art in the Age of Technoscience: Genetic Engineering, Robotics, and Artificial Life in Contemporary Art.* Vienna: Springer, 2009.

Roberts, Lissa. "A Word and the World: The Significance of Naming the Calorimeter." *Isis* 79, no. 2 (1988): 199–232.

Rochas de Aiglun, Albert de. *L'Extériorisation de la sensibilité: Étude expérimentale et historique.* Paris: Chamuel, 1895.

Rollins, Mark. "What Monet Meant: Intention and Attention in Understanding Art." *Journal of Aesthetics and Art Criticism* 62, no. 2 (2004): 175–88.

Rosapelly, Charles. "Inscription de mouvements phonétiques." *Physiologie expérimentale: Travaux du laboratoire de M. Marey* (Paris: G. Masson) 2 (1875): 109–31.

Roslak, Robyn. *Neo-Impressionism and Anarchism in Fin-de-Siècle France: Painting, Politics, and Landscape.* Burlington, VT: Ashgate, 2007.

Rothermund, Dietmar. *The German Intellectual Quest for India*. New Delhi: Manihar, 1986.

Rousseau, Pascal. "Confusion des sens: Le Débat sur la synesthésie dans les débuts de l'abstraction en France." *Le Cahiers du Musée nationale de l'art moderne* 74 (2000–2001): 5–33.

Rousselot, Abbé. "Introduction a l'étude des patois." *Revue des patois gallo-roman*s 1 (1887): 1–23.

———. *La Méthode graphique appliquée à la phonétique*. Paris: Macon, 1890.

———. "La Méthode graphique appliquée à la recherche des transformations inconscientes du langage." In *Comptes rendues du Congrès scientifique internationale des Catholiques tenu a Paris de 1er au 6 Avril 1891*, 109–12. Paris: A. Picard, 1891.

———. *Les Modifications phonétiques du langage étudiée dans le patois d'une famille de Cellefrouin*. Paris: H. Welter, 1891.

———. *Principes de phonétiques expérimentale*. 2nd ed. Paris: H. Didier, 1924.

Rousselot, Abbé., and Fauste Laclotte. *Précis de pronunciation française*. Paris: H. Welter, 1902.

Rupke, Nicholas A. "*Bathybius Haeckelii* and the Psychology of Scientific Discovery." *Studies in the History and Philosophy of Science* 7, no. 1 (1976): 53–62.

Russell, E. S. *Form and Function: A Contribution to the History of Animal Morphology*. 1916. Chicago: University of Chicago Press, 1982.

Ryan, Judith. *The Vanishing Subject: Early Psychology and Literary Modernism*. Chicago: University of Chicago Press, 1991.

Sadoul, Georges. *L'Invention du cinema*. Paris: Denoël, 1946.

Saint-Saëns, Camille. *Harmonie et mélodie*. Paris: Calmann Lévy, 1885.

Sapp, Jan. *Beyond the Gene: Cytoplasmic Inheritance and the Struggle for Authority in Genetics*. Oxford: Oxford University Press, 1987.

Sarafianos, Aris. "The Contractility of Burke's Sublime and Heterodoxies in Medicine and Art." *Journal of the History of Ideas* 69, no. 1 (2008): 23–48.

———. "Pain, Labor, and the Sublime: Medical Gymnastics and Burke's Aesthetics." *Representations* 91 (2005): 58–83.

Sarasin, Phillip, and Jacob Tanner, eds. *Physiologie und industrielle Gesellschaft: Studien zur Verwissenschaftlichung des Körpers im 19. und 20. Jahrhundert*. Frankfurt: Suhrkamp, 1998.

Satie, Eirk. "What I Am." In *The Writings of Erik Satie*, translated and edited by Nigel Wilkins, 58. London: Eulenburg, 1980.

Saussure, Ferdinand de. *Mémoire sur le système primitif des voyelles dans les langues indoeuropéenes*. Leipzig: Vieweg, 1878.

Scarry, Elaine. *On Beauty and Being Just*. Princeton, NJ: Princeton University Press, 1999.

Schabas, Margaret. *The Natural Origins of Economics*. Chicago: University of Chicago Press, 2005.

Schaffer, Simon. "Astronomers Mark Time: Discipline and the Personal Equation." *Science in Context* 2 (1988): 115–45.

———. "Babbage's Intelligence: Calculating Engines and the Factory System." *Critical Inquiry* 21, no. 1 (1994): 203–27.

———. "Late Victorian Metrology and its Instrumentation: A Manufactory of Ohms." In *Invisible Connections: Instruments, Institutions, and Science*. Edited by Susan Cozzens and Robert Bud, 23–56. Bellingham, WA: SPIE Optical Engineering Press, 1992.

———. "Machine Philosophy: Demonstration Devices in Georgian Mechanics." *Osiris* 9 (1994): 157–82.

———. "Nebular Hypothesis and the Science of Progress." In *History, Humanity, and Evolution: Essays for John C. Greene*, edited by James Moore. Cambridge: Cambridge University Press, 1989.

———. "Self-Evidence." *Critical Inquiry* 18, no. 2 (Winter 1992): 327–62.

Schäffner, Wolfgang. "Bewegungslinien: Analoge Aufzeichnungsmaschinenen." In *Electric Laokoon: Zeichen und Medien, von der Lochkarte zur Grammatologie*, edited by Michael Franz, Wolfgang Schäffner, Bernhard Siegert, and Robert Stockhammer, 130–46. Berlin: Akademie Verlag, 2007.

Schapiro, Meyer. "The Liberating Quality of Avant-Garde Art." *Art News* 56, no. 4 (Summer 1957): 36–42.

Sherry, Vincent. *Ezra Pound, Wyndham Lewis, and Radical Modernism*. Oxford: Oxford University Press, 1993.

Schiff, Richard. "Grave Seurat." In *Seurat Re-viewed*, edited by Paul Smith. University Park: Pennsylvania State University Press, 2009.

———. "Realism of Low Resolution: Digitisation and Modern Painting." In *Impossible Presence: Surface and Screen in the Photogenic Era*, edited by Terry Smith, 124–56. Chicago: University of Chicago Press, 2001.

———. "Representation, Copying, and the Technique of Originality." *New Literary History* 14 (1983): 332–63.

Schleich, Carl Ludwig. *Besonnte Vergangenheit: Lebenserinnerungen, 1859–1919*. Berlin: Rowohlt, 1924.

Schloegel, Judy Johns, and Henning Schmidgen. "General Physiology, Experimental Psychology, and Evolutionism: Unicellular Organisms as Objects of Psychophysiological Research, 1877–1918." *Isis* 93, no. 4 (2002): 614–45.

Schmidgen, Henning. *Bruno Latour: Zur Einführung*. Hamburg: Junius, 2011.

———. "The Donders Machine: Matter, Signs, and Time in a Physiological Experiment, ca. 1865." *Configurations* 13 (2005): 211–56.

———. *Die Helmholtz-Kurven: Auf der Spur der verlorenen Zeit*. Berlin: Merve, 2009.

———. "The Materiality of Things? Bruno Latour, Charles Péguy, and the History of Science." *History of the Human Sciences* 26 (2013): 3–28.

———. "1900—The Spectatorium: On Biology's Audiovisual Archive." *Grey Room* 43 (2011): 42–65.

———. "Physics, Ballistics, and Psychology: A History of the Chronoscope in/as Context, 1845–1890." *History of Psychology* 8 (2005): 46–78

Schnapp, Jeffrey T. "Propeller Talk." *Modernism/modernity* 1, no. 3 (1994): 153–78.

Schuchardt, H. Review of *Étude sur les changements phonétiques et leurs caractères généraux*, by Paul Passy; and *Les modifications phonétique du language étudiée dans le patois d'une famille de Cellefrouin*, by Abbé Rousselot. *Literaturblatt für germanische und romanische Philologie* 9 (1892): 303–15.

Schultze, Max. "Die Gattung Cornuspira unter den Monothamien und Bemerkungen über die Organisation und Fortpflanzung der Polythamien." *Archiv für Naturgeschichte* 26 (1860): 287–310.

Schwartz, Hillel. *The Culture of the Copy: Striking Likenesses, Unreasonable Facsimiles.* New York: Zone Books, 1996.

Scott, Clive. *Vers Libre: The Emergence of Free Verse in France, 1886–1914.* New York: Oxford University Press, 1990.

Scott, Joan Wallach. "'L'Ouvrière! Mot impie, sordide . . . ' Women Workers in the Disourse of French Political Economy, 1840–1860." In *Gender and the Politics of History*, 139–63. New York: Columbia University Press, 1988.

Scripture, Edward Wheeler. *The Elements of Experimental Phonetics.* New York: Charles Scribner's Sons, 1902.

———. "On the Nature of Vowels." *American Journal of Science* 161 (1901): 302–9.

———. "Report on the Construction of a Vowel Organ." *Smithsonian Miscellaneous Collections* 47 (1905): 360–64.

Séailles, Gabriel. *Essai sur le génie dans l'art.* Paris: Baillière, 1883.

Sedgwick, Eve Kosofsky, and Adam Frank, eds. *Shame and Its Sisters: A Silvan Tomkins Reader.* Durham, NC: Duke University Press, 1995.

Seeley, W. P. "What Is the Cognitive Neuroscience of Art . . . and Why Should We Care?" *Aesthetics* 31, no. 2 (2011): 1–4.

Segal, Harold B. *Turn of the Century Cabaret: Paris, Barcelona, Berlin, Munich, Vienna, Cracow, Moscow, St. Petersburg, Zurich.* New York: Columbia University Press, 1987.

Segalen, Victor. "Les Synesthésies et l'École symboliste." *Mercure de France* 42, no. 148 (April 1902): 57–90.

Semon, Richard. *Die Mneme als erhaltendes Prinzip im Wechsel des organischen Geschehens.* 5th ed. Leipzig: Wilhelm Engelmann, 1920.

Séris, Jean-Pierre. *Machine et communication.* Paris: Vrin, 1987.

Serres, Michel. "Turner Translates Carnot." In *Hermes: Literature, Science, Philosophy*, translated by Josué Harari. Baltimore: Johns Hopkins University Press, 1982.

Shapin, Steven, and Simon Schaffer. *Leviathan and the Air-Pump. Hobbes, Boyle, and the Experimental Life.* Princeton, NJ: Princeton University Press, 1985.

Shattuck, Roger. *The Inner Eye: On Modern Literature and the Arts.* New York: Farrar, Straus and Giroux, 1984.

Shimamura, A. P., and S. E. Palmer, eds. *Aesthetic Science: Connecting Minds, Brains, and Experience.* New York: Oxford University Press, 2011.

Shryock, Richard. "Becoming Political: Symbolist Literature in the Third Republic." *Nineteenth-Century French Studies* 33, nos. 3–4 (2005): 385–98.

Sibum, Heinz Otto. "Reworking the Mechanical Value of Heat: Instruments of Precision and Gestures of Accuracy in Early Victorian England." *Studies in History and Philosophy of Science* 26, no. 1 (1995): 73–106.

———. *Shifting Scales: Microstudies in Early Victorian Britain.* Berlin: Max-Planck Institute for History of Science Pre-print, 2001.

Sieburth, Richard. "The Music of the Future." 1885. In *A New Literary History of French Literature,* edited by Denis Hollier, 789–98. Cambridge, MA: Harvard University Press, 1994.

Signac, Paul. *D'Eugène Delacroix au néo-impressionnisme.* 1899. Paris: Hermann, 1964.

———. "Excerpts from the Unpublished Diary of Paul Signac, pt. 1." Edited and translated by John Rewald. *Gazette des beaux-arts* 91 (July–December 1949): 166–74.

———. "Extraits du journal inédit de Paul Signac, I (1894–1895)." Edited by John Rewald. *Gazette des Beaux-Arts* 36 (July–September 1949): 97–128.

———. "Fragments du journal de Paul Signac." *Arts de France* 11 (1947): 97–106.

———. "Variétés: Impressionnistes et révolutionnaires." *La Révolte* 4 (June 13–19, 1891): 3–4.

Silverman, Deborah. *Art Nouveau in Fin-de-Siècle France: Politics, Psychology, and Style.* Berkeley: University of California Press, 1989.

Simonsz, H. J., and I. Den Tonkelaar. "19th Century Models of Eye Movements, Donder's Law, Listing's Law and Helmholtz's Directional Circles." *Documenta Opthamologica* 74 (1990): 95–112.

Skov, M., and O. Vartanian, eds. *Neuroaesthetics.* Amityville, NY: Baywood Publishing Co., 2010.

Smith, Crosbie. *The Science of Energy: A Cultural History of Energy Physics in Victorian Britain.* Chicago: University of Chicago Press, 1998.

Smith, Judy. "Genealogies of Desire: 'Uranianism,' Mysticism, and Science in Britain, 1889–1940." Master's thesis, University of British Columbia, 2008.

Smith, Paul. *Seurat and the Avant-Garde.* New Haven, CT: Yale University Press, 1997.

Smith, Roger. *Inhibition: History and Meaning in the Sciences of Mind and Brain.* Berkeley and Los Angeles: University of California Press, 1992.

Snyder, Charles. "Clarence John Blake and Alexander Graham Bell: Otology and the Telephone." *Annals of Otology, Rhinology and Laryngology* 83, no. 2, S13 (1974): 3–31.

Société des psychologie physiologique de Paris. *Congrès international de psychologie physiologique.* Paris: Société d'Éditions Scientifique, 1890.

Söderstrom, Göran. *Strindberg och bildkonsten.* Uddevalla, Sweden: Forum, 1972.

Soury, Jules. Review of *Anatomie et physiologie comparée de la pholade dactyle,* by Raphaël Du Bois. *Revue philosophique* 40 (1895): 541–51.

Spae, Virginia *Orphism: The Evolution of Non-figurative Painting in Paris, 1910–1914.* Oxford: Clarendon Press, 1979.

"Speech Automatically Transmitted in Short Hand by the Telegraph." *Scientific American* 37, no. 18, S96 (November 3, 1877): 273.

Spencer, Herbert. *Les Bases de la moral évolutionniste*. Paris: Ballière, 1880.

———. *Essays: Moral, Political, and Aesthetic*. New York: D. Appleton, 1889.

———. "The Origin and Function of Music." *Fraser's Magazine* 56, no. 334 (October 1857): 396–407.

———. *The Principles of Psychology*. 2 vols. New York: D. Appleton & Co., 1877.

———. *The Works of Herbert Spencer*. Vol. 2, part 9. 3rd ed. Osnabrueck, Germany: Otto Zeller, 1966.

Spire, André. *Plaisir poétique et plaisir musculaire: Essai sur l'évolution des techniques poétiques*. Paris: José Corti, 1949.

Stafford, Barbara Maria. "Presuming Images and Consuming Goods: The Visualization of Knowledge from the Enlightenment to Post-modernism." In *Consumption and the World of Goods*, edited by John Brewer and Roy Porter, 462–77. London: Routledge, 1992.

———. *Symbol and Myth: Humbert de Superville's Essay on Absolute Signs in Art*. London: Associated University Presses, 1979.

Staley, Richard. *Einstein's Generation: The Origins of the Relativity Revolution*. Chicago: University of Chicago Press, 2008.

———, ed. *The Physics of Empire*. Cambridge: Whipple Museum Publications, 1994.

Stein, Gertrude. *The Autobiography of Alice B. Toklas*. New York: Random House, 1961.

Stenersen, Rolf. *Edvard Munch: Close-Up of a Genius*. Translated and edited by Reidar Dittmann. Oslo: Gyldendal, 1969.

Sterne, Jonathan. *The Audible Past: Cultural Origins of Sound Reproduction*. Durham, NC: Duke University Press, 2003.

Stewart, Balfour, and Peter Guthrie Tait. *The Unseen Universe; or, Physical Speculations on a Future State*. New York: Macmillan and Co., 1875.

Stirling, John Hutchinson. *As Regards Protoplasm: In Relation to Professor Huxley's Essay "On the Physical Basis of Life."* New Haven, CT: Charles C. Chatfield, 1870.

Storch, Wolfgang, and Josef Mackert, eds. *Die Symbolisten und Richard Wagner*. Berlin: Edition Hentrich, 1991.

Strindberg, August. *Antibarbarus I oder die Welt für sich und die Welt für mich*. Berlin: Verlag des Bibliographischen Bureaus, 1894.

———. "The New Arts! Or the Role of Chance in Artistic Creation." In *Selected Essays by August Strindberg*, translated and edited by Michael Robinson, 103–7. Cambridge: Cambridge University Press, 1996.

———. "Das Seufzen der Steine." In *Verwirrte Sinneseindrücke: Schriften zu Malerei, Fotografie und Naturwissenschaften*, 141–74. Dresden: Verlag der Kunst, 1998.

———. *Strindberg's Letters*. Vol. 2, *1892–1912*. Translated and edited by Michael Robinson. Chicago: University of Chicago Press, 1992.

———. "Ueber die Lichtwirkung in der Fotographie: Betrachtungen aus Anlass der

X-Strahlen." In *Verwirrte Sinneseindrücke: Schriften zu Malerei, Fotografie und Natur-wissenschaften*, 122–30. Dresden: Verlag der Kunst, 1998.

———. "Wo sind die Nerven der Pflanzen?" *Verwirrte Sinneseindrücke: Schriften zu Malerei, Fotografie und Naturwissenschaften*. Dresden: Verlag der Kunst, 1998.

Tarde, Gabriel. *Les Lois de l'imitation: Étude sociologique*. Paris: F. Alcan, 1890.

———. *Les Lois sociales: Esquisse d'une sociologie*. Paris: F. Alcan, 1898.

———. "Les Vers impairs." *Le Semeur* 19 (1890): 598–601; and 20 (1890): 639–43.

Taylor, Frederick W. *The Principles of Scientific Management*. 1911. New York: Harper and Brothers, 1967.

Terrall, Mary. "Frogs on the Mantelpiece: The Practice of Observation in Daily Life." In *Histories of Scientific Observation*. Edited by Lorraine Daston and Elizabeth Lunbeck, 185–205. Chicago: University of Chicago Press, 2011.

Thiebaut, Phillippe. "Art nouveau et néo-impressionnisme: Les Ateliers de Signac." *Revue de l'art* 92 (1991): 72–78.

Thomson, Richard. *Seurat*. Oxford: Phaidon Press, 1985.

Thurow, Gerald D. "Art and Politics: Wagnerism in France." In *Wagnerism in European Culture and Politics*, edited by David C. Large and William Weber, 134–66. Ithaca, NY: Cornell University Press, 1984.

Thurtle, Phillip. *The Emergence of Genetic Rationality: Space, Time and Information in American Biological Science, 1870–1920*. Seattle: University of Washington Press, 2007.

Tillman, Hans Günter. "Early Modern Instrumental Phonetics." In *Concise History of the Language Sciences: From Sumerians to the Cognivitists*, edited by E. F. K. Koerner and R. E. Asher, 401–15. Oxford: Pergamon, 1995.

Tourtual, Kaspar. *Die Sinne des Menschen in den wechselseitigen Bezeihungen ihres psychischen und organischen Leben: Ein Beitrag zur physiologischen Aesthetik*. Münster, Germany: Friedrich Regensburg, 1827.

Tresch, John. "The Prophet and the Pendulum: Sensational Science and Audiovisual Phantasmagoria around 1848." *Grey Room* 43 (2011): 16–41.

———. *The Romantic Machine: Utopian Science and Technology after Napoleon*. Chicago: University of Chicago Press, 2012.

Tucker, Jennifer. *Nature Exposed: Photography as Eyewitness in Victorian Science*. Baltimore: Johns Hopkins University Press, 2005.

Turner, R. Steven. *In the Eye's Mind: Vision and the Helmholtz-Hering Controversy*. Princeton, NJ: Princeton University Press, 1994.

Tzara, Tristan. "Dada Manifesto 1918." Translated by Ralph Mannheim. In *The Dada Painters and Poets: An Anthology*, edited by Robert Motherwell, 76–82. Cambridge, MA: Belknap Press of Harvard University Press, 1981.

Vachon, Marius. *Les Musées et les écoles d'art industrielle en Europe*. Paris: Imprimerie Nationale, 1890.

———. *Pour la défense de nos industries d'art*. Paris: Lahure, 1899.

———. "Rapport de M. George Berger." *Revue des arts décoratifs* 12 (1891–92): 360–61.

Vaïsse, Léon. "Discours du président." *Bulletin de la Société de linguistique* 1–5 (1869–85): clj–cljiii.

———. "Notation des sons du langages." *Bulletin de la Société de linguistique* 1–5 (1869–85): clv–clviii.

———. "Notes pour servir à l'histoire des machines parlantes." *Mémoires de la Société de linguistique de Paris* 3 (1878): 257–68.

Vaisse, P. *La Troisième Rèpublique et les peintres: Recherches sur les rapports des pouvoirs publiques et de la peinture en France de 1870 à 1914.* Paris: Sorbonne, 1980.

Valéry, Paul. *Degas, Manet, Morisot.* Princeton, NJ: Princeton University Press, 1960.

———. "Existence du symbolisme." 1936. In *Paul Valéry: Œuvres*, vol. 1, edited by Jean Hytier. Paris: Gallimard, 1957.

———. "Introduction à la methode de Léonardo de Vinci." 1894. In *Paul Valéry: Œuvres*, vol. 1, edited by Jean Hytier. Paris: Gallimard, 1957.

———. "On Literary Technique." 1889. In *The Art of Poetry*, edited by Jackson Mathews, translated by Denise Foliot. Princeton, NJ: Princeton University Press, 1989.

———. *Paul Valéry: Œuvres.* 2 vols. Edited by Jean Hytier. Paris: Gallimard, 1957–60.

———. *Variété.* 5 vols. Paris: Nouvelle Revue Française, 1924–44.

Valéry, Paul, et al., eds. "Hommage à Charles Henry." Special issue, *Cahiers de l'étoile* 13 (January–February 1930).

van de Velde, Henry. "Die Linie." *Die Zukunft* 40, no. 49 (September 6, 1902): 385–88.

———. "Notes sur l'art: Chahut." *La Wallonie* 5 (May 1890): 123–25.

van Gogh, Vincent. *The Complete Letters of Vincent van Gogh.* 2nd ed. 3 vols. Boston: New York Graphic Society, 1978.

Vatin, François. "À quoi rêvent les polypes? Individuation et sociation d'Abraham Trembley à Émile Durkheim." In *Trois essais sur la genèse de la pensée sociologique*, 123–220. Paris: Le Découverte, 2005.

———. *Le Travail: Économie et physique 1780–1830.* Paris: Presses Universitaires de France, 1993.

Veder, Robin. "The Expressive Efficiencies of American Delsarte and Mensendieck Body Cultures." *Modernism/modernity* 17, no. 4 (2010): 819–38.

Veder, Robin Maremant. *The Living Line: Modern Art and the Economy of Energy.* University Press of New England, forthcoming.

Verdin, Charles. *Catalogue des instruments de précision pour la physiologie et la médicine.* Paris: Verdin, 1890.

Vignon, P. *Recherches de cytologie générale sur les épithéliums.* Paris: Schleicher Frères, 1912.

Vogl, Joseph. "Becoming Media: Galileo's Telescope." *Grey Room* 29 (2008): 14–25.

Voland, Eckart, and Karl Grammer, eds. *Evolutionary Aesthetics.* Berlin: Springer, 2003.

von Dobschuetz, Ernst. *Christusbilder: Untersuchungen zur christlichen Legende.* Leipzig: Hinrichs, 1899.

von Hanstein, Johannes. *Das Protoplasma als Träger der pflanzlichen und tierlichen Lebensvorrichtungen.* Heidelberg: Winter, 1880.

Wagner, Ph. "Über die Verwendung der Grützner-Marey'schen Apparats u.d. Phonographen zur phonetischen Untersuchungen." *Phonetische Studien* 4 (1890): 68–82.

Wagner, Richard. "The Arts of Poetry and Tone in the Drama of the Future." In *Opera and Drama,* translated by William Ashton Ellis, 2nd ed., 123–88. London: Kegan Paul, Trench, Trubner & Co., 1900.

———. *"The Art-Work of the Future," and Other Works.* Translated and edited by William Ashton Ellis. Lincoln: University of Nebraska Press, 1993.

Wahrig-Schmidt, Bettina. "'Irgendwie-jedenfalls physiologisch': Friedrich Nietzsche, Alexandre Herzen (fils) und Charles Féré 1888." *Nietzsche-Studien* 17 (1988): 434–74.

Warrain, Francis. *L'Œuvre psychobiophysique de Charles Henry.* Paris: Gallimard, 1931.

Webb, Daniel. *Observations on the Correspondences between Poetry and Music.* London, 1769.

Weber, Eugen. *Peasants into Frenchmen: The Modernization of Rural France, 1870–1914.* London: Chatto and Windus, 1979.

Wechsler, Judith. *A Human Comedy: Physiognomy and Caricature in Nineteenth-Century Paris.* Chicago: University of Chicago Press, 1982.

Weibel, Peter, and Ljiljana Fruk. *Molecular Aesthetics.* Cambridge, MA: MIT Press, 2013.

Weindling, Paul. "Ernst Haeckel, Darwinismus and the Secularization Nature." In *History, Humanity and Evolution: Essays for John C. Greene,* edited by James R. Moore, 311–28. New York: Cambridge University Press, 1989.

———. "Theories of the Cell State in Imperial Germany." In *Biology, Medicine and Society, 1840–1940,* edited by Charles Webster, 99–155. New York: Cambridge University Press, 1981.

Weissbach, Lee Shai. "Artisanal Response to Artistic Decline: The Cabinetmakers of Paris in the Era of Industrialization." *Journal of Social History* 16, no. 2 (1982): 67–83.

Wells, H. G. "The Limits of Individual Plasticity." 1895. In *H. G. Wells: Early Writings in Science and Science Fiction,* edited by R. M. Philmus and D. Y. Hughes, 36–39. Berkeley: University of California Press, 1975.

White, Erdmute Wenzel. *The Magic Bishop: Hugo Ball, Dada Poet.* Columbia, SC: Camden House, 1998.

White, Paul. *Thomas Huxley: Making the Man of Science.* Cambridge: Cambridge University Press, 2003.

Whitehead, Alfred North. *An Enquiry Concerning the Principles of Natural Knowledge.* 1919. London: Forgotten Books, 2013.

Whiting, Steven Moore. *Satie the Bohemian: From Cabaret to Concert Hall*. Oxford: Oxford University Press, 1999.

Wickhoff, Franz. "On the Historical Unity in the Universal Evolution of Art." In *German Essays on Art History*, translated by Peter Wortsman, edited by Gert Schiff, 165–71. New York: Continuum, 1988.

Wiener, Otto. *Die Erweiterung unserer Sinne: Akademische Antrittsvorlesung*. Leipzig: J. A. Barth, 1900.

Willis, Robert. "On Vowel Sounds, and on Reed Pipes." *Transactions of the Cambridge Philosophical Society* 3 (1830): 231–68.

Wilson, Catherine. *The Invisible World: Early Modern Philosophy and the Invention of the Microscope*. Princeton, NJ: Princeton University Press, 1995.

Wimsatt, W. K., Jr., and Monroe Beardsley. "The Concept of Meter: An Exercise in Abstraction." *PMLA* 74, no. 5 (1959): 585–98.

Winner, Langdon. "Do Artifacts Have Politics?" *Daedelus* 109 (1980): 121–36.

Winthrop-Young, Geoffrey. *Kittler and the Media*. Cambridge: Polity, 2011.

Winthrop-Young, Geoffrey, Jussi Parikka, and Ilinca Iurascu, eds. "Special Issue: Cultural Techniques." *Theory, Culture, and Society* 30, no. 6 (2013).

Wise, M. Norton. "Machines without Kraft: On the Cultural Meaning of Automata." In *Zeichen der Kraft: Wissensformationen 1800–1900*, edited by Thomas Brandstetter and Christof Windgaetter, 81–107. Berlin: Kulturverlag Kadmos, 2008.

———. "Mediations: Enlightenment Balancing Acts; or, The Technology of Rationalism." In *World Changes: Thomas Kuhn and the Nature of Science*, edited by P. Horwich, 207–56. Cambridge, MA: MIT Press, 1993.

———. "Work and Waste: Political Economy and Natural Philosophy in Nineteenth-Century Britain." *History of Science* 27 (1989): pt.1, 263–301; pt. 2, 391–449; pt. 3, vol. 28 (1990): 221–61.

Wolf, Stewart. *Brain, Mind, and Medicine: Charles Richet and the Origin of Physiological Psychology*. New Brunswick, NJ: Transaction Publishing, 1993.

Woodcock, George. *Anarchism*. Peterborough, ON: Broadview, 2004.

Wright, Barbara, ed. *Seven Dada Manifestoes and Lampisteries*. London: John Calder, 1977.

Wronski, Josef Hoëné de. *Introduction à la philosophie des mathématiques et technie de l'algorithmie*. Paris: Courcier, 1811.

Wyzewska, Isabelle. *"La Revue wagnérienne": Essai sur l'interpretation esthétique de Wagner en France*. Paris: Perrin, 1934.

Yates, JoAnne. *Control through Communication: The Rise of System in American Management*. Baltimore: Johns Hopkins University Press, 1989.

Zeki, S. *Inner Vision: An Exploration of Art and the Brain*. New York: Oxford University Press, 1999.

Zimmerman, Michael. *Les Mondes de Seurat: Son œuvre et le débat artistique de son temp*. Translated by J. Ferry, S. Schnall and K. F. Willems. Paris: Fonds Mercator/Albin Michel, 1991.

CPSIA information can be obtained
at www.ICGtesting.com
Printed in the USA
BVHW052306300820
587603BV00007B/24

9 780295 993201